Want to Start a Revolution?

D1483799

Want to Start a Revolution?

*Radical Women in the
Black Freedom Struggle*

*Edited by Dayo F. Gore,
Jeanne Theoharis, and
Komozi Woodard*

NEW YORK UNIVERSITY PRESS

New York and London

NEW YORK UNIVERSITY PRESS
New York and London
www.nyupress.org

Library of Congress Cataloging-in-Publication Data

Want to start a revolution? : radical women in the Black freedom
struggle / edited by Dayo F. Gore, Jeanne Theoharis, and Komozi
Woodard.
p. cm.
Includes bibliographical references and index.
ISBN-13: 978-0-8147-8313-9 (cl : alk. paper)
ISBN-10: 0-8147-8313-9 (cl : alk. paper)
ISBN-13: 978-0-8147-8314-6 (pb : alk. paper)
ISBN-10: 0-8147-8314-7 (pb : alk. paper)
1. African American women civil rights workers—History—20th
century. 2. African American women political activists—History—
20th century. 3. Women radicals—United States—History—20th
century. 4. African American radicals—History—20th century. 5.
African Americans—Civil rights—History—20th century. 6. Civil
rights movements—United States—History—20th century. 7. Black
power—United States—History—20th century. 8. Feminism—United
States—History—20th century. 9. Communism—United States—
History—20th century. 10. United States—Race relations—History—
20th century. I. Gore, Dayo F. II. Theoharis, Jeanne. III. Woodard,
Komozi.
E185.615.W328   2009
323.1196'073—dc22   2009029215

New York University Press books are printed on acid-free paper,
and their binding materials are chosen for strength and durability.
We strive to use environmentally responsible suppliers and materials
to the greatest extent possible in publishing our books.

Manufactured in the United States of America
c   10 9 8 7 6 5 4 3 2 1
p   10 9 8 7 6 5 4 3 2 1

Contents

Acknowledgments

This book is dedicated to the women whose activism is the subject of this collection. Through all manner of economic, physical, and psychic repression, they continued to believe a different world was possible and worked tirelessly to make it so.

We would like to thank all the contributors to this book for their dedication to this project, their marvelous chapters that return the story of women's radicalism to the history of the postwar era, and the political commitments that guide their work. Debbie Gershenowitz is the kind of visionary editor all scholars wish for. She has been with us since the beginning, and we are immensely grateful. Gabrielle Begue shepherded this project through its myriad stages, a Herculean task for a collection with fifteen authors. Despina P. Gimbel's careful attention to detail guided this book through production. Leroy Henderson agreed to allow us to use his striking photo on the cover—an essay in and of itself. The Program in Women's Studies and the Shirley Chisholm Center at Brooklyn College helped us hold a conference that brought us together for a productive two days of discussion and reflection.

DFG, JT, and KW

A number of friends and colleagues have provided deep insight and unflagging support. In particular, my new work on Rosa Parks has only been possible through a wide community of people who have impressed upon me the need for this project and helped me see the radical Rosa in new ways. Infinite gratitude goes to Gaston Alonso, Susan Artinian, Adina Back, Matthew Countryman, Emilye Crosby, Prudence Cumberbatch, Johanna Fernandez, Arnold Franklin, Brenna Greer, Wesley Hogan, Ira Katznelson, the Honorable Judge Damon Keith, Chana Kai Lee, Alejandra Marchevsky, Karen Miller, Mojubaolu Okome, Annelise Orleck, Celina Su, and the entire Theoharis family. Finally, in a profession that does not always encourage collectivity, Dayo Gore and Komozi Woodard stand in stark contrast. They show me again and again the power of collaboration in creating richer intellectual work and in modeling the kind of academy we can be proud to be a part of.

JT

Vicki Garvin dedicated her life to the protracted struggle for liberation. Her willingness, almost ten years ago, to share some of this history with me has served as continued inspiration and motivation. My work on Garvin has been greatly enriched by the insights of those who knew her. Miranda Bergman and Lincoln Bergman have been unbelievably generous with their support, sharing personal memories, responding to numerous e-mails, and providing invaluable documentation of Vicki Garvin's life. I am also grateful to Thelma Dale for talking with me about her work and friendship with Vicki, and to Ajamu Dillihunt and Dennis O'Neil.

Friends, colleagues, and loved ones have provided much needed professional and personal support, as well as helpful insights as the project has moved along. Thanks to the "Forbes Posse," Jamila Gore and the entire Gore family, Christina Hanhardt, Lili Kim, Andy Terranova, and the faculty and staff of the Women's Studies Program at the University of Massachusetts–Amherst. Jeanne Theoharis and Komozi Woodard's unwavering commitment to this project has been inspiring. Their generosity and investment in the collective process serve as a powerful reminder that scholarship—at its best—is grounded in community and exchange. Finally, a special acknowledgment is due Arianne Miller. Her intellect, encouragement, and love have helped me to stay the course.

DFG

I mourn the loss of Vicki Garvin, Adina Back, Aunt Mary Woodward, and Bonnie Shullenberger. Adina Back's work on women in the black freedom movement helps set the pace for this scholarship. And I mourn the loss of Bonnie Shullenberger, who spent a rich life fighting for social justice. Aunt Mary helped me understand the Long Black Renaissance. For me, Vicki Garvin was the beginning of my insight into revolutionary women's history and the organizing tradition they fashioned for black liberation. She was not only my teacher but also a comrade of Malcolm X, W. E. B. Du Bois, Paul Robeson, and Claudia Jones.

The Woodard family has always supported my intellectual development, including the insights about history in this volume. My father, Theodore Woodward, and my uncle, Thomas Woodward, listened and guided me though my rethinking of black social history last year. My Sarah Lawrence College community is always at the center of my intellectual work; but special thanks goes to the yearlong class I taught, "Women in the Black Revolt." Alongside that class was the annual Women's History conference at Sarah Lawrence in March 2008, directed by Priscilla Murolo and Tara James. In the Black liberation movement, the leading women of the Congress of African People taught me some of my first lessons in this history. Fannie Lou Hamer of SNCC was one of the earliest inspirations that helped me understand a radical grassroots tradition pioneered by Harriet Tubman and Ida B. Wells. And Vicki Garvin was my mentor in teaching me the "hidden transcript" of the freedom struggle at a formative period in my life. And, finally, the sisters and brothers in the Solidarity Club, including Sarah, Shamara, Brenda, Juliana, Florence, Anna, Sam, Justin, Tariq, Amiri, and Jennifer, taught me that the struggle continues, and that we will win liberation without a doubt.

Working with Jeanne Theoharis and Dayo Gore is one of the sweetest joys in a writer's life. And their hunger for freedom and thirst for justice graces each page of this important book.

KW

Introduction

Dayo F. Gore, Jeanne Theoharis,
and Komozi Woodard

The day has ended when white trade union leaders or white leaders in any organization may presume to tell Blacks on what basis they shall come together to fight for their rights. . . . Three hundred years has been enough of that. We Black people in America ask for your cooperation—but we do not ask for your permission.
Vicki Garvin, written for National Negro Labor Council, 1951

I had decided I would not go anywhere with a piece of paper in my hand asking white folks for any favors.
Rosa Parks, *My Story*, 1992

Legend has it that when the notoriously charismatic Representative Adam Clayton Powell Jr. from Harlem heard that fellow organizer Vicki Garvin had joined the Communist Party, he went to the Party's Harlem leadership to plead for Garvin's return: *"Can't we share her?"* Garvin—a master strategist whose political career spanned more than a half century of leadership—seized the political stage in the 1930s working alongside Powell in the pioneering Harlem Boycott Movement. Vicki Garvin's epic trajectory in the black freedom struggle reveals the distinct but hidden contours of the black radical tradition. Her activism took her from public school in working-class Harlem to the elite all-women's Smith College; on to work as a vice president with the United Office and Professional Workers of America helping to build CIO unionism; and then to

1

membership in the Communist Party USA and leadership of the National Negro Labor Council during the 1950s. In the 1960s, Garvin embraced an expatriate's life as a Third World internationalist in Nkrumah's Ghana and Mao's China, and then returned to the United States in 1970, where she mentored a group of activists in the African Liberation Support Committee and the National Black United Front.

In Harlem, Ghana, and Egypt, Malcolm X sought her revolutionary guidance; W. E. B. Du Bois, Paul Robeson, Robert F. Williams, Maya Angelou, and Communist Party USA leader Claudia Jones also looked to her political acumen and cherished her camaraderie. In fact, in describing African American politics in Ghana, expatriate Leslie Lacy proclaimed, "Want to start a revolution? See Vicki Garvin and Alice Windom."[1] Yet, this sentiment—that a black woman would be a commanding presence, indeed the "go-to" person, for revolution—sits at odds with popular perceptions of the black freedom struggle. In most studies of the period the impact of radical women's leadership has been neglected. While it is now commonly understood that Malcolm X inspired a broad community of radicals, the circle of women who inspired and mentored him—and countless others—are much less known. Moreover, in standard understandings of the struggle, there is no place to imagine a black revolutionary like Garvin and "the mother of the civil rights movement" Rosa Parks joined in common struggle. However, in June 1956, Parks wrote a letter of thanks to Garvin's revolutionary colleagues in the National Negro Labor Council, evoking the need for struggle over empty sentiments: "It awakens within our mind the fact that there are people of good will in America who are deeply concerned about justice and freedom for all people, and who are willing to make the noble precepts of Democracy living facts lifted out of the dusty files of unimplemented and forgotten court decisions."[2]

Although a new generation of scholars has greatly expanded our knowledge of black radicalism and the black freedom struggle, they have left largely intact a "leading man" master narrative that misses crucial dimensions of the postwar freedom struggle and minimizes the contributions of women. These narratives have centered men and located women at the margins of great social change—visible at times in the mass demonstrations but obscured in the ranks of revolutionaries and radical theoreticians. Such histories have neglected crucial dimensions of the postwar black radical tradition that held black women's self-emancipation as pivotal to black liberation.[3]

Most of the women examined in this book were not obscure figures of their day. In fact, many were nationally known activists. Rethinking the historiography of the Black Revolt requires interrogating a narrative of black radicalism that casts these radical women in supporting roles. This volume furthers that critical task, telling the stories of veteran leaders such as Vicki Garvin and Rosa Parks, as well as writer Toni Cade Bambara, 1972 presidential candidate Shirley Chisholm, feminist lawyer Flo Kennedy, welfare rights leader Johnnie Tillmon, and political prisoner Assata Shakur—among others—to introduce new dimensions to the concept of radical black politics.

Highlighting these women's radical politics makes visible their convergence at the center of the Black Revolt. For example, as Black Panthers Elaine Brown, Bobby Seale, and Ericka Huggins campaigned for local political office in March 1972, some 16,000 people gathered at a rally in Oakland, California, to hear Tillmon and Chisholm support the grassroots politics and voter registration efforts of the Black Panther Party.[4] For other women detailed in this anthology, their radicalism was hidden in plain sight. The cover photo of this book, taken by photographer Leroy Henderson, depicts Rosa Parks at the Gary Convention gazing at a poster of Malcolm X, whom she had long admired. Henderson photographed numerous demonstrations and Black caucuses in the 1960s and 1970s. "Like the time I was at the Black Political Convention in Gary Indiana. . . . [S]tanding at this poster table was a lady nobody even seemed to know who she was. . . . I knew it was Rosa Parks."[5] Pulling together the stories of Parks, Garvin, Bambara, Chisholm, Tillmon, and Shakur in one collection uncovers an obscured history of postwar radicalism. Their experiences reveal major contours of black radicalism that have been impossible to see because the political commitments, radical alliances, and expansive vision of these women have rarely been given center stage.

Just as the work of these radical women in the political arena changed the complexion of black political culture, the examination of women's activism in this volume will reorient studies of black radicalism by expanding its boundaries beyond self-defense and separatism and by articulating its roots in labor, civil rights, and early autonomous black feminist politics that came to flower in the postwar era. Often defined in vastly different terms, these women seem to represent separate, mutually-exclusive political movements. Yet bringing their work together presents a powerful demonstration not only of their individual achievements but also of the collective force of black women activists as strategic thinkers, leaders, and architects of postwar radicalism.

Key Interventions of Our Book

In delving behind each of these women's symbolic representations, significant commonalities emerge in their politics and visions for liberation. These are personal stories of self-transformation in the "white heat" of the struggle for social, economic, and political change.[6] Each woman proved a long-distance runner and embraced a range of strategies. Each woman traversed a host of movements and invested in innovative coalition building; and each woman articulated an intersectional analysis that made connections between multiple movements for social justice: black freedom, women's equality, anticolonialism, and the redistribution of wealth. Taken together, they show the day-to-day work necessary to sustain a radical movement, women's intellectual contributions to the advancement of the struggle, and the broad vision of black liberation that was forged in the postwar era.

This volume reframes women in black radicalism by consciously not categorizing these women within one movement (whether the Left, Black Power, "second-wave" feminism, or Third World liberation movements) but tracing their work across many spaces.[7] Bringing them together in one collection challenges the framework that has long presented the radical activism of the 1960s and 1970 in separate and distinct movements. Therefore, while it is clearly viable to organize these women's contributions based upon their affiliation with the civil rights, Black Power, "second-wave" feminism, and U.S. communist movements, such a framework obscures the full breadth of their contributions to black radicalism. Rosa Parks's iconic status within the civil rights movement overshadows her lifelong radical commitments; Johnnie Tillmon's interventions in Black Power politics are often lost when viewed through the lens of welfare rights activism; and national radicals such as Florynce Kennedy and Vicki Garvin drop out altogether as their varied political affiliations resist neat categorization. In highlighting Rosa Parks's brand of Black Power politics, Vicki Garvin's journey from the Old Left to black liberation and Third World solidarity, and Denise Oliver's radical roots and feminist politics in the Young Lord's Party, this anthology intentionally resists marking these women as activists defined exclusively within any singular movement and makes visible the ways these black women radicals redefined movement politics.[8]

Thus, the essays in this book present three key interventions into contemporary understandings of postwar black radicalism. First, they expand the boundaries of black radicalism. In the postwar period, electoral politics, antipoverty activism, and trade union organizing, as well as mobilizing against Congress, setting up independent black schools, and creating art that asserted an intersectional notion of beauty, power, and self, all constituted the work of radical social transformation. These essays begin to tell that expansive story of black radicalism whose roots in labor, civil rights, and community organizing in the 1930s came to flower in the postwar era.

Second, these chapters examine women's work in the movement and, in doing so, the labor of radical politics. This anthology takes as its starting point the twin assertions that women organized in the national and international arena as well as leading on the local level, and that women shaped the radicalism that developed in the postwar period by working as key strategists, theorists, and activists. Expanding beyond the "men led but women organized" paradigm of women's leadership, these essays demonstrate how women's leadership took many forms in the black freedom struggle and detail the work it took to sustain a radical vision and political engagement over the long haul.[9] Challenging the limits of the "bridge leader" framework for understanding the breadth of black women's roles in the movement, these essays show the diversity of black women's experiences, roles, and philosophies.[10] Some women assumed the position of charismatic leader; others stood philosophically opposed to such models for movement building and helped instead to build democratic organizing structures; still others had to create new structures and political movements free from racism, sexism, classism, and homophobia to nourish their visions of liberation. They show us the ways activists reemerged after the devastation of anticommunism, forged ties internationally, mentored younger activists, imagined new strategies, and then created institutions to promote these new directions.[11] Not the least of that difficult work was the often unacknowledged intellectual labor of challenging old ideas and rethinking strategies, as they navigated the shifting U.S. political landscape over several decades.

Third, these essays help us see black women's gender politics in expanded ways. Formative in developing the politics of the Black Revolt, many women produced pioneering gendered analyses of economic, social, and political conditions that proved crucial to advancing the black struggle. Their feminisms developed in multiple spaces, many emerging from within civil rights, left, or Black Power organizations. By complicating the idea that black women felt they had to choose their race over their gender, these essays highlight the diversity of strategies and approaches black women employed and the differing ways black women imagined and enacted their "freedom dreams."[12] While scholars studying the feminism of women of color have largely focused on the creation of separate, more inclusive spaces like the Third World Women's Alliance and the Combahee River Collective, many of the essays collected here reveal the ways women negotiated race, gender, class, and sexuality *within* the black left, Black Power, and women's movements. They show the early roots of black feminist politics and its influence on an emerging women's liberation movement, challenging the still prevalent notion that black feminism was simply a reaction to the exclusions of Black Power and what has been framed as "second-wave" feminism.[13]

Thus, the purpose of this collection is not simply to broaden the roster of known activists but also to enlarge the scope of how black radicalism is understood. This anthology is more suggestive than definitive—to expand what is known about women's roles as theorists, leaders, strategists, and organizers, rather than lay out a strict definition of women's leadership in the Black Revolt. Many women leaders and political mobilizations are left out of these pages: women of the Student Nonviolent Coordinating Committee (SNCC) like Diane Nash, Gloria House, and Ruby Doris Smith Robinson; Mississippi militants such as Fannie Lou Hamer and Unita Blackwell; organizing campaigns that foregrounded black women's right to defend their own bodies, such as those for Rosa Lee Ingram and Joan Little; leading black feminist organizations such as the groundbreaking Combahee River Collective, the Third World Women's Alliance, and the National Black Feminist Organization; women of the Nation of Islam; peace activists such as Coretta Scott King; black women active in the gay and lesbian politics, such as Audre Lorde and Barbara Smith; and a host of well-known and lesser-known women radicals from Grace Lee Boggs, Mae Mallory, and Pauli Murray to Frances Beale, Sonia Sanchez, Amina Baraka, and Charlotta Bass. We hope, however, in presenting these three key interventions to create more space and interest for expanding scholarship in these areas.

Where Is the Black Woman?
An Analysis of the Current Historiography

By uncovering the political and intellectual contributions of women radicals to the postwar black freedom struggle, this anthology engages a number of debates within the historiography. First, these essays begin to expand the boundaries of what is understood to encompass black radicalism. In most historical studies, postwar black radicalism has been defined by a limited set of principles: self-defense tenets and tactics, separatist organizations, Afrocentric cultural practices, and anticapitalist philosophies, as well as a rejection of the practice of lobbying the state. Thus, early histories on postwar radicalism often located radical politics solely within a narrowed time frame of Black Power politics that ostensibly emerged with the Watts riot of 1965 and Stokely Carmichael's call for Black Power during the Meredith March of 1966.

This historical framing has taken shape through a number of prominent studies. One of the most lasting definitions of black radicalism emerged in Harold Cruse's book *The Crisis of the Negro Intellectual* (1967), which drew a rigid distinction between nationalist and integrationist politics and sharply critiqued black communists. Indeed, by Cruse's gauge for Black Power, Robert F. Williams explicitly and Gloria Richardson implicitly did not make the cut.[14] This boundary has been taken up in a number of more recent works that have helped to popularize a limited vision of black radicalism that excludes activists who affiliated themselves with electoral politics, civil rights desegregation demands, majority-white organizations such as the communist, socialist, and labor organizations, or feminist and gay rights groups.[15] The impact of these constricted definitions has rendered a host of women leaders, artists, and strategists historically invisible and implicitly insignificant. Yet, while Cruse's critique engaged women's contributions, particularly the work of black feminist Lorraine Hansberry, black women radicals have dropped out of sight in more recent studies that have furthered Cruse's arguments.[16] These works tend to focus solely on the militancy of black men and often define black radical ideologies from self-defense to black nationalism as exclusively male (and often masculinist) domains. From this scholarship, there is little sense that African American women also shared a philosophical commitment to and practice of self-defense and armed resistance.[17]

A number of new studies have introduced significant revisions to the traditional narrative of black radicalism in the United States. Fueled by a growing emphasis on the "long movement," this new scholarship argues for a more inclusive view of black radicalism and Black Power politics.[18] Through monographs such as Timothy Tyson's *Radio Free Dixie*, Nikhil Singh's *Black Is a Country*, Martha Biondi's *To Stand and Fight*, Robert Self's *American Babylon*, and Peniel Joseph's *Waiting 'Til the Midnight Hour*, a different picture of postwar black radical politics and its impact on the broader black freedom struggle has emerged.[19] Such revisions have extended the periodization of black radicalism well before 1965 and recalibrated our understanding of the intersections of Black Power, black leftist, and nationalist ideologies, as well as the civil rights organizing and transnational solidarity efforts. Moreover, they have recouped important leaders of the Black Revolt previously marginalized in Cold War scholarship such as Robert F. Williams, Paul Robeson, and Ewart Guiner and highlighted the radical politics emerging from those active in a range of organizations from the Communist Party to the National Association for the Advancement of Colored People (NAACP).

Such insights support a new framework for defining black radicalism, which takes into account the multitude of strategies that activists took up to challenge the structures of U.S. power, build coalitions, and claim liberation. Yet, for the most part, these studies are curiously silent on revisioning women's radicalism. While several of these works acknowledge the contributions of women radicals, these women emerge as subsidiary or symbolic figures.[20] Rather than examining women as pivotal historical actors, far too many of these studies simply acknowledge various women as key participants and note the damage of sexism and the relevance of gender politics.[21] Critical theorist Michael Apple has defined this narrative technique as "dominance through mentioning."[22] In the current historiography, many radical women are mentioned, the sexism in many Black Power organizations is mentioned, black feminism is mentioned. However, a full exploration of these women's lives and philosophies and the ways their contributions shaped all the movements of the postwar era has largely not been forthcoming.

Recent scholars of the civil rights movement have provided a strong model for revisioning the male-centered story of social change.[23] Groundbreaking studies such as Charles Payne's *I've Got the Light of Freedom*, John Dittmer's *Local People*, Barbara Ransby's *Ella Baker and the Black Freedom Movement*, and Belinda Robnett's *How Long? How Long?*, along with a burgeoning scholarship on local organizing and women of the SNCC,

Highlander Folk School, and Montgomery's Women's Political Council, have demonstrated the pivotal role women played in the development and execution of modern civil rights activism. This scholarship has convincingly argued for the centrality of black women as long-distance runners and on-the-ground activists in the black freedom struggle. Accounting for traditional notions of male leadership that dominated during this period, these works have popularized the idea of black women as "bridge leaders" within black communities. However, these histories have largely focused on the southern civil rights struggle and often framed women within the gendered image of the backbone of the movement, reinforcing the construction of woman activists as respectable, stoic, and operating behind the scenes. This perspective makes less visible the radical politics and vision embedded in these women's activism and often ignores their roles as central leaders and strategists. Pioneering biographies of Ella Baker, Fannie Lou Hamer, and Gloria Richardson have documented the breadth and expanse of these women's work and radical philosophies; however, presented as individual stories, these women are often read as the exceptional women to stand alongside the great men.

Moreover, as scholars explored the rise of feminist politics in the postwar period, they often defined it as a movement emerging from white women's experiences with civil rights activism but wholly separate from the Black Power movement or black radicalism more broadly. Such a definition is misleading in agency, substance, and chronology. The dominant perception that feminist politics and the fight for women's equality occurred largely outside of the black freedom struggle and with little engagement from black women has emerged implicitly and explicitly in numerous studies, including Sara Evans's early work *Personal Politics: The Roots of Women's Liberation in the Civil Rights Movement and the New Left*, Alice Echols's *Daring to Be Bad: Radical Feminism in America*, and Ruth Rosen's *The World Split Wide Open*.[24] Such framing has been reinforced by growing scholarship on sexism within the Black Power movements. These studies foreground the ways positions of formal or public leadership were often reserved for men, and many Black Power activists emphasized male leadership as a way to free black people from the emasculations of slavery and Jim Crow. These studies also uncover the pressures of Black Power discourses, national debates around the Moynihan Report, and many white women's myopia about the parameters of women's liberation. Works such as Winfred Breines's *The Trouble between Us* and Deborah Gray White's *Too Heavy a Load* reflect the continued dominance of this interpretation. These books center an important discussion of the movement's sexism—of what women were *not* able to do—but do not necessarily provide a full portrayal of the significant political work radical black women did do within the Black Power and women's movements and the ways many black women carried feminist politics into and raised gender issues from within these organizations.[25] This outlook has led to the perception that black women activists were summarily excluded from leadership roles and generally found it difficult, if not impossible, to raise gender concerns within black organizations.

As part of a larger body of work critiquing second-wave feminism as a framing device, this anthology contributes to an interpretive framework that positions black women radicals as central voices in feminist politics in both the women's movement and black liberation organizations. Such an intervention builds upon the work of a number of studies, such as Kimberly Springer's *Living for the Revolution,* Jennifer Nelson's *Women of Color and the Reproductive Rights Movement,* V. P. Franklin and Bettye Collier-Thomas's *Sisters in the Struggle,* and Benita Roth's *Separate Roads to Feminism,* that produce a more nuanced view of black women's feminist politics both outside and within the frameworks of civil rights activism and Black Power politics.[26] These studies illustrate the ways black women challenged the direction of Black Power and black radicalism from within the ranks of those political movements, not only in opposition to these ideological dynamics.[27] New work on black women's antipoverty organizing by Rhonda Williams, Premilla Nadasen, Felicia Kornbluh, and Annelise Orleck has expanded beyond a southern movement focus by examining the ways black women drew attention to the fissures of race, class, and gender in deindustrializing America and built a web of local movements to challenge this inequality.[28] Such scholarship has produced a series of important local studies of black women's feminist politics but largely been treated separately from discussions of 1960s feminist movements. With this anthology, we hope to broaden this conversation by bringing together these disparate strands of black feminism and women's activist politics.

Enlarging the Boundaries of Radicalism

Want to Start a Revolution? restores the contributions of leading women activists—and particularly black women radicals—into the history of U.S. social movements from the 1930s through the 1970s. Drawing on extensive new research on women's contributions to a range of postwar social movements, these scholars have taken the paradigms forged out of pathbreaking studies that have begun rethinking the civil rights movement, black radicalism, Black Power, and women's liberation movements to examine women radicals' work as critical organizers, strategists, and leaders in a host of movements and mobilizations. In so doing, this collection not only enriches our understanding of the long black freedom struggle and postwar U.S. politics but also expands dominant conceptions of black radicalism.

Indeed, examining these women's experiences reveals far more than their presence in the ranks of the Black Revolt and encourages us to re-map the movements of the 1960s and 1970s. The chapters here on Vicki Garvin, Shirley Graham Du Bois, and Esther Cooper Jackson challenge contemporary notions that the anticommunism of the 1950s destroyed the black left. Red-baiting took an immense personal and material toll on these women, but they continued their activism in the sixties, thus revealing important yet neglected continuities between Cold War radicalism, Black Power, and black feminism. Serious analysis of these women's political lives also refuses the strict binaries between integrationist and black separatist politics, nationalism and socialism, and feminism and Black Power and reveals that such dichotomies often hide important commonalties and connections that people forged across and between ideologies and movements. In other words, what has been framed as hard sectarian divisions are not so hard-and-fast when we put Rosa Parks, Vicki Garvin and Esther Cooper Jackson, Florynce Kennedy, Denise Oliver, and Ericka Huggins side-by-side and examine their activism over a half century.

The political work of many of these women thus complicates the simplistic binary between reformist and radical and illustrates the connections between civil rights and Black Power politics. By some gauges of the period, people like Shirley Chisholm were criticized for not being radical enough. Yet Chisholm's presidential candidacy was simultaneously about working within the political system and transforming it. With the perspective of history, Chisholm's historic candidacy for the presidency of the United States, endorsed by the Black Panther Party, can be seen as a bold attempt to force open corridors of power. Hoping to amass enough delegate power to force the Democratic Party to have to deal with black issues, Chisholm's run charted a different path to social transformation rather than simply making a reformist compromise with power.[29]

These essays also ask us to rethink the simplistic binary between respectable and radical. The focus on respectability in much of the literature on middle-class black women has obscured the ways many working women hewed to *and* reshaped dominant notions of respectability as a vehicle to promote radical change.[30] Rosa Parks and a generation of civil rights women waged struggle in ways that both adhered to and destabilized notions of respectability. This had as much to do with negotiating and transforming intraracial gender dynamics and creating a space for more militant protest as with an individual adherence to the politics of respectability. Graciously but firmly, Rosa Parks explained her decision not to join a group of civil rights activists in the summer of 1955 when they met with city officials months before her bus stand: "I had decided I would not go anywhere with a piece of paper in my hand asking white folks for any favors." The respectable Parks had firm lines beyond which she "would not be pushed"; a devoted churchgoer *and* believer in self-defense, this shy woman spent nearly sixty years of her life vociferously advocating for the rights of black prisoners. Similarly, clad in stylish coat and hat, Juanita Jackson Mitchell journeyed in 1936 to meet with the imprisoned Scottsboro boys, strategically using her middle-class status to promote justice in this case and other campaigns.

Expanding the boundaries of black radicalism not only marks one of the key historiographical interventions of this collection but also reflects what happened on the ground within many of these movements. Women radicals often pushed their comrades to broaden their conception of liberation. Indeed, one of the strands that unite the disparate assortment of women in this book is the ways they prodded the organizations they worked with to take a more inclusive view of the struggle. For instance, the fight for welfare rights was not only about pushing local agencies and the federal government to expand access to welfare but also about getting other black organizations to see public assistance as a right of social citizenship and a path to self-determination and self-respect. Johnnie Tillmon and the National Welfare Rights Organization (NWRO) asserted a very different notion of rights that foregrounded entitlement to economic security as a key aspect of citizenship. Such politics pushed a diverse array of black leaders, from Martin Luther King, Jr. to Amiri Baraka, to see self-protection as a woman's and family right and public assistance as a key to self-determination.

Women's Work: Women Radicals as Long-Distance Runners,
Strategic Thinkers, Behind-the-Scenes Organizers,
and Charismatic Leaders

This anthology's second intervention moves the history of women's work in the movement beyond a view of women as solely behind-the-scenes, local activists. Challenging the limits of the bridge leader concept and any single framework of black women's leadership, a number of the essays look at a wider spectrum of women's leadership roles. On one end of the spectrum, this included charismatic leadership. Women like Lillie Jackson, Shirley Chisholm, and Denise Oliver took public leadership roles, pushing aside barriers of sexism in their organizations. Indeed, as demonstrated in these pages, black women's activism was not only local but also national and international. Shirley Chisholm had the audacity as a first-term congress-woman to challenge her placement on the Agricultural Committee and then to run for president at a moment when most political organizations—be they black or white—saw this kind of national leadership as the exclusive purview of men. She built a national organization run largely by women that made her presidential campaign a potent one, laying the groundwork for future progressive political campaigns. Similarly, Johnnie Tillmon, who began her welfare activism in Los Angeles, helped launch a national move-ment of welfare recipients and became a regular, disruptive presence on Capitol Hill. Along with such national presence, a number of these activists also spent a portion of their activist careers overseas. Vicki Garvin, Shirley Graham Du Bois, and Denise Oliver moved to Africa and joined the anti-colonial struggles there—to help forge a global politics of black liberation that linked anti-imperialist liberation struggles around the world.

On the other end of the spectrum, many women (and men) believed in participatory democracy and resisted public leadership and national roles. Activists like Yuri Kochiyama and Rosa Parks understood that no move-ment could be built without people creating an infrastructure, without the day-to-day work to enable the dramatic public action.[31] These movement organizers rejected notions of the charismatic individual and instead in-vested heavily in building democratic organizing structures and complet-ing the behind-the-scenes work the struggle entailed. Still others, like Toni Cade Bambara and Ericka Huggins, created alternate structures and institutions to nourish themselves and others in order to provide political spaces free from racism, classism, sexism, and homophobia.

However, these women's contributions to the movement were rarely static. This volume follows a host of women who demonstrated a lifelong commitment to radical change that entailed embracing multiple roles to sustain the movement. Women radicals helped to create the groundwork for the movement by operating as local organizers in key periods. At other moments, they stood as national and international voices of resistance and charismatic leadership, founded numerous groups, took up or were thrust into the public spotlight, and then stepped aside to mentor younger activists.

In highlighting these multiple forms of women's leadership, this collection of essays brings new texture to the work entailed in building and sustaining these movements. Such aspects are too often ignored in the literature or relegated to organizational histories, yet these articles reveal the day-to-day work of radical organizing. For example, while nearly every study of the Black Panther Party mentions its school, little attention has been paid to how people envisioned and enacted liberatory education. An analysis of the Oakland Community School (OCS), the longest-lasting Panther program, demonstrates the ways these Panther women created an institution of their own and made Black Power real at the educational grassroots. Such detail on Panther organizing has been overshadowed by discussions of the ideological contributions, internecine struggles, and federal repression that predominate in scholarly work on the Panthers.

Uncovering Black Feminist Politics in Black Power Politics and the Women's Movement

This anthology joins a growing literature that pushes students to rethink the origins of black women's feminism, women's liberation, and the framing device of "second-wave" feminism more broadly. For many black women radicals, feminist politics did not simply emerge in the 1960s through white women's experiences in the civil rights and student movements, nor did black women's feminism develop primarily as a reaction to the limits of white feminism and black nationalism. Indeed, a number of women profiled here raised issues of sexism, called for greater attention to the specific struggles of black women, and put forth theories of more equitable gender relationships within Left organizations in the 1940s and 1950s. For instance, Esther Cooper Jackson's master's thesis, "The Negro Woman Domestic Worker in Relation to Trade Unionism" (1940), advanced an intersectional analysis that outlined the interconnections of class, race, and gender oppression for black women domestics—the kind of analysis that most people associate with the 1970s. While Vicki Garvin advocated for the rights of black women workers as an important "litmus test of American democracy," Juanita Jackson pushed the NAACP to recognize the value of "women's work." Uncovering the politics of women's equality that emerged among the black left and civil rights groups in the 1940s and 1950s, these essays reperiodize our understandings of the trajectory of postwar women's liberation struggles and highlight black women's attacks on sexist discourse that often predated the emergence of majority-white feminist organizations in the 1960s.

Black women radicals continued this fight for equality into the 1960s and 1970s. Unwilling to keep silent about gender issues within all-black organizations, many of these women highlighted gender oppression as part of their political analysis. They opened up conversations about gendered structures and assumptions in the organizations in which they worked. Johnnie Tillmon's organizing around welfare rights challenged and transformed the political agenda of women's liberation by articulating a radical black feminism of bodily integrity and economic self-determination. Flo Kennedy did not see her radical feminism precluding her role in the Black Power movement, from her work with NOW to mounting the legal defense strategies for H. Rap Brown and Assata Shakur, who were both targeted by COINTELPRO.[32] And she thought Black Power had much to teach her white feminist colleagues, which in part was why she brought them (and insisted upon their right) to attend Black Power meetings. When Shirley Chisholm ran for Congress in 1968 and James Farmer anchored his candidacy to the need for masculine leadership, Chisholm did not let him get away with it. And voters did not automatically gravitate to Farmer's masculinist appeal but elected Chisholm to Brooklyn's Twelfth District seat in 1968, making her the first African American woman in Congress. Such feminist praxis makes clear that many black women did not feel they had to pick their race over their gender, and that such politics enjoyed a mass constituency.

Black women radicals fought to make feminist politics an intrinsic part of the black left and Black Power mobilizations, just as they pushed white feminists to address racism and economic exploitation as crucial to women's liberation. Centering the roles and experiences of women in Black Power organizations, their contributions to the majority-white women's movement and the separate organizations and campaigns black women built allows for a clearer view of black women radicals' political

interventions in these spaces. Writer Toni Cade Bambara sought to challenge conservative notions of manhood and womanhood in Black Power
politics and pulled together the anthology *The Black Woman* (1970). This
book created an important space for women to articulate a black gender
politics that challenged both Black Power's masculinist politics and mainstream feminists' privileging of white women's experiences. In addition
to articulating a diversity of black feminisms in *The Black Woman*, as a
teacher and mentor, Bambara shaped a generation of younger artists ranging from the writer Pearl Cleage to performance poet Sekou Sundiata to
filmmakers Louis Massiah and Spike Lee. Women in Atlanta's Black Arts
movement—like Bambara, Cleage, and Alice Lovelace—did not languish
on the margins of the artistic world but brought their feminist-nationalist
politics to the center of the black arts scene in that southern city, where
Shirley Franklin became the first black woman mayor in 2001.

Finally, the women examined in this book are not all the same—they
do not gender themselves similarly, nor do they necessarily imagine liberation in the same ways. They are gender nonconforming and conven-
tionally feminine, queer and straight, brash and shy, comfortably middle-
class and profoundly poor. While Juanita Jackson Mitchell sought a paid
position in the NAACP to affirm her value to the organization and her
need for paid child care, women like Tillmon fought for the choice to be
able to stay home to raise their own children. Women like Shirley Graham Du Bois and Yuri Kochiyama saw mothering other movement activists as crucial to the longevity of the struggle; yet Denise Oliver and Shirley Chisholm resisted this role as too gendered. While some women in
the movement, like Rosa Parks, attempted to maintain a judicious privacy
about their personal lives, artists like Toni Cade Bambara, Audre Lorde,
and other writers in *The Black Woman* fashioned art—and the weapons of
social change—from the many strands of their selves.

In widening the boundaries of black womanhood, these histories also
expand our ideas of how sexism affected women's lives and political work
at the time. The experiences of both Rosa Parks and Juanita Jackson Mitchell reveal the difficulties women had getting paid for their political work.
Indeed, the Parks family plunged into a decade of economic insecurity after her Montgomery bus arrest; no civil rights organization offered her a
job until newly elected John Conyers hired her as an assistant in his Detroit office in 1965. In addition to those economic dimensions, women also
faced organizational challenges to their liberation and created structures
within these organizations to root out sexism. While most work on the

Young Lords mentions the discussions of "machismo" that arose out of the Party's thirteen-point program, there has been little attention to the structures that rank-and-file members built to address gender issues within the organization. Denise Oliver and other women in the Young Lords Party created separate men's and women's caucuses, built formal structures for disciplining misogynist behavior, and instituted affirmative action policies for including gender issues in the organization's newspaper *Palante* and building women's participation in multiple organizational roles.

Organizational Design of This Book

For the most part, these fourteen chapters, covering a vast range of women's strategies, organizations, and leadership, are presented chronologically, spanning roughly five decades of turbulent struggle, from the labor and community organizing of the 1930s to the resistance to Nixon's repressive law-and-order politics of the 1970s. Those years witness the rise and fall of the U.S. left during the Great Depression and Cold War era, the explosion of civil rights and Black Power in the 1950s and 1960s, the rise of the gay and lesbian movement, and the growth and decline of Black Power and Latino liberation organizations like the Black Panther Party and the Young Lords Party. The first four chapters present the early roots of black women's radicalism, which sprout in the 1930s and incubate despite the anticommunist backlash of the 1950s. Chapter 1, "'No Small Amount of Change Could Do': Esther Cooper Jackson and the Making of a Black Left Feminist," by Erik S. McDuffie, focuses on Esther Cooper's embrace of communist politics and her early feminist analysis. In the second chapter, "What 'the Cause' Needs Is a 'Brainy and Energetic Woman': A Study of Female Charismatic Leadership in Baltimore," Prudence Cumberbatch examines the assertive politics of mother and daughter Lillie Carroll Jackson and Juanita Jackson Mitchell. For two generations, the Jacksons boldly challenged the racial structures of the city of Baltimore and the gender strictures of male-dominated leadership within the NAACP. The next two chapters explore women who set their sights on the international struggle for black liberation. In the third chapter, "From Communist Politics to Black Power: The Visionary Politics and Transnational Solidarities of Victoria "Vicki" Ama Garvin," Dayo F. Gore examines the rich political career of Vicki Garvin. Garvin's leadership linked radical labor politics to community mobilization and women's self-emancipation in the groundbreaking National Negro Labor Council and continued to fashion such strategic political connections while she was in exile in Ghana and China. The fourth chapter, "Shirley Graham Du Bois: Portrait of the Black Woman Artist as a Revolutionary," coauthored by Gerald Horne and Margaret Stevens, investigates the life of Shirley Graham Du Bois and her work in Ghana and China. Vicki Garvin and Shirley Graham Du Bois, both of whom mentored Malcolm X, returned to the United States to share the revolutionary lessons they had learned on their journeys as they mentored a new generation of activists in the Black Revolt of the 1970s and 1980s.

By contrast, the next three chapters present a rethinking of several of the women and organizations that stand as iconic figures in the civil rights and Black Power movements. Jeanne Theoharis's "'A Life History of Being Rebellious': The Radicalism of Rosa Parks" presents a careful rereading of Rosa Park as the quiet and stoic "mother of the civil rights movement." Situating Parks's bus protest in a lifetime of activism, this chapter uncovers Parks's radical past as well as her continued investment in black liberation and self-determination post-Montgomery. Chapters 6 and 7 turn our attention to the Black Panther Party. In chapter 6, "Framing the Panther: Assata Shakur and Black Female Agency," Joy James pushes beyond the iconic image of Assata Shakur as a black fugitive to examine her political contributions as a prison intellectual, including her theorizing of prison industry and black women's resistance. In chapter 7, "Revolutionary Women, Revolutionary Education: The Black Panther Party's Oakland Community School," Angela D. LeBlanc-Ernest and former Black Panther leader Ericka Huggins provide an important detailed account of women's leadership roles in formulating and fostering the Black Panther Community School specifically and its survival programs more generally. In many ways, the Black Panther Party drew attention to the depth of the urban crisis for black America; the survival programs the organization created provide a basic outline of the material exclusions from the robust social citizenship introduced by the New Deal and of the segregated and unequal education black children were receiving in northern cities. This chapter reveals not only the power of this local organizing but the ways it shaped the politics of the Black Panther Party more broadly and fundamentally challenged the dismal education system most black children endured.

Black Arts movement politics are the subject of the next two chapters. During that critical period of identity formation, women artists challenged both blinders and barriers to their self-discovery and self-determination within the black community and American society at large. Chapters 8 and 9 examine black women's contributions to postwar black radical culture in general and the Black Arts movement more specifically, as well as exploring the impact of debates over gender and sexuality in shaping black cultural politics. Margo Natalie Crawford's chapter, "Must Revolution Be a Family Affair? Revisiting *The Black Woman*," reminds us that black male writers also brought an intersectional paradigm to their writing, seeing black liberation as intrinsically connected to issues of black masculinity and the restoration of the black family. Black women writing in *The Black Woman* thus sought to reframe intersectionality to demonstrate the interlocking nature of sexism, racism, economic inequality, and homophobia and push black liberation outside the narrow parameters of a "black family affair." James Smethurst's "Retraining the Heartworks: Women in Atlanta's Black Arts Movement" examines the central contributions of Atlanta's Black Arts women and the ways writers like Toni Cade Bambara and Pearl Cleage saw their feminism and nationalism as politically compatible.

The essays that make up the final five chapters of the anthology bring to light a number of women traditionally excluded from the pantheon of the Black Revolt to reorient the ways we define black radicalism and feminist politics during the 1960s and 1970s. Sherie M. Randolph's "'Women's Liberation or . . . Black Liberation, You're Fighting the Same Enemies': Florynce Kennedy, Black Power, and Feminism" and Joshua Guild's "To Make That Someday Come: Shirley Chisholm's Radical Politics of Possibility" look at two black women—lawyer Florynce Kennedy and New York congresswoman Shirley Chisholm—whose feminism in the 1960s and 1970s was boldly pronounced and publicized. While both women were household names in the 1970s, they have faded into obscurity, Randolph and Guild argue, because their feminist radicalism and connections to Black Power seem at odds with prevalent histories of Black Power and "second-wave" feminism.

Rethinking the boundaries of the Black Revolt even further are the stories in chapters 12 through 14 of a black woman in the leadership of the Young Lords Party, a Japanese American member of Malcolm X's Organization of Afro-American Unity, and Johnnie Tillmon's Black Power politics in welfare rights. Johanna Fernández's "Denise Oliver and the Young Lords Party: Stretching the Political Boundaries of Struggle" and Diane C. Fujino's "Grassroots Leadership and Afro-Asian Solidarities: Yuri Kochiyama's Humanizing Radicalism" reveal that the ethnic boundaries of black radicalism were porous and permeable. African American Denise Oliver emerged as a leader of the Puerto Rican Young Lords Party, and Japanese American Yuri Kochiyama served as an organizer of Malcolm X's Organization for Afro-American Unity. In chapter 14, "'We Do Whatever Becomes Necessary': Johnnie Tillmon, Welfare Rights, and Black Power," Premilla Nadasen provides an important corrective to the presumed whiteness of the mass base of 1960s feminism. Nadasen examines NWRO leader Johnnie Tillmon's philosophies, demonstrating the traditions of self-defense and self-determination at the heart of the struggle for welfare rights. In concert, these final chapters show that black radicalism, feminism, and Black Power flowered in the midst of Third World frameworks where African American, Puerto Rican, Chicano, Native American, and Asian American radicals developed common antiracist and anti-imperialist politics, as well as welfare rights campaigns for economic justice.

Taken together, these fourteen essays push us to refocus how we understand the history of the black freedom struggle and to reconceptualize the trajectory and cross-fertilization in radical movements of the 1960s and 1970s. Centering women in this anthology provides a wider lens on the range of postwar black radicalisms and thus a much-expanded view of postwar U.S. social movement history.

NOTES

1. Leslie Alexander Lacy, "Black Bodies in Exile," in *Black Homeland/Black Diaspora: Cross-Currents of the African Relationship*, ed. Jacob Drachler (London: Kennikat Press, 1975), 147.

2. Rosa Parks, letter to Ernest Thompson [chair of the National Negro Labor Council] from the Montgomery Improvement Association, June 15, 1956, Ernest Thompson papers, National Negro Labor Council File, Rutgers University Special Collection at Alexander Library, New Brunswick, box 1C.

3. Rhonda Y. Williams, "Black Women and Black Power," *Magazine of History* 22 (July 2008): 22–27; Kevin Gaines, "From Center to Margin: Internationalism and the Origins of Black Feminism," in *Materializing Democracy: Toward a Revitalized Cultural Politics*, ed. Russ Castronovo and Dara Nelson (Durham, NC: Duke University Press, 2002), 294–313; Ruth Feldstein, "'I Don't Trust You Anymore': Nina Simone, Culture and Black Activism in the 1960s," *Journal of American History* 91 (2005): 1349–1379.

4. This gathering reflects one of numerous shared political actions and meetings black women radicals attended or held during this period. For example, at the "Symposium on Black Women" on January 7–8, 1972, a number of elder leaders met in Chicago on the eve of the Gary Convention in order to pass on black radical traditions to the younger political generation. Septima Clark of the Citizenship Schools and Fannie Lou Hamer and Unita Blackwell of the Mississippi Movement, as well as Charlayne Hunter and Johnetta Cole, met with Amina Baraka of the Congress of African People and Nikki Giovanni, Audre Lorde, Jayne Cortez, and Mari Evans of the Black Arts movement to fashion an agenda for Black women's struggles within the larger Black national agenda. See Report: "A Symposium on Black Women," January 7 and 8, 1972, Deering Special Collection (7–22–91), Northwestern University, Evanston, Illinois.

5. For Leroy Henderson's full description of the photo, see http://www.youtube.com/watch?v=OrCUgW6Qw40.

6. This paraphrases Robert P. Moses, *Radical Equations: Civil Rights from Mississippi to the Algebra Project* (Boston: Beacon Press, 2002), 22.

7. The Left is that broad array of ideas, as well as social, cultural, and political movements, that have stood in opposition to exploitation and have debated ways to end injustice. There have always been many factions with conflicting definitions of what constitutes the U.S left. The 1960s witnessed endless debates about an Old Left, including earlier generations of socialists, communists, and pacifists as well as feminist and civil rights activists, and a New Left, including a wide array of radicals initially in support of the 1960s civil rights activism and opposed to the war in Vietnam. The New Left introduced a host of social and cultural issues that may have had less political status and emphasis than economic exploitation in the Old Left. The origin of the term "Left" as a political definition is more obscure. It may be traced back to the French Revolution and seating arrangements in the Legislative Assembly. Those factions who supported the monarchy sat on the right wing of the assembly and became known as the Right—and, by that measure, counterrevolutionary. By contrast, the factions who advocated the overthrow of the French king were seated on the left wing and became known as the Left—and, by that measure, radical.

8. In its broadest meaning, inside the United States, "Third World" refers to oppressed people of color such as African Americans, Native Americans, Asian Americans, and Mexican Americans, as well as Puerto Ricans and other peoples from the Caribbean. However, beyond the United States and in terms of world geography, the term emerged during the Cold War when the great military powers attempted to divide the world into two spheres of power. The influential former British premier Winston Churchill defined the First World as the West, headed by the United States, and the Second World as the sphere of communist nations headed by the Soviet Union. What was the Third World? According to Vijay Prashad, the peoples and nations emerging from colonialism were termed, in 1952, the Third World by French journalist Albert Sauvy when he insisted that beyond the heated Cold War conflict, there was an "ignored, exploited, scorned Third World" that "demands to become something as well." The idea of a Third World further crystallized at the Afro-Asian political summits in Bandung, Indonesia (1955) and Cairo, Egypt (1961). See Vijay Prashad, *The Darker Nations: A People's History of the Third World* (New York: New Press, 2007), xvi, 11.

9. Charles Payne forwarded this idea in his groundbreaking work on Mississippi, "Men Led, but Women Organized: Movement Participation of Women in the Mississippi Delta," in *Women in the Civil Rights Movement: Trailblazers and Torchbearers, 1941–1945*, ed. Vicki L. Crawford, Jacqueline Anne Rouse, and Barbara Woods (Bloomington: Indiana University Press, 1993). But he now has revised it and spoken to the limitations of this paradigm in capturing women's roles in the movement.

10. Belinda Robnett, *How Long? How Long? African American Women and the Struggle for Freedom and Justice* (New York: Oxford University Press, 1997).

11. McCarthyism, which draws its name from the staunchly anticommunist Senator Joseph McCarthy, refers to the government-supported harassment and political repression of a wide range of activists, artists, and intellectuals who were accused of being affiliated with, sympathetic to, or members in the Communist Party during the early Cold War period, roughly the late 1940s to the 1960s.

12. We borrow this formulation from Robin Kelley, *Freedom Dreams: The Black Radical Imagination* (Boston: Beacon Press, 2002)

13. In this introduction and throughout the collection of essays, we use the term "second-wave" feminism as a shorthand to refer to the rise of feminist activism in the 1960s and 1970, yet we also seek to problematize the term. Indeed, several of the authors in this volume join a growing number of scholars who critique this term for its framing of feminist politics through moments of upsurge and decline within white women's organizing.

14. Harold Cruse, *The Crisis of the Negro Intellectual: A Historical Analysis of the Failure of Black Leadership* (New York: Quill Press, 1984 [1967]). For important alternatives to Cruse's limited racial lens, see Jeffrey B. Perry, ed., *The Hubert H. Harrison Reader* (Middletown, CT: Wesleyan University Press, 2001); Winston James, *Holding Aloft the Banner of Ethiopia: Caribbean Radicalism in Early Twentieth-Century America* (New York: Verso, 1999); Jeffrey B. Perry, *Hubert Harrison: The Voice of Harlem Radicalism* (New York: Columbia University Press, 2008).

15. William L. Van Deburg, *New Day in Babylon: The Black Power Movement and American Culture, 1965-1975* (Chicago: University of Chicago Press, 1993); Sundiata Keita Cha-Jua and Clarence Lang, "The 'Long Movement' as Vampire: Temporal and Spatial Fallacies in Recent Black Freedom Studies," *Journal of African American History* 92 (2007): 265–288.

16. Jama Lazerow and Yohuru Williams's most recent collection, *In Search of the Black Panther Party: New Perspectives on a Revolutionary Movement* (Chapel Hill, NC: Duke University Press, 2006), includes little examination of women Panthers in any of the essays despite the fact that the conference the collection came out of had many papers on and much discussion of women Panthers.

17. In Christopher Strain's study of self-defense in the civil rights era, *Pure Fire: Self-Defense as Activism in the Civil Rights Era* (Athens: University of Georgia Press, 2005), for instance, there is no consideration of the countless militant women who claimed the right of self-defense as they organized to fight white terror and rape. In these years women like Mae Mallory were legendary in black self-defense from New York to North Carolina, and they served prison sentences for their militant political work in supporting Robert F. Williams and in protesting the murder of Congolese premier Patrice Lumumba. For other women, like Daisy Bates, a show of force was not tactically sound, but concealed self-defense weapons were crucial and effective. For still others, women as well as men, self-defense involved issues of racial and class "respectability." For them, a black woman openly advocating self-defense was seen as "lower-class." Still, insisting on their own definitions of womanhood, many women carried or owned weapons for self-defense as a crucial tool of political survival and self-determination.

18. See Jacquelyn Dowd Hall, "The Long Civil Rights Movement and the Political Uses of the Past," *Journal of American History* 91 (2005): 1233–1263, for a discussion of the long movement.

19. Timothy Tyson, *Radio Free Dixie* (Chapel Hill: University of North Carolina Press, 1999); Nikhil Pal Singh, *Black Is a Country: Race and the Unfinished Struggle for Democracy* (Cambridge, MA: Harvard University Press, 2004); Martha Biondi, *To Stand and Fight: The Struggle for Civil Rights in Postwar New York* (Cambridge, MA: Harvard University Press, 2003); Peniel Joseph, *Waiting 'Til the Midnight Hour: A Narrative History of Black Power* (New York: Henry Holt, 2006); and Peniel Joseph, ed., *The Black Power Movement: Rethinking the Civil Rights–Black Power Era* (New York: Routledge, 2006); Robert Self, *American Babylon: Race and the Struggle for Postwar Oakland* (Princeton, NJ: Princeton University Press, 2003); Matthew Countryman, *Up South: Civil Rights and Black Power in Philadelphia* (Philadelphia: University of Pennsylvania Press, 2005); Martin Bauml Duberman, *Paul Robeson* (New York: Knopf, 1988); Glenda Gilmore, *Defying Dixie: The Radical Roots of Civil Rights, 1919-1950* (New York: Norton, 2008); Murali Balaji, *The Professor and the Pupil: The Politics of W. E. B. DuBois and Paul Robeson* (New York: Nation Books, 2007); Tom Sugrue, *Sweet Land of Liberty: The Forgotten Struggle for Civil Rights in the North* (New York: Knopf, 2008); Patrick Jones, *The Selma of the North: Civil Rights Insurgency in Milwaukee* (Cambridge, MA: Harvard University Press, 2009); Peter Levy, *Civil War on Race Street: The Civil Rights Movement in Cambridge, Maryland* (Gainesville: University Press of Florida, 2003); Kelley *Freedom Dreams*; Carole Boyce Davies, *Left of Karl Marx: The Political Life of Black Communist Claudia Jones* (Durham, NC: Duke University Press, 2007); Jeanne Theoharis and Komozi Woodard, eds., *Freedom North: Black Freedom Struggles Outside the South, 1940-1980* (New York: Palgrave Macmillan, 2003); Theoharis and Woodard, *Groundwork: Local Black Freedom Movements in America* (New York: NYU Press, 2005); Judson Jeffries *Black Power*

in the Belly of the Beast (Urbana: University of Illinois Press, 2006); Charles Jones, ed., *The Black Panther Party Reconsidered* (New York: Black Classic Press, 1998).

20. Important works that still do not do full justice to women's radicalism include Kevin Gaines, *American Africans in Ghana: Black Expatriates and the Civil Rights Era* (Chapel Hill: University of North Carolina Press, 2006); Joseph, *Waiting 'Til the Midnight Hour*; Singh, *Black Is a Country*; and Biondi *To Stand and Fight*.

21. Indeed, as historian Robyn Spencer has observed, "Black women have remained on the outskirts of Black Power [historiography]: their marginality central to the movement's definition, but their agency and empowerment within the movement effectively obscured." Robyn Spencer, "Engendering the Black Freedom Struggle: Revolutionary Black Womanhood and the Black Panther Party in the Bay Area, California," *Journal of Women's History* 20 (Spring 2008): 91.

22. Apple argues, "Dominance is partly maintained here through compromise and the process of 'mentioning.' Here limited and isolated elements of the history and culture of less powerful groups are included in the texts. Thus, for example a small and often separate section is included on 'the contributions of women' and 'minority groups,' but without any substantive elaboration of the view of the world as seen from their perspective." Michael Apple, *Official Knowledge: Democratic Education in a Conservative Age* (New York: Routledge, 2000), 61.

23. Charles Payne, *I've Got the Light of Freedom* (Berkeley: University of California Press, 1995); Robnett, *How Long? How Long?*; John Dittmer, *Local People: The Struggle for Civil Rights in Mississippi* (Urbana: University of Illinois Press, 1995). See also Joanne Grant, *Ella Baker: Freedom Bound* (New York: Wiley, 1999), Chana Kai Lee, *For Freedom's Sake: The Life of Fannie Lou Hamer* (Urbana: University of Illinois Press, 1999); Cynthia Fleming, *Soon We Will Not Cry: The Liberation of Ruby Doris Smith Robinson* (New York: Rowman and Littlefield, 1998); Bettye Collier-Thomas and V. P. Franklin, eds., *Sisters in the Struggle* (New York: NYU Press, 2001); Barbara Ransby, *Ella Baker and the Black Freedom Movement: A Radical Democratic Vision* (Chapel Hill: University of North Carolina Press, 2003); Peter Levy, *Civil War on Race Street: The Civil Rights Movement in Cambridge, Maryland* (Gainesville: University Press of Florida, 2003); Christina Greene, *Our Separate Ways: Women and the Black Freedom Movement in Durham, North Carolina* (Chapel Hill: University of North Carolina Press, 2005); Gilmore, *Defying Dixie*.

24. Sara Evans, *Personal Politics: The Roots of Women's Liberation in the Civil Rights Movement and the New Left* (New York: Vintage, 1980); Alice Echols, *Daring to Be Bad: Radical Feminism in America, 1967–1971* (Minneapolis: University of Minnesota Press, 1989); Ruth Rosen, *The World Split Wide Open: How the Modern Women's Movement Changed America* (New York: Viking, 2000). For studies that disrupt aspects of this historiography by including activism by women of color or challenging the periodization, but continue to center white women's feminism, see Flora Davis, *Moving the Mountain: The American Women's Movement since 1960* (New York: Simon and Schuster, 1991); and Kate Weigand, *Red Feminism: American Communism and the Making of Women's Liberation* (Baltimore: Johns Hopkins University Press, 2001).

25. Winfred Breines, *The Trouble between Us: An Uneasy History of White and Black Women in the Feminist Movement* (New York: Oxford University Press, 2007); Deborah Gray White, *Too Heavy a Load: Black Women in Defense of Themselves, 1884–1994* (New York: Norton, 1999). Gray White argues that these conflicts "left black women at odds with both black men and white women . . . now race and gender issues seemed oppositional" (222).

26. Kimberly Springer, *Living for the Revolution: Black Feminist Organizing, 1968–1980* (Duke, NC: Duke University Press, 2005); Jennifer Nelson, *Women of Color and the Reproductive Rights Movement* (New York: NYU Press, 2003); Franklin and Collier-Thomas, *Sisters in the Struggle*; Benita Roth, *Separate Roads to Feminism: Black, Chicana and White Feminist Movements in America's Second Wave* (Cambridge: Cambridge University Press, 2004); Alexis De Veaux, *Warrior Poet: The Biography of Audre Lorde* (New York: Norton, 2004); Anne M. Valk, *Radical Sisters: Second Wave Feminism and Black Liberation in Washington, D.C.* (Urbana:

University of Illinois Press, 2008); Cheryl Clarke, *"After Mecca": Women Poets and the Black Arts Movement* (New Brunswick, NJ: Rutgers University Press, 2005); Danielle McGuire, "'It Was Like All of Us Had Been Raped': Black Womanhood, White Violence, and the Civil Rights Movement," *Journal of American History* 91 (2004): 906–931.

27. Historian Stephen Ward makes this point in his essay on the Third World Women's Alliance, where he writes: "I aim to challenge the notion that black feminism and Black Power were ideologically incompatible or locked in an inherently antagonistic relationship. To the contrary, the Third World Women's Alliance's feminism was not simply a critique of Black Power politics but a form of it." Stephen Ward, "The Third World Women's Alliance: Black Feminist Radicalisms and Black Power Politics," in *The Black Power Movement*, ed. Peniel Joseph (New York: Routledge, 2006), 120. While Benita Roth argues that these black women represented a "vanguard center" in the civil rights/Black Power movements, she also marks the rise of Black Power with a move to northern organizing and increasing sexism that limited black women's roles in these movements.

28. Rhonda Y. Williams, *The Politics of Public Housing: Black Women's Struggles against Urban Inequality* (New York: Oxford University Press, 2005); Premilla Nadasen, *Welfare Warriors: The Welfare Rights Movement in the United States* (New York: Routledge, 2004); Annelise Orleck, *Storming Caesar's Palace: How Black Mothers Fought Their Own War on Poverty* (Boston: Beacon Press, 2005); Felicia Kornbluh, *The Battle for Welfare Rights: Politics and Poverty in Modern America* (Philadelphia: University of Pennsylvania Press, 2007).

29. Historians of Reconstruction have used more sophisticated gauges when examining the political work of those black political leaders who had autonomous bases of power but who ran on the Republican or later Populist tickets. By contrast, the more complex Second Reconstruction requires even finer standards of measurement. See Hasan Kwame Jeffries, *Bloody Lowndes: Civil Rights and Black Power in Lowndes County, Alabama* (New York: NYU Press, 2009); Komozi Woodard, *A Nation within a Nation: Amiri Baraka (LeRoi Jones) and Black Power Politics* (Chapel Hill: University of North Carolina Press, 1999); Ronald W. Walters, *Black Presidential Politics in America: A Strategic Approach* (Albany: State University of New York Press, 1988); Ronald Dellums, *Lying Down with the Lions: A Public Life from the Streets of Oakland to the Halls of Power* (Boston: Beacon Press, 2000); Cedric Johnson, *Revolutionaries to Race Leaders: Black Power and the Making of African American Politics* (Minneapolis: University of Minnesota Press, 2007); Hanes Walton and Robert C. Smith, *American Politics and the African American Quest for Universal Freedom*, 3rd ed. (London: Longman, 2005).

30. In an important exception, Victoria Wolcott has written about the ways black women remade respectability in the radical 1930s Housewives League in *Remaking Respectability: African American Women in Interwar Detroit* (Chapel Hill: University of North Carolina Press, 2001).

31. Inadvertently, this has contributed to their own obscurity, since "backgrounding" oneself makes the record more difficult for scholars to follow. Charismatic leaders such as King and Malcolm X are always already understood as important and left a public record for scholars to follow.

32. COINTELPRO is the name given to a set of secret Federal Bureau of Investigation (FBI) counterintelligence programs. Between 1956 and 1971, the FBI designed a series of illegal counterintelligence programs aimed at American citizens and their political activities. Initially focused on the Communist Party, the programs came to include Dr. Martin Luther King Jr., the Southern Christian Leadership Conference, Assata Shakur and the Black Panther Party as well as Rap Brown and the Student Nonviolent Coordinating Committee. Under the leadership of J. Edgar Hoover, the FBI defined the aims of the civil rights movement and many of the social movements of the 1960s as subversive activity. They attacked activists in a number of ways, ranging from misinformation, disruption, and psychological warfare, to targeting activists for the loss of employment, for IRS harassment, and for political and physical attacks by other activists. These efforts at their most destructive included the torture, murder, and assassination of leaders. The specific impact of this FBI program on radical women is discussed in several of the chapters that follow.

1

"No Small Amount of Change Could Do"

Esther Cooper Jackson and the Making of a Black Left Feminist

Erik S. McDuffie

On April 18, 1942, a twenty-three-year-old African American woman named Esther Cooper delivered the opening address of the Fifth All-Southern Negro Youth Conference held on the campus of historically black Tuskegee Institute in Tuskegee, Alabama.[1] An activist trailblazer, she was the newly elected executive secretary of the gathering's sponsoring organization: the Birmingham, Alabama-based Southern Negro Youth Congress (SNYC), a pioneering, World War II era civil rights group with links to the Communist Party, USA (CPUSA).[2] Opening her speech by emphasizing black southern youth's importance "to the resolute prosecution of the war for a speedy victory," she called for a "Double Victory," the defeat of fascism abroad and Jim Crow at home.[3] She also called special attention to how the SNYC "recognize[d] the importance of [black] women in winning the war . . . for the preservation of democracy in the world." Stating that black women were "an important part of the total woman labor supply needed in this crisis," she argued that their inclusion in trade unions and extending social security and old-age benefits to domestic workers would be crucial for defeating Nazi Germany, Japan, and Italy.[4]

Her address embodied the CPUSA's 1930s and 1940s era Popular Front agenda of racial and economic justice, antifascism, internationalism, anticolonialism, women's rights, and the protection of civil liberties. Her position as the SNYC's titular head highlighted the ways in which Black Popular Front organizations of the 1940s provided black women with unique

Esther Cooper Jackson speaking in 1968 in Great Barrington, Massachusetts, at a ceremony in which the site of W. E. B. Du Bois's childhood home was officially designated as a National Historic Landmark. Esther and James Jackson's Personal Papers, Brooklyn, New York.

opportunities to hold formal, visible leadership positions. Above all, her speech illustrates one of the trademarks of her political activism that spanned the New Deal through the civil rights and Black Power era: her belief that black women's status was the gauge for measuring democracy in the United States and across the world, and that progressives needed to foreground black women's struggles in the left-wing agenda.[5]

Until recently, the involvement of black women like Esther Cooper Jackson[6] in the Communist Left and their connections to 1960s radicalism have received only cursory treatment from scholars interested in African American women's history, black radicalism, and the twentieth century black freedom movement.[7] Tracing her radicalization, enlistment in the CPUSA, and activism highlights the importance of the Popular Front as a site—albeit a contested one—for black feminist knowledge production and activism. Cooper Jackson—like other women drawn to the Communist

Left during the 1930s and 1940s—formulated what literary scholar Mary Helen Washington has termed "black left feminism," a distinct politics that combined Communist Party positions on race, gender, and class, and black nationalism with black women radicals' own lived experiences that focused on working-class women. Paying special attention to the intersectional, transnational nature of black women's multiple oppressions, black left feminists put forth gender liberation as inextricably connected to race and class liberation. In doing so, they attempted to recenter the Communist Left by arguing that African American working-class women's concerns were central, not peripheral, to the socialist struggle.[8]

Cooper Jackson's story also provides a lens for reassessing the impact of the Cold War on black movements and for reperiodizing postwar black feminism.[9] Her work shows how black left feminism not only survived the politically repressive McCarthy era but also helped cultivate a new generation of black feminists in the 1960s and 1970s. This history, however, remains largely untold. Instead, much of the recent scholarship on 1960s and 1970s black feminism by Kimberly Springer, Benita Roth, and Premilla Nadasen either has focused on recovering black women's involvement in "second-wave feminism" or has charted the ways in which black women fashioned their own distinct feminist politics during these years.[10] For the most part, these works identify the civil rights movement, New Left, and Chicano/a movement as the "parent" movements to 1960s and 1970s black feminism. This scholarship also locates the emergence of black feminist groups such as the Third World Women's Alliance and the Combahee River Collective as a counter to the infamous 1965 Moynihan Report and to the "resurgent masculinism of Black Liberation."[11] My intention here is to broaden these scholarly narratives by locating how black left feminism helped to lay the groundwork for 1960s and 1970s black feminism.[12] In doing so, Cooper Jackson's life and activism call into question the usefulness of the wave metaphor for understanding U.S. feminist struggles, which "neatly package[s] the women's rights movement into peaks and troughs" and excludes women of color's involvement in feminist struggles by "reinscribing gender as the primary category of analysis that defines feminism."[13] Cooper Jackson's work and legacy offer an alternative narrative to the wave metaphor, for her activism highlights both the breaks and the continuities in black feminist struggles from the 1930s through the 1980s.

This chapter begins with a discussion of Cooper Jackson's formative years, illustrating how her family's commitment to racial uplift was critical to her political awakening as a young woman. It then focuses on the impact of Popular Front movements on campus in radicalizing her. Next, the chapter examines her black left feminist stance embedded in her 1940 master's thesis, "The Negro Woman Domestic Worker in Relation to Trade Unionism."[14] The story shifts to her leadership of the Southern Negro Youth Congress and how it served as an important site for black left feminism until Cold War repression crushed the group. The essay concludes with a discussion of her journalistic work in *Freedomways: A Quarterly Review of the Negro Movement*. The journal represented the continuation of black left feminism into the civil rights–Black Power era and served as an important but understudied site for the cultivation of a new generation of black feminists. Excavating Cooper Jackson's life is important not simply because it tells a fascinating story of a remarkable activist and thinker but because her work has important implications for rethinking the origins, contours, and periodization of postwar black feminism, black radicalism, and U.S. women's movements.

Early Years

Esther Cooper Jackson's lifelong career as a radical activist was not inevitable. However, growing up in a politically conscious, talented-tenth black family committed to racial uplift prepared the ground for her life's work and black left feminist sensibility. By the time she reached early adulthood, she was already well aware of racial inequality and her place in the world as a young African American woman.[15]

Esther Victoria Cooper Jackson was born on August 21, 1917, in Arlington, Virginia, to George Posia Cooper (1885–1937) and Esther Irving Cooper (1888–1970). Cooper Jackson was the second of the couple's three daughters (Kathyrn, Esther, and Pauline). Her parents were part of the upwardly mobile group of black people who came of age during the so-called nadir of African American life.[16] A strong, independent-minded woman, Irving Cooper was an educator, a community activist, and a major figure in the Arlington and Washington, D.C., chapters of the National Association for the Advancement of Colored People (NAACP) and in local school desegregation campaigns. She inspired in her daughter a sense of independence and an "interest in struggle and doing something about the Jim Crow situation in which we lived," as Cooper Jackson recalled.[17] Her father was a Spanish-American War army veteran and a decorated World War I army officer who became a pacifist and atheist later in life. She credited her staunch pacifist and secular views to his influence.[18]

Given the realities facing blacks in the Jim Crow South, her family instilled in the young Cooper Jackson an interest in racial justice along with the value of education. The family read religiously the NAACP's magazine, the *Crisis*, and debated columns by the magazine's editor, W. E. B. Du Bois. Enrolled in the prestigious all-black Paul Lawrence Dunbar High School in Washington, D.C., she graduated near the top of her class in the spring of 1934.[19]

Oberlin, Fisk, and the Popular Front

Popular Front movements on college campuses were critical in radicalizing Cooper Jackson during the latter half of 1930s, one of the most dynamic moments in U.S. student protest prior to the 1960s. Galvanized by social and political upheavals of the Depression, the growing menace of fascism and the looming world war, Communist, Socialist, Trotskyite, and Christian student movements proliferated on college campuses across the country by the mid-1930s. Groups focused on free speech, labor organizing, civil rights, unemployment, social relief, peace, and antifascism. It was in this context that in the fall of 1934 Cooper Jackson enrolled in Oberlin College, a prestigious liberal arts school that was the first college in the United States to admit African Americans and white women.[20]

Radical politics on campus sparked her initial interest in the Left. She arrived at Oberlin a committed pacifist; in fact, she sometimes argued with students, especially Young Communist League members, who called for "collective security" to stem the spread of fascism.[21] However, the Spanish Civil War (1936–1939) was critical in moving Cooper Jackson toward the left and in sparking her burgeoning feminist politics. The global Left viewed the devastating conflict between the democratically elected, left-wing Spanish (Republican) government and the forces of Francisco Franco backed by Nazi Germany and fascist Italy as an epic struggle between fascism and democracy. Support for Spain on American college campuses peaked in 1938 following a nationwide student strike in support of the Republican government led by the American Student Union (ASU), a Popular Front antiwar group. While she still maintained her pacifism, Cooper Jackson nevertheless attended ASU rallies in support of the embattled Republican government. Her admiration for Dolores "La Pasionaria" Ibarruri, the beloved, highest-ranking Communist in the Spanish government, was key to bolstering Cooper Jackson's interest in Spain and her interest in women's involvement in revolutionary movements around the world. She idolized Ibarruri because "she was a leader and not just a follower . . . of women. She was the revolution."[22]

At the same time, Cooper Jackson developed a strong sense of solidarity with workers and the newly founded Congress of Industrial Organizations (CIO), especially after the sit-down strikes of rubber workers in nearby Akron in 1936 and autoworkers in Flint, Michigan, the following year.[23] As graduation approached, she had no plans on becoming a professional, left-wing activist. Instead, she planned to pursue a career in social work, prompting her to major in sociology. After she graduated from Oberlin in 1938, she headed that fall for historically black Fisk University in Nashville, Tennessee, to earn a master's degree in sociology.[24]

Cooper Jackson's two-year graduate experience drew her into the Communist Party. Her graduate fellowship required that she live in and work at the Bethlehem Community Center, a Methodist settlement house located in an impoverished black Nashville neighborhood near Fisk. Many of her social work cases involved impoverished black women who toiled as domestics in wealthy white homes. Here "for the first time I saw southern poverty of blacks . . . where people were living in very horrible conditions." These experiences "helped steer me to radical politics. I felt that no small amount of change could do . . . to really advance the people who were the most oppressed."[25] Her sentiments at this time marked a key turning point in her thinking, as she was becoming increasingly aware of the intersections of race, gender, and class and the structural inequalities of capitalism. These conclusions demanded a shift from the largely race-based strategies of uplift ideology toward a more radical politics that understood racial justice and economic equality as inextricably connected.

While working at the settlement house, Cooper Jackson also befriended several left-wing professors on campus who profoundly influenced her nascent radical thought, including painter Aaron Douglas and white economics professor Addison T. Cutler, who was the adviser for her master's thesis and a Communist Party member. She also befriended the more mainstream politically minded Charles Johnson, the prominent black sociologist and former head of the Urban League. Upon Cutler's invitation, she joined a left-wing faculty study circle. During one meeting, one of her instructors signed her up as a member of the Communist Party. Joining the CPUSA marked a significant break from her parents' racial uplift politics that did not call for the dismantling of capitalism as a prerequisite for realizing racial equality.[26] Even more, by enlisting in the Party she joined a small community of African American women across the country, including Louise Thompson Patterson, Audley Moore, Claudia Jones, Thelma Dale, Bonita Williams, and Dorothy Burnham, who moved into the Communist Left during the Depression because they saw in CPUSA-affiliated social movements and their links to the global stage unique opportunities to pursue racial justice and social equality, especially for black women.[27]

"The Negro Woman Domestic Worker in Relation to Trade Unionism"

Cooper Jackson's master's thesis, "The Negro Woman Domestic Worker in Relation to Trade Unionism" (1940), stands both as her first major achievement as a left-wing activist intellectual and as the most thorough study of black women household workers' unionizing during the Depression. Inspired by her burgeoning interest in Marxism, CIO industrial unionism, the New Deal, the Soviet Union, and black women's status, the thesis's black left feminist approach historicized African American women domestics' exploitation and called attention to their agency in fighting for their well-being and respect. Part of a growing body of Popular Front era writings focused on women's rights, the thesis was also in conversation with black left feminist writings and politically mainstream black periodical articles focused on the plight of African American household workers. The most famous of these works was the muckraking exposé "The Bronx Slave Market" (1938), published in the *Crisis* by future civil rights activist Ella Baker and journalist Marvel Cooke, both of whom had ties to the Left.[28] They vividly described the infamous "slave markets," select Bronx street corners where African American women stood to be hired for household day labor by white housewives. Baker and Cooke discussed the backbreaking nature of household work and the sexual assault black women often encountered from white men on the job.[29] Moreover, mass street protests in Harlem—often led by black Communist women—focused on the high price of food, poor housing, and other pressing community concerns during the latter half of the 1930s fueled black women writers' interest in domestic workers. These campaigns and their writings illustrate that black women radicals understood that no one but themselves would lead the struggle for their well-being and dignity.[30]

Positing that the support for black women's freedom was the litmus test for the Communist Left's and labor's commitment to democracy in New Deal America, her main argument asserted that "the problems faced by

Negro women domestic workers are responsive to amelioration through trade union organizations." She rejected the mainstream American labor movement's position that domestic workers were "unorganizable" by pointing to the success in unionizing household laborers in Western Europe and, above all, in the Soviet Union. In stark contrast to the United States, she stressed that in the U.S.S.R. "the social standing of domestic workers is equal to any other worker."[31] She saw advances made by Soviet household laborers as a model for improving black women domestics' lives and an example of how socialism liberated women.

The study briefly discussed the miserable conditions and low status of African American women domestics from slavery to the Depression, paying careful attention to relations of inequality historically between black women and white women in whose homes they worked. Moreover, she stressed that black women, in contrast to white women, "have been discriminated against and exploited with double harshness." "Negro women," she added, "often have to face discrimination and prejudice in addition to the problems which domestic workers as a whole must face."[32] These latter issues included the "social stigma" of domestic labor, long hours, low wages, poor work conditions, lack of job security, mainstream labor's neglect of domestic workers, absent job standards, the isolating nature of household work, and the exemption of domestics from old age insurance and unemployment benefits under the Social Security Act of 1935. Criticizing the American Federation of Labor, the largest U.S. union, for its refusal to organize black women domestics, she charged that mainstream labor and the U.S. state were complicit in black women's marginalization.[33]

Despite these obstacles, Cooper Jackson remained optimistic about black women domestics' future. She cited New Deal legislation—Section 7a of the National Industrial Recovery Act (1933) and the National Labor Relations Act (1935)—as important potential tools for enabling black women to unionize. While she credited the CIO and the National Negro Congress, a Popular Front civil rights federation, for their support for black women domestics' unionization, she urged these organizations to devote more attention to collectively organizing black women household workers.[34] For her, the limited success of the New York–based Domestic Workers Union, an organization led by black household workers, was the most encouraging sign that unionization was possible and that black women were key agents in advancing their rights and dignity. She found that the union had won higher wages and better work conditions for its members. However, she was also realistic about the union's prospects for success. It counted only 2,000 members in New York, Chicago, and Washington, D.C., out of a total of 600,000 black domestic workers nationwide. Given the tremendous obstacles that prevented household workers from organizing, especially in New York, where a large pool of domestics made it easy for white employers to find black women who would work for the smallest pittance, she understood that unionization was a formidable task.[35]

"The Negro Woman Domestic Worker" also critiqued Popular Front era writings by white Communist women, who often posited "woman" as a universal, ahistorical category and provided only glancing discussion of African American women. *Women and Equality* (1936) by Margaret Cowl, chair of the CPUSA National Women's Committee, for example, posited that "all women are in unequal position with men in all countries."[36] Mary Inman, author of the widely read *In Woman's Defense* (1940), which generated considerable controversy within the Communist Left for arguing that women's household labor was as exploitative and necessary to reproducing capitalist inequalities as working-class men's factory work, asserted that (white) prostitutes constituted the most oppressed segment of society.[37] She also drew the Communist Left's common but problematic comparison of women's oppression as analogous to racism, and she equated "women" with white and "Negroes" with men.[38]

Although Cooper Jackson's thesis did not explicitly reference these works, "The Negro Woman Domestic Worker" challenged propositions advanced by white Communist women that rendered black working women invisible in left analysis.[39] Like Baker and Cooke, Cooper Jackson singled out the Bronx slave market to make the case that African American women encountered unique forms of exploitation and that intersections of race, gender, and class positioned black and white women differently vis-à-vis one another. The Bronx slave market, she argued, constituted "one of the worst types of human exploitation . . . found in New York City, and one of its ugliest aspects is the way in which girls are shipped up in car loads from the South to stand on corners waiting for work at 25 to 35 cents per hour." White women not only enjoyed a degree of comfort and freedom from alienating, time-consuming household labor at the expense of black women; she charged that white women were complicit in black women's exploitation, arguing: "Housewives, knowing they can get domestic workers at almost starvation wages, have played employee against employee." For Cooper Jackson, the Bronx slave market was emblematic of black women's historic economic and social marginality in

American society and a glaring example of the race and class divisions between black and white women. However, while African American domestics were victimized, she emphasized that they did not wallow in their oppression. Instead, "these women formed the nucleus of the [Domestic Workers Union] in New York," and she detailed the ways in which black women built their union.[40]

For Cooper Jackson, then, black women's location at the bottom of the U.S. political economy positioned them as the vanguard for radical social change, a point she insisted that the white Left had failed to appreciate. Implicit in her thesis was an argument that black women's freedom could only be achieved through the destruction of all forms of domination, underscoring how black women's status was the barometer for measuring American democracy. These ideas would be further developed after the late 1960s by black feminist organizations, especially the Third World Women's Alliance and the Combahee River Collective.[41]

"The Negro Woman Domestic Worker" not only illustrated how black women in the Popular Front formulated their own distinct brand of feminist politics. The thesis also showed how black women radicals during the 1930s prefigured the "triple oppression" paradigm popularized in the postwar Communist Left by black Party leader and theoretician Claudia Jones. Her influential article "An End to the Neglect of the Problems of the Negro Woman!" (1949), published in the CPUSA's theoretical journal *Political Affairs*, argued that triply exploited black women constituted both the most exploited and most revolutionary segment of the U.S. working class, thereby challenging orthodox Marxist postulations that industrial (white male) workers represented the vanguard of the working class. (Jones's ideas gained some traction in the postwar Communist Left, especially among black and white women in the Party-affiliated Congress of American Women and the Sojourners for Truth and Justice, an all-black women's left-wing protest group.) Cooper Jackson made similar arguments nearly ten years earlier.[42]

In the spring of 1940, "The Negro Woman Domestic Worker" gained the attention of Robert Park, a nationally renowned University of Chicago sociologist, who offered Cooper Jackson a doctoral fellowship. Park's invitation came at the same time as she became interested in civil rights organizing and began courting James E. Jackson Jr., a Howard University pharmaceutical graduate who had joined the Communist Party at the age of sixteen and had cofounded the Southern Negro Youth Congress in 1937. They met in 1939 when he came to Nashville to conduct research on behalf of Gunnar Myrdal for his study on U.S. race relations, later published as *The American Dilemma*. After Jackson left Nashville, he invited Cooper Jackson to attend the SNYC's 1939 convention in Birmingham, Alabama. Impressed with the group's militant antiracist agenda, she turned down Park's invitation and opted instead to work for the Youth Congress in Birmingham. She intended to complete her graduate studies one day but got "busy organizing in the South."[43] The chance to materialize her commitment to racial justice and democracy was just too good an opportunity to pass up. Her growing romantic relationship with Jackson also kept her in Birmingham. They were married on May 7, 1941.[44]

While her thesis gained Park's attention, it received little notice from the American labor movement or the Communist Left. For example, Jackson urged her to send the thesis to CIO officials at the union's Washington headquarters, believing that it would make a useful manual for organizing black domestics. She followed his advice. However, she never received a reply from the union. Deprived of a larger audience, the thesis mainly sat on the shelves at Fisk University's library for decades to come until Cooper Jackson began receiving scholarly attention in the 1980s. The CIO's silence was indicative of black women's marginal position in the Popular Front. However, Cooper Jackson's ideas did not fall on deaf ears among black Communist women and men during the 1940s and beyond. Rather, black left feminist articulations made their way into other spaces in the coming years, namely, the SNYC and later *Freedomways*.[45]

The Southern Negro Youth Congress

Under Cooper's leadership as executive secretary during most of World War II, the SNYC cultivated a black left feminist stance, encouraging the group's black Communist couples—Esther Cooper and James E. Jackson Jr., Edward Strong and Augusta Jackson, and Dorothy and Louis E. Burnham—to think critically about the politicized nature of personal life. That feminist stance also promoted black women in leadership who were in many respects ahead of their time. Due to CPUSA initiatives on what the Party called the "Woman Question," which emphasized the need to root out "male chauvinism" within its ranks, along with black Birmingham Communists' intense discussions of Frederick Engels's *Origins of the Family, Private Property, and the State*, SNYC leadership, according to Cooper Jackson, "took very seriously [the Woman Question], and it was an integral part of the whole struggle to change society."[46] In an effort to assert their independence, black Party women with the support of their spouses continued using their maiden names in public for years to come. In Cooper's case, she began using Cooper Jackson during the 1950s, when her husband faced persecution from Cold Warriors. Given that she spoke publicly in his defense, she adopted Cooper Jackson so that she would be associated with him. This was a courageous move in light of the times, speaking to her nondogmatic application of black feminist politics.[47]

Black Communist couples also challenged traditional sexual divisions of labor at home. James Jackson and Louis Burnham, for example, often shared child-rearing and household chores. They, however, did not "always live up to this [their antisexist politics]," as Cooper Jackson insisted. Still, that black Party women and men attempted to grapple with prevailing gender conventions shows not only that they believed that the personal was political but also that the SNYC created space for black radicals to rethink dominant notions about gender.[48]

The visibility of black women in formal leadership positions from the group's very inception was another example of the SNYC's progressive gender politics. In addition to Cooper Jackson, the group counted a cadre of Communist and non-Communist women leaders: Rose Mae Catchings (president), Thelma Dale (vice president), Dorothy Burnham (educational director), and Augusta Jackson (editor of the Youth Conference newspaper, *Cavalcade*). Wartime dislocations helped to create opportunities for women to lead. Ed Strong and James Jackson, for instance, both joined the army and served overseas. But it was the SNYC's sensitivity to gender equality and, more important, black women's determination to lead that best explain the large number of high-ranking African American women officials in the organization.[49]

Echoing concerns drawn in Cooper Jackson's thesis, the Youth Conference devoted special attention in recognizing black working-class women's issues. The SNYC's 1946 conference in Columbia, South Carolina, for example, featured a speech by Miami SNYC official Florence Valentine in which she argued that black women had "been discriminated against and exploited . . . with double harshness." Calling attention to how African American women had "played an important part in winning the war" and yet still worked disproportionately in domestic service, she demanded decent-paying jobs in unionized blue- and white-collar professions for black women in postwar America. Improving black women's status, she argued, was critical to advancing black freedom and postwar U.S. democracy.[50]

Serving as the SNYC's director enabled Cooper Jackson to expand her networks with leading Communist and non-Communist black women activists across the country. She befriended Claudia Jones during the early 1940s. While there are no records of correspondence between them about women's rights, it seems difficult to imagine how they would not have discussed gender matters. Cooper Jackson also worked closely with the distinguished educator Mary McCleod Bethune, educator Charlotte Hawkins Brown, and South Carolina–based civil rights activists Septima Clark and Modjeska Simpkins on SNYC-related projects. Cooper Jackson also met Ella Baker, then the NAACP director of branches, who would play a pivotal role in founding the Student Nonviolent Coordinating Committee (SNCC) in 1960. Surely these encounters bolstered Cooper Jackson's black woman selfhood and knowledge about African American women's plight. As World War II came to a close, Cooper Jackson acquired a national reputation as a leading civil rights spokesperson. Moreover, she and her SNYC comrades looked optimistically toward the postwar period, believing that a new, democratic racial order was coming. However, growing anticommunist hysteria soon dashed their hopes.[51]

The McCarthy Period

The McCarthy period, as those in the Communist Left called the postwar red scare, was a tumultuous time for Cooper Jackson. Growing prosegregationist sentiment coupled with anticommunist hysteria prompted the SNYC to disband in 1949.[52] The Cold War also marked an extremely difficult time in Cooper Jackson's personal life. Indicted along with eleven other "second-string" Communist national leaders under the Smith Act, James Jackson went "underground" to avoid arrest in June 1951.[53] After James was placed on the FBI's "Most Wanted List," she had no contact with him for almost five years. In his absence, she raised the couple's two daughters (Harriet and Kathryn) under constant FBI surveillance and harassment. FBI agents conspicuously followed the family everywhere they went and pressured Kathryn's nursery school into expelling her.[54] Additionally, Cooper Jackson's 950-page FBI file, most of which covers the 1950s, highlights authorities' obsession with capturing her "fugitive" husband and surveilling her. In a move anticipating 1960s COINTELPRO surveillance of black militants, authorities compiled several hundred pages of reports detailing her and her children's every move, her involvement in Party-affiliated groups, her biographical history, her employment, and newspaper clippings about her plight. Despite this harassment, her political resolve, together with support from family and friends, enabled her to weather McCarthyism. She also remained politically active. She became a national spokesperson for the Families of Smith Act Victims, an organization composed largely of wives of CPUSA officials indicted under the Smith Act, which called for Party leaders' freedom and for the protection of civil liberties, linking these campaigns to struggles for peace and civil rights. But the stifling anticommunist political climate largely prevented Cooper Jackson from successfully building broad-based movements around these issues.[55]

On December 2, 1956, the day after the launching of the Montgomery Bus Boycott that marked the beginning of the civil rights movement, Jackson turned himself in to federal authorities in New York and spent nearly the next two years in pitched legal battles for his freedom. As this new phase in the black freedom movement gained momentum, the Jacksons and many of their black left-wing allies sat mainly on the sidelines. Cold War repression crushed Popular Front organizations and isolated some of the most dedicated antiracist activists for a brief but key moment as new black freedom struggles unfolded.[56]

Freedomways

As Robin Kelley has observed, "The collapse of an organization does not necessarily signify the destruction of a movement or the eradication of traditions of radicalism."[57] These conclusions have important implications for appreciating the impact of the Cold War on the trajectory of black feminism and in appreciating the links between Popular Front era and 1960s black radicalism. As destructive as the red scare was on CPUSA-affiliated organizations and on the lives of black women radicals, it squelched neither their freedom dreams nor their black left feminism. Rather, many emerged from the McCarthy period committed to building new antiracist, antisexist, anti-imperialist struggles and in doing so helped lay the foundations for 1960s and 1970s black feminism.[58]

Nothing better epitomized this than Cooper Jackson's role in cofounding *Freedomways* and serving as its managing editor from 1961 to 1985. The journal marked her most significant achievement and stood as "probably the most notable and enduring institution established in the 1960s by African Americans who had been active in the Popular Front."[59] An important site of intergenerational exchange between an ideologically diverse group of black thinkers during the civil rights–Black Power era, the journal published articles by such black luminaries as W. E. B. Du Bois, James Baldwin, and Paul Robeson, left nationalist historian John Henrik Clarke, and younger civil rights leaders like Martin Luther King, Southern Christian Leadership Council organizer Jack O'Dell, SNCC leader Julian Bond, Black Power spokesperson Stokely Carmichael (Kwame Toure), and future presidential hopeful Jesse Jackson. Diasporic in vision, *Freedomways* printed essays by Trinidadian revolutionary theoretician C. L. R. James and President Julius Nyerere of Tanzania. Moreover, Cooper Jackson drew on her broad networks among black writers and artists with the left-wing Harlem Writers Guild, such as actors Ossie Davis and Ruby Dee along with Harry Belafonte, to organize fund-raisers and to write for the journal.[60]

In both its staffing and its editorial content, *Freedomways* revealed the continuation of Cooper Jackson's belief first articulated in her 1940 master's thesis that black women's dignity and rights were vital to American democracy and black freedom. The magazine prominently featured black women on its staff, which was atypical of magazines, even African American periodicals, during the early 1960s. In addition to Cooper Jackson, older radicals such as playwright Shirley Graham Du Bois and Chicago artist Margaret Burroughs served as the journal's associate editor and first art editor, respectively. Younger women such as Jean Carey Bond, who had lived in Ghana during the mid–1960s, coedited the journal during its final years.[61]

During its entire run, *Freedomways* featured articles, visual art, and poetry by and about black women and also reported on their contributions to black freedom movements across the diaspora. Veteran progressive activist intellectuals such as Shirley Graham Du Bois, Eslanda Robeson, Alice Childress, Louise Thompson Patterson, Maude White Katz, and Lorraine Hansberry, for instance, wrote for the journal. It published visual art by Elizabeth Catlett and Margaret Burroughs. Anticipating late 1960s and early 1970s black feminist critiques of the masculinist assumptions embedded in black nationalism, the magazine printed comments from a 1965 New School for Social Research conference panel, "The Negro Woman in American Literature," in which presenters Alice Childress, Paule Marshall, and Sarah Wright critically discussed denigrating representations of African American women in black-authored novels and in popular culture. Moreover, *Freedomways* promoted a new generation of black women militants. Some of the earliest work by Alice Walker, Toni Morrison, June

Jordan, Audre Lorde, and Nikki Giovanni, all whom would go on to make names for themselves as leading black literary feminist voices, appeared in the journal.[62] The prominence of black feminist voices in *Freedomways* from its very inception illustrates the ways in which 1960s and 1970s black feminism was not, as commonly believed, mainly a response to black nationalists' misogyny or to white feminists' racism. Rather, black feminism emerged in part from longer, richly textured feminist conversations within the Communist Left dating back to the Popular Front, revealing how black left feminism survived the Cold War.

Freedomways has important implications not only for rethinking the roots of 1960s and 1970s black feminism but also for providing an alternative narrative to the wave metaphor. The journal preceded by two years the publication of Betty Friedan's seminal *Feminine Mystique* (1963), a text widely regarded as "a major turning point in the history of modern American feminism" and "a key factor in the revival of the women's movement."[63] Moreover, Cooper Jackson's black left feminism at this moment stood in stark contrast to the rightward turn of Friedan, who had worked for several years after World War II as a reporter for the *UE News*, the newspaper of the CPUSA-affiliated United Electrical Radio and Workers union that was attentive to race, gender, and class. "Reacting to the terror of anti-communism, redbaiting, and naming names," Friedan, according to her biographer Daniel Horowitz, "sought a safer haven in the suburbs," downplayed her radical past, and reinvented herself into an alienated, middle-class housewife following the height of the McCarthy period. In a break from postwar Popular Front feminism, Friedan's *Feminine Mystique* was inattentive to both race and class and devoid of an internationalist perspective.[64] As a black woman radical whose husband had been on the FBI's "Most Wanted List," retreating to staid, lily-white suburbs was not an option for Cooper Jackson, nor could she have easily found a home in politically mainstream black protest groups that still were intent on keeping Communists and even former ones at arm's length out of fear of being charged by the government as subversive. In this light, her social location coupled with the ways in which she was situated in the political landscape of the early 1960s played a crucial role in shaping the articulation of her feminist politics in ways that were very strikingly different than her more famous counterpart. Indeed, Cooper Jackson's and Friedan's stories not only reveal how black and white feminists formulated different feminist politics but also how the wave narrative fails to capture black women's centrality to early 1960s U.S. feminism and its connections to Popular Front era feminism.[65]

Freedomways published its last issue in the winter of 1985. Strains of operating the magazine on a limited budget were an important factor in ending its run. In addition, Cooper Jackson was approaching her seventies, and the political climate had swung to the right.[66] The journal's demise does not erase its important legacy, for it underscores the continuum of black feminist struggle from the 1930s through the 1980s.

Conclusion

In recent years, Esther Cooper Jackson—along with her husband—has practically gained celebrity status among scholars, filmmakers, and activists interested in the origins of the modern black freedom movement, W. E. B. Du Bois and Paul Robeson, and African Americans and Communism.[67] Now more than ninety years old, she remains actively involved in progressive political causes. She sits, for example, on the executive board of the Louis E. Burnham Award, a foundation named for her dear friend that funds scholarly work and grassroots community projects focused on African American youth, social justice, and human rights.[68]

Cooper Jackson's work sheds invaluable light on the Communist Left's importance as a site for cultivating a distinct black feminist politics that called on the CPUSA to appreciate the black working class's issues as central to the left-wing agenda. In addition, her work, especially in *Freedomways*, calls attention to the debt modern black feminism owes to Popular Front era black women radicals. The journal promoted leading young black feminist voices and created a unique space for intergenerational dialogue that has yet to receive close scholarly attention.

Future scholarship needs to appreciate black women radicals' complicated relationship with the Communist Left. It created both unique opportunities for black women radicals to theorize and to promote their black left feminist agenda while at the same time the CPUSA often marginalized their work. In addition, scholars need to excavate the links between black women radicals before and after the McCarthy period. Cooper Jackson's life provides a lens for understanding the Cold War's destructive impact on black radical women and how they often found creative ways to survive it. At the forefront since the 1940s in leading black radical protest and literary groups that were committed to internationalism and attentive to race, class, and gender, her work helped lay the groundwork for civil rights, Black Power, and 1960s and 1970s black feminism. The life and activism of Esther Cooper Jackson, then, not only disrupt standard narratives of the black freedom movement, U.S. feminist movements, and American Communism but also point scholars toward exciting new areas of inquiry for appreciating the genealogies of postwar black feminism.

NOTES

1. "Negro Youth Fighting for America," program, Fifth All-Southern Negro Youth Conference," April 17–19, 1942, Edward E. Strong Papers, box 3, folder 3, Moorland-Spingarn Research Center, Howard University, Washington, D.C.; Esther V. Cooper, "Negro Youth Organizing for Victory," April 18, 1942, Strong Papers, box 3, folder 3; Erik S. McDuffie, "Long Journeys: Four Black Women and the Communist Party, USA, 1930–1956" (Ph.D. diss., New York University, 2003), 371–375.

2. McDuffie, "Long Journeys," 363–395; Peter F. Lau, *Democracy Rising: South Carolina and the Fight for Black Equality since 1865* (Lexington: University Press of Kentucky, 2006), 156–173; Robin D. G. Kelley, *Hammer and Hoe: Alabama Communists during the Depression* (Chapel Hill: University of North Carolina Press, 1990), 195–219; Johnetta Richards, "The Southern Negro Youth Congress: A History" (Ph.D. diss., University of Cincinnati, 1987).

3. Beth T. Bates, "'Double V for Victory' Mobilizes Black Detroit, 1941–1946," in *Freedom North: Black Freedom Struggles Outside the South, 1940–1980*, ed. Jeanne F. Theoharis and Komozi Woodard (New York: Palgrave Macmillan, 2003), 17–33.

4. Cooper, "Negro Youth Organizing for Victory." For discussions of the gendered and racial implications of and the exclusion of domestics, migrant farm laborers, and other occupations from receiving benefits and protections under the 1935 Social Security Act, see Linda Gordon, *Pitied but Not Entitled: Single Mothers and the History of Welfare* (Cambridge, MA: Harvard University Press, 1994), 4–6, 253–263, 293–297.

5. "Women Urged to Attend Tuskegee," n.b., James E. Jackson and Esther Cooper Jackson Papers, Tamiment Library/Robert F. Wagner Labor Archives, New York University, SNYC Box, Documents, Publications Folder. Note that I first accessed the Jackson Papers in August 2006 before they were reorganized in June 2007; the term "Black Popular Front" is borrowed from Martha Biondi, *To Stand and Fight: The Struggle for Civil Rights in Postwar New York* (Cambridge, MA: Harvard University Press, 2003).

6. Readers should note that Esther Cooper made a conscious, political decision not to use her married name, Esther Cooper Jackson, until the 1950s, during the McCarthy period; such decisions marked the contours of her politics. However, to avoid confusion, we use Esther Cooper Jackson hereafter in this chapter.

7. This essay joins a growing body of scholarship on black women's encounters with the U.S. Old Left; see Erik S. McDuffie, "A New Freedom Movement of Negro Women": Sojourning for Truth, Justice, and Human Rights during the Early Cold War," *Radical History Review* 101 (Spring 2008): 81–105; Carole Boyce Davies, *Left of Karl Marx: The Political Life of Black Communist Claudia Jones* (Durham, NC: Duke University Press, 2008); Erik S. McDuffie, "'[She] Devoted Twenty Minutes Condemning All Other Forms of Government but the Soviet': Black Women Radicals in the Garvey Movement and in the Left during the 1920s," in *Diasporic Africa: A Reader*, ed. Michael A. Gomez (New York: NYU Press, 2006), 219–250; McDuffie, "Long Journeys"; Jacqueline Ann Castledine, "Gendering the Cold War: Race, Class and Women's Peace Politics, 1945–1975" (Ph.D. diss., Rutgers, State University of New Jersey, 2006); Dayo Falayon Gore, "To Hold a Candle in the Wind: Black Women Radicals and Post World War II U.S. Politics" (Ph.D. diss., New York University, 2003); Rebeccah E. Welch, "Gender and Power in the Black Diaspora: Radical Women of Color and the Cold War, *Souls* 5, no. 3 (2003): 71–82; Claire Nee Nelson, "Louise Thompson Patterson and the Southern Roots of the Popular Front,"

in *Women Shaping the South: Creating and Confronting Change*, ed. Angela Boswell and Judith N. McArthur (Columbia: University of Missouri Press, 2006), 204–228; Mary Helen Washington, "Alice Childress, Lorraine Hansberry, and Claudia Jones: Black Women Write the Popular Front," in *Left of the Color Line: Race, Radicalism, and Twentieth Century Literature of the United States*, ed. Bill V. Mullen and James Smethurst (Chapel Hill: University of North Carolina Press, 2003), 183–204; Kate Weigand, *Red Feminism: American Communism and the Making of Women's Liberation* (Baltimore: Johns Hopkins University Press, 2001), 97–113; Gerald Horne, *Race Woman: The Lives of Shirley Graham Du Bois* (New York: NYU Press, 2000); Rebecca Hill, "Fosterites and Feminists, or 1950s Ultra-Leftists and the Invention of the Amerikkka," *New Left Review* 228 (1998): 67–90.

8. Washington, "Black Women Write the Popular Front," 185, 193–194.

9. For discussions and debates about the impact of the Cold War on black radicalism and postwar black freedoms struggles, see Gerald Horne, *Black and Red: W. E. B. Du Bois and the Afro-American Response to the Cold War, 1944–1963* (Albany: State University of New York Press, 1986); James Edward Smethurst, *The Black Arts Movement: Literary Nationalism in the 1960s and 1970s* (Chapel Hill: University of North Carolina Press, 2005); Cynthia Young, *Soul Power: Culture, Radicalism, and the Making of a U.S. Third World Left* (Durham, NC: Duke University Press, 2006); Fanon Che Wilkins, "Beyond Bandung: The Critical Nationalism of Lorraine Hansberry, 1950–1965," *Radical History Review* 95 (Spring 2006): 191–210; Nikhil Pal Singh, *Black Is a Country: Race and the Unfinished Struggle for Democracy* (Cambridge, MA: Harvard University Press, 2004); Carol Anderson, *Eyes Off the Prize: The United Nations and the African American Struggle for Human Rights, 1944–1955* (Cambridge: Cambridge University Press, 2003); Glenda Elizabeth Gilmore, *Defying Dixie: The Radical Roots of Civil Rights, 1919–1950* (New York: Norton, 2008); James H. Meriwether, *Proudly We Can Be Africans: Black Americans and Africa, 1935–1961* (Chapel Hill: University of North Carolina Press, 2002); Mary L. Dudziak, *Cold War Civil Rights: Race and the Image of American Democracy* (Princeton, NJ: Princeton University Press, 2000); Thomas Borstelman, *The Cold War and the Color Line: American Race Relations in the Global Arena* (Cambridge, MA: Harvard University Press, 2001); Biondi, *To Stand and Fight*; Brenda Gayle Plummer, *Rising Wind: Black Americans and U.S. Foreign Affairs, 1935–1960* (Chapel Hill: University of North Carolina Press, 1996).

10. Kimberly Springer, *Living for the Revolution: Black Feminist Organizations, 1968–1980* (Durham, NC: Duke University Press, 2005); Premilla Nadasen, *Welfare Warriors: The Welfare Rights Movement in the United States* (New York: Routledge, 2005); Benita Roth, *Separate Roads to Feminism: Black, Chicana, and White Feminist Movements in America's Second Wave* (Cambridge: Cambridge University Press, 2004).

11. Roth, *Separate Roads to Feminism*, 16; Stephen Ward, "The Third World Women's Alliance: Black Feminist Radicalism and Black Power Radicalism," in *The Black Power Movement: Rethinking the Civil Rights–Black Power Era*, ed. Peniel E. Joseph (New York: Routledge, 2006), 121, 122–123.

12. I should note that I am not the first scholar to identify the importance of Old Left Communism in shaping 1960s and 1970s black feminism; see also Boyce Davies, *Left of Karl Marx*; Gore, "To Hold a Candle in a Wind."

13. Premilla Nadasen, "Black Feminism: Waves, Rivers, and Still Water" (unpublished paper in author's possession). For other texts that reassess the usefulness of the "wave analogy" for interpreting black women's movements, see Roth, *Separate Roads to Feminism*; Springer, *Living for the Revolution*, 7–10.

14. Esther V. Cooper, "The Negro Woman Domestic Worker in Relation to Trade Unionism" (M.A. thesis, Fisk University, 1940); McDuffie, "Long Journeys," 284, 295–302; Kelley, *Hammer and Hoe*, 204.

15. Kevin G. Gaines, *Uplifting the Race: Black Leadership, Politics and Culture in the Twentieth Century* (Chapel Hill: University of North Carolina Press, 2006); Stephanie J. Shaw, *What*

a Woman Ought to Be and to Do: Black Professional Women Workers during the Jim Crow Era (Chicago: University of Chicago Press, 1996).

16. Rayford Logan, *The Negro in American Life and Thought: The Nadir, 1877–1901* (New York: Dial Press, 1954); Pauline Cooper Moss, "At Home and at War, 1917–1919," *Negro History Bulletin* 45, no. 2 (1982): 43–45; Esther Cooper Jackson, telephone interview by author, February 19, 2002.

17. James and Esther Jackson, interview with Louis Massiah, W. E. B. Du Bois Film Project, June 2, 1992 (hereafter Jacksons with Massiah), 10–11; *Northern Virginia Sun*, February 10, 1970, 1–2, Esther I. Cooper Papers, Moorland-Spingarn Research Center, Howard University, Washington, D.C., box 4, Death of Esther Cooper Folder; Esther Cooper Jackson and James Jackson, interview with author, August 13, 1998, Brooklyn, NY.

18. Della Scott, "Interview with Esther Jackson," *Abafazi: Simmons College Journal of Women of African Descent* 9, no, 1 (1998): 2–3; Esther Cooper Jackson and James E. Jackson Jr., interview by author, April 2, 1998, Brooklyn, NY (hereafter Jacksons April 2, 1998, interview).

19. Jacksons 2 April 1998 interview; Jacksons, interview by Massiah, 3–4; "America's Best Negro High School," *Ebony*, June 1954, 71–76; Jacksons April 2, 1998, interview; Esther Cooper Jackson, telephone interview by author, November 17, 2002 (hereafter Cooper Jackson phone interview).

20. Robert Cohen, *When the Old Left Was Young: Student Radicals and America's First Mass Student Movement, 1929–1941* (New York: Oxford University Press, 1993), 139–154, 207–208; Daniel Horowitz, *Betty Friedan and the Making of "The Feminine Mystique": The American Left, the Cold War, and Modern Feminism* (Amherst: University of Massachusetts Press, 1998), 33–68.

21. Jacksons, interview by author, 2 April 1998, 1; Scott, "Interview with Esther Jackson," 4; Cooper Jackson phone interview; Cohen, *When the Old Left Was Young*, 134–187; Kelley, *Hammer and Hoe*, 204–205.

22. Cooper Jackson, interview with author, November 17, 2002.

23. Ibid.; Cohen, *When the Old Left Was Young*, 177–201.

24. Jacksons, interview with Massiah, 1992, 16–17; McDuffie, "Long Journeys," 290–292.

25. Scott, "Interview with Esther Jackson," 4; Kelley, *Hammer and Hoe*, 205.

26. Cooper Jackson phone interview; Esther Cooper Jackson, telephone interview, January 23, 2003.

27. McDuffie, "Long Journeys"; Boyce Davies, *Left of Karl Marx*; Weigand, *Red Feminism*, 97–113; Hill, "Fosterites and Feminists."

28. Although never central to the CPUSA's overall agenda during the Popular Front, women's rights did receive more attention than ever before during these years. The Party's National Women's Committee sponsored conferences and encouraged the Party to prioritize "women's work." Communists performed outreach to more politically mainstream, middle-class women in the YWCA, League of Women Voters, and Parent Teachers Association and threw their weight behind national campaigns in support of birth control and the "Women's Charter," a progressive alternative to the National Woman's Party's equal rights amendment. In addition, Party activists mobilized women around cost-of-living issues. Weigand, *Red Feminism*, 28–45; Horowitz, *Betty Friedan and the Making of the Feminine Mystique*, 33–87; Van Gosse, "'To Organize in Every Neighborhood, in Every Home': The Gender Politics of American Communists between the Wars," *Radical History Review* 50 (1991): 109–141; Ella Baker and Marvel Cooke, "The Bronx Slave Market," *Crisis* 42 (November 1935): 330–331, 340; Ransby, *Ella Baker and the Black Freedom Movement* (Chapel Hill: University of North Carolina Press, 2003), 77–79; Marvel Cooke, interview with author, April 1, 1998, 11 June 1998, New York, NY.

29. Baker and Cooke, "The Bronx Slave Market"; see also Louise Thompson, "Toward a Brighter Future," *Woman Today*, April 1936, 14, 30.

30. McDuffie, "Long Journeys," 209–212; Mark Naison, *Communists in Harlem during the Depression* (Urbana: University of Illinois Press, 1983), 119.

31. Cooper, "The Negro Woman Domestic Worker," 27, 29, 30.

32. Ibid., 6, i.

33. Ibid., 1–16.

34. Ibid., 104, 83.

35. Ibid., 31–77, 84, 90–93.

36. Margaret Cowl, *Women and Equality* (New York: Workers Library, 1935), 3.

37. Mary Inman, *In Woman's Defense* (Los Angeles: Committee to Organize the Advancement of Women, 1940), 81; Weigand, *Red Feminism*, 28–45.

38. Inman, *In Woman's Defense*, 8; Weigand, *Red Feminism*, 28–45.

39. Esther Cooper Jackson, interview by author, June 12, 2007.

40. Cooper, "The Negro Woman Domestic Worker," 98.

41. Springer, *Living for the Revolution*, 45–64; Nadasen, *Welfare Warriors*; Roth, *Separate Roads to Feminism*, 76–128.

42. Claudia Jones, "An End to the Neglect of the Problems of the Negro Woman!" *Political Affairs* 28, no. 6 (June 1949): 51–67; Boyce Davies, *Left of Karl Marx*, 29–68; McDuffie, "A New Freedom Movement of Negro Women."

43. Scott, "Interview with Esther Jackson," 4; Kelley, *Hammer and Hoe*, 205.

44. Jacksons with author, August 13, 1998, 6; Jacksons 2 April 1998 interview; Cooper Jackson phone interview; Kelley, *Hammer and Hoe*, 204; Erik S. McDuffie, "Esther V. Cooper's 'The Negro Woman Domestic Worker in Relation to Trade Unionism': Black Left Feminism and the Popular Front," *American Communist History* 7 (2008): 203–209.

45. McDuffie, "Long Journeys," 305, 433–434.

46. Jacksons August 13, 1998 interview; Esther Cooper Jackson and James Jackson, interview by author, April 10, 1999, Brooklyn, NY (hereafter Jacksons April 10, 1999, interview).

47. Jacksons April 10, 1999, interview.

48. Jacksons August 13, 1998, interview; Kelley, *Hammer and Hoe*, 206.

49. "Women Urged to Attend Tuskegee"; Kelley, *Hammer and Hoe*, 203.

50. Florence J. Valentine, "Remarks on Jobs and Training for Negro Women delivered at the panel on Youth and Labor, Youth Legislature," SNYC Papers, box 6, SNYC Folder; "Southern Youth Legislature Souvenir Journal" program, Southern Youth Legislature, Columbia, South Carolina, October 18–20, 1946, SNYC Papers, box 6, SNYC Folder; Lau, *Democracy Rising*, 167–168.

51. "Souvenir Bulletin, Sixth All-Southern Youth Conference," November 30–December 3, 1944, Atlanta, GA, Jackson Papers; "Keynote Session," Sixth All-Southern Negro Youth Legislature" flyer, Jackson Papers; "Proceedings: Sixth All-Southern Negro Youth Conference," program; Strong Papers, box 3, folder 4; Cooper Jackson, interview by author, June 27, 2007; Kelley, *Hammer and Hoe*, 223; Ransby, *Ella Baker and the Black Freedom Movement*, 239–272.

52. Kelley, *Hammer and Hoe*, 220–231; Ellen Schrecker, *Many Are the Crimes: McCarthyism in America* (Princeton, NJ: Princeton University Press, 1998).

53. The 1940 Smith Act banned teaching and advocating the violent overthrow of the U.S. government. Schrecker, *Many Are the Crimes*, 97–98, 104–105.

54. The best example of Cooper Jackson's efforts to free Jackson is her booklet *This Is My Husband: Fighter for His People, Political Refugee*, 3rd ed. (Brooklyn: National Committee to Defend Negro Leadership, 1953).

55. See FBI, "Esther Cooper Jackson," New York Bureau File, 100–402509–63, February 29, 1956.

56. *Amsterdam News*, 10 December 1955, 3; *Daily Worker*, 5 December 1955, 2; *United States v. George Blake Charney, et al.*, 136–137 (2nd Cir. 1956); *United States v. James E. Jackson, et al.*, 24445 (2nd Cir. 1957), in Jackson Papers, Smith Act Box, Legal Documents folder; McDuffie, "Long Journeys," 463–468; Horne, *Black and Red*, 201–253; Penny M. Von Eschen, *Race against*

Empire: Black Americans and Anticolonialism, 1937–1957 (Ithaca: Cornell University Press, 1997), 109–121.

57. Kelley, *Hamer and Hoe*, 220.

58. Kelley, *Freedom Dreams*, 58.

59. Smethurst, *Black Arts Movement*, 45.

60. Esther Cooper Jackson, *Freedomways Reader: Prophets in Their Own Country* (Boulder, CO: Westview Press, 2000), xvii–xxx.

61. Bond, interview with author.

62. "The Negro Woman in American Literature," *Freedomways* 6, no. 1 (1966): 8–25; Jean Carey Bond, interview with author, November 9, 2001; Audre Lorde, "Rites of Passage," *Freedomways* 10, no. 3 (1970), reprinted in Cooper Jackson, *Freedomways Reader*, 355; Nikki Giovanni, "The Lion in Daniel's Den," *Freedomways* 11, no. 2 (1971): 191; June Jordan, "For Beautiful Mary Brown," *Freedomways* 11, no. 2 (1971): 191; Alice Walker, "Rock Eagle," *Freedomways* 11, no. 4 (1971): 367; Walker, "Facing the Way," *Freedomways* 15, no. 4 (1975): 265; Walker, "The Abduction of Saints," *Freedomways* 15, no. 4 (1975): 266–267.

63. Horowitz, *Betty Friedan and the Making of the Feminine Mystique*, 197.

64. Ibid., 153, 121–223.

65. Ransby, *Ella Baker and the Black Freedom Movement*, 263–264.

66. *Freedomways* 25 (1985): 134.

67. James E. Jackson passed away on September 1, 2007, at the age of ninety-two.

68. Invitation to inaugural Louis E. Burnham Award, February 18, 2002, in author's possession; Louis E. Burnham Award form letter, Dorothy Burnham, November 15, 2005, in author's possession.

2

What "the Cause" Needs Is a "Brainy and Energetic Woman"

A Study of Female Charismatic Leadership in Baltimore

Prudence Cumberbatch

I don't want anybody to give me love, just give me my constitutional rights.

Lillie May Jackson

We do not beg for civil rights as crumbs from the table of democracy. We insist on our right to sit at the table.

Juanita Jackson Mitchell

On November 20, 1936, Juanita Elizabeth Jackson and two members of the Birmingham, Alabama, National Association for the Advancement of Colored People (NAACP) "visited the Scottsboro youth in the Jefferson County jail."[1] Representing the NAACP, Jackson pledged to the nine young men that the group would continue to fight for their freedom. The photograph of the meeting in the January 1937 issue of the *Crisis* showed Jackson shaking the hand of Clarence Norris, one of the imprisoned men. That handshake between Juanita Jackson, a petite University of Pennsylvania–educated middle-class black woman, and Norris, a poor rural black male accused of rape, represented a transformation in the sense of how black women participated in racial politics. Instead of the

Juanita E. Jackson and Lillie May Jackson. Photo from the Jackson-Mitchell Collection courtesy of Michael B. Mitchell Sr.

concerns about maintaining respectability as a "lady" that previous generations of black women had fought hard to establish, a socially competent and confident Jackson used her cultural and social status and dominant society's notion of "womanhood" to bridge class differences and take up the banner of the most oppressed black men in the country. In one simple gesture, she created a symbol of the type of civil rights movement and the politics of gender that characterized her public career.

While earlier twentieth-century black reformers often left the masses behind in their political campaigns, a new generation of civil rights leaders emerged in the 1930s that lacked the class antipathies of their respectable elders. They worked to build intraracial bridges across class differences through concrete political action.[2] Black women, like Juanita Jackson (Mitchell) and her mother, Baltimore activist Lillie May Carroll Jackson, played key roles in this political formation. However, few are recognized today for their public roles or for contributing to this shift. The dominance of African American male leadership during the 1930s and 1940s has become iconic, partly because concerns about "the race" during that period were addressed in masculinist terms, as in discussions of racial violence.[3] As a result, there is a dearth of information on women's community activism. Even though Dorothy Height, Ella Baker, and Anna Hedgeman began their careers at this moment, they gained widespread national recognition only during the traditional civil rights movement.

At a time when the NAACP's branch leadership was overwhelmingly male and the national influence of black clubwomen was fading, Juanita Jackson was familiar to readers of the NAACP magazine the *Crisis*. Her portrait appeared on the cover of the September 1935 issue announcing her appointment to the national staff. At twenty-two years of age, she was already active in both Methodist and NAACP circles. Jackson was recruited to mobilize young people nationally, as she had done in her hometown of Baltimore, Maryland. Although some would consider Jackson, with a bachelor's and a master's degree from the University of Pennsylvania, representative of the "talented tenth's second generation," she was also a member of the first generation of the modern civil rights movement.[4]

Our historical attention to women, like Juanita Jackson in the 1930s, redefines the political wing of the New Negro movement as not merely a phenomenon of the 1920s or 1930s but an awakening that extended into the 1940s. In political terms, it became the pre–civil rights movement. On the cover of the *Crisis*, Jackson embodied an emerging ideal of black middle-class womanhood. She was beautiful, extremely intelligent, confident, and socially competent—perhaps the last attribute being the key to the political consciousness that drove her to reorganize and refocus the struggle for racial justice. Moving beyond older models of politically active black women, Jackson did not have to prove her womanhood or her class standing. These challenges had been answered by the previous generation of black female activists.[5]

Social competency and confidence in her social role allowed Jackson, and women like her, to speak to multiple audiences, crossing racial, religious, and class lines to convey political messages that were important, relevant, accessible, and inspirational. Jackson's status as a black female icon was accentuated by her lifelong determination to fight for all African Americans' political rights, regardless of their social standing. Jackson's social confidence mirrored that of her mother, Lillie Jackson, who prided herself on creating an interclass Baltimore NAACP as its president from 1935 to 1969.

The militancy of black women who came of age during this period has often been overlooked because of the traditional ways in which they conducted themselves in public. Their outward conservative appearance masked a fierce political determination that challenged the restrictions placed on women, although they were not always successful. The Jacksons were part of a new generation of black women leaders who, like Ella Baker, Daisy Bates, Septima Clark, and Gloria Richardson, were no longer satisfied with supporting men's activism. They rejuvenated organizations like the fledgling Baltimore NAACP and made them into powerful political institutions. They were not only the backbone of the movement—they were its stewards.

Juanita and Lillie Jackson refashioned Baltimore's civil rights movement at the height of the Great Depression. The local NAACP was in decline when Juanita began organizing thousands into the City-Wide Young People's Forum to discuss pressing political and economic concerns. These women employed new leadership strategies, which culminated in the revival of the Baltimore NAACP, the reinvention of its membership composition, and a redefinition of the organization's functions. Their new leadership built the NAACP steadily from a few hundred members to 3,000 by the late 1930s to more than 17,000 members after World War II. In contrast to the elite male leadership of the Baltimore NAACP, the Jacksons revealed the roots of the Young Turks of the New Crowd, emphasizing mass mobilization and direct action as well as boycotts for black employment despite the economic downturn. They fashioned a Popular Front leadership strategy that reached churches, labor organizers, and the Left. The Jacksons organized forums, rallies, and demonstrations that drew regular crowds ranging from several hundred to 2,000 people to campaign for jobs and mobilize against discrimination. Their aim was to develop a politically minded and race-conscious activist contingent that worked in concert in the struggle for racial justice. Under the Jacksons' leadership, the NAACP challenged segregated attendance at the colleges and universities and Jim Crow employment, including within the public library and wartime defense industries. The New Crowd politics became visible locally in the March on Annapolis against police brutality and killer cops and nationally in the March on Washington Movement that challenged Roosevelt's White House on fair employment.

During the 1930s, Juanita and Lillie Jackson worked to transform political activism in Baltimore's African American community. The successful desegregation of the University of Maryland Law School in 1935 demonstrated the potential to win in the courts against state-supported Jim Crow. Starting in the 1940s, black Marylanders who had taken interest in these cases took to the streets. They marched on the state capitol, registered new voters, and picketed segregated theaters. At the center of the struggle was the rejuvenated Baltimore NAACP led by its dynamic president, Lillie Jackson, and supported by her daughter Juanita.

Scholars have long acknowledged the importance of the black church to community organizing, but as their focus shifted to radicalism with roots in the 1920s and the interaction between African Americans and the Left, discussions of the role of the institutionalized church and politicized religious visions have faded into the background.[6] Rather than lament the failure of Baltimore's black activists, like Lillie Jackson, to adopt "more secularistic and socialist-tinged policies," it is important to explore why and how laypeople continued to draw upon the familiar language of religion that had sustained their community despite their continued racial oppression.[7] Grounded in the church, the Jacksons' organizing styles made them charismatic leaders, a concept that is generally reserved for men.[8] Using powerful rhetoric that was both emotional and intellectual, their message emphasized equality and the sanctity of the law and directly challenged the power of the state and moved away from discussions of community racial uplift as a site for women's work.[9] For Juanita and Lillie, the solutions to the problems of the black community demanded a confrontation with the systematic exclusion of African Americans from equal opportunities and the oppression of white supremacy.

The Jacksons' relations with and historical understanding of city churches gave them an instinct for the possibilities of an interorganizational civil rights struggle in Baltimore, where a traditional group, like the NAACP, could be the umbrella for a number of organizations involved in struggles for racial and economic equality. Using the NAACP as a spring-board, Jackson and Mitchell were able to gather the support of thousands across organizational boundaries—from church groups and fraternal or-ganizations to labor unions. Creating a living model of democracy, black women in Baltimore joined their male counterparts to encourage political engagement, a proactive legal strategy, and direct-action campaigns.

As in many southern states, most whites in Maryland considered the local racial situation benign, and Baltimore wore the public face of a modern southern city with few racial conflicts. However, white resistance to integration in Maryland was both historical and modern despite the status of the "Old Line State" as a border state where African Americans could vote. Historically in the Civil War era, Maryland was ambivalent; in the modern era, the state was reluctant to acknowledge racial inequality. Confronted with the idea that Maryland was not as bad as Mississippi, ac-tivists were forced to both educate political leaders on race relations and call on them to take action.

Although prior scholarship on women in civil rights organizations has focused on their limitations and frustrated ambitions, Juanita and Lillie Jackson serve as two examples of women leaders that emerged from local movements.[10] Jackson's success stemmed from her demanding, and some-times dictatorial, leadership style. Her daughter Juanita, though equally passionate, was instrumental in forging interracial and interclass political connections. Their stories are multilayered because they personally fol-lowed conventional gender roles. Their religious base, with its seeming personal and social conservatism, supported rather than negated a radical political praxis that promoted gender equality in their struggle for racial justice. The Jacksons were women who, with the assistance of supportive family, carved out a new space where they could be radical and religious, confrontational and "ladylike."

The women's strategies for success did not go unchallenged. Both were subjected to criticism during their tenure with the Baltimore NAACP. Lillie Jackson could be "aggressive, arrogant, demanding, commanding [and] insulting," traits not usually associated with a respectable middle-class woman.[11] In particular, her ironfisted rule caused the loss of several key members and occasionally infuriated national NAACP officers. For example, Barbara Ransby's biography of Ella Baker projects an unflatter-ing view of the Jackson family. Baker developed this opinion when she coordinated the Baltimore branch's membership drive in 1941. She com-plained about the Jackson family's tactics in securing memberships and the seeming bias toward their own relatives in awarding prizes to dedicated branch campaign workers.[12] Ransby uses Baker's assessment to conclude that the local branch was "run like an exclusive social club."[13]

Lillie Jackson had her own criticisms of Baker. The conflict between the two women erupted at the conclusion of the membership drive when Jackson wrote to Walter White claiming Baker was "discourteous and contemptible" and possessed an "attitude" that was "not conducive to the best interests of all concerned."[14] Jackson had worked to fashion a cross-class coalition of supporters with a range of political and social views and managed to organize this delicately balanced machine in a black community known for its political apathy. As a result, she saw Baker's complaints as a threat that could destabilize this tenuous coalition. Jackson did not welcome criticism from Baker or the national office that empowered disgruntled and disaffected members.

Ransby's work, which contrasts "elite" members and those with traditional values to those involved in radical politics, describes Lillie Jackson as "an unapologetic socialite." Ransby cites the "ostentatious wedding she hosted for her daughter, Juanita," as evidence of the branch president's "elitism and snobbery" but ignores her political appeal.[15] Drawing a dichotomy between radical and traditional women obfuscates overlap in the history of black women's politics. While Lillie Jackson's style offended Ella Baker, her approach was practical. After years of dysfunction, it was Jackson's nearly single-minded determination that raised membership levels to "nearly 3000," even if "they were members in name only," as Ransby claimed.[16] Jackson was also able to weather criticism and defections because she believed deeply in the cause and was focused on recruiting members and donations for the national office. Her long political career reflects the coexistence of traditional (and at times conservative) social values and radical activism. Prior to the 1930s, membership in the Baltimore NAACP had been small, and professional men dominated the leadership.[17] The Jacksons' leadership styles, reflecting their confidence and competence, if at times dictatorial and nepotistic, brought the Baltimore NAACP to new audiences, maintained an open dialogue with male-headed institutions, and empowered the civil rights movement in Baltimore.

Lillie Jackson was hardly a typical middle-class lady. Both she and her daughter were tested and became comfortable as leaders "on the road," so to speak. Although she was trained as a teacher, Lillie left the public school system to travel throughout the South with her husband, who showed religious films, while she sang and lectured before church audiences. It was here that the accomplished vocalist learned how to address both large and small crowds, in both urban and rural areas. By 1919, the family returned to Baltimore, and Lillie Jackson began to invest in real estate, becoming an economically independent businesswoman.[18] Jackson encouraged her children to become active in the church and supported their participation in "youth conferences" sponsored by the Methodist Church.[19]

Juanita forged a path of academic excellence. At fifteen, in her freshman year at Morgan College, she won first place for an "original oration."[20] Juanita left Morgan in 1929, largely because her mother felt that she could receive a better education outside Maryland.[21] Arriving at the University of Pennsylvania, Juanita expanded her extracurricular activities to both religious and secular organizations. She joined the Alpha Kappa Alpha sorority, which in 1931 organized a Paul Robeson concert at the Philadelphia Metropolitan Opera House. Juanita was active in a number of organizations, such as the Young Women's Christian Association, the Social Service Club, and the settlement house at the university. She was also involved in religious groups that promoted interracial and interdenominational relationships.[22] Juanita's education in Philadelphia provided her with the tools to move comfortably in interracial spaces and offered her a model for life in a city without state-sanctioned segregation.[23]

Individual responsibility and collective action were infused into Juanita's political consciousness. She recalled that she and her siblings "were reared with a sense of destiny, a mission," and that their parents "told [us] as children that we were important because we were getting the training whereby we could help to free our people—ourselves and our people."[24] It was her mother's expectation that after graduation, her children would "get out in the streets and help the masses of your people win freedom."[25] While their lives did not reflect those of the "masses," each woman understood that their freedom was tied to that of the larger black community. Both mother and daughter echoed the importance of organizing efforts in private reflections and public pronouncements, partly to differentiate themselves from previous generations of black leaders in Baltimore who failed to mobilize a sustaining movement.

Graduating with honors in 1931, Juanita Jackson and her less well-known sister, Virginia, returned to Baltimore and hoped to find work. Instead, their return was marked by increasing unemployment and underemployment amid the Great Depression. Juanita had a B.S. in education and worked in the city's public schools as a substitute teacher during the day and taught French at night. While Virginia found work as an art teacher, Juanita found it more difficult to settle into quiet middle-class respectability or achieve the financial independence of her mother. The summer after graduation, Virginia attended a Methodist Epworth League Institute and, encouraged by this program and dismayed by the lack of dialogue in the black community concerning racial and economic issues, suggested forming a similar group for young African Americans.[26] The two sisters organized the City-Wide Young People's Forum, which hosted two-hour meetings each Friday night in the fall through the spring in area churches from 1931 until 1938, and with less regularity until 1942.[27]

From the forum's inception, the meetings attracted audiences that ranged from several hundred to 2,000 people who came to hear both local and national leaders speak on issues that affected black Baltimoreans. The forum not only raised the political consciousness of the community and provided a social outlet for youths but also embarked on its own political program that campaigned against lynching and promoted consumer boycotts that secured jobs for African Americans. Most important, the Jackson sisters voiced the concerns of young people, simultaneously creating a distinct youth political culture and engaging in a transformative dialogue with the larger black community. There were other forums in Baltimore at that time, but Juanita and Virginia's group infused their community with a revitalizing excitement about the possibility for civil rights in Baltimore that filled the void left by the moribund NAACP and the more traditionalist Urban League.[28]

While it is generally believed that Lillie Jackson's pre-1931 political activity was limited to membership in the Baltimore NAACP, she briefly served as a vice president in the organization in 1928. The experience proved to be unsatisfying, however, because the local president failed to call a meeting. Lillie's resignation not only reveals her frustration with local black political activism but also provides insight into why she structured the branch as she did, with multiple committees active on many fronts, when she was elected president.[29] As a person of action, her productivity was better measured in the late 1920s by her church work. For example, her activities within Sharp Street Memorial ME Church led to her election to its trustee board in 1930. Lillie was the first woman to hold this position at Sharp Street, and she later served for nine years as chairperson.[30]

Lillie Jackson's religious devotion was heightened in 1919 after a medical procedure left her with a severed facial nerve, and a subsequent infection sent her to the hospital for emergency surgery.[31] Her life was saved, but one side of her face was partially paralyzed. Her health crisis was so serious that Lillie Jackson pledged to "Him a life of service" if God would spare her life so she could "rear [her] three daughters." Known for her religious moderation, she did not allow drinking, smoking, card playing, or dancing in her home.[32] Lillie's religious beliefs were infused with a political consciousness that combined Christianity with race responsibility. She saw the omnipresent racial discrimination that African Americans lived with as a sign "that people were not helping God to do something about it."[33] She raised her children with "a sense of mission that some day, somehow, somewhere God was going to use [them] all and that [they] must prepare for it."[34] Rather than a reform-minded Christianity, however, Jackson understood her religion as having the potential to effect political change as well. The message that Lillie imparted to her children was that racism "wasn't God's doing" but that of man, and it was man's responsibility to rectify the situation: "God helps those who help themselves."[35]

One of the first major direct-action campaigns that the Jacksons participated in together was led by a faith healer, Prophet Kiowa Costonie, where black citizens in West Baltimore successfully organized a consumer boycott against several A&P stores to secure jobs for young black men.[36] This victory was followed by an attempt to gain jobs for black women in stores located on Pennsylvania Avenue, the main shopping thoroughfare in black West Baltimore. Taking on a more public role in the movement, Lillie Jackson (the forum's principle mentor), along with Costonie and Elvira Bond, president of the Housewives League, surveyed several local businesses to ascertain whether or not African Americans were employed. In the ensuing boycott, Lillie and Juanita served as observers, making sure that participants were orderly. Neither woman actually picketed any stores, but both mother and daughter were named defendants in a lawsuit filed by the targeted store owners, who claimed that the pickets had hurt their businesses and were illegal.[37]

The entrepreneurs were successful in their quest for a permanent injunction, but Lillie and Juanita were energized by the campaign. Juanita's success as president of the forum caught the attention of the NAACP's national office, and Walter White asked her to organize a meeting for "a small group of younger people" who could potentially assist in the work of the local branch.[38] In 1935, after receiving a master's degree in sociology, Juanita was hired by the association as the special assistant to White; her first assignment was to organize, along with veteran NAACP officer Daisy Lampkin, Baltimore's fall membership drive.[39] Juanita divided her time between organizing branches and developing youth chapters. Organizing youth provided Jackson with her greatest sense of purpose, and she believed much of the association's promise lay in cultivating a politically oriented race consciousness among young people.

In many ways Lillie Jackson was the ideal candidate for branch president. She was committed to civil rights, had flexible work hours, possessed business acumen, and was economically independent. She also possessed the fortitude to battle against the historic apathy that had plagued the Baltimore branch since the 1920s. Setting their goal at 5,000 members, the campaign garnered fewer than 2,000. What is most revealing from this campaign is that the "women's division" was much more effective in mobilizing the community, bringing in almost twice as many memberships as its male counterpart. Lillie Jackson played an integral role, serving as chairperson of the awards committee and personally securing 214 members. In their concurrent reorganization of the branch, members turned away from the traditional male leadership and chose Lillie Jackson as their new president.[40]

Joining the ranks of a select few female branch presidents, Jackson catapulted the chapter onto the local and national civil rights scene. Her leadership began the reorientation of the group, taking the local chapter from being just an organization to a movement. Under her direction, the executive board was composed of people she knew to be hard workers and those she considered to be "'pure of heart' . . . embracing the whole program of the N.A.C.P. [sic]."[41] She recruited board members who were willing to dedicate substantial amounts of time and energy to the organization's success. This group included a mixture of prominent individuals in the community and citizens who had successfully recruited large numbers of members to the organization.[42] The board composition demonstrated Jackson's belief that the chapter relied on the social and cultural legitimacy that emanated from both prestige and practical organizational skills. Jackson also used her position in the community and called upon family and friends to increase the number of active women in the local branch. Drawing on their experience in the second echelons of church leadership and in women's groups, under Jackson's presidency, women emerged into the first echelon of leaders in the NAACP. Jackson's ability to tap into women's resources and networks was key to making the branch successful.

With the mottoes "You Can't Win by Yourself" and "Every Day a Membership Day," Jackson and her staff of volunteers carried on a mission to increase memberships and raise funds for the NAACP.[43] Where previous presidents had failed, Jackson's financial situation enabled her to devote full attention to the campaign for racial justice. While scholars have given equal weight to the influence of the NAACP, the *Afro American* newspaper, and black churches in Baltimore's civil rights movement, it was only under Lillie's leadership that these forces began to successfully work together. Jackson and the NAACP served as the glue that held Baltimore's early civil rights campaign together, bridging the worlds of the *Afro American* and the black religious community and merging the religious and secular spheres into a dynamic political campaign.[44]

One of the keys to Jackson's success was fostering strong relationships with black churches throughout the city.[45] Her previous work within the church gave her legitimacy and access to many religious institutions. She used these opportunities to recruit volunteers and secure memberships, but her relationship with black ministers provided her with a regular weekend audience of congregants to which she could preach the NAACP's mission. She was known for attending several churches each Sunday to spread the association's message, laying the groundwork for soliciting memberships and donations to support NAACP activities.[46] Jackson was able to navigate through a complicated network of religious authority, acting as a steward for racial justice without posing a threat to the leadership of ministers who gave her access to their pulpits. The branch held meetings in the churches and organized "citizenship training schools" that promoted a partnership with local ministers to educate their congregants about their "rights as citizens" and identify ways to "implement their citizenship in the community."[47] Lillie and Juanita came from a tradition where segregation and religious discrimination were unchristian and contrary to their religious beliefs. In contrast, voter registration and citizenship were concrete applications of radical ideas embedded in Christianity.

While the campaigns of the 1930s boosted support for the local branch, Lillie Jackson's tireless efforts and determination sustained its growth through the 1940s. From a position of demonstrated organizational strength, she moved to incorporate black Baltimore into the NAACP program in the wake of the Great Depression. Her daughters, Juanita and Virginia, met with labor leaders and targeted workers for memberships. Working together in an unofficial partnership, the local branch joined with the Baltimore Urban League (BUL) to increase African Americans' union memberships and find them employment on various city projects. Under her leadership the Baltimore branch integrated the librarians' training program at Enoch Pratt Public Library, the University of Maryland's undergraduate, graduate, and professional schools, and public beaches. Her efforts increased membership in the Baltimore NAACP from nearly 2,000 when she was elected to more than 17,600 in 1946 and transformed the branch into one of the largest and most active in the country.[48]

Lillie and Juanita were able to speak to multiple audiences, based inside and outside religious institutions. Lillie, the orator, called upon her roots in the church, while Juanita merged her church-based foundation with her work in secular groups to build a black, women-led political organization. The Jacksons built on these connections to organize successfully where others, including the Communists, had failed. Lillie and Juanita Jackson offered an equal, if not more powerful, alternative in the form of religiously-grounded, militant political action. They promoted active citizenship and a radical understanding and application of democracy. They used the state's tools—the law, the courts, and the right to vote—to push forward a political agenda that fought for justice and fairness.

If later historians mistakenly place them in the "conservative" ranks or chide them for their "middle-class orientation," at the time, as activists from the black church and traditional civil rights organizations, they were viewed as radicals by the white power structure, and in many cases they self-identified as radical "freedom fighter[s]."[49] Their alternative for militant political action was well aligned with the community's religious beliefs. Lillie and Juanita led secular organizations, *and* their Christian faith was apparent. Their personal moderation and religious beliefs gave them legitimacy and made their radical stance more acceptable to Baltimore's black community. Above all they were crusaders for racial justice. Indeed, Lillie Jackson, in particular, saw civil rights as a divine mission, her workers as messengers, and individuals as responsible for effecting change.[50]

Juanita Jackson left Baltimore to become one of the most recognizable African American youth leaders in the country. She spent two summers, in 1933 and 1934, traveling across the country conducting classes for religious organizations. In 1934, she was elected as a vice president of the National Council of Methodist Youth and inspired the organization to take an official stance on race discrimination.[51] For the NAACP, she traveled around the nation organizing youth and senior chapters, as well as routinely serving as a speaker in both secular and religious forums, promoting the idea of racial justice. She also was active in the national antilynching campaign and joined Dorothy Height, later president of the National Council of Negro Women (NCNW), in organizing the United Youth Committee against Lynching.[52]

By 1940, however, twenty-seven-year-old Juanita Jackson Mitchell, who almost single-handedly spearheaded the revitalized NAACP youth movement, was no longer a "youth" in terms of age or professional and personal experiences. She had spent nearly half of her young life organizing, both officially and unofficially, for the cause of racial justice and equality. She resigned from the NAACP, in August 1938, to marry a former vice president of the forum, Clarence Mitchell Jr., who was by then executive director of the Urban League in St. Paul, Minnesota. Their marriage was announced in a press release from the national office and noted in black newspapers.[53]

Being Mrs. Mitchell did not alter Juanita's beliefs and support for racial justice; however, her venues changed. She was thrilled to be married but recognized her husband's competing emotions of admiration and insecurity about her national stature. At the time of the marriage, he was less accomplished in their chosen field. Juanita did "not go to Minnesota to inactivity" but, instead, negotiated her husband's emotions and her own desires skillfully.[54] As husband and wife, they continued their activities and instilled their political passion in their children; the Jackson-Mitchell family became one of the most important dynasties in racial politics.[55]

In the 1940s through 1960s, Lillie Jackson and Juanita Mitchell would be integral to developing Baltimore's civil rights movement strategies. Prior to the birth of her first son in December 1939, Mitchell remained active through speaking engagements, selling NAACP Christmas seals, and representing the youth of "the race" at President Franklin D. Roosevelt's Conference on Children in a Democracy. She was one of four African American women at the conference, and the only one who lacked an official title with a race organization.[56] Her activities were classified as an unpaid "volunteer" for the cause. She, like many other women before the mid-1940s, was relied on by race organizations, such as the NAACP. These women were generally excluded from the top leadership positions in mixed-gender groups, and their contributions were viewed as a normal part of their volunteerism. In contrast, men's sacrifices were considered extraordinary and status enhancing.

Mitchell's status as a "volunteer" changed after she was asked to lead Baltimore's fall membership campaign in 1940. She insisted that she would only return as a paid organizer. Writing to Walter White that she needed the income to pay for professional child care, she emphasized that her "time is not [my] own." She could have drafted a relative to provide child care. Instead, she valued her labor as a wife and mother, insisting on a pay rate of fifty dollars per week, nineteen more than her initial salary at the NAACP. Mitchell successfully reentered the field as a contract worker with a salary from the national office that legitimized her professional activities.[57]

In 1941, Juanita Mitchell returned to Baltimore with her family, where she reignited the formal partnership with her mother. Using NAACP as their base, and adopting a more expansive Popular Front strategy, they were able to gather the support among thousands across organizational boundaries. In 1942, Mitchell and Dr. J. E. T. Camper headed the Citizens Committee for Justice (CCJ) and brought together 2,000 people representing 150 groups to march on Annapolis, the state capital.[58] The March on Annapolis was prompted by several issues, most immediately the fatal shooting of a black soldier by a white police officer on Pennsylvania Avenue, the main strip in black West Baltimore.[59] Over the previous four years, nine other African Americans had been killed and fifteen "wounded by blazing guns of Baltimore's wild policemen."[60] Although Mitchell claimed the Baltimore NAACP was prepared to join A. Philip Randolph's 1941 March on Washington, once the conflict was resolved, the group moved to organize a broad-based coalition that focused on black Marylanders.[61]

Juanita Mitchell was one of the chief organizers of the march on Annapolis and called on the black community to press for their democratic rights. The 2,000 marchers demanded more African American police officers, an end to police brutality, a "colored magistrate," and the inclusion of black representatives on state regulatory boards.[62] The march reflected an expansion of the direct-action component of the civil rights movement. Crowds that were marshaled to support the court-based campaigns would be called upon to gather for mass marches.

During the 1940s, issues of housing, employment opportunities, and job training became central to discussions about civil rights and economic justice.[63] Traditional histories of the NAACP have most often focused on its larger legal campaigns to desegregate schools and secure voting rights, even at the local level. Critics have highlighted its middle-class orientation. The case of Baltimore demonstrates, however, that local stories are often complex, reflecting multilayered campaigns that were responsive to members' needs and national office directives.

This march reflected more than Jackson and Mitchell's charismatic leadership. It also demonstrated the broader appeal of their conceptualization of democracy. In their eyes, the system was flawed but provided a means to change it and improve the lives of black Marylanders. Adopting a multifaceted strategy and using the tools of the state, Jackson and Mitchell understood that African Americans had rights and would force the state to fairly exercise the law and remove barriers to equal opportunities for economic, educational, political, and social advancement. In discussing their 1930s political strategy, Mitchell said, "We began to try to sue Jim Crow out of Maryland." [64] They also used the ballot. With their leadership, emphasizing their roles and rights as citizens, black Marylanders demanded that the state not only recognize their contribution but also adhere to the democratic principles on which the nation was founded.

The march had two important outcomes. First, Governor Herbert R. O'Conor created the Commission to Study Problems Affecting the Negro Population. Jackson had already served on the previous governor's Interracial Commission, and she was allowed to complete the two years left in her appointment.[65] Like many invested in the civil rights struggle, Jackson was hopeful that the new commission would be an active one. She and some of the other African American members of the group were disappointed. Jackson concluded that the group was "a do-nothing commission."[66]

Second, following the march, the NAACP aggressively promoted voter registration. In addition to increasing the political participation of veterans, the NAACP goals included "put[ting] a committee in every church to get the people on Sundays to educate them as to the importance of registering and voting."[67] Virginia Jackson Kiah, Lillie's firstborn daughter, often appeared before a variety of groups, including longshoreman, to spread the message of the power of the vote.[68] Lillie preached the slogan, "A Voteless People Is a Hopeless People" in the "Votes for Victory" campaign. Bringing national politics to black Baltimore, Kiah secured the First Lady, Eleanor Roosevelt, to speak at a mass meeting in 1944.[69] In its voter registration drive that lasted from the fall of 1943 to the spring of 1944, some 9,000 new voters were added to the rolls.[70] The Baltimore branch housed a mock voting machine in its office and provided "guides" at the courthouse for those who came to register.[71] To increase the numbers of African American police officers, the Baltimore NAACP organized its own school to prepare candidates for the police officer examinations in 1943.[72] Lillie Jackson also directed attention to the state network of branches, and she and Juanita would serve as presidents of the Maryland State Conferences of NAACP branches, organized in 1940.

During World War II, Lillie Jackson and the NAACP worked with the BUL, labor unions, ministers and fraternal organizations to create new campaigns for economic justice. The branch fought to increase job opportunities and housing options for African Americans employed in the defense industry. Through Mitchell and Dr. Camper (by way of the CCJ and the Total War Employment Committee), the NAACP was involved in struggles for a permanent Fair Employment Practices Committee. It encouraged black workers to pressure the government and the defense industry to provide more opportunities for African Americans. In looking at the personnel of the CCJ and its subcommittees, women were well represented and often held leadership positions. In many cases, these committees reflect the interorganizational interests of black Baltimore; a number of individuals involved in the CCJ were also quite active in the local NAACP. While some might consider the NAACP as politically elitist, Jackson's leadership promoted the development of hard workers interested in a holistic approach to the race problem.

That holistic approach involved Jackson's neighborhood politics. For instance, she was the driving force behind the Northwestern Residential Protective Association (NRPA), organized in 1937, which represented residents' concerns in its predominantly black neighborhood.[73] The NPRA fought for environmental rights, protested the overconcentration of taverns in black communities (along with the NAACP), and filed a lawsuit to change dangerous traffic patterns.[74] Jackson was such a powerful leader that her son-in-law Clarence Mitchell Jr. encouraged her to "run for one of those legislative offices because you are a clear thinker and have more fight than most people."[75] She and Juanita often lent their support to umbrella organizations like the Associated Groups for Repeal of Jim Crow Laws, the Institute on Race Relations, and the Baltimore Interracial Fellowship to promote racial justice holistically.

In addition to mobilizing voters, promoting economic equality, and awakening neighborhood activism, Jackson led the branch's use of strategies from letter writing, telegrams, and phone call campaigns to petitions and lawsuits to change other public institutions. It fought for a high school in Baltimore County for African American students, attacked school overcrowding, and secured the removal of "colored" signs on the bathrooms at the airport and racial identifiers "from Maryland State employment" forms. In the postwar period, the branch continued its fight against police brutality, pressed for the prosecution of police officers who shot unarmed African Americans, and assisted in the prosecution of a white man who raped a pregnant African American woman.[76] The branch served as an information clearinghouse regarding the black community and routinely took its complaints, often with a delegation of clergy and an *Afro American* newspaper representative, to local politicians and law enforcement for redress.[77]

In 1946, the Baltimore NAACP launched a six-year picketing campaign in front of Ford's Theater protesting its discriminatory seating policies that restricted black patrons to the balcony.[78] That same year, Juanita Mitchell enrolled in law school, graduating in 1950. She became the first African American woman to practice law in Maryland, and her goal was to attack segregation.[79] In the areas of education, entertainment, recreation, and employment the concept of "separate but equal" was unacceptable to Lillie Jackson and Juanita Mitchell. The Baltimore NAACP did not challenge every aspect of discrimination, but the organization was often involved either through direct participation or through the actions of its members in a total war against racial oppression.

By 1959, the Baltimore branch had won the NAACP's Thalheimer Award five times for having "the most active and well-rounded program."[80] When Jackson stepped down as president in January 1970, at the age of eighty-one, Baltimore and Maryland were free of official signs of segregation.[81] African Americans had the right to integrated education and to equal employment and housing options, as well as the freedom to spend their leisure time at any recreational area that they chose.

According to Bayard Rustin, Jackson "follow[ed] in the noble tradition of heroic Negro women."[82] Challenging both the black community and the state to take an active role in the elimination of racial segregation, Jackson and Mitchell stood at the nexus of the Baltimore civil rights movement from 1931 to 1968. As Martin Luther King Jr. wrote to Lillie Jackson in 1956, "I have watched with pride the great leadership you have given. Every American of good will is proud of the contribution that the Jackson family has rendered in the quest for civil rights."[83] The Jackson women articulated a concept of democracy that was both powerful and accessible to an African American community suffering under Jim Crow segregation. Their fearlessness and belief in the Constitution inspired many generations of Marylanders to participate in the civil rights movement. "Ma Jackson," as Lillie was called around the city, was known as "candid, . . . forthright, and fearless and courageous." She said: "I don't want anybody to give me love, just give me my constitutional rights."[84] Juanita reflected this character in a 1952 speech at Howard University, saying: "We do not beg for civil rights as crumbs from the table of democracy. We insist on our right to sit at the table."[85] Working in groups traditionally dominated by men, Lillie May Jackson and Juanita Jackson Mitchell built an organization that remained relevant to local politics for four decades. Although younger activists moved to the forefront in the 1960s, Jackson and Mitchell remained politically active and supportive of the activities of young people. Building on the tradition of women's activism during the clubwomen's movement, Jackson and Mitchell challenged the prevailing notions of female leadership and left a desegregated city as a living tribute to the struggle.

NOTES

I want to thank the editors of this volume as well as George P. Cunningham and Nicole Trujillo-Pagan for their comments and suggestions. Additionally, I want to thank Michael B. Mitchell Sr., who generously provided access to his family's personal papers as well as his memories of these two civil rights leaders.

1. The title comes from the following letter: George F. Bragg to Robert W. Bagnall, November 1, 1932, National Association for the Advancement of Colored People Records (NAACP), Library of Congress (LOC), group I, box G85. Reverend Bragg, a noted historian and civic worker wrote, "The cause would make better headway with a woman at the head . . . especially, if a brainy and energetic woman could be secured to Head the whole scheme." For information on Jackson's visit to Birmingham, see "Youth Council Leader Visits Scotsboro Boys," *Crisis*, January 1937, 26.

2. Beth Tompkins Bates "A New Crowd Challenges the Agenda of the Old Guard in the NAACP, 1933–1941." *American Historical Review* 102 (1997): 340–377.

3. For discussions on women's leadership after World War I, see Victoria W. Wolcott, *Remaking Respectability: African American Women in Interwar Detroit* (Chapel Hill: University of North Carolina Press, 2001); Anne Meis Knupfer, *The Chicago Black Renaissance and Women's Activism* (Urbana: University of Illinois Press, 2006).

4. Eben Miller, "Born along the Color Line: The Second Generation of the Talented Tenth and the 'Problem of the Twentieth Century'" (Ph.D. diss., Brandeis University, 2004).

5. Jackson and Mitchell were members of the National Council of Negro Women (NCNW), founded in 1935. Mitchell, a NCNW life member, suggested the institution of National Council Day in 1937. NCNW Records series 2, box 1, folder 3: Correspondence, Minutes, Press Releases 1937, 3.

6. The history of Communist advocacy for racial justice is both important and compelling, but it has often overshadowed other forms of local activism in traditional civil rights organizations. For studies of blacks and the Communist Party, see Robin D. G. Kelley, *Hammer and Hoe: Alabama Communists during the Great Depression* (Chapel Hill: University of North Carolina Press, 1990); Mark Solomon, *The Cry Was Unity: Communists and African Americans, 1917–1936* (Jackson: University Press of Mississippi, 1998). For a discussion of the relationship between African American religion and political action, see Angela D. Dillard, *Faith in the City: Preaching Radical Social Change in Detroit* (Ann Arbor: University of Michigan Press, 2007).

7. While Skotnes acknowledges Jackson's triumphs, he bemoans what he considers to be a lost opportunity for progressive interracial activism. Andor Skotnes, "The Black Freedom Movement and the Workers' Movement in Baltimore, 1930–1939" (Ph.D. diss., Rutgers University, 1991), 428.

8. Skotnes labels Jackson as a charismatic leader, but not Mitchell; I argue that both women possessed a powerful and persuasive leadership style. Ibid., 426.

9. See Merline Pitre, *In Struggle against Jim Crow: Lulu B. White and the NAACP, 1900–1957* (College Station: Texas A&M University Press, 1999); Barbara Ransby, *Ella Baker and the Black Freedom Movement: A Radical Democratic Vision* (Chapel Hill: University of Chapel Hill Press, 2003); Stephanie J. Shaw, *What a Woman Ought to Be and Do: Black Professional Women Workers during the Jim Crow Era* (Chicago: University of Chicago Press, 1996); Lee Sartain, *Invisible Activists: Women of the Louisiana NAACP and the Struggle for Civil Rights, 1915–1945* (Baton Rouge: Louisiana State University Press, 2007).

10. Belinda Robnett, *How Long? How Long? African American Women in the Struggle for Civil Rights* (New York: Oxford University Press, 1997).

11. Rev. Marion Bascom interviewed by Richard Richardson, June 18, 1976, McKeldin-Jackson Collection, Maryland Historical Society (hereafter MJC-MHS) OH 8128, 22.

12. Roy Wilkins noted that Florence Snowden (Lillie's sister) "ha[d] 'won' a trip to the Conference almost every year in recent years." He wrote, "[Baker] declares that the system which the Jacksons have used to favor themselves has discouraged the rest of the people." Memo, Wilkins to Walter White, October 21, 1941, NAACP Records, LOC, group II, box C76.

13. Ransby, *Ella Baker and the Black Freedom Movement*, 124.

14. Lillie M. Jackson to Walter White, October 19, 1941, NAACP Records, LOC, group II, box C76.

15. Ransby, *Ella Baker and the Black Freedom Movement*, 122, 394; see Ransby note 65 on p. 394.

16. Ibid., 123.

17. The only female president before Jackson, Lillian Lottier, was elected in 1924 and served one year. Lottier was also active in the Baltimore Urban League. Branch membership reached 2,000 in 1920, but the numbers fell soon thereafter. Mark Robert Schneider, *"We Return Fighting": The Civil Rights Movement in the Jazz Age* (Boston: Northeastern University Press, 2002), 57.

18. Juanita Jackson Mitchell and Virginia Jackson Kiah, interviewed by Charles Wagnant, July 15, 1975, MJC-MHS OH 8094, II: 24–27. For more on Jackson's real estate business, see Juanita Jackson Mitchell, interviewed by Charles Wagnant, July 25, 1975, MJC-MHS OH 8095, V: 4–5.

19. Mitchell interview, July 25, 1975, V: 8. Juanita and Virginia taught Sunday school.

20. Juanita's composition "Hot-House Plants" won the "Baldwin Hughes oratorical contest." Clipping, Baltimore *Afro American* (hereafter BAA), June 1928, Jackson-Mitchell Collection (hereafter JMC).

21. The only four-year institution in Maryland open to African Americans was Morgan College. When it was financially possible, African Americans often chose to attend colleges and universities outside Maryland. See Mitchell and Kiah interview, July 15, 1975, III: 37.

22. Undated news clipping, 1931, and Juanita Jackson's scrapbook, JMC.

23. Skotnes, "The Black Freedom Movement," 188.

24. Juanita Jackson Mitchell interviewed by Charles Wagnant, December 9, 1976, MJC-MHS OH 8183, III: side 1: 55–56.

25. Mitchell interview, December 9, 1976, III: side 1: 56.

26. Mitchell and Kiah interview July 15, 1975, III: 40–41. Virginia, a graduate of the Philadelphia Museum and School of Art, adamantly claimed the forum as her idea but acknowledged that Juanita was more experienced in organizing.

27. Forum programs (various years), JMC. Initially the forum was held at Sharp Street Memorial ME Church, moving to Bethel AME in fall 1932. In its later years, the forum was held at various churches.

28. For more on the forum, see Genna Rae McNeil, "Youth Initiative in the African American Struggle for Racial Justice and Constitutional Rights: The City-Wide Young People's Forum

of Baltimore, 1931–1941," in *African Americans and the Living Constitution*, ed. John Hope Franklin and Genna Rae McNeil (Washington, DC: Smithsonian Institution Press, 1995), 56–80; Skotnes, "The Black Freedom Movement"; Juanita Jackson Mitchell and Virginia Jackson Kiah, interviewed by Charles Wagnant, January 10, 1976, MJC-MHS OH 8097 I: 1–2. Jackson family members regularly attended Forum events. Marion, the youngest daughter, sang with the Forum Trio and was a vice president in the group.

29. Lillie M. Jackson to Moorefield Storey, June 8, 1928, NAACP Records, group 1, box G84, LOC.

30. Jackson was also a trustee of Sharp Street Community House, which was a meeting place that provided housing and job assistance to unemployed young women. Sharp Street Community House pamphlet, National Urban League Records, LOC, series 6, box 85, folder: Early Surveys. During Jackson's tenure on Sharp Street Church's trustee board, the church dispensed a $64,000 debt. See clipping, BAA, "Mrs. Jackson Quits Post: Resigns as Chairman of Sharp St. Board," JMC. According to her grandson Michael B. Mitchell Sr., Jackson agreed to help the church with its finances in exchange for the position of chairperson. Interview with Michael B. Mitchell Sr., July 2007.

31. Virginia Jackson Kiah, "Mamma's Life," handwritten, July 15, 1965, JMC.

32. Mitchell interview, July 25, 1975, V: 5–7; Mitchell and Kiah interview, July 15, 1975, II: 30–33.

33. Mitchell and Kiah interview, July 15, 1975, III: 34.

34. Ibid..

35. Ibid., III: 34–35; Skotnes, "The Black Freedom Movement," 426. See also "Dr. Lillie M. Jackson: Lifelong Freedom Fighter," and "A Tribute," *Crisis*, October 1975, 297–300.

36. Lillie Jackson did not picket the A&P, but she spoke to the "proper authorities" after receiving complaints that the police forced the picketers to leave the area. See *Aaron Samuelson, trading as Tommy Tucker 5 &10 Cent Store et. al. v. Tony Green, Otherwise Known as Kiowa Costonie etc., et al.* (hereafter *Samuelson v. Green*), Maryland State Archives (MSA), Baltimore City Circuit Court 1 (Equity Papers A) box: 3955, folder: A19400, Location: 3/9/6/16, 574–576. See also Andor Skotnes, "'Buy Where You Can Work': Boycotting for Jobs in African-American Baltimore, 1933–1934," *Journal of Social History* 27 (1994): 735–761. For details on boycotts in other cities, see Bates, "A New Crowd Challenges the Agenda of the Old Guard in the NAACP"; Cheryl Lynn Greenberg "*Or Does It Explode?" Black Harlem in the Great Depression* (New York: Oxford University Press, 1991), chap. 5.

37. Complaint filed by Samuelson et al., December 15, 1933, Baltimore City Circuit Court 1 (Equity Papers A, Miscellaneous) 1933, box: 3954, folder: A19400, series: T53-4596, Location: 3/9/6/15. Forum legal adviser W. A. C. Hughes Jr. and Warner T. McGuinn, the famed black lawyer, former city councilman, and 1920s Garveyite, represented the defendants.

38. Walter White to Juanita Jackson, November 28, 1933, series I, box G 85, NAACP Records. Juanita's organizing achievements were also reflected by her invitations to the second Amenia conference (1933) and to testify before the Costigan-Wagner hearings (1934).

39. Later her title expanded to national youth director.

40. Mitchell recalls that her mother was asked by Murphy to lead the branch's reorganization campaign. Mitchell interview, July 25, 1975, V: 4; "NAACP's Drive Ends with 1927 Memberships," BAA, October 19, 1935.

41. Mitchell interview, December 9, 1976, II: side 2: 51.

42. The executive board included "domestic workers who had gotten a hundred members for the N.A.A.C.P." along with "longshoremen" and "union leaders." Mitchell interview, December 9, 1976, II: side 2: 51.

43. Mitchell and Kiah interview, July 15, 1975, IV: 49. Kiah coined the slogan "Every Day a Membership Day."

44. Sandy M. Shoemaker, "'We Shall Overcome, Someday': The Equal Rights Movement in Baltimore 1935–1942," *Maryland Historical Magazine* 89 (1944): 260–273; George H. Callcott, *Maryland and America, 1940 to 1980* (Baltimore: Johns Hopkins University Press, 1985), 146. This idea of the triumvirate comes from Juanita Mitchell: "My mother and the *Afro American* and the clergy were really the triple generals in the struggle." But she follows with the comment "*She* [Jackson] *made the churches feel important*" (emphasis added) Mitchell interview, July 25, 1975, VI: 22.

45. Another component to her success was the support of Carl Murphy, president and editor of the Baltimore *Afro American*, who often mediated between the local branch and the national office and provided extensive coverage of branch activities in his newspaper.

46. In a 1953 list of donors, several churches appear, including Enon Baptist, Faith Baptist, Bethel AME, Douglass Memorial, Union Baptist, Knox Presbyterian, and Providence Baptist, along with unions such as UPA CIO Local 3, UAW, and Hod Carriers AFL Local 194. "Contributions to Legal Defense Fund," Mitchell Papers, LOC, folder: Legal Redress.

47. Edward Wilson interviewed by Leroy Graham, June 25, 1976, MJC-MHS OH 8127, I: 9.

48. Langston Hughes, *Fight for Freedom: The Story of the NAACP* (New York: Berkley, 1962), 177. Between 1935 and 1962, Baltimore sent more than $290,000 to the national office; most notable is the more than $174,000 sent between 1954 and 1962. "Money Sent to National Office by Baltimore Branch NAACP," JMC.

49. In the 1960s, Juanita Mitchell was elected as a delegate to the Maryland Constitutional Convention. Her campaign poster identified her as "NAACP State President; Constitutional Lawyer; Freedom Fighter," JMC. See also Andor Sktones, "Narratives of Juanita Jackson Mitchell: The Making of a 1930s Freedom Movement Leader," *Maryland Historian*, 2nd ser. 1, no. 1 (Fall/Winter 2001): 47–48.

50. Skotnes, "The Black Freedom Movement," 426.

51. Mary Jenness, *Twelve Negro Americans* (New York: Friendship Press, 1936), 126–135

52. Dorothy Height, *Open Wide the Freedom Gates: A Memoir* (New York: Public Affairs, 2003), 61.

53. Jackson and Mitchell Jr. married on September 7, 1938, seven days after her official resignation.

54. Juanita Jackson to Walter White, June 25, 1938, JMC.

55. Clarence Mitchell Jr. became a nationally known civil rights leader when he joined the Washington bureau of the NAACP. His brother, Parren J. Mitchell, was the first African American from Maryland elected to the U.S. House of Representatives in 1970. Clarence Mitchell III, the oldest son of Mitchell Jr. and Juanita, was elected to the Maryland House of Delegates in 1963 and the state's senate in 1967, where he was the youngest person to ever serve. Michael B. Mitchell Sr., their third son, was elected to the Baltimore City Council in 1975 and to the state's senate in the 1980s. Two grandsons were elected to political office in Maryland.

56. Mary McLeod Bethune, director of the Negro Division of the National Youth Administration and president of the NCNW, Jennie B. Moten, president of the NACW, and Mable K. Staupers, executive secretary of the National Association of Colored Graduate Nurses, also attended.

57. Juanita Jackson Mitchell to Walter White, August 27, 1940, NAACP Records, LOC, group II, box C 76. In addition to child care, Jackson insisted that she had to pay someone to care for her home in St. Paul.

58. 1943 pamphlet "Baltimore Branch NAACP in Action," 4, JMC

59. The shooting of U.S. Army private Thomas E. Broadus was the second fatal shooting of an African American by policeman Edward Bender; the first took place in February 1940. Governor O'Conor's Commission to Study the Problems Affecting the Negro Population investigated the incident and the failure to indict Bender. See "Report on Questions Affecting the Police by the Sub-committee of the Commission to Study Colored Problems in Maryland, 1943," folder

"Report of the Subcommittee * Questions Affecting Police," Mitchell papers, LOC. See also Mitchell interview, December 9, 1976, II: side 2: 41–44.

60. Citizens Committee for Justice flyer (undated), JMC.

61. Mitchell interview, December 9, 1976, II: side 2: 41–42.

62. B. M. Phillips, "2,000 Join in March on Annapolis," BAA, April 28, 1942; "Let Freedom Ring!" editorial, BAA, April 28, 1942.

63. Advertisement, BAA, August 12, 1944, late city edition. The 1944 Baltimore NAACP membership drive linked the issues of war, work, and civil rights. In small print, the advertisement read: "Help keep your job after the war. Help us have jobs for our soldier boys when they return home, protect your rights—Fight for a Real Democracy. sign up now."

64. She also attributes this idea to Charles H. Houston. Mitchell interview, July 25, 1975, VII: 46, 44.

65. The Interracial Commission was created by Democratic governor Albert C. Ritchie in 1927 and was continued by Republican governor Harry W. Nice, elected in 1935. Jackson joined the commission in 1936. Governor O'Conor credited Marie Bauernschmidt with the idea for the interracial group, rather than the marchers. Clipping, *Baltimore Sun*, "Negro Problem Probe Set," MSA Governor (general file) 1940–1942 Neg-Nu; Series: S 1041; Accession no. 8955–62; Location: 2/32/5/25 folder: NEGRO POPULATION, Commission to Study Problems of (membership) 1942. See Bauernschmidt to Governor O'Conor, March 11, 1942, MSA Governor (General File) 1940–1942 Nat-Neg; Series: S 1041; Accession no. 8955–61; Location: 2/32/5/25 folder "Negro Problems, Commission to Study, 1942."

66. Mitchell interview, July 25, 1975, VI: 26. Although Jackson and two other black members threatened to resign, she left when her term expired.

67. Mitchell interview, July 25, 1975, VIII: 51.

68. Mitchell and Kiah interview, July 15, 1975, IV: 53.

69. The First Lady experienced the realities of Jim Crow when both the Lyric Theater and Ford's Theater refused to open their doors to an event sponsored by African Americans for a predominantly African American audience. Instead, Roosevelt spoke at Sharp Street Memorial, which could not hold the more than 2,000 people in attendance. According to Juanita, "very few whites" attended the event. The mayor and the governor were noticeably absent. Once again, the local context was more salient than professional obligations or party loyalty. See Mitchell interview, December 9, 1976, II: side 1: 34–35; Mitchell and Kiah interview, July 15, 1975, III: 45

70. 1943 Pamphlet, "Baltimore Branch NAACP in Action," JMC.

71. Voter registration campaigns continued through the 1960s. By 1959, there were more than 105,000 registered black voters, spurred by the Baltimore NAACP with the assistance of "ministers in churches, supported by *Afro American* newspapers and women's groups." 1959 NAACP pamphlet, JMC.

72. 1943 pamphlet "Baltimore Branch NAACP in Action," JMC. Marse Calloway, real estate entrepreneur and Republican leader, organized the first "Police Training School" in 1937. "Report of the Executive Secretary for the February Meeting of the Executive Board N.A.A.C.P.," NAACP Records, LOC, group II, box C76.

73. Jackson's sister, Florence Snowden, was the NRPA's president.

74. Interview with Michael B. Mitchell Sr., July 2007. See also Skotnes, "The Black Freedom Movement," 412–414.

75. Clarence Mitchell Jr. to Lillie Jackson, undated letter (Saturday afternoon) postmarked October 29, 1938, JMC.

76. Baltimore NAACP pamphlet late 1940s, JMC.

77. Mitchell interview, July 25, 1975, VI: 22

78. Hughes, *Fight for Freedom*, 178. African American patrons bought their tickets at the box office and walked around back, through an alley, and upstairs to reach a rear entrance to the

"top balcony," known as "the 'pit.'" Mitchell and Kiah interview, January 10, 1976, I: 3–4. See also folder: Theatres—Jim Crow (Pickets, Protests), Mitchell papers, LOC.

79. Mitchell became a lawyer, in part, because of encouragement from Charles H. Houston. She was to function as Houston's "Baltimore arm," initiating the lawsuits, while "he would . . . process them through" the courts. Mitchell interview, July 25, 1975, VII: 44–45. Mitchell was cocounsel in the 1953 school desegregation lawsuits that many credit as one of reasons Baltimore was the first school district in the South to integrate after *Brown v. Board*. Mitchell interview, July 25, 1975, VIII: 56–57.

80. "Mrs. Lillie M. Jackson," folder: Jackson, Lillie M. NAACP, Mitchell papers LOC. Jackson received a number of awards, including an honorary doctorate from Morgan State College in 1956.

81. Despite losing the 1969 election for branch president to Enolia P. McMillan, Mitchell called for continued unity in the struggle for racial justice. In 1984, McMillan became the first woman to head the national NAACP.

82. Bayard Rustin to Bishop Edgar A. Love, May 21, 1969, folder: 80th Birthday Tribute Luncheon—Telegrams and Letters, Mitchell papers, LOC.

83. Martin Luther King Jr. to Lillie Jackson, December 20, 1956, JMC.

84. As recalled by Mitchell. Mitchell interview, December 9, 1976, III: side 1: 55.

85. Handwritten speech notes. Most likely this speech was given on November 7, 1952, when Mitchell was the featured speaker at the "30th Howard University Women's Dinner." folder: Speech, Mitchell papers, LOC.

3

From Communist
Politics to Black Power

The Visionary Politics and Transnational
Solidarities of Victoria "Vicki" Ama Garvin

Dayo F. Gore

As recounted in this collection's introduction, when listing the key figures in Ghana's expatriate community during the 1960s, writer Leslie Lacy referenced Vicki Garvin, a longtime labor activist and black radical, as one of the people to see "if you want to start a revolution."[1] While several recent studies on Black Power politics have acknowledged Vicki Garvin's activism and transnational travels, she is often mentioned only as a representative figure, a "radical trade unionist," or a "survivor of McCarthyism," with little attention given to the specific details of her life and political contributions.[2] Yet Vicki Garvin played a leading role in the six decades of struggle that marked the shift from Negro civil rights to black liberation. Politicized in the upheavals of Depression-era Harlem and active in the U.S. left well into the 1980s, Garvin provides an important window for understanding the significant channels of influence between the Old Left and the New Left and between black radicalism and the black freedom struggle.

Vicki Garvin arrived in Africa in 1961 as a single woman, a seasoned organizer, and a radical intellectual, who persevered through McCarthyism (the government-supported political repression of the U.S. left during the late 1940s and 1950s) with her political commitments intact, even as her spirits were tattered. She had served as leadership in several national organizations, including as staff for the Congress of Industrial Organization's (CIO) United Office and Professional Workers of America Union

Victoria "Vicki" Garvin preparing to speak at the founding convention of the Harlem Trade Union Council, 1949. Courtesy of Miranda Bergman, Vicki Garvin's stepdaughter.

(UOPWA), a founding member of the National Negro Labor Council (NNLC), and a member of the editorial board of Paul Robeson's *Freedom* newspaper. In 1970, after almost ten years of living in Ghana and China, Garvin returned to Newark and New York to work alongside a younger generation of activists in the New Left and Third World solidarity movements.

Recent scholarship has begun to acknowledge the role of black leftists such as Harry Haywood and Nelson Peery, or journals such as *Freedomways* in the development of student radicalism and the New Left in the 1960s and 1970s.[3] However, few scholars have addressed the important influence that Vicki Garvin, and other black women radicals, had in channeling political knowledge from the U.S. Communist Party–affiliated black left to transnational solidarity efforts in Ghana and China and back to Marxist factions in the Students for a Democratic Society (SDS) and black nationalist politics of the National Black United Front (NBUF). Garvin's life is part of the untold story of black liberation politics in a global arena. Her distinct political legacy rests not in official titles but in revolutionary experience and solidarity efforts that always combined local organizing with a global vision.

Garvin has remained an illegible figure in black radicalism, in part because her activism does not fit neatly into the convenient paradigms of the black freedom struggle. Garvin was a skilled theorist and strategic thinker, who wrote for movements and organizations but never produced a definitive text outlining her own political philosophy. She worked as a labor activist and was a proponent of black nationalism and Marxist-Leninism, even though these movements are often seen as incompatible. Garvin joined the Communist Party (CP) and served as a leader in New York's black left during the height of McCarthyism. She continued to be politically active in the U.S. left amid these anticommunist attacks and well beyond her own departure from the Communist Party in 1957.[4] She became an expatriate and international activist as the U.S. civil rights movement exploded onto the national arena and worked diligently as a behind-the-scenes mentor, strategist, and advocate for unity during a Black Power movement that often celebrated charismatic male leadership and a New Left embroiled in factional debates. Along the way, Garvin could count such luminaries as Paul Robeson, Claudia Jones, Harry Haywood, W. E. B. Du Bois, Shirley Graham Du Bois, Robert Williams, and Malcolm X as allies and mentors. Such diverse political engagements and sustained activism reveal Garvin as a central figure in the post–World War II struggle for black liberation, even as they speak to the reasons she has remained invisible within the historical record.

In examining Vicki Garvin's long history of activism, this chapter challenges some of the dominant narratives that inform the historiography of black radicalism. First, Garvin's ability to operate as a significant radical voice during the height of Cold War anticommunism and remain politically active well into the 1980s not only calls for a more nuanced understanding of the impact of U.S. Cold War politics on the black left but also highlights some central continuities in black radical politics from the 1950s to the 1970s. Second, Garvin's lifetime of engaged activism provides a powerful example of a "long-distance runner" and the difficult (and at times costly) work that is crucial to sustaining a radical movement in the United States. Finally, Garvin's leadership and radical vision, as reflected in her organizing work, present an important counterpoint to the still dominant tendency to depict black radicalism more as an ideology defined by great texts and fiery speeches than as a movement sustained through institutions and organizing.

The evidence supporting these interventions emerges in the details of Vicki Garvin's life as an activist and strategist in the black freedom struggle. She articulated a brand of radicalism that always carried with it a critique of white supremacy and capitalist exploitation, as well as a dedication to building community, an investment in transnational solidarity, and a deep belief in women's equality, if not explicit feminist politics. Garvin's commitment to the protracted struggle for revolutionary change led her to join with those who shared her overall political goals even if they were not always in tune with her specific political strategy. This is not to imply that Garvin was politically malleable or ideologically uncommitted but instead to highlight a political vision that was expansive, intersectional, and responsive to changing conditions. She valued political debate as a necessary part of building a radical movement and learned to negotiate the personal, ideological, and organizational differences that arose during this process. Garvin developed her politics and ideology not only in theory but also in action. She applied her ideas on the terrain of actual struggle in such political arenas as labor, socialism, civil rights, Pan-Africanism, and Black Power politics. Such broad political reach allowed Garvin to remain politically relevant for more than six decades.

"I Began to Get My Formal Training in Marxism-Leninism"

Born Victoria "Vicki" Holmes on December 18, 1915, in Richmond, Virginia, Garvin grew up in a working-class family where both parents labored outside the home. Her father, Wallace J. Holmes, worked as a plasterer in a black trade union, and her mother worked as a domestic for white families. The Holmeses migrated north in 1926 with hopes of providing better opportunities and education for their two daughters. Arriving in New York City, the family joined the swell of southern migrants settling in Harlem just as the Great Depression hit and struggled to sustain themselves through the downturn. Garvin's father found it impossible to continue his trade as a plasterer and could only support his family with menial jobs, while Garvin's mother continued to work as a domestic, sometimes even bargaining for wages on a street corner in the brutal New York day laborers' market, often referred to as the "slave market."[5] In oral interviews, Garvin vividly recalls her father's humiliation at his limited job opportunities and her mother's stories about the harsh working conditions and disrespect she suffered at the hands of her white employers. The feelings of embarrassment and anger Garvin experienced witnessing her parents' exploitation and the family's descent into poverty had an indelible impact and fueled her desire to understand the intersections of labor and race.[6]

It was in the radical milieu of Harlem that Vicki Garvin began to develop her early political voice and analysis. Her family joined Harlem's Abyssinian Baptist Church (ABC), and Garvin became active in its youth program run by left-leaning future congressman Adam Clayton Powell Jr.[7] Formal education also proved an important part of Garvin's political development, as it helped to deepen her knowledge of black history and radical resistance. At the age of sixteen Garvin graduated from Wadleigh High School in Harlem and began attending Hunter College for Women full-time. While at Hunter, Garvin served as president of the black history club, named the Toussaint L'Ouverture Society, and encountered a range of radical student organizations, including a very active CP-affiliated Young Communist League.[8]

After graduating from college in 1936, Garvin found employment as a switchboard operator for the American League for Peace and Democracy, a broad-based antiwar and antifascism group with ties to the CP, and became an active member in the CIO's United Office and Professionals Workers of America union. She also continued her activism with ABC and Adam Clayton Powell Jr. In fact, Garvin joined her first picket line in Powell's "Don't Buy Where You Can't Work" protest that fought to gain employment for black workers in the shops along 125th Street in Harlem.[9]

In 1940 Garvin decided to move to Northampton, Massachusetts, to pursue a master's degree in economics at the elite all-women's Smith College. It was during her two years at Smith that Garvin garnered a "formal introduction to Marxism-Leninism" and emerged with what she considered a "qualitative" change in her viewpoint on world politics and economics.[10] Garvin worked closely with faculty member Dorothy Douglass, a progressive economist who proved a radicalizing influence on a number of undergraduate women attending Smith during the 1940s.[11] Garvin produced a thesis entitled "The American Federation of Labor and Social Security Legislation" that reflected her growing commitment to labor organizing and radical politics.[12] As she studied Marxist economics, Garvin also participated in student activism, serving as a Smith representative at the Congress of Negro Youth held in Washington, D.C., in 1941.[13] Armed with a master's degree, Garvin returned to New York City in the midst of War World II. She took up a position with the National War Labor Board (NWLB) that directed her toward a career in labor. At the NWLB, Garvin gained familiarity with the national labor scene and became involved in local labor activism, helping to organize an independent in-house union of the professional and clerical staff and serving as union president.[14]

With the war's end, Garvin moved on to a union staff position as the national research director and co-chair of the Fair Employment Practices Committee of the UOPWA. It was within this left-leaning CIO union that Garvin became immersed in CP-supported activism. In early 1947, recruited by a former coworker in the NWLB, Garvin officially joined the Communist Party. Later that year she would also marry Clinton Arthur Garvin Jr., a black union activist. Garvin's decision to join the CP during a period many historians mark as a time of increasing isolation for the Party, as well as her marriage to a fellow activist, reflected her own idealism and growing political commitment to working-class struggles.[15] Nearly forty years later, in recounting her decision to join the CP, Garvin remembers it as a "key development" in her life. "I knew from that point," recalls Garvin, "where my focus would be in terms of work . . . certainly something related to white workers and black workers or the general working-class movement."[16]

Throughout the late 1940s, Vicki Garvin emerged as a central player in New York's black left. Thelma Dale (Perkins), the acting executive secretary of the National Negro Congress (NNC) from 1943 to 1946, remembers her as a key leader within the labor movement and black left more broadly.[17] As an active member of the CP, a leading labor organizer, and executive secretary of the Manhattan Council of the NNC, Garvin brought her political skills to a range of organizing efforts. In all these spaces, Garvin presented herself as a strong advocate for black women workers and black liberation, and a powerful voice of resistance to emerging Cold War policies. Yet, even as she found a political home in the CP's Harlem chapter, Garvin also encountered conflict in the Party, including negotiating the racism of some white members and political disagreements over strategies for fighting anticommunist attacks. Garvin's decision to remain in the CP despite these conflicts reflected not only her belief in radical organizations but also her political philosophy of building unity with those who shared her political ideals and goals, if not her strategic vision.

As the decade came to a close, Garvin encountered increasing anticommunist pressure for her union activism. In 1949, the UOPWA joined a list of left-led unions expelled from the CIO for communist affiliations. While the CP encouraged its members to work within established procedures, Vicki Garvin, along with many other leftists, refused to accept the purging of her union without a fight.[18] During the 1949 convention, Garvin took the floor to read from a six-page prepared speech. She delivered an incisive critique of the CIO, including its move away from supporting the "militant struggle for the rights of Negro workers" and its failed leadership in building a southern organizing drive.[19] Although her fellow labor activists praised Garvin for her "extremely courageous leadership" during the convention, the expulsions went forward.[20] This more or less marked Garvin's final days as trade union staff.

"I Never Felt Surrounded by Better Comrades in My Life"

Faced with narrowing opportunities as a union activist, Garvin, alongside other black leftists, turned to community-based labor organizing. In 1950, Garvin joined black radicals Paul Robeson, William Alphaeus Hunter, and Louis Burnham as a founding board member of *Freedom* newspaper. In the paper's inaugural issue Garvin penned an article focused on African American women workers. The piece addressed the combined impact of race and gender oppression that positioned black women at the "very bottom of the nation's economic ladder." "Raising the level of women generally and Negro women in particular," Garvin argued, served as an "acid test for democracy at this crucial point" in U.S. history. Such language reflected a common theme among black activists who challenged the United States' Cold War positioning as the model of democracy. Garvin saw the failures in U.S. democracy reflected in the plight of black women workers who were "forced into the dirtiest, least desirable jobs," earned the lowest wages, and were often excluded from leadership in and the benefits of workplace unions.[21] She concluded the article by calling on "progressive trade unions and women's organizations to spearhead" a program that would address the concerns of black women workers and promote "Negro women leadership at all levels of trade union activity."[22]

As the *Freedom* article suggests, Garvin remained invested in union activism, yet her work increasingly emphasized the fight for racial equality. She was an active member of the Harlem Trade Union Council (HTUC), a mass-based black labor organization founded in 1949 with radical labor leaders Ferdinand Smith as executive secretary, Ewart Guinier as chairman, Revels Cayton as co-chairman, and Pearl Laws as treasurer. The work of the HTUC would lead directly to the formation of the NNLC, a nationwide labor organization supported by black leftists like Paul Robeson and led by black workers and activists.[23]

Putting aside her work with *Freedom*, Garvin dedicated much of 1951 to organizing the first NNLC convention to be held in Cincinnati.[24] Introduced at the October 1951 gathering as the person "who has done more . . . than any one individual in order to make this Convention possible," Garvin took the stage to present the opening remarks. "We are making history here today in the struggle of the Negro people for freedom and equality," Garvin boldly proclaimed.[25] The impetus for her enthusiasm could be traced to the broad appeal of the founding convention. The gathering drew more than 1,000 delegates, a third of them women, from major cities throughout the nation, including Cleveland, Birmingham, San Francisco, and Denver.[26] Such success came despite surveillance from the Federal Bureau of Investigation (FBI) and pressure from a number of forces, including the Cincinnati City Council, which passed a resolution condemning the convention.[27]

Merging the struggle for black civil rights and the fight for "better jobs," the NNLC became one of the most significant black-led labor organizations of the 1950s. It also emerged as an important space for black women labor radicals. Unlike most labor organizations, the NNLC proudly counted a number of black women labor activists among its national and regional leadership, including Garvin; Viola Brown, who had been a leader in the Food, Tobacco and Allied Workers Union (FTA-CIO) in Winston-Salem; and Pearl Laws of New York's Fur Workers Union (FWU-CIO).[28] Such welcoming gender politics were visible from the first day of the NNLC's founding convention, which included a resolution titled "Negro Women's Equality" and a report on the need to organize domestic workers.[29]

Garvin would put her on-the-ground organizing and leadership skills to great use in the NNLC. Serving as a national vice president, she helped spearhead the council's first national campaign directed at garnering clerical and sales clerk positions for black women in the Sears-Roebuck department stores. The campaign made its first breakthrough in San Francisco in early 1952, soon after Garvin completed an organizing visit out west.[30] Bill Chester of the International Longshoremen's Union in California praised Garvin's contributions, declaring, "We were very glad to have had Vicki here. . . . she did work among the women that no man could have done and she straightened out a lot of things."[31] By March 1952 Garvin would also be appointed executive secretary of the New York Labor Council. In this position she not only continued to shape national campaigns but also became a visible face of the NNLC and its prominent New York chapter.

Although the NNLC proved supportive of black women organizing, and Garvin argued that the male leadership "never tried to run roughshod over me," she did encounter sexist tendencies. Garvin laughingly remembered having to assert herself to have her voice heard beyond "women's issues": "I wanted my say not in a pigeonholed way only on certain issues . . . you know I would stand up and fight for my position."[32] Thus Garvin pushed the NNLC to accept black women's leadership not only when addressing the concerns of women workers but in all aspects of building a radical labor movement.

For Garvin, the NNCL represented "a very high point" of her development and "the closest collective" she had ever experienced. Reflecting her belief in building unity through an organized struggle, Garvin recalled, "I never felt surrounded by better comrades in my life, where we would have really strong ideological fights, really sharp but we would leave as friends." Such a positive recollection stands in sharp contrast to many of the accounts of the U.S. left during the 1950s and the intense surveillance and harassment the NNLC endured from the Subversive Activities Control Board (SACB) that eventually led the council to close its doors in 1956. Despite its short life span, the sense of accomplishment Garvin, and many of her fellow activists, found in the NNLC and the vibrant range of labor activists drawn to its work highlight the ways that many African American leftists produced powerful moments of resistance and lasting bonds with one another in spite of, or perhaps as a protective measure against, anticommunist attacks.[33]

Such bonds provided a central impetus for Garvin's work with *Freedom* and the community of New York–based black leftists who rallied around the newspaper and a number of other CP-affiliated black organizations throughout the early 1950s. This community of activists provided an important base of support for Paul Robeson, W. E. B. Du Bois, and other

black radicals, who faced intense government surveillance and travel restrictions.[34] Garvin gained important sustenance from these allies, and
in return she provided a warm welcome for many activists as her apartment often served as both a formal and an informal meeting place for
the black radicals. Thelma Dale recalls with great fondness Garvin's generosity; Garvin even offered her a place to stay when Dale arrived in the
New York City in 1943 to start work with the National Negro Congress.[35]
These investments endured as Garvin negotiated continued anticommunist pressures and political setbacks.

With the support of her fellow activists and a resolve honed in the CIO
purges, Garvin steadfastly refused to let the threat of government surveillance silence her political beliefs.[36] She often pushed the CP to provide
stronger resistance to McCarthyism, particularly attacks on organizations
and activists within the black liberation movement. Thus, it is not surprising that Garvin took the stage alongside Paul Robeson and previously
jailed CP member Elizabeth Gurley Flynn during a 1954 May Day rally in
New York City's Union Square, to call for peace and the freeing of jailed
CP members. Or that Garvin also joined NNLC activists in leafleting the
AFL-CIO merger convention in 1956, urging the new organization to continue the CIO tradition of supporting black workers.[37] These moments of
resistance illustrated not only Garvin's dedication to radical politics but
also her refusal to temper her political beliefs.

Such sustained resistance did come at a cost, both personally and politically. Days before the founding of the NNLC, Garvin was not only putting in long hours on last-minute details but also negotiating the painful
dissolution of her four-year marriage to Arthur Garvin. "This was a crisis
for me in terms of my personal and family relations," recounted Garvin,
"but I had no real choice so I remained at my post."[38] Less than a year
later, in 1953, Garvin was called before the House Un-American Activities
Committee (HUAC). Her testimony was brief as she followed the Party
members' practice of invoking the Fifth Amendment when asked about
their political views, yet her appearance reflected the encroaching pressure of anticommunism.[39]

By 1956, at the age of forty-one and in the prime of her career, Garvin
found herself closed out of union work, disillusioned with a Communist
Party experiencing major political upheavals, and invested in a range of
black left organizations, from the NNLC to *Freedom*, that were unable to
sustain financially. A recently-divorced Garvin also felt the increased "psychological, social, and financial insecurity as a single woman."[40] Struggling

to chart a new path for employment and political organizing, Garvin moved through a range of clerical and temporary office jobs. She worked as a cashier at New York's progressive-owned restaurant the Cooker and even briefly returned to graduate school to study marketing at New York University.

Despite these hard times, Garvin's experiences present a more nuanced example of the impact of Cold War anticommunism on CP-affiliated activists. For Garvin, being called before HUAC clearly limited her job opportunities. The decline of left institutions after 1955, however, appeared to have a greater impact as it left Garvin with employment options that made little use of her skills and education. In addition, this work often did not reflect her politics or her desire to avoid the boredom of a conventional nine-to-five job. Furthermore, although battered by "the difficulty and despair of the McCarthy period" and frustrated with her paid work, Garvin still remained committed to radical politics and connected to a supportive community of New York–based black leftists.[41]

"While I Was a Pan-Africanist, I Was a Proletarian, Working Class, Internationalist"

As the decade came to a close, Garvin discovered an opportunity for political rejuvenation when her close friend Thelma Dale Perkins approached her with an offer of employment in the newly independent African nation of Nigeria. The job, working for a Nigerian businessman, was available through Perkins's uncle Dr. Frederick Patterson, the former president of Fisk University. Relocating to Nigeria proved an enticing option.[42] Vicki Garvin arrived in the country in May 1961, just one year after the nation gained formal independence from Britain. She hoped that living in Nigeria would, in her words, "reinforce my resolve and confidence in our ultimate victory."[43] Such hope was captured in Garvin's writing, as she remarked on feeling "a real sense of being at peace with myself" upon landing in Africa.[44] Her optimism for the trip was also fueled by the enthusiasm of her new employer, a well-established businessman and parliamentary official named Chief Ayo Rosiji, who assured Garvin that "you are coming here to your true home and to your own people."[45]

Garvin's desires for a rejuvenating homecoming would be tempered by the political and gendered realities of daily life in Lagos, Nigeria's capital city. Garvin's brief diary entries, written sporadically during her initial months on the continent, provide some insights into her struggles to adjust to the cultural and economic demands of life in Lagos, including disorganized work conditions, the demands of being an "Amer[ican] woman living alone," and her consequent loneliness. She was also forced to negotiate the realities of neocolonialism as she noted "beggars, men with facial tribal marks, people lying and sleeping on streets (unemployed, homeless)" alongside "many modern bldings [sic] big Chase Man. Bank & other, Amer. oil companies, etc & remaining big British firms."[46] Garvin's stay in Nigeria lasted two trying years. In recounting her time in the country Garvin succinctly noted, "2 years in Nigeria neocolonialism-disillusionment."[47] This shorthand can be read as her critique of the simmering internal political divisions and concessions to Western Cold War interests, which would soon send Nigeria into civil war.

Yet it also speaks to the limited community and political opportunities she found in what she had imagined as her "homeland." Garvin noted this point in her diary. "It is interesting (and significant I think)," she wrote, "that I (& possible other American Negroes) who feel while in the U.S. a kinship with brother-sister Africans experience some preliminary difficulty in assimilating." During her time in Nigeria, Garvin had come to realize that even with the "intellectual-political sympathy" between African American and African activists that she believed to be "theoretically true," there was still "nothing automatic" about building such diasporic solidarity.[48] Throughout her stay in Nigeria, Garvin struggled to not "remain aloof" from local culture, yet ironically she found her strongest community among a number of African American women working with the U.S. State Department. By 1963, faced with unstable employment, Garvin decided to head back to the States with a quick stopover in Accra, Ghana, to meet up with W. E. B. and Shirley Graham Du Bois, who had recently arrived in the city.

By 1960, Ghana had emerged as the site for black activists from throughout the diaspora. Kwame Nkrumah broadly defined Pan-African politics as unity among continental Africans, as well as solidarity with the struggles against racial discrimination faced by Africans in the diaspora.[49] In this vein, unlike Nigeria, Nkrumah argued that Ghana faced "neither East nor West but forward." The African nation's central positioning in the diaspora was amplified for communist-affiliated African Americans with the growing number of leftist expatriates, particularly William Alphaeus Hunton and W. E. B. Du Bois, who settled in Ghana as Nkrumah's invited guests.[50]

The possibility of reconnecting with allies from New York clearly fueled Garvin's attraction to Ghana, and she soon decided to stay on in

Accra. Garvin settled into sharing a house with two single African American women, Alice Windom and Maya (Angelou) Make. Although both Windom and Make were younger than Garvin, all three women could be counted among the group of African American radicals with a history of association with the U.S. black left. These activists, generally in their thirties and forties, became known in Ghana as the "politicals" of the Afro-American set—or, as one expatriate described them, "professional protestors."[51] Disquieted by the domestic Cold War, they refused to embrace defeat and instead turned to newly independent African nations as vital sites for sustaining a black radical movement.[52] As a result, they held a profound loyalty to Nkrumah's project of African socialism and cheered his sharp critiques of U.S. domestic and foreign policy. In contributing their skills and talents to Ghanaian development, these African American radicals sought to do their part to "hasten socialism and African unity."[53]

In Africa, Garvin hoped "to be really useful, to represent the best of thinking Negro Americans."[54] However, the gender and political dynamics of life in Ghana made it impossible for Garvin to find work that made use of her skills as a labor activist and organizer. Believing she "had no special skills to contribute to Ghana," Garvin could only find employment as an English teacher through the Foreign Language Institute.[55] Nonetheless, her claims of "no special skills" ring false given Garvin's history of activism and contributions to strengthening the bonds of solidarity between African nationalist struggles and black liberation organizing in the United States. One example of this activism was the August 1963 protest at the U.S. embassy. As the civil rights March on Washington occurred in the States, Garvin, alongside Alice Windom and Alphaeus Hunton, organized expatriates in Ghana to participate in a solidarity protest picketing the embassy. The demonstration criticized U.S. intervention in Vietnam and Cuba and included a declaration against racial discrimination addressed to President Kennedy.[56] Such activism unnerved U.S. policy makers, who from the early years of decolonization feared Africans' exposure to African Americans critical of U.S. racial policies, especially those who invoked connections between domestic and international politics.[57] The State Department placed these activities and activists under intense surveillance. This scrutiny, however, did not prevent the protest from receiving extensive coverage in Ghana and among black radical publications in the United States.[58]

Garvin also worked to politicize the visits of a growing number of black activists seeking to experience for themselves one of the first independent black nations in Africa. The local community of black radicals served as a welcome center of sorts for newly arriving African Americans. Malcolm X, who arrived in Ghana in May 1964, became the most celebrated of these African American activists. Pulling together an ad hoc committee that included Vicki Garvin, Alice Windom, Maya (Angelou) Make, Julian and Ava Livia Mayfield, and several others, the expatriates organized a "refugee night" for "Afro-Americans" to meet and talk with Malcolm X. Vicki Garvin recalls of Malcolm's visit that "Maya, Alice and I became his guardian three musketeers—mother hens who accompanied him to many affairs."[59]

Garvin, however, proved more than a "guardian." As historians Gerald Horne and Kevin Gaines have noted, Malcolm X's visit to Ghana and exchanges with black radicals broadened his ideas of coalition and the importance of unity in the black liberation struggle.[60] Garvin played an important role in facilitating Malcolm's introductions to these politics as well as a range of international revolutionaries. She arranged meetings for Malcolm X with officials at the Algerian and Cuban embassies and with the Chinese ambassador, Huang Hua. She also served as the interpreter during Malcolm's meeting with Algerian officials. For both Garvin and Malcolm X, such connections proved crucial in shaping their future transnational travels and alliances. Soon after these meetings, Ambassador Hua extended an invitation for Garvin to visit China, while Malcolm X's meeting with Algerian officials would soon lead him to visit that nation.[61] These conversations also seemed to mark an important exchange between Malcolm and Garvin as she shared her political wisdom with and learned from the powerful young leader. Garvin admired Malcolm's ability to take in other people's insights, "he believed in listening to other people. He was not a know it all. I greatly appreciated that."[62]

Garvin's description of herself as a "mother hen" when discussing her organizing around Malcolm X's visit suggests some of the limits on and possibilities for African American women radicals negotiating the complicated politics of gender and nation in Ghana.[63] On the one hand, such a statement can be read as downplaying her role by embracing a more acceptable gendered construct to define her political work. Intertwined within the work of this community of expatriates was a gender politics that reflected a male dominance, which shaped many of these diasporic networks. African American activist Sylvie Boone angrily addressed this exclusion, contending that in Ghana it was "fixed so that there is no meaningful way for an Afro woman to participate."[64] On the other hand, such framing also defined an important mentoring relationship with Malcolm X. In this context Garvin's use of the term "mother hen" reflected an effort to mark her role as knowledgeable elder (a role long gendered male) within the black liberation movement, mentoring a younger generation just as she had been mentored.

In this context, African American women expatriates encountered and negotiated a range of masculinist politics in their travels. However, there is little evidence that these women organized against such exclusionary gendered politics. This is surprising considering that many of them, Vicki Garvin in particular, had incorporated a strong gender analysis within their U.S.-based activism and championed black women's equality as a crucial part of black liberation. Such gender dynamics reflected the complicated ways masculinist politics also shaped transnational black liberation activism in the 1960s, erecting barriers to black feminist politics even as black women proved crucial political voices, leaders, and organizers within these movements.

Nkrumah's efforts at building African socialism and Pan-African unity "officially" ended on March 3, 1966, as a military coup ousted him from power. Many African American radicals experienced the coup as an opportunity lost.[65] "Nothing seems possible to me," bemoaned Alice Windom following the coup, "all the purpose has gone out of being in Africa now that it has turned into a bloody minstrel show, but I can't yet face going back to the States."[66] Vicki Garvin joined those who read the writing on the wall and left Ghana before the coup occurred. In 1964 Garvin turned her hopes to China, moving there to take up the offer from the Chinese ambassador to work as an English-language teacher in Shanghai.[67]

Although Garvin would arrive in the People's Republic of China alone and not knowing the language, she would not remain isolated for long. In traveling to China, Garvin joined with a number of African American radicals who sought to develop ties with the communist nation. Shirley Graham Du Bois would continue to strengthen her connections to China, traveling there frequently although she remained based on the African continent. In addition, Robert F. Williams, the black radical from North Carolina who was forced into exile for advocating armed self-defense, also found a new home in China in 1965. Although Garvin's reputation as a revolutionary and behind-the-scene strategist did not garner her the lavish treatment afforded Graham Du Bois and Williams, they all contributed to solidifying China's reputation as a powerful supporter of the black liberation struggle. In turn,

China provided these black radicals a base from which to continue to participate in transnational communist politics and stay connected to the emerging U.S. Black Power movement that advocated Third World solidarity and a revolutionary nationalist vision inspired by the Chinese Revolution and the writings of Mao Tse-tung.[68]

While in Shanghai, Garvin honed her skills as a teacher working at the Shanghai Institute of Foreign Languages teaching advanced classes in English and establishing her own course on African American history. By 1966, as the Cultural Revolution brought the closing of schools, Garvin found herself out of a job and one of the few foreign visitors still residing in Shanghai's Peace Hotel. After meeting and marrying Leibel Bergman, a fellow American living in Beijing, Garvin relocated to the bustling capital city to work for the English-language translation of the *Peking Weekly Review*. In Beijing she became "close friends and allies" with Robert and Mabel Williams and with Gerald (Gerry) Tannenbaum. During these years they "shared countless hours recounting the history of the revolutionary struggle" as together they watched, debated, and honed their analysis of the social and political upheaval occurring in China and the United States.[69]

In all, Garvin spent six years in the People's Republic. One of Garvin's most powerful experiences in China was being invited by students back to the Shanghai Institute of Foreign Language in 1968 to address a pre-rally meeting to celebrate Chairman Mao's second statement on the black liberation movement, "In Support of the Afro-American Struggle against Violent Repression," issued after the assassination of Martin Luther King. Recounting the experience, Garvin remembers it as a "privilege" and a moment of overwhelming support that moved her to tears. Such experiences led Garvin to view China as "a valuable resource for exploited and oppressed peoples everywhere who have so much in common."[70] Thus Garvin's embrace of China reflected not only her continued commitments to socialist revolution and her broad vision of transnational solidarity but also an attendant black nationalist politics that led her to frame herself as "a pan-Africanist," and "a proletarian, working class, internationalist."[71] Although Garvin wrote about her experiences in China, she rarely addressed the turbulence she must have witnessed during the early days of the Cultural Revolution. Garvin simply credited her time in the country with teaching her much about "the working of imperialism, neo-colonialism and socialism" and remained a staunch supporter of the Chinese Communist Party.

"Whatever as a So-Called Veteran You Can Add . . . Do It"

In 1970, Vicki Garvin returned to the United States and to a markedly changed country and political scene. Yet Garvin's credentials as a long-time black radical and Third World internationalist would find strong resonance with the radical politics taking shape in the 1970s. Garvin and her husband initially settled in Newark, New Jersey. As she adjusted to living in the States again, she would reconnect with members of New York's black left, including allies from the NNLC and *Freedom*, and deepen her commitment to mentoring a younger generation of activists. In New Jersey, Garvin worked with former NNLC comrade Ernest "Big Train" Thompson, replacing an ailing Thompson as director of the Tri-City Citizens Union, a community organization based in New Jersey that he had helped to develop.[72] The job introduced Garvin to the vastly different political landscape of 1970s urban life, yet stymied by the intricate terrain of New Jersey politics, she left Tri-City after several years. Garvin moved on to work as area leader of community action at the Center for Community Health Systems at Columbia University. Hired to connect with neighboring black and Latino communities, Garvin was excited to be back in New York City and for "a chance to move around and sort of get up to date with what was happening in Manhattan."[73] The Columbia job also proved short-lived, as her mother's impending death forced Garvin to take a leave of absence.

As Garvin recovered from her mother's death, she sought to reestablish her political activism. A longtime member of the U.S. China Friendship Network, in 1974 she joined the editorial committee of *New China*, a journal published by the newly reconstituted US China Peoples Friendship Association (USCPFA). Perhaps not surprisingly, fellow American expatriates Gerald Tannenbaum and Shirley Graham Du Bois also worked with the USCPFA. In addition, Garvin reached out to black activists she had worked with in supporting Paul Robeson, such as author Alice Childress, who penned an article on Robeson for *New China*.[74]

In the late 1970s, Garvin relocated to Chicago to live with her husband, Leibel Bergman. There she began to put into practice her skills as a mentor honed from her time in Ghana and China, as she join Bergman in the Revolutionary Communist Party (RCP), one of the largest of the New Left party formations. Garvin had reservations about the RCP, a Maoist-oriented organization made-up of young activists from the Revolutionary Union and the SDS. Still a committed communist, Garvin hesitated in joining the Party because of her sense that it lacked a clear theory on the struggle for black liberation in the United States and that it was "basically a young movement." Nonetheless, Garvin's commitment to mentoring a younger generation of radicals proved one of the driving forces in her decision to join. As she recalled, "I said, maybe don't work on it 100 percent of your time, but whatever as a so-called veteran you can add and stories you can share and to whatever extent you can participate, then do it."[75] Garvin's decades of political knowledge and experiences proved a vital resource as she mentored young activists, theorized black liberation, and advocated for left unity. "I use to be a sprinter and she made me into a long-distance runner," stated one black man and former member of the RCP who credited Garvin with helping him to sustain a lifelong commitment to revolutionary politics. This guidance proved crucial as Garvin helped younger activists to weather a split in the RCP in 1977 and the founding of the Revolutionary Workers Headquarters (RWH).[76]

By 1980, with her marriage coming to an end and her father's health deteriorating, Garvin left Chicago and the RWH to return to her parents' home in Jamaica, Queens, New York. Garvin soon reconnected with former CP comrades such as Harry Haywood, a leading theoretician on the "national question." She began working with a new group of black leftist and revolutionary nationalists active in the National Black United Front (NBUF). Founded in June 1980, NBUF sought to bring together the disparate array of black radicals, from communists to black nationalists, who had helped to build black revolutionary politics during the 1960s and 1970s. NBUF activist Komozi Woodard credited Garvin with bringing an invaluable range of talents to the organization: "You would see her at meetings doing the on-the-ground work, and she would be providing behind-the-scenes leadership." Woodard remembered Garvin as a central adviser in the NBUF founding convention, providing keen insights during tense negotiations over ideological differences and the vagaries of building political unity. "She had one of the most strategic minds," declared Woodard.[77]

Some thirty years after her fight for black women workers, Garvin also continued to advocate for women's equality and workers' rights. She guided the NBUF's Women's Committee, urging women in a March 1981 article to "insist on the elimination of all fetters to our functioning in equality and dignity as full human beings alongside men" and to resist being pitted against "black men and other oppressed women."[78] Garvin also participated in the formation of the Black Workers Committee of the NBUF. She not only provided detailed feedback on initial drafts of the organizational statement but also helped to organize a workers conference and served as a keynote speaker for the conference's opening plenary on women's activism.[79] In 1985, almost twenty-five years after she first visited the continent, Garvin, now seventy, joined the NBUF's Women's Committee on a trip to Nairobi, Kenya, to attend the United Nations World Conference on Women.

Conclusion

By the mid-1980s, Garvin had "retired from paid employment, but not political activity."[80] She carried on her role as a mentor and activist throughout the 1980s, and in doing so maintained her long-standing investments in black radical politics and black women's activism. Garvin continued to participate in on-the-ground organizing, lending her support to numerous activities from Sisters Against South African Apartheid and the Black Workers for Justice to the Committee to Eliminate Media Offensive to African People and the 1998 founding convention of the Black Radical Congress. Garvin also shared her insights with larger audiences, contributing an essay titled "Step Up the Offensive Today for Victory!" to the collection *In Defense of Mumia* (1996), which lent support to Mumia Abu-Jamal, a political prisoner on death row and former Black Panther Party member. Garvin viewed such broad-ranging work as a necessary part of contributing to the ongoing struggle for liberation. "One must educate, organize, and agitate," Garvin proclaimed in a 1977 video interview, and this slogan encompassed the multiple threads of her political life.[81] Vicki Garvin struggled with declining health during the later years of her life and passed away on June 11, 2007, at the age of ninety-one. Garvin's decades of political engagement and mentoring made real the bonds that connected black radicalism of the 1950s to the transnational solidarity efforts and Black Power politics in the 1960s, and the New Left in the 1970s and 1980s. Such longevity reflected not only Garvin's expansive political vision but also the significant continuities that shaped black radical politics after World War II.

NOTES

1. Leslie Alexander Lacy, "Black Bodies in Exile," in *Black Homeland/Black Diaspora: Cross-Currents of the African Relationship*, ed. Jacob Drachler (London: Kennikat Press, 1975), 143.

2. Recent books that mention Garvin include Kevin Gaines, *American Africans in Ghana: Black Expatriates and the Civil Rights Era* (Chapel Hill: University of North Carolina Press, 2006); Peniel Joseph, *Waiting 'Til the Midnight Hour: A Narrative History of Black Power in*

America (New York: Holt, 2006); and James Campbell, *Middle Passages: African American Journeys to Africa, 1787–2005* (New York: Penguin, 2006). Martha Biondi, *To Stand and Fight: The Struggle for Civil Rights in Postwar New York City* (Cambridge, MA: Harvard University Press, 2003), includes a more extensive discussion of Garvin's labor activism, with little attention to her other radical politics or her membership in the CP.

3. Max Elbaum, *Revolution in the Air: Sixties Radicals Turn to Lenin, Mao and Che* (New York: Verso, 2002); James Smethurst, *The Black Arts Movement: Literary Nationalism in the 1960s and 1970s* (Chapel Hill: University of North Carolina Press, 2005); Ian Rocksborough-Smith, "'Filling the Gap': Intergeneration Black Radicalism and the Popular Front Ideals of *Freedomways* Magazine's Early Years (1961–1965)," *Afro American in New York Life and History* 31 (January 2007): 7–36; Esther Cooper Jackson and Constance Pohl, eds., *Freedomways Reader: Prophets in Their Own Country* (Boulder, CO: Westview Press, 2000); Robin D. G. Kelley and Betsy Esch, "Black Like Mao: Red China and Black Revolution," *Souls* 1 (Fall 1999): 6–41; Nikhil Pal Singh, *Black Is a Country: Race and the Unfinished Struggle for Democracy* (Cambridge, MA: Harvard University Press, 2004); Harry Haywood, *Black Bolshevik: Autobiography of an Afro-American Communist* (Chicago: Liberator Press, 1978); and Nelson Peery, *Black Radical: The Education of an American Revolutionary* (London: New Press, 2007).

4. Historians have long marked the rise of McCarthyism and the Cold War, as decimating the U.S. left and limiting black civil rights activism. See Ellen Shrecker, *Many Are the Crimes: McCarthyism in America* (Princeton, NJ: Princeton University Press, 1998); Penny M. Von Eschen, *Race against Empire: Black Americans and Anticolonialism, 1937–1957* (Ithaca, NY: Cornell University Press, 1996); Fraser M. Ottanelli, *The Communist Party of the United States from the Depression to World War II* (New Brunswick, NJ: Rutgers University Press, 1991); and Maurice Isserman, *Which Side Where You On? The American Communist Party during the Second World War* (Middletown, CT: Wesleyan University Press, 1982).

5. "Biography Resume," box 1, Biographical Information, Vicki Garvin Papers, Schomburg Center for Research in Black Culture, New York Public Library (hereafter VGP); Vicki Garvin interview with Lincoln Bergman, tape 1, n.d., Oak Park, IL, Freedom Archives Collection, San Francisco; Ella Baker and Marvel Cooke, "The Bronx Slave Market," *Crisis* 42 (November 1935): 330–331, 342.

6. Garvin interview with Lincoln Bergman, tape 1; and Vicki Garvin, "Celebrating Women's History Month with Vicki Garvin," transcription of speech on February 14, 1996, Women's Commission of the Black Workers for Justice, in author's possession.

7. "The Young People's Forum," *ABC Advance*, March 10, 1929.

8. "Toussaint L'Ouverture," *Wistarion: Hunter College of the City of New York* 34 (1936): 171, Hunter College Archives, New York; "Biography Resume," VGP. The YCL was the youth wing of the CP.

9. Miranda Bergman, interview with author, June 28, 2007; Garvin, "Celebrating Women's History Month"; Wil Haygood, *King of the Cats: The Life and Times of Adam Clayton Powell Jr.* (Boston: Houghton Mifflin, 1993).

10. Vicki Garvin interview with Lincoln Bergman, tape 2, n.d., Oak Park, IL, Freedom Archives Collection, San Francisco; "1942 Smith College Commencement Program," box 1, Education and Accomplishments, VGP.

11. Betty Friedan, who graduated with a B.A. in 1942, was also influenced by Douglass's teachings. Daniel Horowitz, *Betty Friedan and the Making of "The Feminine Mystique": The American Left, the Cold War, and Modern Feminism* (Amherst: University of Massachusetts Press, 2000), 50–55.

12. Victoria Holmes Best, "The American Federation of Labor and Social Security Legislation: Changing Policy toward Old Age Pensions and Unemployment Insurance, 1900–1932" (M.A. thesis, Smith College, 1942). Best was Garvin's last name from her first marriage, although she rarely mentioned her first husband.

13. Garvin interview with Lincoln Bergman, tape 1; author interview with Miranda Bergman; "V. Best Represents Smith at Negro Youth Congress" and "V. Best Will Be Interviewed about Anti-strike Legislation," *Smith College Weekly*, n.d., box 1, newspaper articles, VGP; Ernest E. Johnson, "Youth Group Assails Hitlerism," *New York Amsterdam News*, November 22, 1941, 1.

14. A. M. Wendell Malliet, "Race No Barrier—They Made It on Merit," *New York Amsterdam News*, January 29, 1944, 3A.

15. Historians point to the CP's support of failed presidential candidate Henry Wallace in 1948 and its "ultra-left" turn that emphasized organizing for an impeding downturn in the U.S. economy. Ottanelli, *Communist Party*; Isserman, *Which Side Where You On?*

16. Garvin interview with Lincoln Bergman, tape 2.

17. The NNC was one of the leading and most inclusive mass-based black organizations during the 1940s. Vicki Best to Dear, September 11, 1946, part 2, reel 24, National Negro Congress Papers, Harvard University, Cambridge, MA; Thelma Dale Perkins interview with author, October 3, 2007, Chapel Hill, NC. I would like to thank Martha Biondi and Erik Gellman for directing me to Perkins.

18. Vicki Garvin, "The Participation of UOPWA in This Conference," n.d. 1, box 1, Trade Union Writings, VGP; Robert H. Zeiger, *The CIO, 1935–1955* (Chapel Hill: University of North Carolina Press, 1995), 253–293; and Philip S. Foner, *Organized Labor and the Black Worker, 1619–1981* (New York: International Publishers, 1974), 281.

19. Garvin, "The Participation of UOPWA in This Conference," 1.

20. Thomas Richardson to Vicki Garvin, November 7, 1949, box 1, Trade Union Correspondence 1949–1951, VGP.

21. Vicki Garvin, "Negro Women Workers: Union Leader Challenges Progressive America," *Freedom*, November 1950, 5; Vicki Garvin, "The New South," *Negro History Week*, box 1, Trade Union folder, VGP; Vicki Garvin, "The Economic Status of Negro Women in the U.S.A.," n.d. (1952?) box 1, Trade Union folder, VGP.

22. Garvin, "Negro Women Workers," 5. Similar language is found in Garvin, "The Economic Status of Negro Women in the U.S.A.," and "Announce Job Action Meeting for Saturday," *New York Amsterdam News*, March 8, 1952, 2.

23. "Initiating Sponsors" exhibit no. 148C-D, *Communist Political Subversions Part 2: Appendix to Hearing before the Committee of Un-American Activities House of Representatives 84th Congress* (Washington, DC: Government Printing Office, 1956), p. 7366; "Harlem Trade Union Council Meet Planned," *New York Amsterdam News*, October 21, 1950, 19; Foner, *Organized Labor and the Black Worker*, 294.

24. Woodard, *Nation within a Nation*, 36; *Proceedings of the Founding Convention of the National Negro Labor Council*, 1951, p. 9, box 1, folder 1, Ernest Thompson Papers, Rutgers University Archives, New Brunswick, NJ (hereafter ETP).

25. *Proceedings of the Founding Convention of the National Negro Labor Council*, 79.

26. Yvonne Gregory, "'Big Train' Speaks of the 'New Negro,'" *Freedom*, November 1951, 4; *Proceedings of the Founding Convention of the National Negro Labor Council*, 12; Foner, *Organized Labor and the Black Worker*, 299–300.

27. "Labor Unit Set Up for Negro Rights," *New York Times*, March 2, 1952, 41.

28. *Second Annual Convention Yearbook, National Negro Labor Council*, 1952, box 1, folder 2, ETP. National leadership included William Hood of Detroit's UAW Local 600 as president; labor activist and future mayor of Detroit, Coleman Young, as executive secretary; and Ernest Thompson from the independent Union Electric union as director of organizing.

29. *Proceedings of the Founding Convention of the National Negro Labor Council*, 31, 69–71; "NNLC Officers Elected," *Freedom*, November 1951, 4; "New Council Maps Negro Job Battle," *New York Times*, October 29, 1951, 12; Mindy Thompson, *National Negro Labor Council: A History*, Occasional Paper no. 27 (New York: American Institute for Marxist Study, 1978).

30. "Brownwell Adds to Our Country's Shame," 1956, 7, box 1, folder 5, ETP; Jane Gilbert, "Negro Women and Jobs," December 23, 1951, box 1, NNLC, VGP.

31. Vicki Garvin, "Some Pertinent Facts on the Economic Status of Negro Women in the U.S.," box 1, Trade Union Writings, VGP; National Negro Labor Council, "The Truth about the FEPC Fight," 5, box 1, folder 5, ETP; Bill Chester to Revels Cayton, February 8, 1952, box 1, Trade Union Correspondences, VGP.

32. Vicki Garvin interview with Lincoln Bergman, tape 3, n.d., Oak Park, IL, Freedom Archives Collection, San Francisco.

33. Garvin interview with Lincoln Bergman, tape 2; and "Summary of the Reunion of Former Leaders of the NNLC," December 12 and 13, 1970, box 1, folder 7, ETP.

34. Thelma Dale Perkins interview with author; Vicki Garvin interview with Lincoln Bergman, tape 4; Vicki Garvin, "To Eslanda and Paul Robeson," New World Review, October 1954, 3.

35. Dale Perkins interview with author; Miranda Bergman interview with author.

36. Proceedings of the Founding Convention of the National Negro Labor Council, 9.

37. "May Day," New York Times, May 2, 1954; Garvin interview with Lincoln Bergman, tape 4.

38. "Personal History," 7, box 2, Original Drafts/Notes, VGP.

39. Victoria Garvin, testimony, February 15, 1952, Hearings before the Subcommittee to Investigate the Administration of the Internal Security Act, 92nd Cong., 1st and 2nd sess. (Washington, DC: Government Printing Office, 1952), 205–211.

40. Vicki Garvin, "Personal History-Marriage," 7, box 2, Original Drafts/Notes, VGP; Thelma Dale Perkins interview with author, October 4, 2007, Chapel Hill, NC.

41. Garvin interview with Lincoln Bergman, tape 4; Vicki Garvin, "Personal History," 7, box 2, Original Drafts/Notes, VGP; "Ghana Notes in the 1960s," box 2, Original Draft/Notes, VGP.

42. Garvin interview with Lincoln Bergman, tape 4.

43. "Ghana Notes in the 1960s."

44. Vicki Garvin, "Nigeria Diary," 1961, box 1, VGP; Garvin interview with Gil Nobel, May 23, 1999, transcript, Like It Is, show no. 1153, WABC-TV, in author's possession, 4.

45. Chief Ayo Rosiji to Victoria Holmes Garvin, February 10, 1961, box 1, Correspondence, 1952–1992, VGP.

46. Garvin, "Nigeria Diary," Thursday, May 10, 1961, box 1, VGP.

47. Vicki Garvin, "Personal History-Travels," box 2, Original Drafts/Notes, VGP.

48. Garvin, "Nigeria Diary," 2:30 a.m., Saturday, May 27, 1961.

49. George Padmore, Pan Africanism or Communism: The Coming Struggle for Africa (London: D. Dobson, 1956), 47; "Harlem Hails Ghanaian Leader as Returning Hero," New York Times, July 28, 1958, 4; Ronald W. Walters, Pan-Africanism in the African Diaspora: An Analysis of Modern Afrocentric Political Movements (Detroit, MI: Wayne State University Press, 1993), 120; George Hauser, No One Can Stop the Rain: Glimpses of Africa's Liberation Struggle (New York: Pilgrim Press, 1989), 70.

50. A year earlier, Du Bois traveled to Ghana for its 1960 inauguration as a republic in the British Commonwealth. In April 1962, Nkrumah invited Robeson to settle in Ghana, offering him a chair at the University of Ghana. Martin Bauml Duberman, Paul Robeson (New York: Knopf, 1988), 508.

51. Lacy, "Black Bodies in Exile," 147.

52. See Kevin Gaines, "African-American Expatriates in Ghana and the Black Radical Tradition," Souls 1 (Fall 1999): 69; Gaines, American Africans in Ghana.

53. Sylvie Boone to Julian Mayfield, 1966, 14, box 1, folder 8, Julian Mayfield Papers, Manuscript Collection, Schomburg Center for Research on Black Culture, New York Public Library (hereafter JMP).

54. Garvin, "Nigeria Diary."

55. Garvin interview with Gil Nobel, 4; Campbell, *Middle Passages*, 343.

56. Alice Windom, "Account of the 1963 March on Washington Protest in Ghana," box 6, folder 21, JMP; and Walters, *Pan-Africanism in the African Diaspora*, 120. Such radical critiques were censored from the D.C. March on Washington; see Taylor Branch, *Parting the Waters: America in the King Years, 1954–63* (New York: Simon and Schuster, 1988).

57. Mary Duziak, *Cold War Civil Rights: Race and the Image of American Democracy* (Princeton, NJ: Princeton University Press, 2000); Thomas Borstelmann, *The Cold War and the Color Line: American Race Relations in the Global Arena* (Cambridge, MA: Harvard University Press, 2002).

58. Windom, "Account of the 1963 March"; Gaines, "African-American Expatriates," 68–69.

59. Garvin interview with Gil Nobel, 6.

60. Gerald Horne, *Race Woman: The Lives of Shirley Graham Du Bois* (New York: NYU Press, 2000), 187–188; Gaines, *American Africans in Ghana*, 197–201.

61. Garvin, "Celebrating Women's History Month," 8; Malcolm X with Alex Haley, *The Autobiography of Malcolm X* (New York: Ballantine Books, 1973 [1964]), 353; Vicki Garvin, "Malcolm X in Ghana," session 4, Malcolm X: Radical Traditions and a Legacy of Struggle Conference Proceedings, New York, November 1990, at http://www.brothermalcolm.net/sections/malcolm/contents.htm.

62. Garvin interview with Gil Nobel, 6.

63. These limits are discussed in greater detail in Garvin, "Malcolm X in Ghana," session 4, and Alice Windom, "Malcolm X in Ghana," session 4, Malcolm X: Radical Traditions and a Legacy of Struggle Conference Proceedings, New York, November 1990, at http://www.brothermalcolm.net/sections/malcolm/contents.htm.

64. Boone to Mayfield, 14.

65. Alice Windom to Julian Mayfield, August 23, 1966, box 6, folder 21, JMP; Campbell, *Middle Passages*, 70; Lacy, "Black Bodies in Exile," 146.

66. Alice Windom to Julian Mayfield, August 23, 1966, box 6, folder 21, JMP.

67. "Celebrating Women's History Month," 9.

68. Mao wrote the statement in support of the black freedom struggle after numerous requests from Williams. Mao Tse-tung, "Oppose Racial Discrimination by U.S. Imperialism," August 8, 1963, in *The Political Thought of Mao Tse-tung*, ed. Stuart R. Schram (New York: Praeger, 1969) 409–414; Horne, *Race Woman*, 231–232; Timothy Tyson, *Radio Free Dixie: Robert F. Williams and the Roots of Black Power* (Chapel Hill: University of North Carolina Press, 1999).

69. Mabel Williams, "Memorial Celebration for the Life and Work of Vicki Ama Garvin," September 15, 2007, the House of the Lord Church, Brooklyn, NY, recording in author's possession.

70. Vicki Garvin, "China and Black Americans," *New China* 1 (Fall 1975): 23; Vicki Garvin interview with Lincoln Bergman, tape 6; and "Personal History," 4a, box 1, biography, VGP.

71. Garvin interview with Gil Nobel, 6.

72. Box 4, folder 10, ETP; Komozi Woodard interview with author, December 21, 2008, Brooklyn, NY.

73. Garvin interview with Lincoln Bergman, tape 6; "Memorial Celebration for the Life and Work of Vicki Ama Garvin," House of Lord Church, September 15, 2007, Brooklyn, NY, recording in author's possession.

74. Alice Childress, "Salute to Paul Robeson," *New China* 2 (June 1976): 40; Helen Rose, "Harry Belafonte: An Exception Wants to Change the Rules," *New China* 2 (June 1976): 17–18. Garvin's support of China placed her in a vibrant Third World solidarity movement, but at ideological odds with the CPUSA, which still supported the Soviet Union.

75. Garvin interview with Lincoln Bergman, tape 6; Elbaum, *Revolution in the Air*, 191–193,

76. "Memorial Celebration for the Life and Work of Vicki Ama Garvin."

77. An NBUF flyer for a forum titled "Black Liberation Yesterday and Today" listed Vicki Garvin and Harry Haywood as speakers, box 1, NBUF 1, VGP; Komozi Woodard interview with author.

78. Vicki Garvin, *The Call*, March 1981, 16, box 1, NBUF 1, VGP.

79. "The Time Is Now," August 1981, box 1, NBUF 2, VGP.

80. "Celebrating Women's History Month," 10.

81. Vicki Garvin, "Step Up the Offensive Today for Victory," in *In Defense of Mumia*, ed. S. E. Anderson and Tony Medina (New York: Writers and Readers, 1996), 326–328; "Memorial Celebration for the Life and Work of Vicki Ama Garvin."

4

Shirley Graham Du Bois

Portrait of the Black Woman
Artist as a Revolutionary

Gerald Horne and Margaret Stevens

Shirley Graham Du Bois pulled Malcolm X aside at a party in the Chinese embassy in Accra, Ghana, in 1964, only months after having met with him at Hotel Omar Khayyam in Cairo, Egypt.[1] When she spotted him at the embassy, she "immediately . . . guided him to a corner where they sat" and talked for "nearly an hour." Afterward, she declared proudly, "This man is brilliant. I am taking him for my son. He must meet Kwame [Nkrumah]. They have too much in common not to meet."[2] She personally saw to it that they did.

In Ghana during the 1960s, Black Nationalists, Pan-Africanists, and Marxists from around the world mingled in many of the same circles. Graham Du Bois figured prominently in this diverse—sometimes at odds—assemblage. On the personal level she informally adopted several "sons" of Pan-Africanism such as Malcolm X, Kwame Nkrumah, and Stokely Carmichael. On the political level she was a living personification of the "motherland" in the political consciousness of a considerable number of African Americans engaged in the Black Power movement. That is, if Black—mostly male—radicals saw Africa as the geopolitical epicenter that would "give birth" to the global struggle against racism and colonialism, Graham Du Bois served as a Pan-Africanist matriarch and elder to help guide this process.

Yet Shirley Graham Du Bois's pioneering efforts as an African American female artist, Pan-Africanist, and Marxist have been marginalized in conventional discourse on the "Who's Who" of twentieth-century Black radical figures. Graham Du Bois's historical contribution is often delimited by her prominent status as the wife of W. E. B. Du Bois, towering African American intellectual and honorary "Father of Pan-Africanism." Indeed, her radicalism climaxed *after* the death of her husband in 1963. Remaining in Ghana from 1963 to 1966, Graham Du Bois played a central role in actively supporting Nkrumah's political strategy: namely, gaining full and complete independence from the West by thwarting the economic domination of the North Atlantic powers throughout Africa—and, moreover, championing socialism as an alternative socioeconomic system on the continent. Therefore, she might have been shocked, but she was not necessarily surprised when, on the morning of February 24, 1966, she found herself under house arrest after the Ghanaian military staged a coup to oust Kwame Nkrumah from power. At sixty-nine years of age, Graham Du Bois was about to embark on another life—one of her many lives—by resituating herself geographically, emotionally, and politically, settling in Cairo and spending time intermittently in the United States, China, and Tanzania.

The journey as a political activist began relatively late in Graham Du Bois's life, but the long road she had traveled as Shirley Graham, a working-class—albeit prolific—artist and mother, provided the existential basis for her subsequent commitment to transformative politics. Born in Indianapolis, Indiana, in 1896, Graham had spent much of her adulthood as a Black single mother whose later pursuit of antiracist activism and Marxism was undoubtedly influenced by the personal struggles she faced as a black woman in America's Jim Crow labor market based on the superexploitation of Black women. In short, as the Great Depression left millions of Americans without sufficient employment, shelter, or food, Graham was among the countless Black women who were compelled to work intermittently as household servants in order to feed their families.

As we shall see, in her efforts to become a renowned artist, she was continually negotiating within a dominant cultural apparatus in which she had to adhere to social mores of both "Negro" and female "respectability" if she hoped to secure any recognition from her peers, much less any financial compensation to be put toward her household. Yet she served as a composer, actor, director, producer, and musician all by the age of thirty-eight. Certainly these achievements would be remarkable by any standard, but even more so for a working-class Black woman of her time. Further still, she was positioned from a working-class standpoint that, though not immediately reflected in her art, laid the basis for her intensifying angst with the class-based system of white supremacy in the United States.

But if the material basis for Graham's lifelong dedication to transformative politics was fundamentally rooted in her struggles as an adult, then some seeds of this incipient "race woman" were also sown during her childhood while under the influence of her father, David Graham. Reverend Graham was a "race man" in his own right, serving as a proud member of the National Association for the Advancement of Colored People and promulgating the cause of "racial uplift" championed by its leader and his daughter's future spouse, W. E. B. Du Bois. But her father's affinity for "talented tenth" leadership did not hinder his commitment to organizing everyday Black people for militant direct action against Jim Crow racism. Graham recalled her father once leading a prayer service with a loaded gun over his Bible while they were living in New Orleans, calling upon the women and children to clear the church while he and twenty-one men, locked and loaded, remained and prepared to ward off an encroaching lynch mob.[3]

Because she was a woman, Graham was encouraged by her father to revere the power of the pen over that of the sword to effect social change. Strikingly, in Graham's adulthood, she would come to champion the power of both the pen and the sword, ostensibly gender-bound forms of resistance. While residing in Colorado Springs at the age of thirteen, Graham wrote in to a local paper, unleashing her personal anger with racial segregation after having been denied entry into a Young Women's Christian Association site because she was Black. "You are now thirteen . . . young but not too young to speak out in protest against this kind of evil by a so-called Christian organization," her father advised. And she dutifully adhered.[4] If in her later years Graham Du Bois tended to favor Pan-Africanism over Marxism, perhaps her eyewitness accounts of Black workers struggling against Jim Crow without the support of their white class brethren were an important causal factor; the white female companion who witnessed Graham being denied entry at the YWCA did not come to her defense.[5]

The contradiction, however, is that David Graham inculcated in the young Shirley a responsibility to challenge segregation in the "public sphere" only to enforce normative gender roles in the "private sphere." He instilled in his daughter the commonplace notion that a woman's primary social identity ought to be as a mother and caretaker. She was therefore taken hostage by the norms of "mothering," norms that reinforced the social division of labor between men and women, and thus she spent the better part of her youth caring for her siblings and assisting her mother in household tasks. In time, however, Graham turned her "mothering" skills into a political weapon through which she later—armed with ideologies of Marxism and Pan-Africanism—defended "race men" such as W. E. B. Du Bois and Kwame Nkrumah.

Anchored though she was in the domestic sphere, Graham found the leverage to excel intellectually and artistically as a young adult.[6] But opportunities for African American women, even those as brilliant as Shirley Graham, were slim in the Pacific Northwest during World War II, and after high school she attended a trade school where she qualified as an office clerk, eventually landing in Seattle. There she met and soon after married Shadrach T. McCants in 1921.[7] By the age of twenty-five she transitioned, albeit reluctantly, into the role of a wife and mother, and bore two sons, Robert in 1923 and David in 1925.

The details of her marriage to McCants from 1921 to 1927 are among the most obscure in her life, but she remained relatively stationary both geographically and professionally for the duration of the marriage. She retrospectively obscured her own biography during these years, proclaiming falsely that McCants had died in the 1920s. However, what emerges quite clearly is the fact that their two sons would remain the single most important personal and political anchors in her life. In her words, "Everything I did, everything I planned, everything I tried to do was motivated by my passionate desire to make a good life for my sons."[8] As a mother, Graham factored her sons into the equation of every subsequent calculation. Further still, as an analogue to this ideology of maternalism, she figured influential men into her life choices, making it her business to defend such leaders as Du Bois, Nkrumah, and Malcolm even when her efforts were met with harsh resistance.

But her anchor within the domestic sphere quickly gave way with Graham's divorce from McCants, and she at once became a globe-trotter, taking off for France in 1927, when, according to Tyler Stovall, "blackness became the rage in Paris during the 1920s." In Paris she became acquainted with prominent African Americans such as Eric Walrond, onetime editor of Marcus Garvey's newspaper, *Negro World*, and writer for the Urban League's journal, *Opportunity*.[9] Here too she encountered various forms of African music that she incorporated into her first opera entitled *Tom-Tom*. But Graham remained a single mother who had financial responsibilities associated with her two sons, who remained in the United States under the care of her mother. Therefore, during her ventures in Paris with the Black artist community from 1927 to 1930, she returned to the States intermittently to tend to her children and augment her income, working as a music librarian at Howard University and as a music teacher at what now is Morgan State University, while taking summer classes at Columbia University.

Graham was not directly engaged with the political struggles at Howard that were sharpening in the wake of the Great Depression in 1929, but she was there during a wave of student strikes in the late 1920s.[10] In the process of becoming a pioneering Black woman composer, she produced an early version of *Tom-Tom* in 1929 while at Morgan State with the teamwork of trailblazing Black male artists such as actor Roland Hayes, director Randolph Edmonds, and filmmaker Carlton Moss.[11] Most notable about the opera was the way in which it fused "Harlem cabarets" with African rhythm, representing the "beating heart of a people."[12] In a time when the Jim Crow United States was overwhelmingly averse to taking Africa seriously as an origin of modern culture, this opera boldly placed Africa at the center of the African American experience in North America from slavery to freedom.

But *Tom-Tom* also adhered to the predominant cultural norms of the society because it portrayed Africans as a fundamentally emotional, rather than intellectual, political—much less proletarian—people. Even her female dancers staged a protest prior to one performance by refusing to wear only rags for their bottoms while dancing topless.[13] As we shall see, Graham later abandoned the "striptease" portrayal of women in her creative work only to reinforce such controversial theories as biological determinism and the women's sphere, both of which were evident in *Tom-Tom*.

Needless to say, *Tom-Tom*'s success did not pay the bills; therefore, Graham in the meantime enrolled at Oberlin College in 1931, where she worked at breakneck speed to complete both a B.A. and an M.A. by 1935 while also working part-time as a laundress like so many other Black working-class women of her day. Consider the amazing accomplishment of Graham as a single Black mother in her midthirties who completed college and graduate school while raising two sons and working for negligible pay. She then opted to keep her elevated credentials in the African American community by teaching fine arts at the historically black school now called Tennessee State University, rather than traveling to Vienna, which was an option for her at that time.

Teaching history, music theory, and French with insufficient supplies, little pay, little time for her sons, and even less time for her own artistic endeavors, however, left Graham thoroughly disillusioned. She remained at Tennessee State for only the 1935–1936 academic year, taking up a position in Chicago as director of the Negro Unit at the Federal Theatre Project (FTP), the government-funded sanctuary for progressive cultural workers during the Depression.

While working at the FTP from 1936 to 1938, Graham continued to grow as an artist, venturing away from opera and into the world of theater by directing such critically acclaimed plays as *Swing Mikado* and *Little Black Sambo*. Leftists of the Popular Front milieu such as Black Communist writer Richard Wright, also in Chicago, dismissed her work as an example of the "waste of talent" in FTP productions, since it opted to depict "jungle scenes, spirituals and all" over proletarian struggle.[14] But when she directed Theodore Ward's play *The Big White Fog*, a now unfortunately obscure drama that grappled with Garveyism, African American families, and burgeoning Left, she was met with equal invective from Chicago elites—Black and white alike, including the local NAACP chapter, which dismissed the play as "communist propaganda."[15] With the subsequent disbandment of the FTP for alleged Communist subversive activity in 1938, Graham's later affinity toward the Communist Party was, quite ironically, anticipated—if not precipitated—by this early red scare. All the same, she emerged from the project with an enhanced reputation as a composer, director, and producer, as well as with a little acting experience. She was quickly accepted into the Yale Drama School to study theater even further.

Yale was "all that [she] expected and more," since she also studied German and Italian and even began contemplating a dissertation.[16] But despite the support from such prominent African Americans as Charles Johnson and Adam Clayton Powell Jr., she found that her white patrons, such as Mary White Ovington of the NAACP, were apologetic about her "Negro plays" when seeking investors for her. Moreover, when Graham attempted to perform her plays through African American theater companies, she found herself even more marginalized. Graham's *Coal Dust*, a play that signaled her growing interest in Marxism insofar as it was an "old fashioned type of play about workers," which was performed at the Black-run Karamu Theatre in Cleveland, Ohio, was quickly abandoned because it lacked the financial backing for major—read non-Black—advertising. At the time, white-owned theater houses had the monopoly of theatrical productions, and the emergence of Black-run theater projects was received with considerable hostility from the dominant cultural apparatus. Her work with the FTP prematurely aborted by the anticommunist suspicions of the House Un-American Activities Committee (HUAC), and efforts at Yale frustrated by the racism of her purported mentors, it is no wonder that she would later spend a significant portion of her life fighting the political repression thrust upon "Red" and Black people. Exasperated with the obstacles associated with producing African American theater, by 1941 she had abandoned her work at Yale and her artistic career altogether for a job with the YWCA in Indianapolis.

Graham's transition away from theater, however, was not a political retreat in the face of racism and sexism. Quite pragmatically, she needed a salary increase to support her children, and a change of careers was in order. In 1942, after a brief tenure at the Phyllis Wheatley YWCA in Indianapolis, where she served as a director of adult activities, she was awarded a position as the YWCA-USO director at Fort Huachuca, Arizona, where 5,000 Black enlisted men and 6,000 Black officers formed the "largest contingent of Negro soldiers in the country."[17]

She arrived at Fort Huachuca at an opportune moment; the Black soldiers were in an uproar against a rash of police brutality cases inflicted by the white military police on post. The NAACP was quite active in organizing these soldiers, focusing on the case of Ollie D. North, who was charged with mutiny for using a loaded rifle to terminate a military police beating of a fellow Black soldier.[18] Graham also intervened on behalf of North and "reached the General and influenced him to reopen the case and by military ruling had the soldier's sentence changed to ten years." In the process she was endearingly referred to as "mama" by the Black troops whom she, apparently, both mothered emotionally and defended politically.[19] Needless to say, her Christian employers were far from enamored with her maternal-turned-political actions; she was dismissed shortly thereafter.

Graham understood her dismissal quite clearly (if not literally) in black-and-white terms: "My ladies at the YWCA-USO . . . ordered me to come into New York City for a conference. When I got here they coolly informed me that the USO was not interested in some of my activities which were outside the recreation program of the USO." Her own evaluation of the firing was that "in the final analysis white supremacy has us by [the] throat because the white man has the money. Yet I'll be damned if I'm sorry."[20] Again she had witnessed a scenario in which the militant self-defense against racist terror was carried out by Black people while the perpetrators were white. On a personal level, her reactions to the firing revealed a deep-seated anger that pitted "us" against "the white man," which was a key tenet of the Black Nationalist ideology she would later profess.

As a result of her experience in Arizona, Graham deepened her commitment to the NAACP because it had been the primary organizational ally in her own struggles against racism. Therefore, upon her dismissal from the USO she immediately packed her bags for New York City to work as an assistant field director for the NAACP. She became active in the group when its membership was in the process of reaching an all-time high, from 40,000 in 1940 to 400,000 in 1945, but she was convinced that it could reach "one million."[21]

Her experience organizing NAACP chapters was significant for several reasons. First, it demonstrates that Graham was part of the "long" civil rights movement dating back to the Communist and NAACP organizing campaigns in the South during the Great Depression. Second, it unearths a political transition in her own perspective that would augur her growing affinity for the Communist Party during the war. She was frustrated by what she saw as the capitulation of the southern church constituency to Jim Crow; this was compounded by what she perceived to be chicanery and chauvinism of the preachers, who were far from the legacy of Reverend Graham. "Believe me," she declared, "I can see more clearly why the Russians closed all the churches! Come the revolution—that would be the first thing I should advise—*throughout the south.* These fat, thieving, ignorant preachers! All of them should be put to work" (emphasis in original).[22] By 1943 Graham was not only thinking in terms of a "revolution" in the United States but also sympathizing with the Russian variety of social transformation and even imagining that she might play more than an advisory role. This was a self-fulfilling prophecy. But Graham's decision to resign from her NAACP position despite the fact that she had raised more than $8,000 in 1943 alone was not the apparent result of an ideological pull toward Communism; rather, she felt the "urge to do creative work."[23]

While working at the Open Door Community Center in Brooklyn, she began participating in political campaigns against police misconduct and for better housing, health care, and jobs for the local residents. Remarkably, she also found time to turn out a series of "biographical novels," as she called them, on such figures as George Washington Carver, Paul Robeson, and Frederick Douglass. While these popular biographies had helped Graham accumulate more money than she had ever made to that point, they also placed her more closely in circles with local and international Communist figures who were guiding her artistically and politically. Among these prominent men were actor Paul Robeson, writer Howard Fast, city councilman from Brooklyn Pete Cacchione, and, most notably, W. E. B. Du Bois, who though still far from being a Communist, was also taking an increasing interest in Red activity in the United States.

Cacchione was also there as an emotional comfort to Graham when her son Robert died while living in California in 1944. This devastation propelled Graham into a more intense work frenzy, since she continued churning out biographies and even entered a doctoral program at New York University (though she did not finish). As she noted in a letter, "My entire life was work."[24] Her close interaction with these Communist men was critical to winning her political loyalty to the Communist Party, becoming more overt by 1947. In that year not only was she on a HUAC list of Red "fronts," but she was also photographed at a rally alongside Fast and Cacchione to save the Communist-initiated *New Masses* from being discontinued during the post–World War II crackdown on Communists in the United States, commonly referred to as the McCarthy period.[25]

Graham's personal and political affinities for the Communist movement became increasingly intertwined as Du Bois—her intimate "flame" since she had returned to New York in 1943—was marginalized and altogether ousted from the NAACP in 1948 for challenging the Cold War thrust of the organization's leadership. Relentlessly attacking the United States for human rights violations, W. E. B. Du Bois and Shirley Graham both supported third-party candidate Henry Wallace of the Progressive Party over Harry Truman in the 1948 election, all to the dismay of the NAACP. Graham came to Du Bois's defense, unequivocally decrying what she saw as the NAACP's "'brazen act' of 'sheer persecution' that illuminated the archaic and anti-democratic character of the NAACP's structure," toward her political comrade and lover.[26] This personal commitment to Du Bois aside, Graham's own support for the Progressive Party shows how her maternal experiences spoke to her newfound leftist politics. At the July 1948 convention that nominated Wallace (where she played a leading role), she stated, "I am only one Negro mother who has seen the doors of a great hospital closed against her dying son. . . . What do we want? That our children may dwell in peace."[27]

Du Bois and Graham were increasingly operating as a two-person united front against U.S. foreign policy; the political repercussions of their activity were imminent. In 1949, the couple sent a greeting to Joseph

Stalin, Communist leader of the Soviet Union, lauding his "leadership in uprooting racial discrimination." To this statement they alone were signatories, but it reflected the fact that a considerable number of African Americans had an increased affinity for the Soviet Union—not least because it was most directly responsible for wiping the world's most racist dictator, Hitler, off the map. And in 1949, at a rally sponsored by the Communist-led Civil Rights Congress in Peekskill, New York, she was hit with a rock by an anticommunist heckler. Du Bois, too, was suffering the repercussions of being increasingly seen as a Communist "agent," specifically because of his anti–nuclear weapons stance. So when he and Graham attended the Paris Peace Conference to discuss the prospects for nuclear disarmament, this was no doubt to the chagrin of U.S. authorities. Therefore, when she and Du Bois married in 1951 after the death of his first wife, they did so secretly and hurriedly on February 14 because, only two days later, he was to be charged in court with attempting to aid a foreign power, that is, the Soviet Union. Just as she had been his avid defender in 1948 against the NAACP, so too did she aid him in rallying financial support for his trial after he made bail.

Noteworthy about their whirlwind tour for his case is the fact that her prestige, in fact, enhanced his credibility. For example, in St. Paul, her mother's original home, the arrival of Du Bois drew the largest interracial meeting ever held in that city because he was "Lizzie Etta's little girl Shirley's husband."[28] Fortunately, though indicted, Du Bois was able to escape conviction. After the turmoil of Du Bois's case had passed, Shirley Graham Du Bois and her husband began to settle into a seemingly pacific life in their chic Brooklyn Heights home, formerly owned by writer Arthur Miller, receiving frequent guests from across the globe, ranging from UN representatives to African anticolonialists. Since they were confined to domestic affairs because both of their passports had been revoked throughout most of the 1950s, Graham Du Bois busied herself by caring for her husband and staying in the circle of Black Communists also living in New York at the time.

In particular, Graham Du Bois co-led a feminist collective alongside two other leading Black women of her period, Eslanda Robeson and Louise Thompson Patterson, also betrothed to two of the most prominent Black Communist figures of the twentieth century: Paul Robeson and William Patterson. Graham Du Bois, along with Eslanda Robeson and Louise Thompson Patterson, started a group called the Sojourners for Truth and Justice, which intended to inspire leadership of women of color across the globe.[29] Challenging barriers of race and nation alike, the work of these Black Communist women "sojourners" indeed helped pave the way for the women's liberation movement of the 1960s that thrived on American college campuses and in the workplace, a movement so often attributed summarily to the leadership of such figures as Gloria Steinem.

But above and beyond her work within this Black Marxist feminist collective, Graham Du Bois was also beginning to perform as a key actor on the global stage in this very period when the civil rights movement in the United States was gaining strength. When leftist forces around the world were riled by the execution of alleged Soviet spies Julius and Ethel Rosenberg in the United States, she called upon her mothering skills and directly oversaw the process whereby their children were successfully adopted.[30] These domestic political engagements notwithstanding, the Du Boises leapt at the opportunity to leave the country when, in 1958, their passports were reinstated. For the better part of 1959 and 1960, the couple stayed in Europe, the Soviet Union and China—Graham Du Bois even venturing into Africa.

While the Du Boises were being wined and dined in Moscow, African Americans ought to contemplate more deeply Communism as a viable socioeconomic system because such blatant forms of racial degradation were negligible in the Soviet Union.[31] The caveat, of course, is that the Du Boises were given royal treatment in a supposedly egalitarian state not least because the Soviets understood the positive propaganda associated with catering to such influential African Americans.

Graham Du Bois, reluctantly though excitedly, left her aged spouse in Russia and departed for Africa, visiting Ghana, Egypt, Sudan, and Nigeria with a Soviet delegation. While in Ghana she gave a stirring presentation based on her husband's essay "The Future of All Africa Lies in Socialism," and at an important Pan-African gathering she replaced the flag of Taiwan with that of the Communist regime in Beijing.[32] After having traveled to China and met its Communist leader, Mao Tse-tung, Graham Du Bois proclaimed, "Wonderful! I didn't think any place could be better than the Soviet Union but I must say China takes my breath away."[33] This indicated that she was moving toward a deeper engagement with Beijing's version of socialism. Moreover, her pro-Maoist sympathies in fact anticipated the political association of the militant Black Panther Party in the 1960s with Maoism.

Subsequently, Graham Du Bois's relations with her U.S.-based, pro-Moscow comrades, even those in the Black feminist circles, were to become increasingly strained. Upon returning to the United States to help edit the upcoming Communist-inspired magazine *Freedomways*, a spin-off of the newspaper *Freedom*, she reported in the *Afro American* that even European women had "more guts" than those in the United States.[34] Convinced, apparently, that she might be of more use to international movements than to those in the United States, Graham Du Bois was off again in 1961 (this time without her husband) and back to Ghana to attend the conference "African Women and Women of African Descent."[35]

Back in the States, W. E. B. Du Bois had made the decision to join the CPUSA, which he did in 1961. At first glance, it is curious that the couple would then turn around and move to Ghana that same year, effectively denying them the chance to organize for the American party. And yet, considering Graham Du Bois's inclination toward building an international movement based in Africa coupled with their general resentment of the U.S. government, their move to Accra was entirely fitting. Moreover, Kwame Nkrumah had arranged it so that they would have a house on the hill, complete with a steward, cook, driver, and night watchman, and in close proximity to Flagstaff House, his own home. Graham Du Bois's son David recalled that it was "like living in a glass house when you went to the home there in Ghana because it was a place of pilgrimage for people from all over the world and particularly all over Africa," as well as for Chinese diplomats and African Americans enthralled with Ghanaian state.[36]

The prominent Du Bois family, it seems, was also so enthralled with the Ghanaian state that they failed to counsel Nkrumah on the potentially negative repercussion of marginalizing the Left, much to the chagrin of American and Ghanaian Marxists. On the ideological level, Nkrumah sought to "inculcate in" the Ghanaian "working people the love for labour and increased productivity."[37] In so doing, however, he declared trade unions "obsolete," since to "struggle against capitalists" was now, he felt, an irrelevant matter, and finally mandated that Communists be "banned from entering the civil service in the Gold Coast."[38] Charged with the task of remapping Ghana's entire educational system in support of the new regime, Graham Du Bois was in no position to challenge official policies of the state. In the coming period this would further alienate Graham Du Bois from the "old school" Marxists of the Moscow milieu while deepening her influence on the "new school" radical youth of the Maoist and Pan-Africanist varieties.

Graham, however, would soon be left to wage such battles on her own since, in 1963, W. E. B. Du Bois died. If Graham had remarkably mustered the energy to work throughout the pain after the loss of her son, Graham Du Bois managed to work even harder after the loss of her husband. She was already in the process of embarking on the most politically engaged and professionally productive position in her entire life: directing the television industry in Ghana while indirectly acting as a "first lady" to Nkrumah. Remarkably, Ghana TV would not have any commercials in that its primary function was not to serve big business; instead, Graham Du Bois stated that "the television we are planning will be a tremendous channel for education, for increased understanding and for developing and unifying the peoples of Africa."[39] Though in some ways this education did little to challenge traditional understandings of gender norms insofar as it offered "demonstrations of cooking, dressmaking, exercises, fashion shows, hints," and "interior decorations," it also quite nobly offered an "evening programme for illiterates."[40]

To learn how to run such an operation, Graham Du Bois traveled across Europe from east to west, also stopping in Japan, where she finally brokered a deal with the Japanese electronics company Sanyo to supply Ghana with the televisions for this enterprise. As a result, Graham Du Bois facilitated the effective displacement of the Philips electronics company of the Netherlands, Ghana's colonial era television supplier, and furthered Nkrumah's hope that Ghana might avoid the road toward "neocolonialism" that was the fate of so many postindependence regimes. Graham Du Bois's political ascendancy upset the self-interested Ghanaian elites, since this was the first time that anyone——much less an African American woman and "outsider"——had been given free reign to sever the traditional colonial ties that had sustained their own class positions.

Moreover, they were angered by her personal oversight of Nkrumah's health and well-being, reflected in the evening telephone calls to Nkrumah "each night at bedtime" along with advising him on such matters as his dietary needs.[41] Again, she had elided the personal with the political. As if her interventions in the economic and personal affairs of leading officials were not enough to incite discontent, Graham Du Bois additionally tested her political clout by using her influence within the Ghanaian publishing industry to praise African American Communists such as her comrade William Patterson. Given the wide reach of the Ghanaian press across the continent, Graham Du Bois helped grant distinction to a political milieu that could hardly expect the slightest praise from its own government. On her off time she also took occasion to meet with Black CPUSA leaders Claude Lightfoot and James Jackson when they came to

Ghana, often discussing the content of *Freedomways* and its ideological direction in relationship to the civil rights movement in the States.[42]

But the ties to her CPUSA comrades, especially those involved in the production of *Freedomways*, were noticeably weakened as a result of her political shifts while in Ghana. On a global level, Graham Du Bois's loyalties to the Soviet Union were becoming increasingly strained as she gravitated away from what she saw as the Moscow/King approach to "peaceful coexistence" and toward the Beijing/Black Power call for militant national liberation. She was increasingly vocal in defending China to the point that in 1963 she wrote into the Nation of Islam journal *Muhammad Speaks*, taking both Roy Wilkins of the NAACP and James Farmer to task for their anti-Chinese positions.[43] But the CPUSA had continued to remain committed to the Soviet Union, while China—and by association Graham Du Bois—was becoming anti-Soviet.

Undoubtedly she was fundamental to shaping the internationalist perspective of *Freedomways* insofar as it was she who solicited Tom Mboya of Kenya, Oliver Tambo of South Africa, and Julius Nyere of Tanzania to submit articles for the magazine. This all-star cast of African leaders was placed squarely before an ambivalent "old guard" base of leading Black activists involved with this journal just as a "new guard" representing the Black Power movement in the United States was looking increasingly to Africa and Asia as the centers of national and anticolonial struggles for liberation from Western imperialism. But Du Bois's death in 1963 placed Graham Du Bois and Esther Jackson Cooper, another editor, at odds, since Graham was enraged that Roy Wilkins was allowed to write on Du Bois though they were archenemies, whereas Graham Du Bois's picks such as Malcolm X were not accepted for submission.[44] This apparent hesitation on the part of the Old Left to break with leading Black activists of the time—even those such as Wilkins with whom they were once at odds— rather than embrace the emergent Third World leaders who were inspiring the youth of the Diaspora, would only further distance Graham from her longtime comrades in the CPUSA.

It was not simply that Graham Du Bois's "left Nationalist" tendencies complicated her position in the U.S.-based *Freedomways* circles; additionally, she challenged her political alliances with the left forces within Ghana by hiring only "professional experts" from the United States to work in the Volta region of that country. She confessed, "My heart bleeds when talented young Afro-Americans are brought to my attention and I am asked to give them an opportunity to use their abilities!" Even Robert Williams, the author of *Negroes with Guns*, who helped jump-start the militant self-defense movement as opposed to the nonviolent philosophy of King, did not make the cut because, she said, "Africa doesn't need 'leaders.' It does need the help of skilled technicians, experienced and exceedingly well-trained."[45] Not only did this approach upset Ghanaian—and non-Ghanaian—leftists, but additionally Graham found herself politically defending Malcolm X's perceived "racialist" viewpoint from attacks by Marxist Ghanaians, stating that he was opposed to the "White government and the White ruling class" of the United States.[46]

But Graham Du Bois was also aware of the fact that many of the African American "skilled technicians" who were making their way into Ghana were "well-trained" by the State Department and other government agencies, functioning as self-interested surrogates of imperialism who, in her words, sought "better and easier living and quick profits to take back [to the United States]."[47] These "surrogates of imperialism," coupled with the anti-Nkrumah forces within Ghana, were building their political and military force, growing such that on February 24, 1966, Nkrumah's power was involuntarily abdicated; so too was that of the honorary "first lady."

Graham Du Bois guarded Nkrumah's legacy as she had done for Du Bois after his NAACP ouster. The litmus test for the political righteousness of any self-proclaimed revolutionary was their position on whether or not Nkrumah was unjustly overthrown. Graham Du Bois was to answer, of course, that he was, but many of her CPUSA friends were not quite so decisive. In particular, prominent Communist writer Anna Louise Strong enraged her when she raised the contention that Nkrumah was rumored to have been exceedingly corrupt.[48] But for Graham Du Bois there was no such thing as opposing Nkrumah from the left; to support his overthrow—or even to question his bona fides—was to aid and abet U.S. imperialism. Her days as a "comrade" in the CPUSA were numbered. Her defense of the African national liberation struggle was becoming increasingly unequivocal.

Apparently exasperated with U.S. nationals of many stripes—Red included—Graham decisively hedged her bets on Africa and lowered her political anchor in Maoist China. Although she kept her eye on the developments occurring in the United States, particularly events involving the Black Panthers on the West Coast (where her son David was to edit their newspaper) and the Student Nonviolent Coordinating Committee (SNCC) in the South, Graham Du Bois was now off to Cairo, Egypt, where she would be based for the duration of her life, residing intermittently in China, Tanzania, and the United States.

Cairo was in the midst of its 1967–1968 conflict with Israel when she arrived, and Graham Du Bois had decided to support a regime that, in her words, had quite appropriately "raised a blockade against white imperialism and aggression rather than against Zionism or the Jewish people."[49] As her political hatred of "white" imperialist foreign policy intensified, her political affinities became more "Egypt-centric." Indeed, Egypt in particular and Afro-Centrism in general would become a major theme in the lectures she would deliver to American students when she returned to the United States in the 1970s.

Supporting Egypt's leader, Gamal Nasser, however, also put Graham Du Bois in a delicate and sensitive position as a Red—analogous to her support for Nkrumah in Ghana—precisely because Nasser was receiving aid from Moscow while suppressing the oxygen supply to the Communist movement in Egypt. This occurred as her relations with Beijing became even closer. Because she was never lacking in vanity, it did not hurt that China had not only given her spouse ample airtime on Radio Peking while in Ghana—and most recently, Chinese officials had met her in Tanzania after Nkrumah's overthrow and pulled out the red carpet for her.[50]

Transitioning into a stalwart defender of China was not, however, without its own contradictions for Graham Du Bois, whether or not she recognized this fact. The Chinese-U.S. normalization of diplomatic relations during the Nixon era at first frustrated her. But apparently she opted not to challenge the mandates of Beijing (which was her normal response of late). Perhaps she was wary of once again courting the wrath of a powerful state whose political repression might have been too much at her age. But more likely, she truly believed that China, with all its flaws, promised the one and only "third way" as a state alternative to Soviet and U.S. influence over the "darker races" of the world.

By the 1970s, Graham Du Bois was back in the United States after a huge left-liberal spectrum—including, ironically, Roy Wilkins—garnered support for her right to return and lecture at campuses across the country. While she had refused to sever ties with her CPUSA friends leading the W. E. B. Du Bois Clubs—considered "revisionist" by her newly minted Beijing allies—she did quite pragmatically (perhaps even willingly) disavow her ties to the CPUSA itself in order to regain entry to the United States. This would seem to contradict all of the recent work she had contributed to *Freedomways* and her membership—if only nominal—to the

Party; however, her desire to reach out to the youth in the Black Power movement in the States required that she make political concessions to the same government apparatus whose repression of political dissent had at one time driven her to the left. On her U.S. tour she spoke as a nationalist on questions related to Africa and Afrocentrism, not on class or socialism. Her Afrocentric leanings were also reflected in her novel *Zulu Heart*, which depicted the plight of the South African indigenes in their struggle against apartheid: this book included a European who, upon receiving a heart transplant from a Zulu, emerged from the operation with a new life rhythm. He could even dance! Needless to say, the *New York Amsterdam News*, a prominent Harlem-based weekly paper loved it, biological determinist implications notwithstanding.[51] Indeed, Graham Du Bois was treading the waters of cultural nationalism in the States that would become most associated with such figures as Ron Karenga, founder of the African American ritual Kwanzaa in 1967.

As late as 1975 she was still lecturing in the United States, even working for brief stints in New England at both the University of Massachusetts in Amherst and Harvard University teaching literature. But she could also be found on the West Coast attending gatherings sponsored by the Black Panthers in Oakland and also speaking before the US China People's Friendship Association on "Africa and China."[52] For Graham Du Bois, defending China and Africa was a matter of life and death, quite literally in her case. In April 1977, after fighting the last of her many battles—this time with cancer—Shirley Graham Du Bois was laid to rest in China, a citizen of Tanzania, ending a series of her many lives in only one of her many homes.

NOTES

1. David Gallen, ed., *Malcolm X: The FBI File* (New York: Carroll and Graf, 1992), 331.

2. Maya Angelou, *All God's Children Need Traveling Shoes* (New York: Random House, 1986), 138, 141.

3. Shirley Graham Du Bois article on coup, *Essence*, January 1971, Shirley Graham Du Bois Papers, courtesy of David Du Bois, Cairo, Egypt; Shirley Graham Du Bois, "What Happened in Ghana? The Inside Story," *Freedomways* (Spring 1966): 201–223, 220.

4. Shirley Graham Du Bois, "I Got Wings," short story (ts. draft), n.d., Shirley Graham Du Bois Papers, Subseries F, Fiction works, Schlesinger Library, Radcliffe Institute. See also Robert Dee Thompson Jr., "A Socio-biography of Shirley Graham Du Bois: A Life in the Struggle" (Ph.D. diss., University of California–Santa Cruz, 1997), 14–17.

5. Shirley Graham Du Bois, interview by Abigail Simon, April 10, 1974, Shirley Graham Du Bois Papers; Shirley Graham Du Bois, *His Day Is Marching On* (Philadelphia: Lippincott, 1971), 30, 31; Thompson, "A Socio-biography of Shirley Graham-Du Bois," 22–30.

6. She graduated as the class valedictorian at her Tennessee-based junior high school and later received high honors upon graduation from Lewis and Clark High School in the state of Washington, where her family had relocated in 1915. Too, she was recognized as the class poet and won an essay contest for a piece she composed on Booker T. Washington, indicating an interest in a figure to whom she would later dedicate an entire biography.

7. Elizabeth Brown-Guillory, ed., *Wines in the Wilderness: Plays by African-American Women from the Harlem Renaissance to the Present* (Westport, CT: Greenwood, 1990), 79. However, on her first passport application she listed her date of marriage as July 16, 1918; see file 100–99729–84A, October 28, 1958, Federal Bureau of Investigation.

8. Graham Du Bois, *His Day Is Marching On*, 37–39.

9. Irma Watkins-Owens, *Blood Relations: Caribbean Immigrants and the Harlem Community, 1900–1930* (Bloomington: Indiana University Press, 1996), 156–157; Eric Walrond, *Tropic Death* (New York: Collier, 1972).

10. She might have even crossed paths with Malcolm Nurse. Nurse, alias George Padmore, was a prominent student organizer on the campus, and, as a member of the Communist Party of the United States, he was soon to become a leading Black member of the Communist International commissioned with the task of organizing Black workers, particularly seamen. Differences of age, personal responsibilities to her children, and lack of political interest might have combined to prevent her from allying more closely with this student movement, but she would not have gone unaffected by its political presence.

11. When this opera reached full-scale production in 1932, it was a tremendous success, broadcast over the National Broadcast Company radio station and winning critical accolades in the pages of *Crisis*, the influential periodical of the NAACP.

12. Program for *Tom-Tom*, ca. 1932, Shirley Graham file, Oberlin College, Oberlin, Ohio.

13. *Afro-American*, July 9, 1932. See also *Washington Tribune*, July 8, 1932; *Boston Chronicle*, July 16, 1932.

14. Richard Wright, "I Tried to Be a Communist," *Atlantic Monthly*, September 1944, file 289882, Federal Bureau of Investigation.

15. Rena Fraden, *Blueprints for a Black Federal Theatre* (Cambridge: Cambridge University Press, 1994), 121–122, 134.

16. Shirley Graham to W. E. B. Du Bois, October 23, 1938, Shirley Graham Du Bois Papers, Amistad Research Center, Tulane University, New Orleans, Louisiana.

17. Graham Du Bois, *His Day Is Marching On*, 52. See also Judith Weisenfeld, *African American Women and Christian Activism: New York's Black YWCA, 1905–1945* (Cambridge, MA: Harvard University Press, 1997).

18. *New York Times*, November 28, 1942, February 17, 1943; Leopold Johnson to NAACP, April 8, 1943; Ottis Burns to James Davis, May 5, 1943; Leslie Perry to Charles Browning, September 29, 1944, box b159, group 2, NAACP papers.

19. Albert McKee to Shirley Graham, March 3, 1942, Shirley Graham Du Bois Papers, courtesy of David Du Bois, Cairo, Egypt.

20. Shirley Graham to W. E. B. Du Bois, October 30, 1942, reel 53, no. 1047, W. E. B. Du Bois Papers, University of Massachusetts–Amherst Library.

21. Shirley Graham to Walter White, July 14, 1943, box a585, group 2, NAACP Papers.

22. Shirley Graham to Mary White Ovington, August 1943, Mary White Ovington Papers, Wayne State University Library, Detroit, Michigan; Nat Brandt, *Harlem at War: The Black Experience in World War II* (Syracuse, NY: Syracuse University Press, 1996); Neil Wynn, *Afro-Americans and the Second World War* (New York: Holmes and Meir, 1976).

23. Arthur Spingam to Shirley Graham, October 5, 1943; Shirley Graham to Walter White, September 8, 1943, box a585, group II, NAACP Papers.

24. Shirley Graham to Roselyn Richardson, July 3, 1946, Roselyn Richardson Papers, Indiana Historical Society, Indianapolis, Indiana.

25. *New Masses*, May 13, 1947.

26. Shirley Graham speech, "National Founding Convention of the New Political Party at Convention Hall, Philadelphia, July 23–25, 1948," reel 2, Third Party Presidential Nominating Conventions, Proceedings, Records, etc.

27. Memorandum, September 11, 1950, no. 100–370965–8, FBI; *Daily Worker*, March 26, 1948, May 31, 1948, December 23, 1949; *New York Amsterdam News*, December 31, 1949; *Counter-Attack*, July 1, 1949.

28. Graham Du Bois, *His Day Is Marching On*, 157–164.

29. Gerald Horne, *Communist Front? The Civil Rights Congress, 1946–1956* (London: Associated University Presses, 1988), 208.

30. Robert Meeropol and Michael Meeropol, *We Are Your Sons: The Legacy of Julius and Ethel Rosenberg* (Boston: Houghton Mifflin, 1975).

31. *Pittsburgh Courier*, June 20, 1959; Martin Bauml Duberman, *Paul Robeson: A Biography* (New York: Knopf, 1988), 473. See also Shirley Graham Du Bois, "Heartwarming Memories," in *Paul Robeson*, ed. Brigitte Moegelsack (Berlin: Academy of Arts of the German Democratic Republic, 1978), 56.

32. W. E. B. Du Bois, *The Autobiography: A Soliloquy on Viewing My Life from the Last Decade of its First Century* (New York: International Publishers, 1968); Graham Du Bois, *His Day Is Marching On*, 301.

33. Shirley Graham Du Bois to Cedric Belfrage, April 4, 1959, box 2, Cedric Belfrage Papers, New York University Library.

34. *Baltimore Afro-American*, September 20, 1959. See also Annelise Orieck, *Common Sense and a Little Fire: Women and Working-Class Politics in the U.S., 1900–1965* (Chapel Hill: University of North Carolina Press, 1995).

35. From there she went to another conference while in Cairo called the "Extraordinary Session of the Afro-Asian Solidarity Council," which was specifically focused on the Congo crisis. In Cairo she signed onto an ad in a Trotskyite paper that denounced U.S. foreign policy activity in the increasingly Soviet-aligned Cuba, evidently less worried about undermining the political tensions between the Socialist Workers' Party and the CPUSA than in challenging U.S. imperialism.

36. David Du Bois, interview, June 3, 1992, Louis Massiah Papers, courtesy of Louis Massiah, Philadelphia, Pennsylvania.

37. Jeff Crisp, *The Story of an African Working Class: Ghanaian Miners' Struggles, 1870–1980* (London: Zed, 1984), 134. See also Ebenezer Oiri Addo, "Kwame Nkrumah: A Case Study of Religion and Politics in Ghana" (Ph.D. diss., Drew University, 1994); W. Scott Thompson, *Ghana's Foreign Policy: 1957–1966* (Princeton, NJ: Princeton University Press, 1969).

38. Hakim Adi, *West Africans in Britain: 1900–1960 Nationalism, Pan Africanism and Communism* (London: Lawrence and Wishart, 1998), 163.

39. Shirley Graham Du Bois to Gladys, December 16, 1964, courtesy of David Du Bois, Cairo, Egypt.

40. Shirley Graham Du Bois to Mikhail Kotov, November 7, 1965, courtesy of David Du Bois, Cairo, Egypt.

41. Angelou, *All God's Children Need Traveling Shoes*, 138.

42. Shirley Graham Du Bois to John Henrik Clarke, January 24, 1965, John Henrik Clarke Papers, Schomburg Center, New York Public Library.

43. *Muhammad Speaks*, November 22, 1963.

44. Esther Jackson to Shirley Graham Du Bois, June 20, 1964, Esther Jackson Papers, courtesy of Esther Jackson, Brooklyn, New York.

45. Shirley Graham Du Bois to John Henrik Clarke, December 20, 1964, John Henrik Clarke Papers; Shirley Graham Du Bois to Cedric Belfrage, June 7, 1963, box 2, Cedric Belfrage Papers.

46. *Ghanaian Times*, May 18, 1974.

47. Shirley Graham Du Bois to George Murphy, May 5, 1963, George Murphy Papers, Howard University Library, Washington, DC.

48. Anna Louise Strong to Shirley Graham Du Bois, December 12, 1969. See also Shirley Graham Du Bois, "Nkrumah's Record Speaks for Itself"; Shirley Graham Du Bois, "Kwame Nkrumah: African Liberator," Shirley Graham Du Bois Papers, Subseries G. Clippings and Other Material Collected by SGD, Schlesinger Library, Radcliffe Institute

49. Shirley Graham Du Bois to Kwame Nkrumah, June 1, 1967, Shirley Graham Du Bois Papers, courtesy of David Du Bois, Cairo, Egypt.

50. Mrs. Huang Hua to Shirley Graham Du Bois, August 31, 1962, reel 75, no. 900, W. E. B. Du Bois Papers; Bill Sutherland, interview by author, March 3, 1995.

51. *New York Amsterdam News*, May 18, 1974.

52. *Guardian*, July 9, 1975.

5

"A Life History of Being Rebellious"
The Radicalism of Rosa Parks

Jeanne Theoharis

In all these years . . . it's strange . . . but maybe not . . . nobody
asks . . . about my life . . . if I have children . . . why I moved to
Detroit . . . what I think . . . about what we tried . . . to do. . . .

Something needs to be said . . . about Rosa Parks . . . other than
her feet . . . were tired. . . . Lots of people . . . on that bus . . . and
many before . . . and since . . . had tired feet . . . lots of people . . .
still do . . . they just don't know . . . where to plant them.
Nikki Giovanni, "Harvest for Rosa Parks"[1]

On October 30, 2005, Rosa Parks became the first woman and
second African American to lie in state in the U.S. Capitol. Forty thousand Americans—including President and Mrs. Bush—came to pay their
respects. Thousands more packed her seven-hour funeral celebration at
the Greater Grace Temple of Detroit and waited outside to see a horse-
drawn carriage carry Mrs. Parks's coffin to the cemetery.[2] Yet what is commonly known—and much of what was widely eulogized—about Parks is a
troubling distortion of what actually makes her fitting for such a national
tribute. Remembered as "quiet," "humble," "soft-spoken," and "never angry," she was heralded by the *New York Times* as "the accidental matriarch
of the civil rights movement."[3] Democratic presidential hopefuls Hillary
Clinton and Barack Obama highlighted her "quiet" stance,[4] while Republican Senate majority leader Bill Frist proclaimed her "bold and principled

refusal to give up her seat was not an intentional attempt to change a nation, but a singular act aimed at restoring the dignity of the individual." Indeed, most of the tributes focused squarely, and nearly exclusively, on December 1, 1955, when Parks refused to give up her seat on the bus. A lifetime of more than sixty years of political activism was reduced to a "singular act" on a long-ago winter day.

This process of iconicizing Rosa Parks was not simply a product of her funeral. Nor was the tendency to honor her outside of a lifetime of activism. In his Pulitzer Prize–winning biography of Martin Luther King, Jr., *Parting the Waters*, Taylor Branch lauded Parks as "one of those rare people of whom everyone agreed that she gave more than she got. Her character represented one of the isolated high blips on the graph of human nature, offsetting a dozen or so sociopaths."[5] Yet all Branch cared to include about Parks's political work in his near 1,000-page book was a mention of her position as secretary of the local National Association for the Advancement of Colored People (NAACP) (but nothing about what she did with the chapter) and her 1955 visit to Highlander Folk School at the urging of white Montgomerian Virginia Durr. Indeed, the only sustained scholarly treatment of Parks is Douglas Brinkley's thoughtful but pocket-sized, unfootnoted biography, *Rosa Parks: A Life*.

The breadth of Parks's six decades of activism is thus largely unfamiliar. Politically active for two decades before the boycott, she moved to Detroit after the boycott and remained politically involved there for the next forty years. She stood up to white bullies as a teenager and deeply admired Malcolm X *and* Martin Luther King. Issues of criminal justice (and the treatment of black people within the legal system) were some of her most long-standing political concerns. Insisting on the right of self-defense, Parks recalled: "I could never think in terms of accepting physical abuse without some form of retaliation if possible." Parks had a fierce line of personal dignity and, according to fellow activist Virginia Durr, the "courage of a lion." When a white boy pushed her, a young Parks pushed back; as a forty-two-year-old political activist, when asked by James Blake to give up her seat on the bus, she refused. "I had been pushed as far I could be pushed." In other words, Parks practiced a strategic resistance that avoided white domination when possible. In the summer of 1955 (months before her bus stand), when other civil rights activists went to meet city officials to contest the disrespectful treatment and lack of hiring black drivers on Montgomery's buses, Parks refused. "I had decided I would not go anywhere . . . asking white folks for any favors."

The overlooking of Parks's radicalism stems in part from the ways she was made into an icon during the movement. Working-class by economic position and middle-class in demeanor, she was an ideal person for a boycott to coalesce around. And, indeed, the boycott turned on a strategic image of Parks. Describing Parks as "not a disturbing factor," Martin Luther King Jr. had noted her character at the first mass meeting in Montgomery. "I'm happy it happened to a person like Mrs. Parks," King extolled, "for nobody can doubt the boundless outreach of her integrity, the height of her character."[6] Indeed, Parks's character made her the ideal test case that NAACP leader E. D. Nixon and other black activists in Montgomery had been looking for. "She was not the first," former Southern Christian Leadership Conference (SCLC) organizer Andrew Young explained, "but when she was thrown in jail it said to all of Montgomery that none of us is safe."[7]

Part of the contemporary construction of Parks—and the ways her radicalism has been obscured—thus flows from the strategic uses of her identity at the time.[8] As historians Marisa Chappell, Jenny Hutchinson, and Brian Ward explain:

> In order to reinforce Parks's image of unassailable respectability, movement leaders and the black press consistently downplayed—in fact, rarely mentioned—her involvement with the NAACP or Highlander.... Indeed, at Holt Street, Martin Luther King appeared concerned to distance Parks from her own history of political engagement.... Other published reports referred to her variously as "unassuming," "genteel" "attractive" "soft-spoken" "quiet" and "refined." ... By emphasizing those aspects of Parks's life which conformed most closely to proper womanly behavior as defined by post-war society ... boycott leaders, the black press, and the sympathetic sections of the white press which followed their lead, partially defused, or at least redefined, the full radicalism of Parks's defiance.[9]

The construction of Parks's respectability, which proved key to the success of the boycott and worked to deflect Cold War suspicions of this grassroots militancy, turned, in part, on obscuring her long-standing politics and larger radicalism. Parks's militancy was played down in service of the movement, but this image of her as a simple seamstress would later take on a life of its own.

Parks's militancy has also been overlooked, as Representative John Conyers explained, because of the "discongruity" of her radicalism: "She had a heavy progressive streak about her that was uncharacteristic for a neat, religious, demure, churchgoing lady."[10] In the popular imagination, black militants do not speak softly, dress conservatively, attend church regularly, get nervous, or work behind the scenes. There has been a corresponding tendency to miss the ways these "respectable" radical women were persecuted for their activism. Both Parks and her husband lost their jobs, developed health problems, had their rent raised, received persistent hate calls and mail at their home, and subsequently left Montgomery because of this persecution—yet to highlight these difficulties and the economic insecurity the family faced for the next decade disrupts the Parks fable, with its simple heroine and happy ending.

This misleading image of militancy stems from two problematic assumptions: the masculinization of militancy and the confusion of radicalism with a confrontational outward form. Fetishizing the package of radicalism (the clothes, the stance, the bold and angry presentation) renders radicalism as a performative, emotional act more than a considered political choice, and the people engaged in it a fringe element distinctly at odds with a respectable lady like Parks. The recent flowering of scholarship on Black Power and black radicalism has, in many cases, overlooked women's roles and maintained a near silence around older women's radical politics. With the glamour attached to youthful boldness, there has been an inclination to celebrate those women who can be cast as "revolutionary sweethearts," as political scientist Joy James has termed it.[11] Within this frame, there is the corresponding tendency to regard middle-aged women as staid and compromising, neither sexy nor dangerous—and therefore invisible in the cast of black militancy. Moreover, by ignoring people like Parks who often labored behind the scenes to promote widespread societal transformation, it provides little consideration of the work of radicalism and the ways people sustained this vision over decades. As James explains, the process of iconization has a corresponding depoliticizing effect. The public celebration and heroification of certain women activists help to obscure the actual political work they did.[12] Paradoxically, then, the more Parks was honored, the less her formidable political challenge to American justice and democracy was visible and taken seriously. To see the ways Parks embraced key aspects of Black Power politics (self-defense, demands for more black history in the curriculum, justice for black people within the criminal justice system) gives us another view not just of Parks herself but of the foundations of Black Power and black radicalism and the ways key activists saw its overlap with the civil rights movement.

"I Didn't Want to Be Pushed":
The Early Years of Rosa McCauley Parks

A considered look at Parks's life reveals a "life history of being rebellious," as she liked to explain it.[13] Born on February 4, 1913, in Tuskegee, Alabama, Rosa Louise McCauley was active in civil rights issues long before that fateful December day. Crediting her mother and grandfather for her political will, Parks described her mother's feistiness: "Instead of saying, 'Yes sir,' she was always saying 'No, you won't do this.'"[14] Parks was raised by her mother and grandparents; her father, an itinerant carpenter, left when she was two. Her grandfather was a staunch believer in self-defense and a supporter of Marcus Garvey. When Klan violence worsened, he sat out at night on the porch with his rifle. Growing up in a deeply segregated community, Parks picked cotton as a child. The school for black children operated on a shortened calendar to allow for this work. "I realized that we went to a different school than the white children," Parks recalled, "and that the school we went to was not as good as theirs."[15]

Rosa McCauley stood up for herself as a young person. One day, as she was coming home from school with some other children, a white boy on roller skates tried to push her off the sidewalk. Parks turned around and pushed him back. The boy's mother threatened Parks: "She said she could put me so far in jail that I never would get out again for pushing her children. So I told her that he had pushed me and that I didn't want to be pushed, seeing that I wasn't bothering him at all."[16] Another time, she threatened a white bully who was taunting her. "I picked up a brick and dared him to hit me. He thought better of the idea and went away."

Rosa McCauley was constrained by the family responsibilities and limited job options that many black women confronted in the 1930s. Because Montgomery did not provide high schools for black students, Parks attended the laboratory school at Alabama State but dropped out in the eleventh grade to care for her sick grandmother and went to work as a domestic. She met the politically active Raymond Parks in the spring of 1931, "the first real activist I ever met."[17] Getting married in December 1932, Rosa Parks joined with him in organizing on behalf of the nine young men who had wrongfully been convicted and sentenced to death in Scottsboro, Alabama. Raymond Parks began holding secret meetings at the Parks home to work on freeing the nine young men. Rosa sometimes attended—"the table was covered with guns," she recalled. She also went back to school and earned her high school degree in 1933.

In 1943, after seeing a newspaper picture of a former classmate, Mrs. Johnnie Carr, at an NAACP function, Rosa Parks went to an NAACP meeting. The realization that there were other women working with the NAACP spurred her participation. She became the secretary of the Montgomery chapter and worked closely with E. D. Nixon, the local president. The chapter turned its attention to voter registration (only thirty-one black people were registered in Montgomery) and to the case of a young black serviceman in Georgia accused of rape by a white woman in Montgomery. The young man had no legal representative that dared pursue his case.

From 1943 to 1945, she also tried on numerous times to register to vote, finally succeeding in 1945. She was then forced to pay back poll taxes—$1.50 for each year she had been old enough to vote—a formidable amount of money for a working-class family. Parks met the NAACP's director of branches Ella Baker in March 1945 at an NAACP leadership conference in Atlanta. There, and at another NAACP conference in Jacksonville in 1946, Baker made a huge impression on Parks. "Beautiful in every way," Parks noted how "smart and funny and strong" Baker was. From then on, "whenever she came to Montgomery, she stayed with me. She was a true friend—a mentor."[18]

Beginning with Scottsboro—and lasting throughout her life—Parks focused on the mistreatment of African Americans under the law and organized to seek justice for black people within the criminal justice system. After a twenty-four-year-old black woman was gang-raped by six white men at gunpoint near Abbeville, Alabama, in 1944, Parks helped form the Committee for Equal Justice for Mrs. Recy Taylor. Using the networks built through the Scottsboro case, the committee reached out to labor unions, African American groups, and women's organizations to draw attention to the case and to pressure Governor Chancey Sparks to convene a special grand jury.[19] "We tried to help," Parks wrote, "but there wasn't much we could do."[20] The men were never indicted.

Parks also took interest in the case of Jeremiah Reeves, a sixteen-year-old black young man who was having an affair with a neighborhood white woman. When a neighbor discovered the couple, the white woman cried rape. The Montgomery NAACP worked for years to free Reeves. Parks personally corresponded with him and helped get his poetry published in the *Birmingham World*. But on March 28, 1958, Reeves was executed. "Sometimes it was very difficult to keep going," Parks admitted, "when all our work seemed to be in vain."[21] Parks became the secretary of the

Alabama state branch of the NAACP and in 1948 gave a speech at the state convention on the mistreatment of African American women in the South. Traveling throughout the state, she sought to document instances of white-on-black violence, in the hopes of pursuing legal justice, and issued press releases on these cases to the *Montgomery Advertiser* and *Alabama Journal*. "Rosa will talk with you" became the understanding throughout Alabama's black communities.

Indeed, Rosa Parks had been politically active for more than two decades before the bus incident. Besides her role as secretary of the chapter where she did much of the behind-the-scenes work of the organization, she founded and led the NAACP Youth Council. She encouraged the young people of the branch to engage in a series of protests at the main library. An early precursor to the sit-in movement, these teenagers would go and ask for service, since the Montgomery library for blacks had a much more limited selection, but were consistently denied access. In 1948, when the Freedom Train had come to Montgomery, Parks had taken a group of black young people to visit the interracial monument. The integrated Freedom Train exhibit was highly controversial—blacks and whites viewing the exhibit could mingle freely—and resulted in numerous hate calls to Parks's home. In the summer of 1955, Parks attended the Highlander Folk School, an interracial organizer training school started by Myles Horton in Tennessee, on the suggestion of her white employer and fellow civil rights comrade Virginia Durr.[22]

Parks admired Highlander's founder Myles Horton's "wonderful sense of humor. [H]e could strip the white segregationists of their hardcore attitudes . . . and I found myself laughing when I hadn't been able to laugh in a long time."[23] The visit to Highlander was a transformative one. "I was 42 years old, and it was one of the few times in my life up to that point when I did not feel any hostility from white people. . . . I felt that I could express myself honestly without any repercussions or antagonistic attitudes from other people. . . . It was hard to leave."[24] Part of the discussion focused on the United Nations Universal Declaration of Human Rights; Eleanor Roosevelt participated in the workshop. Participants were encouraged to contextualize the problems facing their communities within a global movement for human rights but also come up with concrete steps to create change at home. Septima Clark remembered, "At the end of the workshops we always say, 'What do you plan to do back home?' Rosa answered that question by saying that Montgomery was the cradle of the Confederacy, that nothing would happen there because blacks wouldn't stick together. But she promised to work with those kids, and to tell them that they had the right to belong to the NAACP, . . . to do things like going through the Freedom Train."²⁵ Because Parks was afraid that white Montgomerians would retaliate since she had attended the workshop, Clark accompanied Parks to Atlanta and saw her onto the bus to Montgomery.²⁶

Like Ella Baker, Clark had a profound effect on Parks. Parks described being "very much in awe of the presence of Septima Clark, because her life story makes the effort that I have made very minute. I only hope that there is a possible chance that some of her great courage and dignity and wisdom has rubbed off on me. . . . [I]n spite of the fact that she had to face so much opposition in her home state and lost her job . . . it didn't seem to shake her. While on the other hand, I was just the opposite. I was tense, and I was nervous and I was upset most of the time."²⁷ Interestingly, Parks casts her own work as "minute" compared with Clark's and felt "tense" compared with Clark's composed presence. Parks looked to Septima Clark and Ella Baker as mentors, as she sought to figure out how to be a woman activist when much of the visible leadership was men and how to continue the struggle despite the vitriol of white resistance and the glacial pace of change.

In spite of many years of political organizing, Parks still felt nervous, shy, and at times pessimistic about the potential for change. Historian Cynthia Stokes Brown describes Parks's feelings before the boycott, "All of the suffering and all of the struggling and the effort that we put forth just to be human beings sometimes seemed a little too much."²⁸ Thus in understanding Parks's long history of political activism, we need to be wary of romanticizing her ability to take a stand against white terror and intimidation on the bus, as if she were some civil rights version of Clark Kent ready for that December day to transform into a race superhero. Septima Clark recalls, "She was so shy when she came to Highlander, but she got enough courage to do that."²⁹ Indeed, the popular view of Parks as either accidental or angelic misses the years of gathering courage, fortitude, anger, and community that would enable her to refuse to give up her seat.

"I Had Been Pushed as Far as I Could Stand to Be Pushed": Rosa Parks on the Bus

By 1955, the Montgomery NAACP was looking for a test case against bus segregation. Two young women—fifteen-year-old Claudette Colvin in March and eighteen-year-old Mary Louise Smith in October—were arrested for refusing to give up their seats. Parks helped raise money for Colvin's case and brought Colvin into the NAACP Youth Council. But ultimately neither Colvin nor Smith was deemed the kind of plaintiff that the NAACP wanted to back for a legal case. While worrying that the press would "have a field day" with a less than upstanding plaintiff, Parks grew frustrated with the lack of change: "I felt that all of our meetings, trying to negotiate, bring about petitions before the authorities, that is the city officials really hadn't done any good at all."[30] After the NAACP's decision that Colvin was not the proper plaintiff for a suit, a group of activists took a petition to the bus company and city officials asking for more courteous treatment and no visible signs of segregation on the bus. Parks refused: "I had decided I would not go anywhere with a piece of paper in my hand asking white folks for any favors."[31]

On December 1, 1955, Rosa Parks boarded a bus on her way home from work. She and three other black passengers were seated in a row toward the middle of the bus when a white man boarded the bus. There were no seats remaining in the white section; by the terms of Montgomery's segregation, all four passengers would have to get up so one white man could sit down. When the driver, James Blake, who had given Parks trouble before, ordered them to give up their seats, the others got up, but Parks refused.[32] Parks had not planned the protest, but, as she recalled, "I had been pushed as far as I could stand to be pushed."[33] Having done a great deal of organizing around the criminal justice system, Parks was well aware of the physical dangers a black woman faced in getting arrested. Yet, in an interview in 1956, she said that she "wasn't frightened at all."[34]

Like other bus drivers in Montgomery, Blake carried a gun. He ordered Parks to move, and when she would not, had her arrested. She was taken to jail, where she was allowed one phone call to her family and was fined fourteen dollars. Hearing that Parks had been arrested, community leaders—including E. D. Nixon, lawyers Fred Gray and Clifford Durr, and Women's Political Council president Jo Ann Robinson—sprang into action. Nixon saw in Parks the kind of plaintiff they had been looking for—middle-aged, religious, and well respected in the community for her political work. Indeed, while the stance she took on the bus was an independent and personal choice, what made it the catalyst for a movement was certainly not a singular act but years of organizing by Parks and others in Montgomery that made people ready for collective action.

But that protest is often reduced to the unwitting action of a tired seamstress, unconnected to a broader quest for justice. Parks herself critiqued these popular mischaracterizations:

> I didn't tell anyone my feet were hurting. It was just popular, I suppose because they wanted to give some excuse other than the fact that I didn't want to be pushed around. . . . And I had been working for a long time— a number of years in fact—to be treated as a human being with dignity not only for myself, but all those who were being mistreated.[35]

Her decision on the bus was also a lonely one. "Getting arrested was one of the worst days of my life," Park explained. "There were other people on the bus whom I knew. But when I was arrested, not one of them came to my defense. I felt very much alone."[36] She contextualized her decision within her role as a political organizer: "An opportunity was being given to me to do what I had asked of others."[37] Parks saw herself as part of a movement and, as an organizer, felt she had a responsibility to act on behalf of this larger community. Indeed, her decision to act arose as much out of her frustration with the lack of change as from a belief that her particular action would change something.

Parks's commitment to advocating for the rights of black people in prison extended to her own jail experience. One of the women in her cell had been in jail for nearly two months. The woman, who had picked up a hatchet against her boyfriend after he struck her, had no money to post bail and no way to let her family know where she was. Parks smuggled out a piece of paper with the woman's brother's phone number. "The first thing I did the morning after I went to jail," Parks recalled, "was to call the number the woman in the cell with me had written down on that crumpled piece of paper."[38] A few days later, she saw the woman on the street, out of jail and looking much better.[39]

Released on bail, Parks wanted to run her regular Thursday evening NAACP Youth Council meeting. Nixon walked her to the meeting, hoping to convince her to be part of a legal case against bus segregation. Parks agreed.

The boycott was actually called by the Women's Political Council (WPC), a local group of black women formed to address racial inequities in the city. Indeed, the year before, the WPC's president, Jo Ann Robinson, a professor of English at Alabama State College, had sent a letter to the mayor demanding action on the buses or people would organize a citywide boycott.[40] After hearing from lawyer Fred Gray about Parks's arrest, Jo Ann Robinson called a meeting of the WPC's leadership and decided to take action. With the help of two students, Robinson stayed up all night making leaflets that called for a boycott the following Monday. The leaflet read: "Another Negro woman has been arrested. . . . If we do not do something to stop these arrests, they will continue. . . . We are therefore asking every Negro to stay off the buses Monday in protest of the arrest and trial." The WPC distributed more than 50,000 leaflets across town to let people know of the boycott. Thus, Parks's action sparked a movement because a number of people and organizations were already in place to run with it. As Parks herself later reiterated, "Four decades later I am still uncomfortable with the credit given to me for starting the bus boycott. Many people do not know the whole truth. . . . I was just one of many who fought for freedom."[41]

Meanwhile, E. D. Nixon began calling Montgomery's black ministers—including Ralph Abernathy and a new young minister in town, Martin Luther King Jr.—to convince them to support the boycott. Although King initially hesitated, worried about being new in town and having a young family, he agreed to meet with the other ministers and spoke about the action in church on Sunday. Parks also sought to keep a low profile. She never made a statement to the local newspaper, the *Montgomery Advertiser*, and on Monday, after her trial, she answered phones in Fred Gray's law office. "The people were calling to talk to me but I never told them who I was. . . . They didn't know my voice so I just took the messages."[42]

That Monday, nearly every black person in Montgomery stayed off the bus. That evening, 15,000 people gathered for a mass meeting at the Holt Street Baptist Church. They decided to continue the boycott indefinitely (originally it was intended to last one day) and formed a new organization called the Montgomery Improvement Association (MIA). Parks was recognized and introduced but not asked to speak, despite calls from the crowd for her to do so.[43] Years later, Parks recounted in an interview, "I do recall asking someone if I should say anything and someone saying, 'Why? You've said enough.'"[44] While Parks imagined that she might speak at the meeting, she was told that she had "said enough," even though she had said very little between her Thursday arrest and the Monday meeting. Similar to the treatment of other women in the movement, she was lauded as a hero but not imagined to have ideas that needed to be heard about her action or subsequent political strategy.

Parks's gendered role as a mother figure of the movement thus emerged early on. Douglas Brinkley explained, "It helped, of course, that at forty-two years old Parks was also a natural maternal figure to the young ministers and lawyers who led the boycott: Gray was twenty-five, King was twenty-six, and Abernathy was twenty-nine."[45] Indeed, Parks's role as the mother of the movement seemed to preclude her from having a *public* decision-making role. Despite her behind-the-scenes work, the scores of appearances she would make on behalf of the boycott, and her extensive political experience, she was not granted a formal position in the MIA.

"It Is Fine to Be a Heroine but the Price Is High": Rosa Parks and the Bus Boycott

The city stood firm in its commitment to bus segregation. People continued to walk and carpool—and the harassment of boycotters continued. On February 21, Rosa Parks was indicted along with eighty-eight others, including King and Abernathy, for their role in organizing a car pool to help maintain the boycott. For the next year, Parks gave speeches on behalf of the NAACP and MIA, attended meetings, helped distribute clothes and food, and served as a dispatcher.[46]

Meanwhile, Parks's action had taken a significant toll on her family's economic stability. On January 7, 1956, Montgomery Fair, the department store where Parks worked as a seamstress, discharged Parks, allegedly because it was closing the tailor shop. She received two weeks' severance pay. A week later, her husband resigned his job; his employer, Maxwell Airforce Base, had prohibited any discussion of the boycott or even of Rosa Parks in the barbershop where Raymond Parks worked. Their landlord raised their rent ten dollars a month. Parks and her family were in a precarious economic state. Parks was doing a great deal of traveling and public speaking, but the money she earned was going to support the work of the NAACP and MIA. Virginia Durr wrote to Myles Horton on February 18, 1956, noting. "It is fine to be a heroine but the price is high." Horton subsequently wrote to Parks, telling her how "proud we were of your courageous role in the boycott."[47] He offered his sympathies regarding her economic situation: "Doing what's right is not always the easy thing to do."[48] Durr wrote Horton again. explaining, "You would be amazed at the number of pictures, interviews etc that she had taken and all of that takes up time, and then too all the meetings and then having to walk nearly everywhere she goes takes times too. . . . [M]ost people want to contribute to the Boycott itself rather than to an individual, but that particular individual is to my mind very important and I think she should certainly be helped."[49]

Parks's economic situation continued to be difficult. Virginia Durr raised $600 for the Parks family and, in November 1956, wrote to Horton again asking for Highlander's help in creating a voter registration campaign in Montgomery with a paid position for Parks. Horton refused to help develop and fund such a voter project in Montgomery, though he did offer Parks a position at Highlander, but because her mother said she did not want to "be nowhere I don't see nothing but white folks," she turned it down.[50]

Along with this economic hardship, the Parks home was receiving regular hate mail and death threats. Callers would repeatedly tell her, "You should be killed" and "Die, nigger. Die." This took a significant physical and emotional toll on her mother and husband, and Parks herself developed stomach ulcers.[51] Yet she continued to play an active role in coordinating the boycott. With the Supreme Court's ruling in *Browder v. Gayle*, the 381-day boycott ended. On December 20, 1956, the day the buses were desegregated in Montgomery, nearly all the media ignored Parks in favor of quotes from and pictures of King.[52] It was *Look* magazine that staged the photo of her sitting in the front seat looking out the window that would come to be iconic.

Receiving constant death threats and with few economic prospects in the city, the Parks family decided to leave Montgomery.[53] Part of the reason for the decision also came from the unfriendly reception Rosa was now receiving from certain members within Montgomery's civil rights community. According to Brinkley, "Suddenly, Parks found herself lauded as a near saint virtually everywhere she went in black communities, and before long some of her colleagues in Montgomery's civil rights movement began to grow jealous of the attention. . . . Much of the resentment sprang from male chauvinism [from many of the ministers and E. D. Nixon]."[54]

"The Northern Promised Land That Wasn't": Rosa Parks in Detroit

In August 1957, the Parks family, including Rosa's mother, moved to Detroit, where Rosa's brother Sylvester McCauley had lived since 1946. Rosa Parks had gone to Detroit the year before at the invitation of the National Negro Labor Council to speak to Local 600, where she had linked northern and southern struggles for civil rights.[55] Referring to the city as "the northern promised land that wasn't," Parks saw that racism in Detroit was "almost as widespread as Montgomery."[56] Still, the city offered them a chance to be near family and the opportunity to get away from the difficulties that Montgomery now presented. Ralph Abernathy, embarrassed by Rosa's decision to leave, apologized and asked her to stay. The MIA raised $800 as a going-away present, and the couple was honored at a service held at Saint Paul's AME Church.

Arriving in Detroit, the Parkses moved to a neighborhood "almost 100% Negro with the exception of about two families in the block where I live. In fact I suppose you'd call it just about the heart of the ghetto."[57] But the family still struggled economically, and both Rosa and Raymond experienced difficulty finding work. The civil rights community did not offer her any paid work. "I didn't get any work, but I went to a lot of meetings and sometimes when they would take up contributions, but that was never high."[58]

In Detroit, Rosa Parks was still considered "dangerous" and an outside agitator by many residents. In 1963, she joined Martin Luther King at the front of Detroit's Great March to Freedom. This march, held weeks before the March on Washington, drew thousands of Detroiters. There, Parks recalled, King "reminded everybody that segregation and discrimination were rampant in Michigan as well as Alabama." Parks also made these connections between southern and northern racism in some of her speeches.[59] Although she found more openness in race relations in Detroit, "there were problems here . . . especially in the school system. The schools would be overcrowded. The job situation wouldn't be none too good."[60]

The lack of recognition and remuneration that Parks was experiencing was a problem throughout the movement. At the 1963 March on Washington, no women were asked to speak. Criticized for the lack of women on the program, A. Philip Randolph included "A Tribute to Women" in which Parks—along with a number of other women activists such as Gloria Richardson, Diane Nash, Myrlie Evers, and Daisy Bates—were asked to stand up and be recognized. No woman got to speak. There is a tendency, given the iconic view of Parks, to believe that she was simply happy to stand on the dais that August day and did not notice the ways women were being relegated to a lesser role. But Parks did notice—and care—about how women were being marginalized. Parks criticized this sexism, telling fellow activist Daisy Bates at the March on Washington that she hoped for a "better day coming." And in her autobiography, Parks describes the march as "a great occasion, but women were not allowed to play much of a role."[61]

In 1964, Parks became interested in civil rights attorney John Conyers's long-shot campaign for Michigan's First Congressional District (renumbered in 1992 to become the Fourteenth District). She had met Conyers years earlier in Montgomery and became an active volunteer in his campaign for "Jobs, Justice, Peace." Thinking strategically, Parks convinced Martin Luther King, who did not want to involve himself in any political races, to make an exception and come to Detroit. According to Conyers, King's visit "quadrupled my visibility in the black community . . . .Therefore, if it wasn't for Rosa Parks, I never would have gotten elected."[62] Conyers won the primary contest of six Democrats by 128 votes.

On March 1, 1965, Parks was hired as a secretary for the newly elected congressman's Detroit office and worked there until she retired in 1988. Tellingly, after more than twenty years of dedicated political work, this was the first time Parks received a paid political position. Still, she would remain largely within a gender-acceptable role: greeting visitors, answering phones, handling constituent needs, and coordinating the office. Conyers recalled, "People called her a troublemaker," and the office and Parks herself received hate mail.[63] Still, Conyers was awed by Parks's electrifying presence in the office, explaining, "Can you imagine coming to work, and you have Rosa Parks sitting in your office?"[64] Parks also continued a busy activist schedule—making public appearances and speeches at scores of church programs, women's day events, and schools and often apologizing to Conyers for having to leave to fulfill these commitments. She served as an honorary member of SCLC and attended the events she could. She also was active in numerous local organizations like the Women's Public Affairs Committee (WPAC) and political campaigns in Detroit, as well as organizing efforts against the War in Vietnam.

In 1965, moved by the photos of marchers being beaten on the Edmund Pettus Bridge in Selma, Parks decided to return to Alabama to join the march herself. Yet during the march, many of the younger organizers did not know her, and because she was not given an official jacket, the police kept pulling her out and making her stand on the sidelines. A number of the whites in the crowd did recognize her, yelling, "You'll get yours, Rosa." Upon returning to Detroit, Parks was incensed by the murder of Viola Liuzzo, a white Detroiter who had attended the march and been killed by members of the Klan (including an FBI informant) as she drove marchers home. Parks saw Liuzzo's murder as further evidence of the need to put pressure on Johnson. "This was no time to be dormant," she declared in a testimonial dinner given by the WPAC.[65] The murder of Liuzzo spurred Parks to be even more active, particularly in the WPAC.

Not the meek and uninformed seamstress that she is portrayed as, Parks was a longtime believer in self-defense and a big supporter of Malcolm X and Robert F. Williams. In 1967 she told an interviewer, "I don't believe in gradualism or that whatever should be done for the better should take forever to do."[66] Parks had imbibed this tradition of self-defense from her grandfather. Indeed, while seeing the tactical advantages of nonviolence during the boycott—finding it "refreshing" and "more successful, I believe, than it would have been if violence had been used"—she found it "hard to say that she was completely converted to it." "As far back as I remember, I could never think in terms of accepting physical abuse without some form of retaliation if possible."[67] Parks was a voracious reader. According to Brinkley, "She read a number of newspapers and magazines daily—including the *New York Herald Tribune, Saturday Evening Post,* and *Pittsburgh Courier*—to stay abreast of the civil rights battles being waged."[68] Parks kept an extensive clippings file, interested in stories related to African Americans (be they civil rights activists or entertainers, on school desegregation, unions, or the Nation of Islam) and in other pressing national issues such as the war in Vietnam and free speech at home.

Parks did not see a contradiction in her deep admiration for both Martin Luther King Jr. and Malcolm X. Describing him as "a very brilliant man," Parks read all she could on Malcolm X's ministry and political program. "This strong-willed man reminded me somewhat of my grandfather. He was full of conviction and pride in his race . . . . The way he stood up and voiced himself showed that he was a man to be respected."[69] Parks's work in 1960s Detroit exemplified the continuities and connections between the civil rights and Black Power movements. She began making appearances at rallies sponsored by the all-black Freedom Now Party,[70] and in February 1965 received an award from the Afro-American Broadcasting Company, started by Milton and Richard Henry, who also helped found the Freedom Now Party and, later, the Republic of New Africa. Malcolm X gave the keynote speech (often referred to as "The Last Message" because it occurred a week before his assassination). Afterward, Parks got Malcolm X to sign her program.[71] Parks was in the mix of a vibrant and diverse radical community in the city. Brinkley explains, "By the turbulent mid-1960s, the gentle Christian woman had become a tough-minded, free-thinking feminist who had grown impatient with gradualist approaches."[72] She became involved in a number of education projects that sought to bring more black history and Afrocentric approaches into the curriculum.

On July 23, 1967, following a Detroit police raid of an after-hours bar, people refused to disperse. This sparked five days of rioting that left forty-three people dead (thirty at the hands of the police) and $45 million of property damage. Parks saw the 1967 riots as an outgrowth of the frustration people felt at the continuing inequities in a putatively liberal city such as Detroit. She did not cast her years of activism or her protest on the bus as utterly distinct from the actions of the rioters: "I would associate the activity of the burning and looting, and so on, with what I had done and would have done. . . . I guess for whatever reasons it came about, I felt that something had to be wrong with the system."[73] Parks grew more despairing after Martin Luther King's assassination. She went to Memphis to participate in the march that King was to have participated in, but after speaking for a few hours with a number of the striking sanitation workers, she was overcome by grief and accepted Harry Belafonte's invitation to ride on his plane to Atlanta for the funeral.

Continuing to work in coalition with activists throughout the country, she attended the Gary Convention convened by Amiri Baraka, Charles Diggs, and Richard Hatcher in March 1972 to help craft an independent black political agenda. Parks also campaigned vigorously for George McGovern in 1972 and she was invited to the sixtieth birthday of former American Community Party official James Jackson in 1974 in New York. Still, nearly twenty years after her bus stand, Parks was receiving hate mail. One 1972 letter from Indiana read, "Why didn't you stay down South? The North sure doesn't want you up here. You are the biggest woman troublemaker ever."[74]

Continuing her long-standing commitment to criminal justice issues, she was one of the founders of the Joanne Little Defense Committee in Detroit. Little was charged with murder when she defended herself against the sexual assault of her jailer Clarence Alligood. The mission statement of the Detroit organization affirmed the right of women to defend themselves against their sexual attackers.[75] Parks also campaigned vigorously on behalf of Gary Tyler, a sixteen-year-old black teenager who had been wrongfully convicted of killing a thirteen-year-old white boy. The youngest person ever given the death penalty, Tyler was riding a school bus when it was attacked by a white mob angry that schools were being desegregated in Louisiana. Police boarded the bus and pulled Tyler off for allegedly shooting a boy outside the bus, even though no gun was found on the bus. Parks gave the keynote address at a packed meeting in Detroit in June 1976 on behalf of Tyler and worked to see his conviction overturned. However, Tyler was never freed.

"I Understand That I Am a Symbol": Being Rosa Parks

> As time has gone by, people have made my place in the history of the civil-rights movement bigger and bigger. They call me the Mother of the Civil Rights Movement. . . . Interviewers still only want to talk about that one evening in 1955 when I refused to give up my seat on the bus. Organizations still want to give me awards for that one act more than thirty years ago. . . . I understand that I am a symbol.[76]

As the years went by, Parks became more and more of a symbol; with the honors increasing, people still "only want[ed] to talk about that one evening in 1955." In a 1978 interview, she explained that she was "somewhat resigned to whatever contribution I can make." Believing in the importance of young people carrying on the movement, she saw her public role as necessary to preserve the history of the struggle and help young people carry it forward but still wished she had more of a private life. She explained the difficulty her public persona caused for her:

> I always have to refer to something Dr. King once said. . . . He asked the question, "Why should I expect personal happiness when so much depends on any contribution that I can make?" But I find myself asking myself, "Why should I expect personal happiness, if people want to find out what, who I am or what I am or what I have done. . . . There are times when I feel I can hardly get up and go, and once I get there and see their [young people's] reaction, I feel somewhat rewarded.[77]

Over the course of her life, Parks seemed to derive her greatest political pleasures from working with young people. Seeing it as part of her contribution to advancing the struggle, Parks was willing to take up the role of "mother of the civil rights movement." Maintaining the history of the movement, she felt, was critical to carrying it on. And so she answered thousands of letters and attended hundreds of programs in her honor.[78] Yet in seeking to carry on the struggle, she often became trapped as a symbol of a movement long since over. "They equate me along with Harriet

Tubman and Sojourner Truth and ask if I knew them."[79] In 1987, worried that adults had become "too complacent," Parks founded the Rosa and Raymond Parks Institute for Self Development. The purpose of the institute was to develop leadership among Detroit's young people, teach black history, and bring young people into the struggle for civil rights.

Then, in September 1994, Rosa Parks was mugged by a black man in her home.[80] Commentators and politicians used this tragic incident as evidence that the problems facing black people now came from the decline of values within the black community. "Things are not likely to get much worse," lamented liberal *New York Times* columnist Bob Herbert.[81] Parks did not agree with this line of thinking. Indeed, she asked that "people not read too much into the attack" and prayed for the man "and the conditions that have made him this way."[82] To the end, Parks remained focused on changing the conditions that limited black people's ability to flourish.

Throughout the 1990s, Parks maintained her active commitment to social and racial justice. She protested Governor George W. Bush's use of the death penalty in Texas. And, on September 19, 2001, a week after the terrorist attacks on the World Trade Center, she joined with Danny Glover, Harry Belafonte, Gloria Steinem, and other human rights leaders to speak out against a "military response" to terror and to call on the United States to act "cooperatively as part of a community of nations within the framework of international law."[83]

While she continued her work at the grassroots, the honors kept flowing in. In 1999, Parks received the nation's highest honor, a Congressional Gold Medal. Calling Parks's action and the resulting triumph of the movement "the quintessential story of the 20th Century . . . the story of the triumph of freedom," President Bill Clinton celebrated Parks as an American hero. Brinkley explained the irony of these tributes: "Now that Rosa Parks's body was too feeble to march and her voice had faded to a whisper, politicians lauded her as a patriotic icon. She had grown . . . safe to exalt."[84]

This would hold tenfold when Parks died. Politicians from both sides of the political aisle rushed to honor Parks, hoping perhaps that "a tired old woman" lying in the nation's Capitol would cover up the federal travesty of inaction around Hurricane Katrina two months earlier. "Everyone wanted to speak," explained her longtime friend federal circuit judge Damon Keith, who helped to coordinate the funeral service.[85] Casting her as a nonthreatening heroine of a movement that had run its course, the fable of Rosa Parks was useful to constructing a view of America as a society that had moved beyond race. Stripping Rosa Parks of her radicalism while celebrating her as the mother of the civil rights movement became part of a larger move to deradicalize the legacy of the movement itself.

While many of the eulogies sought to put Parks's protest firmly in the past, Parks herself had continued to insist on the persistent need for racial justice in the present.[86] Parks had kept on speaking her mind on the ways "racism is still alive"—reminding Americans "not [to] become comfortable with the gains we have made in the last forty years."[87] Indeed, she ended her autobiography observing, "In recent years there has been a resurgence of reactionary attitudes . . . the recent decisions of the Supreme Court that make it harder to prove a pattern of discrimination in employment and by the fact that the national government does not seem very interested in pursuing violations of civil rights. . . . Sometimes I do feel pretty sad about some of the events that have taken place recently. I try to keep hope alive anyway, but that's not always the easiest thing to do."[88]

NOTES

1. This excerpt from "Harvest" by Nikki Giovanni in *Those Who Ride with the Night Winds* (New York: William Morrow, 1983) is courtesy of and copyright to Giovanni.

2. In November 2006, in part due to the pressure it had been under to make an exception for a Parks stamp, the postal service changed its policy; now five years (rather than ten) after a person dies he or she can be memorialized on a stamp.

3. Michael Jonofsky, "Thousands Gather at the Capitol to Remember a Hero," *New York Times*, October 31, 2005.

4. Peter Slevin, "A Quiet Woman's Resonant Farewell," *Washington Post*, November 2, 2005, A3.

5. Taylor Branch, *Parting the Waters: America in the King Years, 1954-1963* (New York: Simon and Schuster, 1988), 125.

6. Kevin Chappell, "Remembering Rosa Parks: The Life and Legacy of 'The Mother of the Civil Rights Movement,'" *Ebony*, January 2006, 126-132.

7. Malcolm R. West, "Rosa Parks: Mother of the Civil Rights Movement 1913-2005," *Jet*, November 14, 2005.

8. I am grateful to Brenna Greer for her insights on the construction of Parks's image. See also Brenna Wynn Greer, "'A Disturbing Factor': The Iconic Rosa Parks and Remaking of the Public Black Image" (paper presented at the Berkshires Conference on Women's History, Minneapolis, Minnesota, June 2008).

9. Marisa Chappell, Jenny Hutchinson, and Brian Ward, "'Dress Modestly, Neatly . . . as If You Were Going to Church': Respectability, Class and Gender in the Montgomery Bus Boycott and the Early Civil Rights Movement," in *Gender and the Civil Rights Movement*, ed. Peter Lin and Sharon Monteith (New Brunswick, NJ: Rutgers University Press, 2004), 72-73.

10. Ibid., 189.

11. Joy James, *Shadowboxing: Representations of Black Feminist Politics* (New York: St. Martin's Press, 2000), 93-122.

12. Ibid., 120.

13. Stewart Burns, *To the Mountaintop: Martin Luther King's Sacred Mission to Save America 1955–1968* (New York: HarperCollins, 2004), 18.

14. Rosa Parks, interview by Cynthia Stokes Brown, *Southern Exposure*, Spring 1981, 16.

15. Rosa Parks, *My Story* (New York: Dial Books, 1992), 34.

16. Ibid., 54.

17. Ibid., 68.

18. Douglas Brinkley, *Rosa Parks: A Life* (New York: Penguin, 2000), 68–69; Barbara Ransby, *Ella Baker and the Black Freedom Movement: A Radical Democratic Vision* (Chapel Hill: University of North Carolina Press, 2003), 142–143.

19. Danielle McGuire, "It Was Like All of Us Had Been Raped," in *The Best American History Essays 2006* (New York: Palgrave, 2006), 126–127; Brinkley, *Rosa Parks*, 70.

20. Parks, *My Story*, 97–98.

21. Ibid., 99.

22. Septima Poinsette Clark and Cynthia Stokes Brown, *Ready from Within: Septima Clark and the Civil Rights Movement* (Navarro, TX: Wild Trees Press, 1986), 32.

23. Parks, *My Story*, 124.

24. Ibid.

25. Clark and Stokes Brown, *Ready from Within*, 33-34.

26. Ibid., 33.

27. Ibid., 16–17.

28. Rosa Parks, interview by Cynthia Stokes Brown, *Ready from Within*, 17.

29. Clark and Stokes Brown, *Ready from Within*, 34.

30. Rosa Parks, *The Black Women Oral History Project*, vol. 8 (subsequently referred to as BWOHP) (Westport: Meckler, 1991), 253.

31. Parks, *My Story*, 129.

32. In 1943, Parks had her first run-in with Blake. Parks had boarded the front of the bus, and Blake insisted that Parks, who had paid her fare, exit and reboard through the back door. When Parks did not move, Blake grabbed her sleeve to attempt to push her off the bus. She purposefully dropped her purse and sat down in a seat in the whites-only section to pick it up. Blake seemed poised to hit her. She told him, "I will get off. . . . You better not hit me." She exited the bus and did not reboard; for the next twelve years, she avoided Blake's bus (Parks, *My Story*, 91–92)

33. Sidney Rogers interview with Rosa Parks, in *Daybreak of Freedom*, ed. Stewart Burns (Chapel Hill: University of North Carolina Press, 1997), 83.

34. Ibid., 84.

35. Interview of Rosa Parks by John H. Britton for the Civil Rights Documentation Project (subsequently referred to as CRDP) (September 28, 1967), 6.

36. Rosa Parks with Gregory J. Reed, *Quiet Strength: The Faith, the Hope, and the Heart of a Woman Who Changed a Nation* (Grand Rapids, MI: Zondervan, 1994), 24.

37. Ibid., 22.

38. Parks, *My Story*, 145.

39. Ibid.

40. While the president of the college initially stood behind Robinson's organizing of the boycott, political pressures led Robinson to resign her position in 1960. Jo Ann Gibson Robinson, *The Montgomery Bus Boycott and the Women Who Started It: The Memoir of Jo Ann Gibson Robinson* (Knoxville: University of Tennessee Press, 1987), 16.

41. Parks, *Quiet Strength*, 27.

42. Rosa Parks, Steven Millner interview, in *The Walking City: The Montgomery Bus Boycott, 1955–1956* (New York: Carlson, 1989), 562–563.

43. Brinkley bizarrely and somewhat contradictorily argues, "Although some cried out for Parks to speak, it would have been wrong to break the spell of King's magnificent oration.

Furthermore, King and the others on the platform noticed her reluctance and assured Parks that she had done enough and said enough already if she didn't want to speak" (*Rosa Parks*, 140).

44. Parks, Millner interview, 563.

45. Brinkley, *Rosa Parks*, 142–143.

46. Parks corresponded with a number of people during this period, trying to get support for the boycott. One letter from Diane Shapiro, whom Parks had met at Highlander, reads, "I can't tell you how pleased I was to receive your letter. Of course we all knew about the bus strike but none of us associated it with you." Rosa Parks Papers, 1955–1976, on file at the Walter Reuther Library of the Wayne State University (hereafter referred to as Rosa Parks Papers), box 1, folder 1–5.

47. *Daybreak of Freedom*, 155.

48. Ibid.

49. Ibid.

50. Parks, *My Story*, 178.

51. According to Cynthia Stokes Brown, "Raymond Parks, reduced to answering death threats on the telephone, began drinking heavily and chain-smoking to cope with his depression" (Kohl, *She Would Not Be Moved: How We Tell the Story of Rosa Parks and the Montgomery Bus Boycott*, (New York: Norton, 2005, 120).

52. Brinkley, *Rosa Parks*, 170.

53. Violence had continued in Montgomery even after the integration of the buses, with snipers firing into the buses, along with the bombing of four black churches and a taxi company. Brinkley, *Rosa Parks*, 171.

54. Brinkley, *Rosa Parks*, 175. Indeed, throughout the boycott, Parks eschewed the fame that had been thrust upon her and, according to Brinkley, "mastered the art of self-deprecation as a survival mechanism" (156).

55. Beth T. Bates, "'Double V for Victory' Mobilizes Black Detroit, 1941–1946," in *Freedom North: Black Freedom Struggles Outside the South, 1940–1980*, ed. Jeanne F. Theoharis and Komozi Woodard (New York: Palgrave Macmillan, 2003), 33.

56. Brinkley, *Rosa Parks*, 67.

57. Parks, CRDP, 28.

58. Parks, BWOHP, 256.

59. See her notes on her speech to the Alabama club found in her papers. Rosa Parks Papers box 1, folder 1–5.

60. Parks, Millner interview, 565.

61. Parks, *My Story*, 186.

62. Brinkley, *Rosa Parks*, 187.

63. Ibid., 189.

64. Kevin Chappell, "Remembering Rosa Parks."

65. Ibid., 202. The WPAC had also arranged a testimonial dinner for Parks in April 1965, with the proceeds going to Parks herself. Calling Parks "a woman of bold and audacious courage," its minutes explained the decision: "She has received many many plaques and awards of merits, etc. from citizens all over the country, but as meritorious as they are, they do no compensate for Mrs. Parks having to move away from her home, for fear of loss of life, and neither do they compensate for the great financial loss of adequate income. WPAC members felt that to honor Rosa Parks in a very material way, would in some measure, say thanks, for spearheading our nation-wide push for freedom." See Rosa Parks Papers, box 4.

66. Parks, CRDP, 33.

67. Ibid., 19.

68. Ibid., 158.

69. Parks, *Quiet Strength*, 51.

70. Brinkley, *Rosa Parks*, 202.

71. I am grateful to Stephen Ward for helping me put these events together. See also Rosa L. Parks papers, box 2; Brinkley, *Rosa Parks*, 191–193.

72. Brinkley, *Rosa Parks*, 191.

73. Parks, BWOHP, 256.

74. Letter found in Rosa Parks Papers.

75. Rosa Parks Papers, box 3, folder 3.

76. Parks, *My Story*, 207.

77. Parks, BWOHP, 258–259.

78. Later in her life, she also got to see how she was being interpreted. For instance, Parks attended a play performed at Western High School in Detroit called *In White America*, where a young woman performed the role of Parks. In the program's cast list, Parks circled the girl's name and wrote, "Rosa Parks excellent and sensitive acting." Rosa Parks Papers.

79. E. R. Shipp, "Rosa Parks, 92, Founding Symbol of Civil Rights Movement, Dies," *New York Times*, October 25, 2005.

80. According to the initial media coverage, the twenty-eight-year-old man did not know who Parks was; after a few days, however, the media started to portray it as if he did.

81. Bob Herbert, "Mrs. Parks's Request," *New York Times*, September 4, 1994.

82. Parks, *Quiet Strength*, 37.

83. "Diverse Coalition of Americans Speak Out against War as Solution to Terrorism," press release, September 19, 2001.

84. Brinkley, *Rosa Parks*, 226.

85. Interview with Sixth Circuit judge Damon Keith in his chambers. June 14, 2007.

86. Parks worked hard to see a national holiday for Martin Luther King and was critical of the ways King was being stripped of his politics and turned into a dreamer. "He was more than a dreamer. He was an activist who believed in acting as well as speaking out against oppression." Shipp, "Rosa Parks, 92, Founding Symbol of Civil Rights Movement, Dies."

87. Parks, *Quiet Strength*, 87.

88. Parks, *My Story*, 209.

6

Framing the Panther
Assata Shakur and Black Female Agency

Joy James

How we imagine a revolutionary is shaped by our ideas concerning gender, sex, and race, not just ideology.[1] How we imagine transformative black political leadership is very much influenced by how we think of gender and agency. The absence or presence of maleness shapes common perceptions of women revolutionaries. The same is not true for femaleness in perceptions of male revolutionaries.

One can easily imagine antiracist revolutionary struggle against the state without (black) women clearly in the picture, but to imagine revolution against state violence in the absence of (black) men often draws a blank. Men appear independent of women in revolutionary struggles; women generally appear as revolutionaries only in association with men, often as "helpmates." As a category, the female revolutionary remains somewhat of an afterthought, an aberration; hence she is an abstraction— vague and not clearly in the picture.

In this regard, former Black Panther Party (BPP) and Black Liberation Army (BLA) member Assata Shakur is extraordinary, as we shall see later. Assata Shakur is unique not only because she has survived in exile as a political figure despite the U.S. government's bounty —"dead or alive"— on her head but also because she may prove to be "beyond commoditization" in a time in which political leadership seems to be bought and sold in the marketplace of political trade, compromise, and corruption. Above all, Shakur is singular because she is a recognizable female revolutionary, one not bound to a male persona.

Assata Shakur booking photo.

Gender Politics and "Panther Women"

Influential male narratives have helped to masculinize the political rebel in popular culture and memory. Nationally and internationally, the most prominently known black political prisoners and prison intellectuals are male. The brief incarceration of Martin Luther King, Jr., in Alabama, produced the "Letter from Birmingham Jail" (1963), which popularized civil disobedience against repressive laws. The imprisonment as a petty criminal of Malcolm X in the 1950s engendered the political man and somewhat fictionalized *Autobiography of Malcolm X* (1965; published posthumously and creatively embellished and edited by Alex Haley, who had worked for the Federal Bureau of Investigation [FBI], which sought to discredit Malcolm X). The 1971 killing by prison guards of George Jackson, author of *Soledad Brothers: The Prison Letters of George Jackson* and the posthumously published *Blood in My Eye*, helped to incite the Attica prison uprising in New York.² The violent and deadly repression by the National Guard deployed by New York governor Nelson Rockefeller created more male martyrs and more closely linked incarceration, repression, and rebellion to the male figure. Current organizing for a new trial for former Black Panther Mumia Abu-Jamal is galvanized by his incisive commentaries and critiques in *Live from Death Row*.³ Conventional political thought and memory associate few women with revolutionary literature or with armed resistance, political incarceration, or martyrdom stemming from struggles against enslavement or racist oppression.

Along with Harriet Tubman, Shakur would become one of the few black female figures in the United States recognized as a leader in an organization that publicly advocated armed self-defense against racist violence. From its emergence in 1966, originally named the Black Panther Party for Self-Defense, given police brutality and police killings of African Americans and cofounded by Huey P. Newton and Bobby Seale, the Black

Panther Party captured the national imagination and inspired its paranoia.[4] The Black Panther Party remains the organizational icon (with Malcolm X the individual icon) for black militant resistance to racial domination and terror.

The average American political spectator was and is more captivated
or repelled by the Black Panthers' stance on armed self-defense and their
battles with local and federal police—and resulting martyrs—than with
the BPP social service programs largely organized and run by women.
Hundreds of women, including Shakur before she was forced underground, served in the Black Panther Party's rank and file, implementing
the medical, housing, clothing, free breakfast, and education programs.
Female Panthers displayed an agency that (re)shaped American politics,
although their stories recede in popular culture before the narratives of
elites or icons.

Violence, race, and sex mark the symbolism surrounding BPP icons.
African American male revolutionaries are not perceived as having been
politicized through their romantic or personal relationships with female
counterparts; rather, their speeches and deeds mark them for public recognition. Each male in the Panther pantheon can stand individually yet
still "possess" a female counterpart: George Jackson was linked to Angela
Davis, Elaine Brown to Huey P. Newton, Kathleen Cleaver to Eldridge.
Only Assata Shakur stands alone as an iconic figure, embodying masculine and feminine aspects. Her hybridity is a confluence of masculine and
feminine (stereotypical) characteristics. Without a towering male persona,
Shakur—unlike the "conventional" black female revolutionary—has no
shadow of a legendary fighter and revolutionary to shade her from full
scrutiny: the speculative or admiring gaze, the curious gawk, the hostile
stare.

Black female icons were recognized as the lovers or partners of black
male revolutionaries or prison intellectuals (Newton, Cleaver, and Jackson all wrote from prison). Kathleen Cleaver's tumultuous marriage to
Eldridge Cleaver; Elaine Brown's devotion to her disintegrating, drug-
addicted former lover, Huey Newton, who installed her as Black Panther
Party chair (from 1974 to 1977); and Angela Davis's relationship with
prison theorist George Jackson, which began while she was organizing
to free the incarcerated Soledad Brothers—all serve as markers, promoting the image of black female militants as sexual and political associates, as beautiful consorts rather than political comrades. The American
public as spectator would recognize in these personal if not political

lives familiar heterosexual dramas of desire, betrayal, abandonment, and battery.

Assata Shakur least fits this scenario, although her memoir speaks volumes about gender politics in the BPP. Shakur was already an incarcerated revolutionary when she conceived and gave birth to her codefendant's daughter (who graduated from Spelman College and whose father's name is eclipsed by the name of her mother). Equally, the names of her BLA comrades linked to her capture at the turnpike police shooting are largely unknown. In the 1973 confrontation with New Jersey state troopers, Shakur was seriously wounded; Zayd Shakur was killed (along with Trooper Werner Foerster, who may have died in police cross fire); and Sundiata Acoli (Clark Squire) escaped to be later apprehended and sentenced to prison.

Assata Shakur's leadership persona keeps considerable distance from problematic relationships to men. Interestingly, there are no men in the East Coast Panthers whose stature equals hers (although some, such as Dhoruba bin Wahad, who was incarcerated for nearly two decades, were political prisoners). Although West Coast Panther leaders Huey P. Newton, Eldridge Cleaver, Geronimo Pratt, and George Jackson and the Chicago leader Fred Hampton are more prominent, they wear the shroud of "martyrs"—the psychological or physical casualties of a liberation war.[5]

In some ways the men's status as icons does not compare favorably with Shakur's, for she has longevity as a living political figure, one not marred by personal "pathology" or voluntary exile from a U.S. black mass. Shakur's narrative marks her flight as a revolutionary act in itself. She escaped from prison as "quietly" as she lived and struggled (she writes in the memoir that she planned the escape); she was not released by the courts as were Malcolm, Newton, Cleaver, Pratt, Hampton, and Davis. *Assata: An Autobiography* makes her continuously (re)appear to progressives, while the police manhunt that commands her reappearance into prison keeps her visible in the conservative or mainstream public mind (to the degree that it is attentive).

Assata Shakur became a fugitive in the only communist country in the hemisphere. Cuba thus shares an "outlaw" status with the black female fugitive it harbors. (Cuba continues to shelter U.S. political dissidents.) The 1959 Cuban Revolution's ability to expel U.S. crime syndicates and corporations from the island was the ultimate act of enduring revolution within America's "sphere of influence." Likewise, Shakur is the only prominent Panther able to "successfully" escape from prison. Her "legend" is augmented through exile and her political sensibilities and literary ability. (That she was trained by the Cubans and received a postgraduate degree at the University of Havana suggests a set of skills that surpass those of her revolutionary colleagues who died or imploded while young.) Unlike the men, there is little notoriety of a personal life lived in excess and criminality. Rather, there is a dignified restraint that must seem confusing when juxtaposed with her advocacy of liberation "by any means necessary."

Shakur is not more reticent than her male compatriots mentioned here; she is more mature—perhaps in part because she lived long enough to see middle age (but so did Newton and Cleaver), perhaps because her political *style* was less personality driven. It is difficult to compare Shakur's political legacy with those Panther- and BLA-imprisoned intellectuals disciplined by decades of incarceration who have not been in the public spotlight.

Unlike her female elite comrades, Shakur never had to explain (or forget) a controversial male partner or have his silent presence trail her throughout her political and private life. Women more famous than she—Kathleen Cleaver, Angela Davis, Elaine Brown—do not possess her iconic stature as a revolutionary either. In "Black Revolutionary Icons and NeoSlave Narratives," I compare in greater detail Black Panther leaders and associates Elaine Brown, Kathleen Cleaver, Angela Davis and Assata Shakur;[6] here, I only note that she differs from both male and female elite leadership connected to armed resistance.

Shakur's background is remarkable for its unremarkable nature. Among the women, Brown grew up in Philadelphia slums, became a Playboy Bunny, and moved in circles that included Frank Sinatra. Cleaver was the daughter of a diplomat and went to elite schools before embracing SNCC and then the *Soul on Ice* author and convicted rapist Eldridge Cleaver. Davis was mentored by the communist leaders the Apthekers in New York City and grew into an international figure in the Communist Party. Shakur came from neither poverty nor wealth or privilege. She was as ordinary a young woman, with the exception of truancy as a teenage runaway, as the working or (lower) middle-class black society would issue. For some, how frightening must be the prospect that *any* ordinary colored girl, within the appropriate context, could grow up to become a revolutionary.

Born in a New York City hospital in 1947, Joanne Chesimard would later reject her birth name as a "slave name" to become "Assata Shakur." In the mid-1960s, according to her memoir, she enrolled at Manhattan Community College to acquire secretarial skills in order to advance in the labor market. Instead, she became a political activist and began working in the

Black liberation struggle, the student rights movement, and the movement against the Vietnam War. Upon graduating from college, Shakur joined the Black Panther Party. Although she was active in the social service aspects of the New York BPP, its breakfast program, sickle-cell testing, and health services, she was forced out of this work and into the underground due to violent police repression against black radicals associated with the Party. *Assata* describes how she sought out the Black Liberation Army, an underground, military wing of largely East Coast Panthers, for self-protection. The BPP had become a primary target of one of the FBI's violent counterintelligence programs (COINTELPRO) and its most murderous intentions. While underground, Shakur became accused of numerous crimes, charges that were eventually dismissed or of which she was exonerated.

However, in March 1977, following a 1973 change of venue and a 1974 mistrial, Assata Shakur was convicted as an accomplice to the murder of New Jersey state trooper Werner Foerster and of atrocious assault on trooper James Harper with intent to kill. Despite the testimony of expert witnesses, who argued that medical evidence showed that Shakur, who herself had been shot by police while sitting in a car, could not have shot either trooper, an all-white jury, with five members with personal ties to state troopers, convicted her. The judge did not allow any evidence of COINTELPRO repression to be entered into the case and refused to investigate a break-in at the office of her defense counsel. Two years after her conviction, Shakur escaped from New Jersey's Clinton Correctional Facility. In 1984, she received political asylum in Cuba, where she remains today, meeting with foreign delegations and working—with a million-dollar bounty on her head.

Waging a People's War:
Violence and Trauma in the Absence of "Victory"

Historically within the United States, black resistance to domination has been pacifist, militarist, or a creative combination of the two. Most of the violence in resistance movements has been from the state. The story of COINTELPRO as a form of state violence is like a Brothers Grimm tale: it is meant to chill and chasten most who hear it. Unlike in the Grimm's fairy tales, however, the victors in American stories of political struggle for a greater democracy are not usually the victims-in-resistance. Deployed since the 1920s in some fashion against communists, workers, artists, women, civil rights and human rights activists, and antiwar organizations, the FBI counterintelligence program destabilized progressive political movements by targeting, intimidating, and killing activists. The program remains in effect today, with the continuing harassment and incarceration of its targets.[7] In 1968, when FBI director J. Edgar Hoover designated the Black Panther Party as the "greatest threat to the internal security" of the United States, imprisonment as well as assassinations of key Panther leaders followed. However, no concerted national outrage emerged in response to the state's violent repression of black insurgency. The lack of concern seemed tied partly to ignorance and partly to the consequence of negative media depictions of black revolutionaries. According to the U.S. Senate's 1976 Church Commission report on domestic intelligence operations: "The FBI has attempted covertly to influence the public's perception of persons and organizations by disseminating derogatory information to the press, either anonymously or through 'friendly news contacts.'"[8]

While Angela Davis's 1972 acquittal proves to some liberals that the "system" works (and, conversely, for some conservatives, that it is dangerously flawed), Assata Shakur's escape from prison in 1979 invalidates that conviction. Shakur's political life reworks the neoslave narrative to invert its deradicalizing tendencies with the testimony of an unreconstructed insurrectionist. She is disturbing because she was never exonerated, because her 1979 prison escape rejects "the system," because she bears witness as an unrepentant insurrectionist and "slave" fugitive. Shakur represents the unembraceable, against whom (and those who offer her refuge) the state exercises severe sanctions. Nevertheless, her case has received support from ideologically disparate African Americans, ranging from incarcerated revolutionaries and prison intellectuals to neoliberal black studies professors. Her narrative, which is more that of the revolutionary slave than the slave fugitive, seems to construct Cuba, not the United States, as the potential site for (black) freedom.[9]

Assata Shakur's political contributions to black liberation are enmeshed in high controversy and life-and-death crises. Scholar Manning Marable writes in his essay "Black Political Prisoners: The Case of Assata Shakur" (1998):

> If Assata Shakur is involuntarily returned to the US . . . she will be imprisoned for life, and very possibly murdered by state authorities. The only other Black Panther who survived the 1973 shoot-out, Sundiata Acoli, is 61 years old and remains in prison to this day. No new trial could possibly be fair, since part of the trial transcripts have [sic] been lost and crucial evidence has "disappeared."

Assata Shakur is less marketable in mainstream culture given that her life and writings present a narrative similar to that of Mumia Abu-Jamal. As the unrepentant rebel, she calls herself "slave," rejects her "slave name," and denounces the white-dominated corporate society and state as "slave-masters." Aspects of her narrative (found in the memoir, interviews, documentaries, and media reports) link her more to the underground Black Liberation Army than to the Black Panther Party, which has become on some levels a cultural commodity. Hence she is not only a rebel but also a militarist.

Shakur thus functions as political embarrassment and irritation for the police and conservative politicians, and conversely as political inspiration, or at least quiet satisfaction, for some of their most ardent critics. Those who worked above ground with the courts saw and see in Angela Davis's release and exoneration a vindication of their political agency. Likewise, those who did advocacy work or worked underground, or who understood that circumstances and police malfeasance required extralegal maneuvers, see in Shakur's self-liberation an affirmation of their political efficacy or the practicalities of resistance. That her escape entailed neither casualties nor hostages obviously helps pacifists to support her strategies.

Assata: An Autobiography depicts a public persona hardly compatible with commoditization by those who romanticize political or revolutionary violence. Rejecting the image of violent black revolutionaries, her account offers a complex portrait of a woman so committed to black freedom that she refused to reject armed struggle as a strategy to obtain it. Even during violent upheavals, community remains central for Shakur. Refusing to make revolutionary war synonymous with violence, she writes of a "people's war" that precludes elite vanguards. *Assata* describes the limitations of black revolutionaries:

> Some of the groups thought they could just pick up arms and struggle and that, somehow, people would see what they were doing and begin to struggle themselves. They wanted to engage in a do-or-die battle with the power structure in America, even though they were weak and ill prepared for such a fight. But the most important factor is that armed struggle, by itself, can never bring about a revolution. Revolutionary war is a people's war.[10]

The "people's war," however, retained a military dimension for Shakur. Her memoir cites the importance of organizing an underground, the serious consideration of "armed acts of resistance" in scenarios that expand black people's support for resistance.[11]

In news interviews and documentaries, narratives have emerged to portray the black revolutionary as a political icon and the lone active survivor of a tumultuous era.[12] Shakur's image in Lee Lew-Lee's documentary *All Power to the People! The Black Panther Party and Beyond* appears with archival footage in an exposé on the murderous aspects of COINTELPRO. What Lew-Lee labeled "death squads" and I term "state violence" operated against both the Black Panther Party and the American Indian Movement in the late 1960s and early 1970s. In the documentary, former New York Panther Safiya Bukhari is one of the few black women— women are not prominently featured in *All Power to the People!*— who discusses the emergence of the BLA as an underground offshoot of the Panthers. According to Bukhari, New York Panthers, accused of breaking with the West Coast leadership, were caught between "a rock and a hard place." Huey P. Newton had allegedly put out a death warrant on them, condemning them as traitors and "government agents"; the New York Police Department (NYPD), assisted by the FBI, had done likewise, marking them as traitors and "terrorists."

The BLA formed against the frightening background memories of Malcolm X's 1965 assassination and healthy paranoia inspired by the unclear roles played by the Nation of Islam, Louis Farrakhan, and NYPD undercover agent who had infiltrated Malcolm's organization to serve as his "bodyguard." Likewise, the 1969 executions of Panthers Fred Hampton and Mark Clark in a predawn raid by the Chicago police coordinated by the FBI (survivors would later collect a large settlement from the government, which admits no wrongdoing) framed the choices of black radicals as life-and-death options.

In *Still Black, Still Strong: Survivors of the War against Black Revolutionaries*, former Panther Dhoruba Bin Wahad offers insights into the underground organization and reveals the complex gender and race dynamics surrounding Shakur. Assata Shakur's revolutionary icon exists *sans* celebrity posing or adulation for past dramatic and traumatic clashes with the state. Her solitude—in prison, as a fugitive, as a revolutionary woman not tied to a dependent relationship with a man—epitomizes the aloneness, if not loneliness, of the unrepentant revolutionary.

Physical violence and battlefield knowledge and fatigue foster a unique black female political being. Her encounters with police both in the street and in "safe havens" such as hospitals are revealing. Shakur was shot while unarmed, with her hands raised, then taken to the hospital, where she was brutally beaten. The memoir describes her being shackled to a hospital bed with bullet wounds, while New Jersey state troopers tortured and threatened to kill her. *Assata* recounts how medical staff and poetry kept her alive despite police assaults:

> They gave me the poetry of our people, the tradition of our women, the relationship of human beings to nature and the search of human beings for freedom, for justice, for a world that isn't a brutal world. And those books—even through that experience—kind of just chilled me out, let me be in touch with my tradition, the beauty of my people, even though we've had to suffer such vicious oppression. . . .it makes you think that no matter how brutal the police, the courts are, the people fight to keep their humanity.[13]

Revolutionary Fugitive and Slave Rebel

At first confined in a men's prison, under twenty-four-hour surveillance, without adequate intellectual, physical, or medical resources during the trial, Shakur was later relocated to a women's correctional facility in Clinton, New Jersey. Sentenced to life plus thirty-three years, after being convicted of killing Werner Foerster by an all-white jury in 1977,[14] she was initially housed in facilities alongside women of the Aryan Nation sisterhood, the Manson family, and Squeaky Fromme, who had attempted to assassinate former president Gerald Ford. Shakur maintains that her escape was motivated by a fear of being murdered in prison. In her memoir she also writes that she ultimately decided to "leave" after dreaming of her grandmother instructing her to do so, and realizing that she would not be able to see her young daughter while incarcerated.

In a 1978 petition concerning political prisoners, political persecution, and torture in the United States, the National Conference of Black Lawyers, the National Alliance against Racist and Political Repression, and the United Church of Christ's Commission for Racial Justice brought Shakur's case before the United Nations. The petition stated that Assata Shakur became a hunted fugitive after and due to: the FBI and NYPD charging her with being a leader of the Black Liberation Army, which the agencies characterized as an "organization engaged in the shooting of police officers"; the appearance of public posters that depicted her as a dangerous criminal involved in fabricated terrorist conspiracies against civilians; and her appearance on the FBI's "Most Wanted List" which rendered her "a 'shoot-to-kill' target."

In 1998, black activist-intellectuals S. E. Anderson, Soffiyah Jill Elijah, Esq., Joan P. Gibbs, Esq., Rosemari Mealy, and Karen D. Taylor circulated, via e-mail, "An Open Letter to New Jersey Governor Whitman." This letter to Christine Todd Whitman (who would later head the Environmental Protection Agency in the first administration of George W. Bush) protested the $50,000 bounty the governor had placed on political exile and fugitive Shakur. (In 2006, Attorney General Alberto Gonzalez, who would later resign from the Bush administration due to abuse of his office, raised the bounty to $1 million.) The letter castigated the Republican governor: "[In] seeking her apprehension by . . . 'kidnapping,' you have engaged in the kind of debased moralism that the former slave masters in this country resorted to when seeking the return of runaway Africans to slavery." For the letter's authors, Assata Shakur "followed in the footsteps of Harriet Tubman, who instructed: there was one of two things I had a right to, liberty, or death; if I could not have one, I would have the other; for no man should take me alive; I should fight for my liberty as long as my strength lasted."[15]

In early 1998, concurrently with the circulation of "An Open Letter to New Jersey Governor Whitman," an "Open Letter from Assata Shakur" circulated online. Shakur's letter begins: "My name is Assata Shakur, and I am a 20th century escaped slave." Of herself and her codefendant, Sundiata Acoli, she writes that they were both convicted in pretrial news media, and that the media were not allowed to interview them although the New Jersey police and FBI gave daily interviews and stories to the press.[16] Shakur's conflictual relationship with mainstream media would be rekindled a decade later. On December 24, 1997, a press conference was held to announce that New Jersey State Police had written a letter (which was never publicly released) to Pope John Paul II asking him to intervene on their behalf and to aid in having Shakur extradited to the United States. In response, Shakur wrote to the pope, explaining her story. Then in January 1998, during the pope's visit to Cuba, Shakur granted an interview with NBC journalist Ralph Penza. For this three-part "exclusive interview series," NBC advertised on black radio stations and placed notices in local newspapers. The series erased or distorted much of the information Shakur and other progressives had presented concerning her case.

However, most striking here is the bizarre polarization of female identities with images so antipodean that the only comparable extremes in

American cultural iconography are the neoslave narratives, those of the white plantation mistress and the black field slave. In a media interview, Governor Whitman expressed outrage at Shakur's happiness about being a grandmother, and her haven or home in Cuba. Shakur's rejoinder notes that she has never seen her grandchild. She argues that if Whitman considers that "50 years of dealing with racism, poverty, persecution, brutality, prison, underground, exile and blatant lies has been so nice, then I'd be more than happy to let her walk in my shoes."

During the NBC special, one interviewee suggested that the New Jersey police would do everything to extradite Shakur from Cuba, including "kidnapping" her and using bounty hunters. Shakur responds in her "Open Letter":

> I guess the theory is that if they could kidnap millions of Africans from Africa 400 years ago, they should be able to kidnap one African woman today. It is nothing but an attempt to bring about the re-incarnation of the Fugitive Slave Act. All I represent is just another slave that they want to bring back to the plantation. Well, I might be a slave, but I will go to my grave a rebellious slave. I am and I feel like a maroon woman. I will never voluntarily accept the condition of slavery.[17]

Leadership without a Vanguard?

What could have protected Shakur and other militant black leaders in liberation organizations from the counterrevolutionary war and murder waged by a democratic state? In theory, the answer to that question is: a politicized mass base that demanded and enforced their human and civil rights, one that could negotiate the end to police surveillance and brutality that sought to undermine legal and productive organizing in black communities ignored by the welfare state. These communities desperately needed what the BPP provided without fostering dependency upon an aloof and depoliticizing bureaucracy: breakfast and educational programs, literacy and newspaper publishing, drug counseling and health care. Yet the problem in leadership would emerge for this black revolutionary woman, and all revolutionaries, if the mass lacked not only the will but also the desire to constitute itself as leaders, as a political vanguard.

During her time in prison, Shakur became familiar with the mass base, or its most depressed sectors, in ways that her organizing outside of prison, providing social services largely denied to blacks at that time by the state, never permitted. While incarcerated, she was housed with the sector of the population most in need of transformative politics or revolutionary struggle. But this sector proved ambivalent toward organized political struggle. In that space, prison, she and the other incarcerated women functioned less as a members of a vanguard and more like social workers. Her writings on her time in captivity are quite revealing about the disparities within black female agency. Throughout her time and trials of being hunted and prosecuted, Assata Shakur would write and publish mostly essays. *Assata* both reveals her skills as a poet and reveals in many ways the triumphal black woman despite institutional trauma.[18] But that memoir was written and published in Cuba, several years after her self-emancipation from prison. The writing during incarceration is filtered with despair for vanguard formations among severely oppressed black women in repressive sites.

A year before Shakur's escape, the *Black Scholar* published her April 1978 essay "Women in Prison: How We Are."[19] Here, Shakur describes New York Riker's Island Correctional Institution for Women, arguing that at the prison "there are no criminals . . . only victims." The environment is uncomfortable and the food inhospitable. The name of the space they occupy, with a heating system whose thermostat cannot be adjusted for more warmth, is the "bull pen." The women held in the pen are "all black" and "all restless" and freezing, according to Shakur. But the physical discomfort is less disturbing then the frightening and embarrassing emotional and psychological decay of the black women caged in the pen. Shakur observes the state of her fellow inmates:

> All of us, with the exception of a woman, tall and gaunt, who looks naked and ravished, have refused the bologna sandwiches. The rest of us sit drinking bitter, syrupy tea. The tall, forty-ish woman, with sloping shoulders, moves her head back and forth to the beat of a private tune while she takes small, tentative bites out a bologna sandwich. Someone asks her what she's in for. Matter-of-factly, she says, "They say I killed some nigga'. But how could I have when I'm buried down in South Carolina?" Everybody's face gets busy exchanging looks. A short, stout young woman wearing men's pants and men's shoes says, "Buried in South Carolina?" "Yeah," says the tall woman. "South Carolina, that's where I'm buried. You don't know that? You don't know shit, do you? This ain't me. This ain't me." She kept repeating, "This ain't me" until she had eaten all the bologna sandwiches. Then she brushed off the crumbs and withdrew, head moving again, back into that world where only she could hear her private tune.[20]

The nameless woman, in comparison to whom all the other incarcerated women can feel superior, appears in the first of several short vignettes. The essay provides a framework for seeing a number of representational black women. There is the mother of teenage children, Lucille, who defends herself from her violent domestic partner. He had mutilated her arm and partially severed her ear the night she finally killed him. But a jury seeing no vulnerability, and hence no need for self-defense, in a black woman with a drinking addiction gives her a felony "C" conviction. Working as "jailhouse legal counsel" on the women's behalf, Assata, rather than the salaried court attorney or judge, informs her that the sentence can carry up to fifteen years. There is "Spikey," a drug addict scheduled for release; her appearance is so altered by her addictions, and her violations and abusiveness have so damaged her relations with her mother and her children, that she prefers to spend the Christmas holidays institutionalized rather than with her family and experience the shame that would follow.

The majority of the women inside are black and Puerto Rican survivors of childhood abuse, abuse by men, and abuse by the "system."[21] Shakur's memoir chronicles suffering from political violence rather than social or personal violence (the most traumatic recorded memory is her escape from a "train," or gang rape, by teenage boys). Yet she expresses empathy with the seemingly apolitical women: "There are no big time gangsters here, no premeditated mass murderers, no godmothers. There are no big time dope dealers, no kidnappers, no Watergate women. There are virtually no women here charged with white collar crimes like embezzling or fraud."[22]

The dependency of the women's criminality strikes her: their dependency on drug addiction, on male "masterminds" for whom they work as runners, mules, prostitutes, and thieves. Shakur radiates a sympathy or perhaps empathy for what she views as impoverished rather than criminal people: "The women see stealing or hustling as necessary for the survival of themselves or their children because jobs are scarce and welfare is impossible to live on. . . . amerikan capitalism is in no way threatened by the women in prison on Riker's Island."[23]

American capitalism and racially driven incarceration coexist with patriarchy and the mystique of "home." And the women are not fans of white supremacy, or even the nation-state, but are loyalists toward consumer-driven capitalism and the fetish of "home." Shakur writes that the "domesticity" of the women's prison, its brightly colored walls, television, plants, rooms with electronic doors (rather than bars), and laundry facilities, produces in the incarcerated a sense of well-being among emotionally and materially deprived women: "Many women are convinced that they are, somehow, 'getting over.' Some go so far as to reason that because they are not doing hard time, they are not really in prison."[24] Yet the women's relationships, not their attachments to material resources, comfort, and structured predictability, unavailable in their lives outside of prison, reveal their convictions to be false. This false consciousness is dispelled by the relations that women have among themselves as prisoners and with their jailers. The women who police the lives of the incarcerated are also black. Their particular type of black female agency in service to and on the payroll of the state works against the agency of both black radical women prisoners such as Shakur and destabilized black women prisoners such as Spikey. This presents a range of contradictions for progressive politics and absolute Manichean divides. Assata Shakur writes disparagingly of the bonds of "affection" exhibited between black female jailers and their black wards:

> Beneath the motherly veneer, the reality of guard life is [ever] present. Most of the guards are black, usually from working class, upward bound, civil service oriented backgrounds. They identify with the middle class, have middle class values and are extremely materialistic. They are not the most intelligent women in the world. . . . Most are aware that there is no justice in the amerikan judicial system and that blacks and Puerto Ricans are discriminated against in every facet of amerikan life. But, at the same time, they are convinced that the system is somehow "lenient." To them, the women in prison are "losers" who don't have enough sense to stay out of jail. Most believe in the boot strap theory—anybody can "make it" if they try hard enough.[25]

American exceptionalism filters down to the lowest reaches of the social strata (which does not mean that black women can be generalized). Shakur's problematic black women manage Frantz Fanon's "wretched of the earth" by ensuring the smooth operation of systems that cage them. As guards, their dispensing of affection for the caged (presumably based on some shared condition or affinity) pacifies the wretched. American exceptionalism worn by the black woman (guard) becomes a form of self-validation and social superiority.

Shakur grimly (or sadly?) notes: "They congratulate themselves on their great accomplishments. In contrast to themselves they see the inmate as ignorant, uncultured, self-destructive, weak-minded and stupid." She next proceeds to identity the source of black achievement for these women (and, by extension, an extensive segment of the black working and middle class): "They ignore the fact that their dubious accomplishments are not based on superior intelligence or effort, but only on chance and a civil service list. . . . no matter how much they hate the military structure, the infighting, the ugliness of their tasks, they are very aware . . . [that if] they were not working as guards most would be underpaid or unemployed." The absence of their employment in the prison industries would mean existential and material losses: "Many would miss the feeling of superiority and power as much as they would miss the money, especially the cruel, sadistic ones."

Among the incarcerated, drug use and abuse provide the topics for most conversations. Hence, Shakur argues: "In prison, as on the streets, an escapist culture prevails." She estimates that half of the prison population is prescribed and required to take a psychotropic drug (what contemporary incarcerated women have referred to as "chemical handcuffs").[26] Other forms of addiction, socially acceptable ones, manifest in television, prison love/sexual relations, and games of distraction. Few women engage in academic, political, or legal studies, and even fewer in radical politics such as feminism, antiracism, or gay liberation politics. Their dependency on institutionalized life moves beyond the borders of physical need expressed in shelter, health care, food, and safety from violent males.

Assata Shakur observes gender disparities as marking the existence and expression of political agency of black incarcerated people: "A striking difference between women and men prisoners at Riker's Island is the absence of revolutionary rhetoric among the women. We have no study groups. We have no revolutionary literature floating around. There are no groups of militants attempting to 'get their heads together.' The women at Riker's seem vaguely aware of what a revolution is, but generally regard it as an impossible dream."[27] Revolution, of course, requires risk, sacrifice, discipline, and work. Ironically, the women seek the "American dream" and find that more attainable than the dream of revolution for a society free of capitalism, institutional racism, and (hetero)sexism.

Noting that some women find prison "a place to rest and recuperate," Shakur sees that the trials of captivity in some ways reflect the outside: "The cells are not much different from the tenements, the shooting galleries and the welfare hotels they live in on the street. . . . Riker's Island is just another institution. In childhood school was their prison, or youth houses or reform schools or children shelters or foster homes or mental hospitals or drug programs and they see all institutions as indifferent to their needs, yet necessary to their survival." Here, there are rings of captivity to be explored, theorized, and resisted. The striking problem, though, is whether or not the women have the agency and energy to undertake such a task. In her inability to assert that they do in this essay, Shakur functions as witness and advocate.[28]

In the final section of the essay, titled "What of Our Past? What of Our History? What of Our Future?," Shakur notes that trauma and grief are not new to black/red women: "I can imagine the pain and the strength of my great great grandmothers who were slaves and my great great grandmothers who were Cherokee Indians trapped on reservations." She then references the pain of contemporary women in liberation movement(s), those supposedly so unlike the "apolitical" women in Riker's Island who are functioning at low levels of consciousness with no level of active resistance. For Shakur, movement women mirrored the dysfunctional attitudes and behaviors of incarcerated or mass women:

> I think about my sisters in the movement. I remember the days when, draped in African garb, we rejected our foremothers and ourselves as castrators. We did penance for robbing the brother of his manhood, as if we were the oppressor. I remember the days of the Panther party when we were "moderately liberated." When we were allowed to wear pants and expected to pick up the gun. The days when we gave doe-eyed looks to our leaders. The days when we worked like dogs and struggled desperately for the respect which they struggled desperately not to give us. I remember the black history classes that did [not] mention women and the posters of our "leaders" where women were conspicuously absent. We visited our sisters who bore the complete responsibility of the children while the Brotha was doing his thing. Or had moved on to bigger and better things. . . . And we had no desire to sit in some consciousness raising group with white women and bare our souls.[29]

According to Shakur, the specificity of oppression that black women, including the most "liberated" who manifested as "revolutionary," faced in the frame of a Black Panther is strikingly unique. The essay focuses on women in prison, but the forms of containment and abandonment that black women face radiate beyond the prison walls. Shakur maintains that women's liberation is predicated on a liberated country and culture, and that capitalism forecloses that possibility. Her final injunction in the 1978 essay, one of the last pieces written for publication while she was incarcerated, was that black women must form a movement: "Under the guidance of Harriet Tubman and Fannie Lou Hamer and all of our foremothers, let us rebuild a sense of community. Let us rebuild the culture of giving and carry on the tradition of fierce determination to move on closer to freedom."[30] But what that "freedom" is, beyond what it is not—that is, capitalist, racist, sexist/misogynist, homophobic—cannot be specified in her essay.

Conclusion: Honoring the Panther Woman

Assata Shakur's power as a narrator of black struggles and freedom movements would become eclipsed itself as she evolved, along with the BPP, into an icon. The reified thing, the icon, replaces the dynamic human being who changes her mind, her practices, her desires as a living entity. As a living entity she grows. A fixed site of notoriety, in which the stories that could be told about freedom struggles increasingly become eclipsed by caricatures of the antisocial black militant, is a conceptual and political grave.

In her "Open Letter," Shakur evokes one of Martin Luther King, Jr.'s sermons from 1968 that alludes to his imminent assassination. King states that he does "not mind" dying because he has been to the "mountain top." Shakur reflects:

> Everybody has to die sometime, and all I want is to go with dignity. I am more concerned about the growing poverty, the growing despair that is rife in America . . . our younger generations, who represent our future . . . about the rise of the prison-industrial complex that is turning our people into slaves again . . . about the repression, the police brutality, violence, the rising wave of racism that makes up the political landscape of the US today. Our young people deserve a future, and I consider it the mandate of my ancestors to be part of the struggle to ensure that they have one.[31]

Arguing for young people's right to "live free from political repression," Shakur—with "a special, urgent appeal" for struggles for the life of Mumia Abu-Jamal, the only political prisoner on death row—urges the readers of her letter to work to free all political prisoners and abolish the death penalty.[32]

Assata Shakur's story depends in part upon the frame that establishes the borders or boundaries for its telling. There is the antiracist feminist,

the prison intellectual, the party member, the underground revolutionary, the lone iconic militant. There is fierce resistance and profound grief.
Shakur's somber, measured response to losses provides a word ritual for
the dying and dead—whether those entombed in Riker's Island twenty
years ago or a recently fallen comrade.

Her eulogy for Safiya Bukhari, given in Havana on August 29, 2003,
is haunting. Bukhari collapsed hours after she buried her own mother—
the grandmother who raised Safiya Bukhari's young daughter the day her
own daughter became a BLA fighter and fugitive, going underground only
to surface for an eight-year prison term. Bukhari survived the maiming
medical practices of prison doctors (although her uterus did not) only to
succumb to the "typical" black women diseases of hypertension, diabetes,
obesity, and heart failure in 2002. The eulogy could also be read as Assata
Shakur's—and that of all revolutionary black women who refused to cir-
cumscribe their rebellion, and paid the costs for that decision:

> It is with much sadness that i say my last goodbye to Safiya Bukhari.
> She was my sister, my comrade and my friend. We met nearly thirty-five
> years ago, when we were both members of the Black Panther Party in
> Harlem. Even then, i was impressed by her sincerity, her commitment
> and her burning energy. She was a descendent of slaves and she inherited
> the legacy of neo-slavery. She believed that struggle was the only way that
> African people in America could rid ourselves of oppression. As a Black
> woman struggling in America she experienced the most vicious forms
> of racism, sexism, cruelty and indifference. As a political activist she was
> targeted, persecuted, hounded and harassed. Because of her political ac-
> tivities she became a political prisoner and spent many years in prison.
> But she continued to believe in freedom, and she continued to fight for it.
> In spite of her personal suffering, in spite of chronic, life-threatening ill-
> nesses, she continued to struggle. She gave the best that she had to give to
> our people. She devoted her life, her love and her best energies to fighting
> for the liberation of oppressed people. She struggled selflessly, she could
> be trusted, she was consistent, and she could always be counted to do
> what needed to be done. She was a soldier, a warrior-woman who did
> everything she could to free her people and to free political prisoners.[33]

For Assata Shakur, the weight of isolation, alienation, and vilification are
scars that are borne. Redemption does not occur on this plane or in this
life. Betrayal by nonblacks and blacks, by men and women, is part of the

liberation narrative. There will be no gratitude, no appreciation, no recognition equal to the insults and assaults. So, Assata Shakur, in true revolutionary fashion, must conclude her testimonial embracing a community that radiates beyond our immediate boundaries and limitations: "I have faith that the Ancestors will welcome her, cherish her, and treat her with more love and more kindness than she ever received here on this earth."[34]

NOTES

1. This chapter is based on "Black Revolutionary Icons and 'Neoslave' Narratives," in Joy James, *Shadowboxing: Representations of Black Feminist Politics* (New York: St. Martin's Press, 2000). In that essay, I discuss gendered differences among and between Black Panther leaders and associates.

For additional writings on Assata Shakur and the Black Panther Party, see Jim Fletcher, Tanaquil Jones, and Sylvère Lotringer, eds., *Still Black, Still Strong: Survivors of the U.S. War against Black Revolutionaries* (New York: Semiotext(e), 1993); J. Dao, "Fugitive in Cuba Still Wounds Trenton: Chesimard Unrepentant at Trooper's '73 Killing; Whitman Is Irate," *New York Times*, May 1, 1998; Lenox S. Hinds, foreword to Assata Shakur, *Assata: An Autobiography* (Chicago: Lawrence Hill, 1987); Charles E. Jones, ed., *The Black Panther Party [Reconsidered]* (Baltimore: Black Classic Press, 1998); H. Kleffner, "The Black Panthers: Interviews with Geronimo ji Jaga Pratt and Mumia Abu-Jamal," *Race and Class* 35 , no. 1(1993): 9–26; Manning Marable, "Black Political Prisoners: The Case of Assata Shakur," *Along the Colour Line*, April 22, 1998; Christian Parenti, "Assata Shakur Speaks From Exile: Post-modern Maroon in the Ultimate Palenque," *Peace Review: A Journal of Social Justice*, 1469–9982, vol. 10, no. 3 (1998): 419–426; Margo V. Perkins, *Autobiography as Activism: Three Black Women of the Sixties* (Jackson: University Press of Mississippi, 2000); Michael Ratner, "Immoral Bounty for Assata," *CovertAction Quarterly*, no. 65 (Fall 1998), http://www.hartford-hwp.com/archives/45a/101.html; Evelyn Williams, *Inadmissible Evidence* (Brooklyn, NY: Lawrence Hill, 1993); Lee Lew-Lee, *All Power to the People! The Black Panther Party and Beyond*.

2. For some of the most incisive literature from the Black Power era, see George Jackson, *Blood in My Eye* (New York: Random House, 1972); Jackson, *Soledad Brother: The Prison Letters of George Jackson* (New York: Random House, 1970).

3. Mumia Abu-Jamal, *Live from Death Row* (New York: Harper, 1996). Abu-Jamal was convicted in 1982 of killing a Philadelphia police officer, Daniel Faulkner. Trial perjury by witnesses, police suppression of evidence that would assist the defense, and inconsistencies in ballistics reports have led to international calls for a new trial.

4. Charles E. Jones, ed. *The Black Panther Party [Reconsidered]* (Baltimore: Black Classic Press, 1998); Jama Lazerow and Yohuru Williams, eds. *In Search of the Black Panther Party: New Perspectives on a Revolutionary Movement* (Durham: Duke UP, 2009); Mumia Abu-Jamal, *We Want Freedom: A Life in the Black Panther Party* (Cambridge: South End Press, 2004); Robyn Ceanne Spencer, "Inside the Panther Revolution: The Black Freedom Movement and the Black Panther Party in Oakland, California," in *Groundwork*, edited by Jeanne Theoharis and Komozi Woodard.

5. In *Still Black, Still Strong: Survivors of the War against Black Revolutionaries*, Dhoruba Bin Wahad offers insights into the underground organization and reveals the complex gender and race dynamics surrounding Shakur. Her solitude—in prison, as a fugitive, as a revolutionary woman not tied to a dependent relationship with a man—epitomizes the aloneness, if not loneliness, of the isolated revolutionary. Physical violence, battlefield knowledge, and fatigue

foster a unique black female political being who is susceptible to being either romanticized or demonized.

George Jackson would be killed in prison. Huey P. Newton would be executed in an Oakland drug deal gone awry. Eldridge Cleaver's drug addiction was followed by conversion to evangelical Christianity before his death. Geronimo Pratt, wrongfully incarcerated for twenty-seven years for murder, received a large financial settlement and settled in Africa to found an educational center.

For an analysis of media coverage of George Jackson's death, see Michel Foucault et al., "The Masked Assassination," in *Warfare in the American Homeland: Policing and Prison in a Penal Democracy*, ed. Joy James (Durham, NC: Duke University Press, 2007).

6. James, *Shadowboxing*. For a discussion of those activists and authors, see Joy James, *Imprisoned Intellectuals: America's Political Prisoners Write on Life, Liberation and Rebellion* (Boulder, CO: Rowman and Littlefield, 2003).

7. Although publicly condemned, the program allegedly remains in effect today with the continuing harassment of "targets" such as the San Francisco Eight.

8. The 1976 Church Committee Reports on Domestic Surveillance and Other Illegal Activities by U.S. Intelligence Agencies was named after Senator Frank Church (D-Idaho).

9. According to Shakur, she has never been "free"; even in Cuba, protected and valorized as a "black revolutionary," she remains a "slave" because of her status as a black or African woman, a status that she sees as inseparable from the state of subaltern Africans throughout the diaspora.

10. Shakur, *Assata*, 242–243.

11. Ibid, 243.

12. Assata Shakur continues to maintain her innocence in the shooting of Werner Foerster. Her case was reintroduced to mainstream black America in the mid-1980s through a segment on New York–based black journalist Gil Noble's television talk show, *Like It Is*. Noble traveled to Cuba to interview Shakur and with archival footage of the civil rights and black liberation movements set the context for their discussions. Following the two-part segment, a panel that included the Reverend Jesse Jackson was convened to talk about her case. In the 1990s, Shakur appeared in various documentaries, including Cuban filmmaker Gloria Rolando's *Eyes of the Rainbow*, which intersperses images of a serene Shakur with African Orisha, or Yoruba female warrior deities and entities of love and community.

13. Shakur, Assata, 206–207.

14. Malfeasance was the norm during her 1973 trial in Middlesex County. It was discontinued because of the blatant racism expressed in the jury room. The court ruled that the entire jury panel had been contaminated by racist comments like, "If she's black, she's guilty." The New Jersey courts then ordered that a jury be selected from Morris County, one of the wealthiest counties in the country, where 97.5 per cent of potential jurors were white. Most in the jury pool believed the defendant guilty based on pretrial publicity. The trial was later moved back to Middlesex County, yet most whites continued to equate 'black militancy' or a 'black revolutionary' with criminality. Shakur's political affiliations as well as her race-ethnicity would mark her as criminally culpable.

15. In closing, the signatories admonish Whitman concerning her civic and political responsibilities:

"The people of New Jersey, particularly people of African descent, other people of colour and the poor, as well as your political aspirations, would be better served by your attention to reducing poverty, unemployment, underemployment, the incidence of AIDS, police brutality and corruption and improving housing, public education and health care." Copy of the letter can be found at www.iacenter.org/cuba/assata.htm.

16. More contemporary media portrayal of victims of the 1973 tragedy that ended in two deaths focused only on whites. Images of Foerster's weeping widow were broadcast (in similar

fashion to *20/20*'s use of images of Daniel Faulkner's distraught widow in a segment, hosted by Sam Donaldson and run in January 1999, was hostile to calls for a new trial for Mumia Abu-Jamal). No references were made to slain Zayd Shakur, or incarcerated Sundiata Acoli, or their families. Images are, of course, the dominant factor for creating icons, particularly demonized ones. NBC repeatedly aired a photograph of a black woman with a gun implying that it was Shakur although the photograph was taken from a highly publicized case where she was accused of bank robbery but later acquitted (during the trial, several witnesses, including the manager of the bank, testified that the woman in that photograph was not Shakur). Despite NBC's extensive resources for research, it failed to establish the photograph as misidentified; although a subsequent fax and e-mail campaign protested the misinformation, the network continued to broadcast the woman in the photograph as Shakur.

17. Open letter from Assata Shakur. http://www.handsoffassata.org/content/assata openletter-text.htm

18. For a comparative reading of the life of a black female activist among incarcerated black women, see Angela Davis, *Angela Davis: An Autobiography* (New York: International Publisher, 1989). Note that Shakur had been convicted when she wrote her essay, while Davis was awaiting trial, and later would be released on bail, during the writing of her reflections on black women in captivity. Editors at Random House, a capitalist, and/or International Publishers, a communist, publishing house have both provided opportunities for Davis's publication.

19. Assata Shakur, "Women in Prison: How We Are," *Black Scholar* 9, no. 7 (April 1978). http://www.itsabouttimebpp.com/Underground_News/pdf/Best_of_The_Black_Scholar.pdf

20. Ibid.

21. As of 2002, the population of New York jails and prisons was 84 percent non-white. (Mother Jones, *Debt to Society* Special Report, available online at http://www.motherjones.com/prisons/index.html; statistics gathered from Bureau of Justice Statistics, Criminal Justice Institute, and U.S. Census Bureau.)

For more information about women in prison see Amnesty International, *"Not part of my sentence": Violations of the Human Rights of Women in Custody* (New York: Amnesty International, 1999), available online from <http://www.amnesty.org>.

22. Assata Shakur, "Women in Prison: How We Are," *Black Scholar* (April 1978): 9. http://www.itsabouttimebpp.com/Underground_News/pdf/Best_of_The_Black_Scholar.pdf

23. Ibid.,10.

24. Ibid.

25. Ibid., 11

26. For more information on the use of psychotropic drugs in prison, see Kathleen Auerhahn and Elizabeth Dermody Leonard, "Docile Bodies? Chemical Restraints and the Female Inmate," *Journal of Criminal Law and Criminology* 90(Winter 2000): 599–634; D. Benson, "Getting High in Jail: Legal vs. Illegal Drugs," *Prison News Service*, no. 52 (September 1995): 5; "Overview of Mental Health Services Provided by State Adult Correctional Facilities: United States, 1988," *Mental Health Statistical Note* 207 (May 1993): 1–13.

27. Assata Shakur, "Women in Prison: How We Are," *Black Scholar* (April 1978): 12.

28. Ibid., 13

29. Ibid.

30. Ibid.

Between 1850 and 1860, escaped slave Harriet Tubman guided several hundred enslaved people to free territories in the North on the Underground Railroad. During the Civil War, she served as liaison between the army and newly freed African Americans, and following the war she raised money for the education of former slaves and founded a home for the old and poor.

Fannie Lou Hamer was fired from her work as a sharecropper after she attempted to register to vote in 1962 as part of the SNCC voting rights campaign. Jailed and severely beaten in

Mississippi in 1963 for her activism, she gave a rousing speech on behalf of the Mississippi Freedom Democratic Party at the 1964 Democratic National Convention. For Hamer's speech, see
http://americanradioworks.publicradio.org/features/sayitplain/flhamer.html (accessed February
16, 2009).

31. Open letter from Assata Shakur. http://www.handsoffassata.org/content/assata openletter-
text.htm

32. Ibid.

33. http://www.itsabouttimebpp.com/memorials/safiya_bukhari.html

34. Ibid.

7

Revolutionary Women, Revolutionary Education
The Black Panther Party's Oakland Community School

Ericka Huggins and
Angela D. LeBlanc-Ernest

Pride in myself as a [young] black man . . . and pride for all
African-Americans and the revolution we are making together by
helping one another. . . . See, when my mommy and daddy were
growing up, black people didn't have no educational system to
teach *them* that. . . . The job of a revolutionary is to learn and to
teach. I try to do that. I've got a lot more learnin' to do.

Keith Taylor, eleven-year-old OCS student, 1977[1]

The Black Panther Party (BPP), a grassroots organization
founded in Oakland, California, in 1966, by Huey Newton and Bobby
Seale, grew from the needs of local African American and poor communities. Throughout its sixteen-year history, the organization addressed and
took action against police brutality, hunger, inadequate education, poor
health, and unemployment in black and poor communities. Community
education, specifically education for young people, was central to its vision. The BPP's original Ten Point Platform and Program emphasized
providing an education that, among other things, taught African American and poor people about their true history in the United States (see
point 5).[2] The Oakland Community School became not only a flagship

Teaching as well as culinary, facilities, and administrative staff of the Oakland Community School (OCS), 1977. Standing, third from left: Donna Howell. Standing, back row, fifth from left (with eyeglasses): Ericka Huggins. Standing, fourth from right: Haven Henderson. Standing, third from right: Carol Granison. Photo Donald Cunningham, Black Panther Party Photographer.

BPP community program but also a locale for a small but effective group of administrators, educators, and youth who cultivated critical thinking skills to challenge the concept of "uneducable youth." Their efforts established a replicable model for education that was designed to empower whole communities.

The Oakland Community School (OCS) was a ten-year institution that provided an alternative instructional model to Oakland's public education system, a system in a deepening crisis. When the precursor to the OCS, Intercommunal Youth Institute (IYI), opened in 1971, the Oakland Unified School District (OUSD) student population was 62,000 and had a budget of $70.37 million. The district's student population was 60 percent black and other students of color, almost half of whom lived in conditions of poverty. At this time Oakland was one of the lowest-scoring school districts in California; it was mired in tensions between the Oakland School Board, parents, and concerned community members who desired community control of the local schools and a representative voice that counted at the school board meetings. Parents and community members expressed concerns that more money was being spent on administration than on student instruction. Other troubling issues for OUSD included school violence, the use of security guards on school campuses, and the highly contested plan to reduce the number of teachers in the district, resulting in larger class size and high student-teacher ratios.[3]

Continuing a Tradition of Radical Educators

In the face of this citywide education crisis, Oakland Community School administrators followed a tradition of revolutionary educators. Historically, African American women have used academic education and "commonsense" experiences to combat social injustice. The activism of BPP women who became the OCS teaching staff and administrators during the 1970s and early 1980s was no less significant than that of women who organized and educated black and poor communities in the nineteenth and early to mid-twentieth centuries. Sojourner Truth, Mary McLeod Bethune, Septima Clark, Ella Baker, and particularly the outspoken and defiant Harriet Tubman and Fannie Lou Hamer were activists and leaders who risked their lives as educators during pivotal historical periods in the early and modern African American freedom struggle. In their resistance to racism and sexism, they embodied a stance of dignity and courage that defeated white and male supremacist attempts to humiliate them and those they served. These powerful nineteenth- and twentieth-century women saw the needs of their communities and stepped forward to initiate change.[4]

In line with this great tradition of resistance, the OCS administrators saw the dire need for *quality* education and stepped forward to change educational conditions for youth of color. Each administrator was a BPP member at the time she became a school leader, organizing and educating communities, feeding and teaching children in before- and after-school programs, selling BPP newspapers, administering health care, organizing for prisoners' rights, and engaging in voter registration and in local political campaigns. OCS women organized their communities by working with fellow BPP members, actively engaged in coalition politics. In terms of their resistance and the organizing tradition, the educational activism of the women staff of the OCS during the 1970s was revolutionary.

OCS administrators were able to apply lessons from their experience as BPP members to their teaching and community outreach. On a national level, within the BPP chapters, men and women confronted the violence of racism and sexism in their activism and personal lives. Women throughout the BPP were called upon to coordinate or support community programs because of their skill and inclination, not their femaleness. Many women played dual roles, coordinating a community program and participating in behind-the-scenes Party fund-raising and activities.

Visible Invisibility

BPP and Black Power scholarship has become increasingly popular since the late 1990s, yet the primary emphasis has remained on the charismatic male leadership and analyses of BPP ideological development. Most often these studies focus on Huey Newton, Bobby Seale, and Eldridge Cleaver and delve into meanings of revolutionary action, violence, and Black Power.[5] By marginalizing the voices and experiences of women in the BPP, the recent literature also marginalizes the work women did within the BPP's more than forty community survival programs, which were a major draw for many BPP women who embraced the Party's call to "serve the people" in the very basic sense.

Heretofore, male scholars who either have not included rank-and-file, nonleader BPP women, or have not explored the subtleties of BPP women's experiences, have written most BPP and Black liberation movement scholarship. While this literature provides a rich body of scholarship on which to build, minimization of women's roles and experiences relegates BPP women, by default, to a separate category. That approach effectively separates BPP women's femaleness from their lives as revolutionaries. Interestingly, it is females, former Party members and non-Party members alike, who have written most literature on female BPP members, with Tracye Matthews and Angela LeBlanc-Ernest publishing the earliest scholarly analyses highlighting the ways women challenged narrow-minded definitions of their roles in a revolutionary organization. Recently, Robin Spencer has expanded BPP scholarship with her attention to women's work and leadership in the Party.[6] In that spirit, this essay is a unique collaboration between the lived experience of Huggins, a former BPP member, and LeBlanc-Ernest, a non-Party member and researcher, to shift BPP women to the center of the conversation about the BPP and black revolutionary activism. Through this, we hope to expand and aid in refining and redefining the legacy of the BPP.

Similarly, scholarship on the community programs, a basis of BPP activism especially after 1970, is slowly emerging. "Serving the people" was the Party's goal, and the programs were developed to meet the people's needs. Former Party members' autobiographies and articles in *The Black Panther (TBP)* emphasize the extensive number and significance of the programs, while academic scholarship on the programs, in particular the OCS, has emerged only sporadically within the past ten years. A select few authors have noted women's central roles. JoNina Abron, a former BPP member, LeBlanc-Ernest, and Charles Jones and Jonathan Gayles have written most directly about the programs and the school. Daniel Perlstein has examined the OCS in a broader context as a comparative analysis with the southern freedom schools. Researchers' recent and increasing focus on recovering details about local BPP chapters, most of which closed after 1972 when the national headquarters centralized operations to Oakland, offers a unique opportunity to explore survival program details and move toward understanding the BPP and women's central roles.[7]

Primary sources during the BPP's sixteen-year history revealed the roles BPP women assumed in the Party in ways that secondary literature has only begun to capture. Party newspaper coverage included both articles authored by women and information about BPP women's experiences. Bobby Seale's *Seize the Time* was the earliest work that publicly noted that women represented a majority of the Party by 1968. As BPP women's numbers increased and they became equal targets of law enforcement, underground press newspaper articles, of which *TBP* was a part, reveal that the women challenged sexist attitudes both within and outside the BPP. By 1970 Party cofounder Huey Newton had written and published "The Women's Liberation and Gay Liberation Movements," an article supporting the women's and gay liberation movements, stating that sexism and homophobia have no place in the human rights struggle. Only one year later, *Look for Me in the Whirlwind: The Collective Autobiography of the New York 21*, provided Afeni Shakur and Joan Bird the opportunity to share their experiences as BPP women who were moved quickly into leadership positions within the community programs.[8] At a time in the earliest years when an inordinate number of BPP men were routinely imprisoned and killed by law enforcement, women who were not incarcerated continued the Party's community organizing efforts, especially regarding education. The BPP leadership, whose political stance challenged the "power structure," encouraged women to take on significant roles in its leadership body and in its programs. BPP women learned communication, administrative, and grassroots organizing skills from hands-on engagement with the community's needs and the systemic oppressive forces.

A historical analysis of the OCS and women's central involvement reveals how the view of community and coalition building through the lenses of gender, race, and class converged to create and sustain an alternative educational institution in the midst of the nationwide urban educational crisis. Therefore, centering the OCS female administrators and their supporters provides a case study in community-building dynamics and reframes the concept of the movement for black political, social, and economic power as not a solely violent or male historical movement.

Exploring these intersections is crucial given that black women have long been positioned at the unique intersection of race, class, and gender. Throughout American history, from slavery forward, many black women have chosen to focus on the uplift of their race. In the face of the violence of institutional racism, this decision in itself was a revolutionary, feminist action. Though women experienced and battled the force of sexism as it appeared in Party work and in intimate relationships, many BPP members, both women and men, were adamant about deconstructing the race, class, and gender socialization of the pre-1960s.

Although BPP women's work was visible within their organization and in the communities they organized between 1967 and 1981, for several reasons BPP women's voices have been relatively silent in published literature. Foremost, with the exception of their BPP newspaper contributions, BPP women did not have time to reflect and write while they were active in the Party. Most Party members worked twenty hours per day, seven days per week. Women's activism was central to Party success. Indeed, women's work in the Party was not separate work. It was seamlessly intertwined with the Party's leadership and activities. Due to the daily trauma women in the BPP experienced from external oppressive forces such as harassment from local law enforcement, shootings, assassinations, arrests, and imprisonment, all of which often caused women to be separated from their children, many privately processed the complexities of being women and mothers, black critical thinkers, and revolutionary activists. It was not until a full decade after the BPP ended and the Oakland Community School was closed that former Party chairman Elaine Brown published her autobiography, noting the central role of women in the organization both as rank and file and as leaders. The time to process and reflect was crucial.[9]

Recovering BPP women's history and lived experience invariably requires consideration of their seeming silence. For instance, Party women, while challenging issues of gender within the organization, did not believe it was necessary to hold this discussion in the public arena. Instead, women worked to dismantle gender inequity from within BPP ranks. Therefore, journalists, scholars, and others interested in the Party were left with a slim body of primary sources, which only underscored the societal tendency to focus on male leadership models, politics, and ideology.

On their own behalf, several former BPP women have written first-person narratives that reveal the intricacies of their experiences. New York BPP member Assata Shakur was the first, publishing while in Cuban exile. Elaine Brown's book *A Taste of Power* soon followed. Charles Jones's groundbreaking anthology, *The Black Panther Party Reconsidered*, contains articles by Regina Jennings and JoNina Abron that focus attention on personal concerns of BPP women and the Party's community programs. Additionally, Abron, Madalynn Rucker, and Kathleen Cleaver each has reflected on her life as a BPP member committed to community and to combating economic and social injustices in the United States and abroad.[10]

Black Power often has been associated with reclaiming black male masculinity in a society that denigrated African Americans. Interestingly, the BPP, with its media-defined male public image, was an institution that in reality forwarded the principle of valuing women in a revolutionary organization. Many male members engaged in the same activities as female members: cooking, caring for children, selling newspapers, and supporting the Party's community survival programs. While there was only one in 1967, by 1977 six women were added to the BPP central committee. Many more were acknowledged as leaders within the Party ranks and the OCS, including Lorene Banks, Asali Dixon, Carol Granison, Veronica Hagopian, Haven Henderson, Donna Howell, Lula Hudson, Adrienne Humphrey, Pamela Ward, Kaye Washington, Jody Weaver, and Tommye Williams. At a time when the women's rights and feminist movements as well as women in organizations such as the Student Nonviolent Coordinating Committee (SNCC) and the Communist Party, USA, were confronting the role women would play in their organizations, women in the Black Panther Party defined and affirmed their roles as frontline soldiers in the revolutionary struggle.

This essay focuses on centering BPP women's experiences in order to reflect the reality that women were an anchoring power within the BPP, whose presence in the membership and the constancy of their work in the community are a testament to revolutionary action. In a society within which African American women daily struggled to speak and be heard, the revolutionary BPP women found a voice and raised it, spoke and were heard.

The Intercommunal Youth Institute (1970–1973)

The OCS emerged out of several earlier BPP educational programs. Members spoke at schools and organized tutorials to combat truancy. BPP activists built political and social momentum by implementing the national Free Breakfast for Schoolchildren programs and Liberation School programs. Most significant was the decision by Party chief of staff David Hilliard and chairman Bobby Seale to withdraw their and other Party members' children from public schools. Hilliard notes that the FBI and teachers harassed the children because of the parents' BPP membership. The outcome was twofold: to provide a safe place for BPP members' children during a time when BPP offices and homes were subject to raids, shoot-outs, firebombings, and FBI COINTELPRO surveillance, and to serve as an informal home-based community school.[11]

In 1970, the BPP's two-house "home school," similar to southern black church schools, soon evolved into a more structured format—the Intercommunal Youth Institute. Brenda Bay, a BPP member from New York with an academic background in education, served as the IYI's director from 1971 to 1973. Unlike a traditional public school, the IYI had minimal enrollment, teaching staff, and BPP-supported funding. The enrollment increased from twenty-eight students in 1971 to fifty by the 1973–1974 school year. The twenty-two new students primarily were children of BPP members who had moved to Oakland. As such, some IYI students and instructors lived together twenty-four hours per day to provide the children with the care they needed while their parents organized and maintained BPP community programs. The children ranged in age from 2½ to 12, and there were no traditional grade levels, only group levels based on their academic performance. The ratio of instructional staff to students was 1:10, which provided each child with individualized attention, a feature often absent from public schools.[12]

In line with the Party's political principles, the IYI's initial nontraditional curriculum incorporated community work. The IYI was distinguished by the fact that the students were taught to be politically aware.

The four- to twelve-year-olds learned and practiced basic skills, such as math, science, and English. As an example, the students learned writing skills by writing poetry and letters to incarcerated BPP members, by attending trials of BPP members and other political prisoners, by distributing food at BPP-sponsored food giveaways, and by selling BPP newspapers. Over this three-year period, the public expression of the institute's purpose evolved from "learning about their slave past and 'their true role in the present-day society'" (1971), to "educate to liberate" (1972), and, finally, to "the youth are our future" (1973). By 1973, the school moved to a larger location to accommodate its growing student population and to have a more visible presence in the Oakland community. Bay expressed the IYI's ultimate mission as trying to "expose the children to a great deal of information and direct experience with the world so they can receive a more realistic view of the world."[13]

Also, unlike traditional public schools, the IYI's operational expenses were covered by a combination of BPP fund-raising efforts and community support. BPP members all worked to raise money to fund and sustain the community programs. Despite its small size and dependence on those nominal funds and volunteerism, from December 1971 on, the IYI offered free tutoring and dance and music classes to the public.[14]

BPP leadership's involvement in the 1972 and 1973 municipal elections in Oakland, California, mobilized public support and financial resources for the entire BPP and marked a major shift in the IYI's abilities to serve the broader community. No longer dependent solely on paltry sums that BPP members could raise on their own, the IYI received exposure through the electoral campaigns of BPP cofounder Bobby Seale and minister of information Elaine Brown. Seale's campaign for Oakland mayor and Brown's for city councilwoman were launched with the goal of "seizing control of Oakland and creating a base of revolution in the United States, which goal was served by the Party's electoral efforts." Both Seale and Brown often spoke at local student rallies and conferences prior to the campaign. Although neither Seale nor Brown won the positions they sought, education was a crucial platform cornerstone, and their campaigns garnered support from a cross section of the community: churches, local businessmen, politicians, the American Federation of Teacher's Union, and private donors.[15]

Brown, a Philadelphia native and former BPP Southern California chapter member, used her prolific writing and speaking skills to continue the BPP tradition of creating and supporting institutions to address children's educational, health care, cultural, and economic needs.

Simultaneously, she raised awareness of important issues and pressed for broader mobilization. Community support helped the IYI move into a larger building both to accommodate an increasing number of new students and to be a visible presence in the East Oakland community, one of the poorest areas of the city. The variety of initial funding sources for the new building included "Daniel J. Bernstein Foundation, Pacific Change, The Youth Project, The Third World Fund, the Genesis Church and Ecumenical Center and private contributors"[16] The IYI became the programmatic springboard for what evolved into the Oakland Community School.

The Oakland Community School

The Oakland Community School blossomed because of community outreach and the new location's visibility. While the IYI had grown in outreach by 1973, during 1974, the administrators changed the school's name to the Oakland Community School. The OCS grew in visibility and popularity between 1974 and 1979 not only because of unique inroads with the local community but also because of its innovative approach to education. Youth continued to be taught *how* to think and not what to think. The core of student instruction consisted of math, science, language arts (Spanish and English), history, art, physical education, choir, and environmental studies. The student population ranged between 50 and 150 from 1974 to 1979, yet each continued to receive an education tailored to his or her specific needs and learning styles.[17]

Community support for OCS was wide-ranging. The former IYI had a limited outreach: primarily parents who lived nearby, the BPP newspaper readership, and local political organizations. In contrast, the OCS, as a result of Brown's campaign and the growth of community awareness of the school's effective teaching model, was supported by the school districts of Oakland, Berkeley, and San Francisco. Over the school's lifetime, supporters included politicians, local, national, and international educators who visited, teachers who did their internships there, and interested individuals not affiliated with a particular organization.

The school was appealing also because it was free. Because the administrators knew poor families could not afford to pay for the school's services, the OCS was tuition-free and funded by private donations, grants from local foundations, city and county resources, and the California State Department of Education. All BPP cadres, including the general membership, the military wing, party leadership and school leadership, raised significant financial support for the school. Parents donated their time and, where possible, personal money. The school's parent-teacher organization planned house parties and other social events, including two radio-thons and numerous community dances and concerts. In addition, community supporters in professional positions often informed the school's administrators or staff about potential funding sources. In turn, the Educational Opportunities Corporation (EOC), the school's nonprofit sponsor, wrote grants and applied for funds.[18] These actions were essential for the school to remain tuition-free and operational.

OCS administrators had varying backgrounds; but their commitment to education, community, and children united them. Born in Washington, D.C., Ericka Huggins became OCS director beginning in 1973. After majoring in education at Lincoln University in Pennsylvania, Huggins left in her junior year to find the BPP. She and John Huggins joined the Party's Southern California chapter. A community survival program organizer and mother when John Huggins was murdered at UCLA on January 17, 1969, she moved to New Haven, Connecticut, to be with John's family. Huggins stayed to start a BPP chapter in New Haven, was arrested in 1969, and was charged and tried with Bobby Seale for alleged conspiracy to commit the murder of fellow BPP member Alex Rackley. In 1971, after the declared mistrial in New Haven, Huggins, with her 2½-year-old daughter, moved to Oakland to resume community organizing. She sold newspapers, taught, spoke at rallies, and edited *TBP*; two years later, the central committee appointed Huggins OCS director.[19]

At the helm of OCS with Ericka Huggins was Donna Howell. Howell joined the BPP Massachusetts chapter in August 1969 and served on the Boston chapter's central committee. Primarily, Howell was lead organizer of a BPP free health clinic. After transferring to the Oakland chapter in January 1972, Howell served briefly in the Bay Area BPP's free health clinic, the child development program for preschoolers, and the IYI, under Bay's leadership. Howell's tireless efforts demonstrated her dedication to children and her considerable organizational abilities.[20]

With this dedicated leadership, the BPP established the Oakland Community School as a model that could be transferred easily to community control and replicated in cities nationwide. The ultimate goal of Elaine Brown, Huggins, Howell, and others was to mentor community teachers and have them assume the school's operations after a number of years. They had the freedom to develop and sustain this approach because the school staff was integral to and yet, because of the children, protected from the everyday BPP operations.

The children who were taught at the OCS came from a variety of geographic locations and economic classes. While most children lived with their parents in poverty conditions, several families were middle-class. Several students were from other states because their parent(s), who were BPP members, transferred from other national offices to the national headquarters. One example was the Armour family, whose children traveled ahead because the school year began before the parents could leave the BPP Southern California chapter. The children's mother and father, Norma and Al, were part of the LA chapter's strength. Norma was a leading member and, later, a member of the BPP central committee.[21] This variety of student backgrounds made the OCS a welcoming, multifaceted institution.

Students were admitted on a first-come, first-served basis. A student's ethnicity, economic class, learning style, or physical ability was never a criterion for entrance or retention. Demographically, OCS students were approximately 90 percent African American. However, Mexican American, Asian American, biracial, and European-American students were also enrolled. Students were divided into seven groups, each designed for students working on that level, each according to their ability, each according to their need. The student population was roughly 55 percent female and 45 percent male.

The staff was as diverse as the student body. OCS staff was primarily African American, although teachers also were Latina, Asian American, and white, and most were between the ages of twenty-two and thirty-five years. Some were newly trained public school teachers, others seasoned educators hoping to be reinspired. Although men were not represented in the OCS administration, their leadership roles as head teachers, food service managers, and senior and teen program staff were apparent in the OCS. It was not uncommon to see a male teacher brushing a child's hair or soothing tears. As well, it was common to see female staff making decisions that impacted facility use, programmatic details, and finances. No duty was beyond any person: administrator, BPP and community teaching staff, party member, or volunteer. Whoever had the skill or ability to do it, did.

The administrators paid particular attention to programmatic details. Elaine Brown, EOC board director, created a committee that she encouraged to write a curriculum. The committee included Huggins, Howell, and

Carol Granison, the OCS curriculum director. Later Dr. William Moore, a local educator, also provided input. The curriculum was based in the dialectical teaching method. The BPP had adopted the philosophy of dialectical materialism, which emphasized and encouraged critical thinking skills and local and global awareness. The students learned to ask questions that fostered discussion and ideas. They were taught that no one person holds the "right" answer. They were encouraged to create solutions and implement those solutions together.[22]

Although the curriculum had many innovative components, most important was the manner in which it was implemented. Individual instructors were encouraged to tailor the culturally relevant curriculum to meet the specific learning styles of each student and the instructors' own teaching style. The curriculum was culturally relevant and fostered critical thinking skills. The curriculum's multilevel flexibility was essential for student success. Granison, a BPP member who became both an instructor and a curriculum developer, after spending a year cooking meals for the children in the kitchen, recalled working with a group of students with reading difficulties. Curriculum and community combined to solve the problem when a special education consultant visited the school specifically to make an offer to help assess any student with reading and/or cognitive difficulties. These children were tested and determined to have different learning styles. Consequently, the plan for their individual learning was adjusted, as was the instructor's teaching strategy.[23]

The OCS nurtured its many students by providing formal and informal outlets for their physical, emotional, social, creative, abstract, and spiritual needs. Physical education, in the form of martial arts and calisthenics, was taught to help students make the link between mind and body. The administrators established an open-door policy for children who needed to talk privately. They encouraged children to ask as many questions as they needed to grasp a concept. The school's remarkable Youth Committee was the formal venue for students to critique faculty, school, and self in an attempt to foster independence, as was the student-generated newsletter. OCS students tutored their peers, hence implementing the essence of the school's "Each One Teach One" philosophy. Students wrote and performed their own plays about socioeconomic and political realities that were both humorous and sobering. In 1979 the school even added a meditation room. Every day after lunch the entire staff and students sat quietly for a few minutes to "honor their own innate greatness."

These and other activities demonstrated the many ways in which children were taught to care for themselves and one another at the school.

Equally important to staff were each child's physical health, cleanliness, and appearance. Donna Howell coordinated the OCS youth's general health care and appearance, overseeing clothing, grooming, nutrition, and doctor visits. This responsibility extended to OCS children living in the children's dormitory. Caretaking was the shared responsibility of male and female members because the administrators had designed the school to function within a collective framework, similar to the BPP. "Weeknights, BPP members who worked in the school served as parents to the BPP children who lived in dormitories," recalled Howell. "Dormitory life was an integral part of how BPP children and staff lived together as a family. The special interconnectedness and sharing that occurred in the BPP extended family life was an integral part of the trademark atmosphere of love, support, and learning that made OCS so special."[24]

The goal to make the OCS a replicable model led Huggins, Howell, Newton, and Brown to assess staff and volunteer choices carefully, according to the children's needs. Huggins and Howell were responsible for assessing employment qualifications through observation and interviews. Although he was not an official administrator, Huey Newton suggested several staff members based on their caring for children, rapport with children and families, love of humanity, and ability to recognize a need and meet it quickly, as well as their educational background. College education was not a requirement for teaching at OCS, although several teachers came to the school with undergraduate or advanced degrees. Instead, the emphasis was on the quality of education the combination of staff could achieve. Caring for children and maintaining the school's daily program required a specific kind of educator. Patience and dedication, among other qualities, were essential due to the long hours and direct contact with small children.[25]

Consequently, the Oakland Community School's reputation attracted educators interested in educating the whole child. The educators represented a mixture of individuals: Black Panther Party members, former Oakland Unified School District teachers, and teachers from other cities, including Berkeley, Richmond, and San Francisco, California, as well as Detroit and Philadelphia. Other volunteers included students from surrounding colleges and universities such as the University of California, Berkeley, San Francisco State University, and Laney College. The instructors and staff were attracted to the OCS because they enjoyed the environment the school fostered and because they knew that OCS was achieving academic, social, and individual results with its students.[26]

Their mentors and friends often referred teachers to the school. Rodney Gillead was one such instructor. A New York native, Gillead was referred to the OCS by the late Dr. Asa Hilliard, then dean of education at San Francisco State University and program consultant to the OCS. Dr. Hilliard encouraged Gillead to apply to teach at the OCS because of the program's innovative approach to elementary education. Gillead, who taught K–3 children, became a pillar of the OCS staff. He recently stated that his OCS experience laid the foundation for his current teaching career. Gillead was so committed to the OCS vision that he drove two families of children roundtrip between San Francisco and Oakland daily.[27]

OCS administrators and staff knew that flexibility was the key to effective functioning, and they demonstrated a range of expertise in aesthetics, programmatic efficiency, and financial management. Individual women, like Norma Armour, Adrienne Humphrey, and Phyllis Jackson, were meticulous about the OCS financial management. Building cleanliness and organization and something as practical as the quality of front-office reception were crucial to the school's image. Therefore, Lorene Banks, the receptionist and school secretary, was someone who represented the community; children and families trusted her. Banks, whose four children attended the school, often kept extra clothes and other items in her office in case children needed them. One former student even recalled that Banks kept extra bus transfers in her desk.[28]

As educator activists, OCS administrators also modeled justice in the broader community. Director Ericka Huggins's appointment in 1976 as the first black person and woman to serve on the Alameda County Board of Education reflected another way OCS administrators affected preexisting institutions. This board was responsible for Alameda County's special schools (for incarcerated youth) and school programs for students with special needs. Huggins saw this position as an opportunity to "help the board become more responsive to human concerns, and more public in its actions." In particular, the OCS director wanted to infuse a sense of humanity into the board's actions, helping the board to adjust its practices to be more responsive to the ongoing special needs of students. During her tenure on the board, she particularly became interested in improving the living conditions and education for youth in juvenile detention centers.[29]

By fall 1977, the Oakland school district was in worse condition than during the 1971–1972 academic year. The OUSD, which had increased from 60 percent to 80 percent African American and many other ethnicities, held the lowest scores locally, statewide, and nationally at the elementary grade levels. The second-grade reading percentile was 19, and sixth graders were scoring at the 12th percentile in reading and the 16th percentile in math. Such statistics revealed depressing educational options for Oakland youth. To complicate matters, within three months of Oakland Community School receiving its state commendation, teachers in the OUSD went on an eight-day strike for higher pay. The strike resulted in eight days of missed instruction for the district's 52,000 students, who were already doing poorly. [30]

Unlike California public schools, OCS did not rely on state standardized testing as a tool for structuring and implementing its curriculum and for grade placement. Rather, standardized testing played a very small part in OCS instruction; students were not placed in traditional grades according to age but assigned to levels with various age ranges. Students did not receive letter grades. Instead, their families received carefully written academic and social evaluations, encouraging the child's effort and highlighting areas of needed improvement. In its later years, the OCS had a twofold purpose for administering the California Test of Basic Skills (CTBS). While the OCS did use some information from CTBS results, the students were tested to satisfy state requirements to receive particular state funding, and to emotionally and academically prepare students for public school testing after OCS graduation. In fact, over time the OCS developed its own assessment tool. [31]

Nevertheless, CTBS test results can be used to make preliminary analyses of OCS and its students. Although the students were not placed in traditional grades, their ages are listed with their test results for November 1977. For example, in level A (the age equivalent of preschool), student ages ranged from 4.8 years to 5.5 years. As testament to the fact that students were placed in levels according to ability, there was one eight-year-old in level A. Also, in level A, a five-year-old student tested in the 95th prereading percentile, and one scored in both the 33rd prereading percentile and the 18th total math percentile. The OCS was supporting preschool students who were achieving at high levels. This group of sixteen students tested on average at the 70th percentile for reading and the 71st percentile for math. Similarly, thirteen level 2 students (aged 8.8 years to 11.5 years—equivalent to fifth and sixth grades) ranged from the 5th to

82nd percentile in total reading and from the 8th to 93rd percentile in total math. On average, level 2 students scored 32.9 percentage points above their OUSD peers in reading and 28 percentage points higher in math. Although the OCS staff did not rely on these scores as determinants of intelligence or "smartness," the statistics reveal, in numerical terms, a level of success that the OCS staff was quietly achieving.[32]

The OCS attracted the attention of other educators and community representatives who saw it as an effective educational program for all children regardless of ability, ethnicity, or geographic location. Indeed, the school educated the students so effectively that a waiting list became standard. Parents often wait-listed their unborn children or siblings of students already enrolled. The Oakland and Berkeley Unified School Districts recommended OCS and collaborated with school staff to serve families whose educational needs could not be met by the districts. In August 1977 the California State Department of Education gave its approval to the school as a *model* elementary school, one of the OCS administrators' goals. When William Whiteneck, deputy superintendent of the California State Department of Education, visited, he gave official approval to the school and acknowledged its outstanding contribution to the Oakland and Bay Area communities. This award led to increased public exposure. The OCS was so successful that, by late summer 1977, it formally requested a meeting with OUSD's superintendent, Ruth Love, to explore ways the school and the district's alternative school umbrella could work more closely together. In addition, the possibility of funding the OCS was discussed, although ultimately this request was not approved. This was another instance of OCS administration pursuing an opportunity to infuse its education model into the larger public school structure, a model designed to incorporate the community in meeting the individual needs of each child.[33]

While the California Department of Education finally acknowledged the effectiveness of the OCS, parents had always appreciated the school's impact on their children. Indeed, parent participation was a critical component of the school's success. The active parent-teacher association provided a direct link between the OCS and the community. The Parent Advisory Board organized dances and other fund-raisers and also advertised student-sponsored events to community members. Parents were required to participate in their child's schoolwork as well as attend parent meetings and were able to meet with teachers without an appointment. Furthermore, parents were active members of the elected School Advisory

Committee, which included interested community members and OCS instructors. The instructors acted as advisers, particularly "in the areas of curriculum development, classroom activities, field trips and school events." Parents were incorporated into all aspects of school structure and were consistently the best volunteers.[34]

Some children who attended the Oakland Community School found sanctuary from the stressors of home and community life. A poignant example of the intersection of this sanctuary and the role female administrators played involves two siblings who both attended OCS. One day Huggins, by now a mother of two, returned to her office to find the two children huddled beneath her office desk. Unknown to OCS staff, their mother had abused the children regularly. Huggins comforted them, then summoned the mother to a meeting at the school. Acting in the capacity of a mother, revolutionary educator, counselor, social worker, and youth activist, Huggins counseled the mother, strongly encouraging her to stop abusing the children and seek help. The mother, who admitted she had never been taught how to raise children with compassion for them or herself, did receive help. The mother received counseling to resolve her own anger about being abused as a child. Incidents like this sparked Huggins's realization of the community's need for peer-facilitated discussion groups, which the school initiated.

Another example that reflects the combined roles of the administrators and teachers was their support of OCS youth in valuing themselves and others. As women, the OCS administrators and teaching staff confronted the impact of American beauty standards on girls and boys. On one occasion, an OCS student walked into Huggins's office to ask whether others considered her beautiful. She asked Huggins if she could become beautiful if she were to bleach her head and body hair blonde. Huggins responded by encouraging the student to adopt a personal and global perspective of beauty. She asked the preteen young woman, "Is there beauty in African hair, skin, or eyes?" The student had neither considered her African ancestral heritage to be beautiful nor been given permission to question American beauty standards. This was a life-affirming lesson for both Huggins and the young woman, one that reflected the school motto, "The World Is Our Classroom." The impact of women in leadership was so strong that decades later, former female and male students recall these women as central in educating and inspiring them. A former OCS student stated it directly: "It was the women of the Oakland Community School—like Donna, Jeannette [Keyes] and Carol—who inspired me to be the woman I am today."[35]

Oakland Community Learning Center

In addition to their work in the school and the BPP, women played many roles in the community. The Oakland Community School had become a landmark community institution by 1974. Yet a school history is incomplete without a discussion of its direct link to the nonprofit Oakland Community Learning Center (OCLC). The center was an umbrella that covered a host of BPP-generated community programs. As the surrounding community's needs were uncovered, BPP leadership, supported by Huggins and Howell, developed programs and used the school's physical space to host them. Such proximity allowed OCS students to reinforce their connections to the community by participating in the programs after school. It was also a way for the BPP women to infuse their revolutionary activism into the academic education.

Joan Kelley, originally from the BPP Southern California chapter, directed the OCLC. This community center sponsored numerous programs: adult education, a teen program, a free film series, self-defense classes, community legal aid, and a community forum for political discussion and action, among others. Seniors Against a Fearful Environment (S.A.F.E.), a BPP-created program that moved into the OCLC, is a powerful example of a community need that linked OCS youth with community elders. Many non-Party OCS children were raised by their grandmothers. Often these elder caretakers needed transportation, advocacy, and protection as they traveled to and from banks, medical appointments, and shopping areas. Although the BPP created S.A.F.E. in 1972, the OCLC became the space to house it. Similarly, the OCLC offered teen programs, dances, and employment opportunities for teen and young adult siblings (and their friends) who longed for programs to broaden their horizons and life options beyond drugs, prostitution, and boredom. Several OCLC-based programs advocated for public housing support and cash assistance for single parents. The BPP's George Jackson People's Health Clinic provided health, dental, and emotional care.[36]

School staff and administrators also worked in coalition with broader community organizations. In 1979 Pastor J. Alfred Smith, of Allen Temple Baptist Church, held a press conference announcing data that showed the city of Oakland had one of the highest infant mortality rates in the world. The African American and Chicano communities experienced 26.3 deaths per 1,000 births. In response, OCS and OCLC leadership summoned community organizations, including the Third World Women's Alliance, to cofound the Coalition to Fight Infant Mortality, an organization composed of forty-four community groups.[37]

The model of community connection envisioned by the OCS administrators became so successful that organizations such as the National Association for Alternative Schools invited Huggins to join its ranks, which included progressive educators such as Jonathan Kozol and Herbert Kohl. ReBop, the Boston, Massachusetts, children's television show, featured the Oakland Community School. Kellita Smith, an eight-year-old OCS student, narrated the OCS segment. She was filmed both with her family and at school. She conducted a historic and remarkable interview with Huey Newton. Many social justice organizations in the United States and globally sent representatives who visited and showed interest in the OCS programs and its curriculum, including a Belgian television station and the Puerto Rican Socialist Party. Additionally, internationally known visitors and supporters included civil rights activists Rosa Parks and Cesar Chavez, poet Maya Angelou, and author James Baldwin, each of whom admired the OCS as a revolutionary model for education.[38] Through these events and activities the school's children became aware of their place in local, national, and international youth communities.[39]

Despite their many successes, the existence of OCS and OCLC faced external and internal challenges. Local and national law enforcement challenged the school's activities, while the FBI's counterintelligence program remained interested in interrupting the school and its community service component by utilizing print and electronic media to discredit OCS. In 1978, as a result of political and governmental pressures on the Party leadership outside the Oakland Community School and the OCLC, the OCS began to suffer from challenges within, due to personal problems and the Party's dwindling membership and funds.[40] In the midst of these pressures, staff remained dedicated to the students and the community until the OCS (and the OCLC) officially closed in 1982.

Passing It On

The OCS's dialectical training was so successful that the students' adjustment to the public schools in communities of color was often a difficult one. Both Newton and Huggins were hopeful that OCS graduates would leave the elementary-level institution prepared to enter the public school system and "do well because we've equipped them." Newton continued, "They will be the political organizers of the future. They [will] make students in the other schools aware." Similarly, in 1974, when noted educator and author Herbert Kohl asked Huggins whether she worried about the children's transition to public school, her main concern was whether the four- to eight-year-olds who had not been exposed to public school would be ready to face future challenges. Huggins was concerned they would encounter teachers unwilling to answer their "why" questions.[41] At such an early stage in the school's development, it was clear to administrators and others that the OCS was training children to have a different worldview.

One such student was Erica Watkins, who attended OCS during the public school equivalent of grades four through six. After attending OCS she enrolled in both Albany Middle and High Schools, small Bay Area schools in a school district known for lower class size and attentive staff. Her OCS education had taught her how critical her voice was in effecting change. Therefore, she questioned her history teacher about using an outdated text with two simplistic chapters on African Americans and Native Americans. When confronted by the principal, Watkins chose suspension instead of compromise. Ultimately, the teacher apologized and asked Watkins to coordinate the school's first Black History celebration, during which she used poetry, songs, and stories learned at the OCS.[42] Erica had taken revolutionary action for her own and her peers' education.

In spring 2008, Zachary Killoran, another former OCS student, recalled the difficulty of his academic and personal transition from OCS to public school. He transferred to an OUSD school during spring 1981 as a fifth grader. Although he learned calculus and algebra at OCS, in OUSD he was in classes with students learning addition and subtraction and with students "who could barely spell." One of the main things Killoran learned to do in public school was use profanity and fight. Killoran, of bicultural heritage, African American and Irish, recalled that at OCS he was not singled out because of his ethnic background. In contrast, this was the basis of some of his fights in public school. Nevertheless, Killoran always remembers the deeper lessons from OCS that taught him to see himself as part of a broader community, caring for others, what he calls "communal thinking." He further explains: "I don't just take care of me, I take care of my community; anybody who happens to be around me."[43] The community-based OCS had accomplished its larger goal: to educate youth to be critical thinkers who, in their own way, would help to transform their world.

NOTES

1. Ken Kelley, "Black Panther, White Lies," *California*, August 1990, 122. Kelley refers to Taylor as Lumumba and, later, as Keith. We determined Taylor's last name by matching dates of Kelley's article with published names of students in issues of *The Black Panther Community News Service (TBP)*. Taylor was eleven years old in 1977. "OCS September 1977 Enrollment (Non-Collective) 6–12 years, page 2," box 5, OCS Enrollment, Dr. Huey P. Newton Foundation Inc. Collection, M864, Department of Special Collections, Stanford University Libraries, Stanford, CA. Throughout the endnotes the authors refer to the original box numbers and folder titles of the Dr. Huey P. Newton Foundation Records (NFR).

2. "We want an education for our people that exposes the true nature of this decadent American society. We want education that teaches us our true history and our role in the present-day society. We believe in an educational system that will give to our people a knowledge of self. If a man does not have knowledge of himself and his position in society and the world, then he has little chance to relate to anything else."

3. "We Want Education for Our People," *TBP* 8/5/72:C; "Add Racism to the Three 'R's," *TBP* 10/28/72:14; "Part XVI Classroom Crisis: We Need Teachers, Not Executives," *TBP* 11/9/72:B; "Vote for the People's Plan," *TBP* 4/14/73:A-B.

4. Nell Irvin Painter, *Sojourner Truth: A Life, a Symbol* (New York: Norton, 1997); Catherine Clinton, *Harriet Tubman: The Road to Freedom* (New York: Back Bay Books, 2002); Audrey Thomas McCluskey and Elaine M. Smith, *Mary McLeod Bethune Building a Better World, Essays and Selected Documents* (Bloomington: Indiana University Press, 2002); Barbara Ransby, *Ella Baker and the Black Freedom Movement: A Radical Democratic Vision* (Chapel Hill: University of North Carolina Press, 2003); Chana Kai Lee, *For Freedom's Sake: The Life of Fannie Lou Hamer* (Urbana: University of Illinois Press, 1999).

5. See numerous articles in Charles Jones, ed., *The Black Panther Party Reconsidered* (Baltimore: Black Classic Press, 1998). Also, see such works as Judson L. Jeffries, *Huey P. Newton: The Radical Theorist* (Jackson: University Press of Mississippi, 2002); Jeffrey O. G. Ogbar, *Black Power: Radical Politics and African American Identity* (Baltimore: Johns Hopkins University Press, 2004); Judson L. Jeffries, ed., *Black Power in the Belly of the Beast* (Chicago: University of Illinois Press, 2006); Curtis J. Austin, *Up against the Wall: Violence in the Making and Unmaking of the Black Panther Party* (Fayetteville: University of Arkansas Press, 2006).

6. See Tracye Matthews, "No One Ever Asks What a Man's Role in the Revolution Is: Gender and the Politics of the Black Panther Party," and Angela D. LeBlanc-Ernest, "'The Most Qualified Person to Handle the Job': Black Panther Party Women, 1966–1982," both in Jones, *Black Panther Party Reconsidered*; Robyn Ceanne Spencer, "Engendering the Black Freedom Struggle: Revolutionary Black Womanhood and the Black Panther Party in the Bay Area, California," *Journal of Women's History* 20 (2008): 90–113.

7. Elaine Brown, *A Taste of Power: A Black Woman's Story* (New York: Pantheon, 1992); David Hilliard with Lewis Cole, *This Side of Glory: The Autobiography of David Hilliard and the Story of the Black Panther Party* (Chicago: Lawrence Hill Books, 2001); Flores Alexander Forbes, *Will You Die with Me? My Life and the Black Panther Party* (New York: Atria Books, 2006); JoNina Abron "'Serving the People': The Survival Programs of the Black Panther Party," in Jones, *Black Panther Party Reconsidered*; see gender section in Jones: Regina Jennings, "Why I Joined the Party: An Africana Womanist Reflection"; Matthews, "No One Ever Asks What a Man's Role in the Revolution Is"; LeBlanc-Ernest, "'The Most Qualified Person to Handle the Job"; Jane Rhodes, "Black Radicalism in 1960s California: Women in the Black Panther Party," in *African American Women Confront the West, 1600–2000*, ed. Quintard Taylor and Shirley Ann Wilson Moore (Norman: University of Oklahoma Press, 2003); Daniel Perlstein, "Minds Stayed on Freedom: Politics and Pedagogy in the African American Freedom Struggle," *American Educational*

Research Journal 39 (Summer 2002): 249–277; Charles E. Jones and Jonathan Gayles, "The World Is a Child's Classroom: An Analysis of the Black Panther Party's Oakland Community School," in *Teach Freedom*, ed. Charles Payne and Carol Strickland (New York: Teachers College Press, 2008); David Hilliard, ed., *The Black Panther Party: Service to the People Programs* (Albuquerque: University of New Mexico Press, 2008); Hilliard, ed., *The Black Panther Intercommunal News Service, 1967–1980* (New York: Atria Books, 2007); Jama Lazerow and Yohuru Williams, eds., *In Search of the Black Panther Party: New Perspectives on a Revolutionary Movement* (Durham, NC: Duke University Press, 2006); Judson L. Jeffries, ed., *Comrades: A Local History of the Black Panther Party* (Bloomington: Indiana University Press, 2007); Yohuru Williams and Jama Lazarow, eds., *Liberated Territory: Untold Local Perspectives on the Black Panther Party* (Durham, NC: Duke University Press, 2008).

8. TBP, 1967–1980; Bobby Seale, *Seize the Time: The Story of Huey P. Newton and the Black Panther Party* (New York: Random House, 1968); Huey P. Newton, "The Women's Liberation and Gay Liberation Movements: August 15, 1970," in *To Die for the People: The Writings of Huey P. Newton* (New York: Writers and Readers, 1995), 152–155; *Look for Me in the Whirlwind: The Collective Autobiography of the New York 21* (New York: Vintage, 1971).

9. Brown, *Taste of Power*.

10. Assata Shakur, *Assata: An Autobiography* (Chicago: Lawrence Hill Books, 1987); Brown, *Taste of Power*; Jennings, "Why I Joined the Party"; Abron, "Serving the People"; Kathleen Cleaver, "Women, Power, and Revolution," in *Liberation, Imagination and the Black Panther Party: A New Look at the Panthers and Their Legacy*, ed. K. Cleaver and George Katsiaficas (New York: Routledge, 2001), 123–127; Madalynn C. Rucker and JoNina Abron, "Comrade Sisters: Two Women of the Black Panther Party," in *Unrelated Kin: Race and Gender in Women's Personal Narratives*, ed. G. Etter-Lewis (New York: Routledge, 1996), 139–168; "Voices of Panther Women," conference at the University of California at Berkeley, October 26, 1990.

11. Angela LeBlanc-Ernest, interview with Malik Edwards, San Francisco, CA August 1996; Hilliard, *This Side of Glory*, 199–201, 208–209.

12. Brenda Bay, correspondence with the authors, October 6, 2008; "'We Have to Attend to Our People,'" *TBP* 9/2/72:13; "'The World Is Their Classroom,'" *TBP* 11/3/73:4.

13. "'We Have to Attend to Our People'"; "'The World Is Their Classroom.'"

14. "The People's Community Survival Programs," *TBP* 10/9/71:9; *TBP* 12/11/71:12; "Educate to Liberate," *TBP* 9/30/72:14.

15. Elaine Brown, correspondence with authors, October 9, 2008; "Dellums and A.F.T. Endorse Bobby," *TBP* 5/5/73:14; "Alameda Students Welcome Bobby Seale," *TBP* 2/17/73:5+.

16. "Youth Institute Opens," *TBP* 9/15/73:16; "Unity Conference Pledges to Support Bobby Seale," *TBP* 5/5/73:3+; "Dellums and A.F.T. Endorse Bobby," *TBP* 5/5/73:3+; "The Seale-Brown 14-Point Program to Rebuild Oakland," *TBP* 5/12/73:4; "Women Organize for People's Candidates," *TBP* 2/10/73:5+; "Educational Opportunities Corporation (a Non-profit Corporation) Intercommunal Youth Institute 'Each One Teach One' Tuition Club," *TBP* 10/6/73:16.

17. These statistics are from NFR OCS Weekly Reports (OCSWR) and *TBP* issues.

18. Funding information: Brown, *Taste of Power*; Hilliard, *This Side of Glory*; March 6, 1974, box 14, Directives; OCS Memos; OCSWR; EOC and EOC-S grant proposals and financial audits. Brown, October 9, 2008.

19. Donald Freed, *Agony in New Haven* (New York: Simon and Schuster, 1973); Yohuru Williams, *Black Politics/White Power* (New York: Brandywine Press, 2000).

20. Angela LeBlanc-Ernest, interview with Donna Howell, San Francisco, CA, January 1992; NFR, box 14, Directives: October 20, 1973 and November 7, 1973; Donna Howell, correspondence with the authors, October 7, 2008.

21. Angela LeBlanc-Ernest, interview with Norma Armour, Los Angeles, CA, September 1996.

22. "OCS Instructors Handbook, September 1977"; "OCS Instructor's Handbook, September 1979"; "OCS Instructor's Handbook, September 1980," NFR.

23. Ericka Huggins, interview with Carol Granison, Oakland, CA, October 1, 2007; *TBP* 2/9/74:4.

24. NFR, box 36, Health Cadre Reports, September 1, 1972; NFR box 10 Central Committee Info., September 27, 1973; NFR, box 14, Directives, October 20, 1973; NFR Health Cadre Reports; Howell, October 7, 2008.

25. NFR, box 2, Section Progress Reports, Committee Heads and Coordinators Report, September 9, 1972:2.

26. "Youth Institute Teachers Have 'Great Love and Understanding,'" *TBP* 2/9/74:4; OCSWR.

27. Ericka Huggins, interview with Rodney Gillead, Oakland, CA, September 2007.

28. Adrienne Humphrey, correspondence with the authors, October 11, 2008; Ericka Huggins, interview with Zachary Killoran, Oakland, CA, September 6, 2007.

29. Michael Ackley, *The Montclarion*, 1976 (no page); reprinted as "Black Panther Wins Seat on County Board: Ericka Huggins on Board of Education," *TBP* 5/22/76:6.

30. "Oakland School Test Results Show Serious Lag," *TBP* 11/19/77:6+.

31. Descriptions of the school's structure are in *TBP* articles; OCS Instructor's Handbooks; "OCS January Report" to Huey from Ericka, 3/11/78; November 11, 1977, box 4 OCS Weekly Report to Huey from Ericka.

32. CTBS test scores, November 1977.

33. OCS enrollment reports and photographs in the NFR; JoNina Abron, "Reflections of a Former Oakland Public School Parent," *Black Scholar* 27, no. 2 15–20; To Ruth Love, from Huey P. Newton, August 30, 1977, box 4 Educational Opportunities Corporation; Brown, October 9, 2008.

34. This information is based on numerous documents found in OCSWR and OCLC memos; OCS Parent Brochure [1980–1981], box 88, Miscellaneous.

35. Ericka Huggins, interview with Ericka Watkins, Berkeley, CA, November 12, 2007.

36. The Black Panther Party, guest editors, *CoEvolution Quarterly*, Fall 1974; box 4, OCSWR; "Seniors against a Fearful Environment," *TBP* 12/16/72:3+; "Funds for Senior Safety," *TBP* 1/13/73:4; OCLC Weekly Reports.

37. "Community Coalition Organizes against Infant Mortality," *TBP* 1/13–26/08:4.

38. "O.C.S. Director Ericka Huggins Highlights Chicago Alternative Schools Conference Part 1," *TBP* 6/19/76:14–15; Part 2, *TBP* 6/26/76:4+; Part 3, *TBP* 7/3/76:4+; To Huey from Ericka, November 4, 1977, NFR, box 4, OCSWR; information about visitors in *TBP* issues between 1971 and 1980.

39. To Huey from Ericka, November 4, 1977:2; November 17, 1974; and January 9–15, 1978, NFR, box 4; NFR, box 4, OCSWR; Kellita Smith, correspondence with the authors, October 12, 2008.

40. JoNina Abron to Huey P. Newton, Correspondence, October 1, 1980, NFR, box 69, no folder title; "A Second Look/Who Got the Money?" *San Francisco Examiner*, August 22, 1983, n.p.; Kate Coleman with Paul Avery "The Party's Over," *New Times*, July 10, 1978, 22–47; Letters to *New Times* editor by OCS staff and students, box 41, Letters from Institute Students; Joel Dreyfuss "Huey in Pinstripes?" *Black Enterprise*, June 1979, 69; Lance Williams, "State Probes Panther School Funds," *TBP* 9/29/82:A1+, "School Aide Says He Warned Official of Misused Funds," and "School Official Stepped into Chaotic Conditions," *TBP* 11/7/82:A1, A4; "Second Look," *San Francisco Examiner*, August 22, 1983, n.p.

41. "'We Have to Attend to Our People,'" *TBP* 9/2/72:13; "Student's Interests Stressed in Learning Center's Music Program," *TBP* 2/16/74:4.

42. Watkins interview.

43. Killoran interview. Zachary Killoran, correspondence with the authors, October 9, 2008.

8

Must Revolution
Be a Family Affair?
Revisiting The Black Woman

Margo Natalie Crawford

The reason we are in the bag we are in isn't because of my mama,
it's because of what they did to my mama.

Stokely Carmichael[1]

Black men, during the 1960s and 1970s black freedom struggles, were very aware of intersectionality, that which Kimberlé Crenshaw
defines as the "need to account for multiple grounds of identity when
considering how the social world is constructed."[2] Indeed, they insisted
on the need to connect manhood and blackness. Their emphasis on black
male power often convinced them that the liberation of black men would
lead to the liberation of all black people. The black struggle, in this point
of view, could not afford to be divided; a black women's movement would
allow the dominant power structure to continue to "divide and conquer."
This subsuming of black women in the black male struggle becomes particularly troubling when we realize that the intersectionality that overdetermined black male consciousness-raising was not extended to black
women. As black women refused to be subsumed in the black male
struggle, they began to think about the black family affair in a more critical manner as they confronted the problems of the "brother and sister"
rhetoric and the Moynihan paradigm (the larger circulation of the idea of

*The Wall of Respect,*1969, Bob Crawford.

pathological black families and gender trouble) that often overdetermined the gender politics of the 1960s and 1970s black freedom struggles. In the common story of the role of women of color in second-wave feminism, the intersectionality of race and gender is the new layer that feminists of color add to the male-dominated protest movements of the 1960s and 1970s. When we acknowledge that Black Power masculinist discourse was deeply intersectional, the signature difference of Black Power feminism is not intersectionality but the seizure of intersectionality from the male stronghold.

Although Benita Roth, in *Separate Roads to Feminism: Black, Chicana, and White Feminist Movements in America's Second Wave* (2004), does not acknowledge Black (male) Power's use of intersectionality (as she sets up intersectionality as the intervention of black feminists and other feminists of color), she does establish that a focus on intersectionality allows 1960s and 1970s black feminists to rewrite the idea that liberation for black women will necessarily arise from black men's liberation. As Roth explains, since black women's lives intersect the oppressive structures of race, gender, and class, 1960s and 1970s black feminists often insisted that once black women were liberated, everyone would be liberated. Roth writes, "Since black women were at the intersection of oppressive structures, they reasoned that their liberation would mean the liberation of all people. This legacy of intersectional feminist theory—of analyzing and organizing against interlocking oppressions—would come to have a profound impact on feminist theory as a whole."[3] On the surface, this understanding of the "liberation of all people" seems to simply replace "black men" with "black women" (in the masculinist thinkers' formula of black male liberation leading to total black liberation). It is significant, however, that 1960s and 1970s black feminists were using black women's lowest position in the social hierarchy as a means of explaining the "freedom for all" mind-set.

In the anthology *The Black Woman* (1970), this analysis of class and race is described in the following manner: "First, that the class hierarchy as seen from the poor Black woman's position is one of white male in power, followed by the white female, then the Black male, and lastly the Black female."[4] Critical thinking about being black and a woman led Toni Cade Bambara, in 1970, to edit *The Black Woman*, which is often recognized as one of the most vivid records of the critical thought of African American women during the 1960s. Although the anthology includes creative writing (five poems and three short stories), essays predominate. There are twenty-five essays, including creative nonfiction, a drama review, and the "working papers" of black women's collectives. The contributors range from very well-known voices such as Nikki Giovanni and Abbey Lincoln to students and community organizers. The anthology sold so quickly that, two months after publication, a new edition appeared. Farah Jasmine Griffin provides a captivating analysis of Bambara's conscious attempt to create a book that would convince publishers that there was a market for more texts with a black woman's point of view.[5] She cites the following passage from an interview, by Toni Morrison, of Bambara:

> I put together this anthology that I felt would open the door and prove that there was a market. Sure enough, within the second month that the book came out, it went into a new edition. The book was everywhere. There were pyramids of *The Black Woman* in every bookstore. All I knew in the beginning was that it had to fit in your pocket and be under a dollar.[6]

The title *The Black Woman* is strategically simple as it rages against the silence and speaks "the black woman" into existence. Bambara aimed to fill the silence surrounding black women with a supple text that would "fit in your pocket" and circulate widely.

Pivotal recent scholarship by Cheryl Wall and Farah Jasmine Griffin testifies to the groundbreaking nature of this anthology.[7] Griffin has noted the contradictions in the anthology that, through our current lens, make it not entirely "black feminist." Griffin reminds us of the contradictions in one of the most captivating parts of the anthology—a transcript from a black women's rap session at the City University of New York. She contrasts statements such as "Men are our leaders, you know," and the rage, in other parts of this recorded dialogue, against the silencing of black women (*The Black Woman*, 186). The words "Men are our leaders" are not only internalized sexism but also, in 1970, a confession, by the black woman in this rap session, that black men were indeed situating their leadership at the center of the movement. The anthology documents Black Power feminism as it also documents black women's deft maneuvers to decenter this black male focus.

The anthology was Bambara's attempt to record many different examples of black women "turning to each other" and defying the outside "experts," whether white or black men. As I compare this anthology and 1960s black male analyses of race, gender, and the black family affair, I demonstrate *The Black Woman's* questioning of the black family affair and the bold refusal, by many of the anthologized women, of the Moynihan paradigm of black matriarchs and emasculated black men. Calvin Hernton's *Sex and Racism in America* (1965) and William Grier and Price Cobbs's *Black Rage* (1968) exemplify Black Power male-authored texts that ostensibly foreground intersections of race and gender but fail to provide a rigorous analysis of the interlocking oppressions affecting black women. Calvin Hernton was a vital Black Arts movement poet and essayist of the Black Power movement. *Sex and Racism in America* generated great excitement during the Black Power movement. Hernton is widely cited throughout the 1960s in journals such as the *Black Scholar, Negro Digest/ Black World*, and *Liberator*, as Black Power scholars and advocates insist that *Sex and Racism in America* exposed the slavery-inflected sexual relations between white and black Americans. Like *Sex and Racism in America*, *Black Rage*, now a Black Power "classic," energized the Black Power movement. Because William Grier and Price Cobbs were African American psychiatrists analyzing African Americans, they helped legitimize a type of internal expertise that was very different from the gaze of outside "experts" such as Moynihan. Both *Sex and Racism in America* and *Black Rage* become most masculinist when invoking the Moynihan paradigm and its overdetermined depictions of race, gender, and sexuality.[8] In contrast, many of the contributors to *The Black Woman* refused to accept the Moynihan paradigm.

In addition to the rhetoric of matriarchy and emasculation, the 1960s and 1970s African American family affair was greatly shaped by the rhetoric of brothers and sisters. Since the Black Power movement, the terms "brothers" and "sisters" have become common language within African American black nationalism; the words are also used as a means of signaling affection for someone, signaling a person's progressive politics, and, sometimes, signaling that a person is black. Only sisters and brothers call each other sisters and brothers. This use of the words is a private, protected space, an insular family affair. The words also invoke a type of incest, when their use, in Black Arts movement poetry, often became linked to the representation of the ideal romantic and husband-wife bonds between black men and women. In order to break out of the incestuous affair, Black Power feminists had to separate "black womanhood" from a patriarchy-defined type of sisterhood.

One of the crucial interventions in *The Black Woman* is the question "from mother and son to brother and sister—what's so hard about being man and woman?" (85), posed by Joanna Clark in her essay "Motherhood." Clark wonders if investments in the black family affair convert simple gender difference into a very toxic type of role-playing. In this same anthology Kay Lindsey insists that the power of the state depends on people's investment in family. The very first pages of the anthology include a poem by Lindsey in which she vehemently critiques the oppression of black women that was naturalized, in 1960s and 1970s black nationalism, when black women were seen, first and foremost, as mothers. On the very next pages, Audre Lorde inveighs against heteronormativity as she screams, "But if he's said— / At some future date— / To have a head / That's put on straight / My son won't care / About his/ Hair / Nor give a damn / Whose wife I am" (19). These voices conjoin as the anthology documents a very vexed black family affair and the need to appreciate the solidarity that spurred the "brother and sister" rhetoric without accepting a family model as the only way to create solidarity between black women and men.

The Moynihan Paradigm

Before analyzing the complications of the black family affair in *The Black Woman*, the anthology's depictions of the Moynihan Report and its effects must be unpacked. Daniel Patrick Moynihan's report "The Negro Family: The Case for National Action" (1965), produced while he was assistant secretary of labor during Lyndon Johnson's administration, placed the African American family affair in the national spotlight. "At the heart of the deterioration of the fabric of Negro society," the report extolled, "is the deterioration of the Negro family. It is the fundamental source of the weakness of the Negro community at the present time."[9] This report helped naturalize the idea of the emasculated black man and the castrating black matriarch. In 1965, President Johnson made the Moynihan Report the focus of a commencement speech delivered at Howard University. As Johnson echoed Moynihan's connection of black poverty and the lack of nuclear families in black communities, he added a critique of what he viewed as African Americans' inability to address their own "failures." Donna Franklin, in *Ensuring Inequality: The Structural Transformation of the African American Family* (1997), explains that President Johnson, in this speech, "urged black Americans to forgive and forget and to look frankly at their own failures."[10] The "blaming the victim" tone of this Moynihan Report–inspired speech, despite the ways it indicted the socioeconomic structures that furthered this "tangle of pathology," shows that as the report circulated, it became a paradigm that was more toxic than the layer of pathology in the actual report. As the report was used by others such as President Johnson during the Howard University speech, the pathologizing of black family structures, and their cast of alleged black matriarchs, emasculated black men, and wanton children, became the disturbing consequence.

As Moynihan insisted on the connections between the economic troubles of black Americans and the lack, in many cases, of a nuclear family structure, he reinforced the idea that families headed by unwed mothers are pathological.[11] African American men are rendered impotent as he argues that they are dominated by a pathological matriarchy of unwed black mothers. Scholars have recognized the pathologizing impulses reverberating from Moynihan's report. These impulses allow us to more fully appreciate the reasons why investments in family structure played such a huge role in the Black Power discourse.[12] Moynihan and many Black Power advocates ironically concurred that a family crisis must be corrected in order to improve the quality of life for black Americans. Whereas Moynihan was mobilized by a belief in assimilation as the means of economic mobility, the Black Power focus on ideal family relations stemmed from the fear of black genocide and the desire for black self-determination. Stronger black families would lead to more empowered black communities, but many black men were reifying the "black family" without honestly addressing the family's problems.

Writers in *The Black Woman* question the psychological effect of Moynihan's economic theory and sociological research. Gwen Patton, in "Black People and the Victorian Ethos," writes, "Daniel Moynihan . . . was partly responsible for dividing black men and women. (And the correct thing for the oppressor to do was to create havoc and discord among the colonized, particularly in internal and family relationships because of the sensitivity)" (145). Patton places an explicit emphasis on Black (male) Power as too often the black male response to the Moynihan paradigm. She writes:

> Black Power!!! If Moynihan introduced and made people aware of the "castration," then Black Power with its so-called African manifestations will move to correct the situation. Moynihan's report was very successful because it invisibly became the guideline under the guise of Black Power for the Black family. (146)

One year after the publication of *The Black Woman*, in a special issue of the *Black Scholar* titled "Black Male," we see both an attack on Moynihan, in Robert Staples's opening essay, "The Myth of the Impotent Black Male," and a lingering investment, in Nathan Hare's essay, "Will the Real Black Man Please Stand Up?," in the Moynihan paradigm of emasculated black men and black matriarchs. The tone and texture of the sexism in Hare's essay capture the reasons why black feminists of this period were spurred to question the need to connect revolutionary thinking and the family affair. Hare explains the black woman's role in the movement as a wifely duty to "stand by her man." He insists:

> This is the era of liberation, and because it is the era of liberation, the black man will be able to bring the woman along in our common struggle, so that we will not need a black women's liberation movement. In the struggle to assert our black manhood, we must sidestep the trap of turning against our women and they, in retaliation, against us. The black woman is, can be, the black man's helper, an undying collaborator, standing up with him, beside her man. The white man, not the black man, is the black woman's oppressor, the oppressor of us all, including his own women; and we must never forget this fact.[13]

The limitation of this discourse emerges in the clear suggestion that the successful "assert[ion] [of] our black manhood" necessitates that black women agree that black men do not oppress black women. In *The Black Woman*, vehement language such as "They [black women] live the reality daily of Black male oppression" challenges this denial of black women's oppression by black men (193).[14]

Revisions in *The Black Woman*

In *The Black Woman*, Bambara forces her readers to ask themselves who really is "The Man," the popular 1960s term for the ultimate oppressive power. As she presents analyses of black male castration anxiety, matriarchy theories, the alternative family created by the state's welfare programs, and the different understandings of genocide, "The Man" cannot be reduced, as Hare argues, to white men. In the preface to *The Black Woman*, Bambara explains the need for the very movement that Hare rejects—a "black women's liberation movement." *The Black Woman* was an outgrowth of black women's consciousness-raising throughout the nation. Bambara, in her preface, emphasizes that black women were "turning to each other." They were actively studying and researching in "work-study groups, discussion clubs, cooperative nurseries, cooperative businesses, consumer education groups, women's workshops on the campuses, women's caucuses within existing organizations, [and] Afro-American women's magazines" (9). The known and unknown voices that the anthology brought together respond to some of the most pernicious aspects of 1960s black masculinist discourse. The critical interventions made in *The Black Woman* become most visible when the anthology's creative writing and essays are contrasted with specific examples of 1960s black masculinism.

Sex and Racism in America is one of the texts that must be remembered in order to gain an understanding of the deeper layers of the 1960s black masculinist discourse. As Calvin Hernton, in quintessential Black Power fashion, unpacks the nature of White Power, white male envy of imagined black male sexual power becomes one central layer of the argument. Hernton then extends this envy to black women as he argues that some black women have black penis envy. Hernton writes:

> It seems to me that many Negro females who complain about Negro men ignoring them for white women are actually unaware that they are jealous of the attention that black men arouse in white women. The

white stereotype of the Negro male's sex image is often the main force that draws some white females toward them. Distorted as it is, the Negro woman envies this image; she cannot compete with it, in reference to either white or Negro males, and like the white man, her ego cannot bear seeing white women and Negro men together.[15]

Hernton's investment in this notion of penis envy leads him to a focus on self-hatred and queerness that occurs when black women and white men become romantic partners. He argues:

Like many white women who become intimate with Negroes, many black women are latent or unconscious homosexuals—the white man's color and unfamiliarity tend to heighten or excite their sense of themselves as females. Such women simply cannot get along with Negroes. In many instances, since he is considered kind, gentle, and compliant, the white man may psychosexually represent a pseudo-female for an otherwise homosexual, or lesbian-inclined, Negro woman. (163)

This language demonstrates that 1960s black masculinist discourse not only situated black women as the castrating matriarchs but also pathologized black women's "sense of themselves as females." If a black woman is "excited" about her womanhood, she is, within this masculinist gaze, always already on the verge of becoming "lesbian" or "white" or self-hating. As Bambara brings together both heterosexual and lesbian voices, she highlights queer thinking as opposed to heterosexual identities and lesbian identities.

As opposed to Hernton's reduction of black female queerness to black woman/white man relationships, Lorde's poem "And What about the Children," in the first pages of *The Black Woman*, depicts queer thinking as the ability of her son to "not give a damn / Whose wife I am" (17). The poem reveals that the feminizing of the son's curly hair ("and how much curl / is right for a girl?") is tied to the same way of thinking that normalizes marriage.

Just as Audre Lorde responds to the pathologizing, in depictions such as Hernton's, of black women's ability to find romantic relationships that allow them to see themselves "as women," Kay Lindsey, in the essay "The Black Woman as Woman," tackles the black masculinist texts that critique the "castrated black male" layer of the Moynihan paradigm without critiquing the ongoing naturalization of family as race. Lindsey connects the family and the state. She presents the family as the "white institution . . . held up to Blacks as a desirable but somehow unattainable goal, at least not in the pure forms that whites have created," and believes that "if the family as an institution were destroyed, the state would be destroyed" (86, 87). From Lindsey's point of view, the destruction of the state and the "recreat[ion] of society at large" is reliant on the destruction of naturalized family roles that lead, inevitably in her estimation, to the naturalized power of the state. When she moves to an analysis of black welfare mothers as the state's creation of an "artificial family" (through the lens of the normative nuclear family), the radicalism of her analysis is the shift from Moynihan's focus on the "Negro family" to the "State's family." The real problem with Moynihan's report is indeed the lapse into a pathologizing of the specifically "Negro" nature of the family structure that is allegedly not economically viable, as opposed to Lindsay's overt focus on the state's role in this nonnormative family structure. Whereas Moynihan underscores the "matriarchal" and the "emasculated," Lindsay makes the "State" the master term.

Lindsey argues that "becoming black" does not happen in the family in the same way that becoming male or female does. She then proposes that racial trauma is more usefully understood as the trauma that occurs "outside the family." She argues:

> For it is immediately within the bosom of one's family that one learns to be a female and all that the term implies. . . . One discovers what it means to be Black, and all that the term implies, usually outside the family, although this is probably less so than it was as the need to politicize all Blacks, including children, has become so obvious. But until recently, the child had only dim revelations about her color within the family and it was only when she moved out into the community and the opposition and reaction of whites to her gave her insight into her place, racially. (87)

Responding to the idea, in Black Power discourse, that being black means being a part of a black family, Lindsey reminds readers that the "need to politicize" and resist outside trauma has led people to the *need* for a racial family "bosom."

As opposed to Lindsey's focus on the racial formations that emerge outside the family, the prominent black male psychiatrists William Grier and Price Cobbs, in *Black Rage* (1968), explore the racialized family trauma that leads to the racialized violence "on the street." They assert, "A great many of the problems of black people in America can be traced back to the widespread crumbling of the family structure."[16] In their book, Grier and Cobbs move from family problems to family romance. This lapse into the romance leads to the bliss of gender normativity. Their inability to problematize the institution of family enables the deeply historical argument to become very fanciful: "But in spite of the problems facing them, black couples continue to marry, establish families, and try to make a worthwhile contribution to the stream of life. The husband works as best he can, the wife mothers as best she can, and they love each other as best they can" (71). In *The Black Woman,* Frances Beale, in the essay "Double Jeopardy: To Be Black and Female," proposes that these dominant gender roles (men working versus women mothering) are simply irrelevant to the lives of most black people. She claims that it is "idle dreaming to think of Black women simply caring for their homes and children like the middle class white model" (91). Beale brings the idea of irrelevance even more to the surface when she foregrounds the difference between the images that have been internalized and the reality: "Though we have been brow-beaten with this white image, the reality of the degrading and dehumanizing jobs that were relegated to us quickly dissipated this mirage of womanhood" (91). In "Black Romanticism," another essay in *The Black Woman,* Joyce Green argues that too many black men "in the revolution" want black women to perform this mirage. She captures the silliness of this desire when she writes, "But sisters don't have no time to be dumb afros as opposed to dumb blondes" (139).

In Black Power images of African American queens, as opposed to "dumb afros," black women are given the *regal* burden of being viewed as always strong and wise. Women in the Black Power movement recognized the dangers of this rhetoric that often romanticized oppression and suffering by understanding survival tactics as inborn strength and courage. The poem "Alafia," in *Black Fire* (1968), ends with the words "Poverty's little girl / Black Woman, Queen of the World."[17] The poet's name is a part of the naming and misnaming that the poem addresses. Instead of only using her new African name, she uses the composite "Odaro (Barbara Jones, slave name)." Like the slave name "Barbara Jones," the words "Queen of the World" prevent self-definition. The poem begins with a letter to the editors of *Black Fire:* "I am writing at the request of / Larry Neal, Ed Spriggs and Harold Foster / Who seem to think that you / Might be interested in my / Poetry" (356). The poem becomes a description of black women's attempt to answer the black male "call" for black art. As Odaro (Barbara Jones) answers this call, her final words ("Poverty's little girl /

Black Woman, Queen of the World") signal that she remains caught in all the names that hail black women.

The Black Woman documents black women's attempts to name themselves during the Black Power movement. This self-naming shifted the very geography of Black Power. Black women's bodies were too often the medium for black male dreams of a nation-state; their bodies were often the canvas for the geography of Black Power. In *The Black Woman*, the new geography of Black Power included a shift to reconsider anti–birth control rhetoric. Writers in *The Black Woman* inveigh against welfare programs that make the state a type of father figure. As they think, however, about the birth control strategies tied to the public aid programs, they refuse to simply propose that black women should not use birth control. In the essay "The Pill: Genocide or Liberation?" Bambara addresses the "national call to the Sisters to abandon birth controls, to not cooperate with an enemy all too determined to solve his problem with the bomb, the gun, the pill" (163). Bambara argues that black women should critique the state's attempt to control black women's reproduction even as they refuse to accept the idea that "having babies for the revolution" is the women's role in the struggle. The link that Bambara draws between the "bomb, the gun, the pill" fully displays the conflict of signs between the work of women situated in both the Black Power movement and the women's movement and the work of white women in the women's movement. Imagine a slogan "No more bombs, guns, pills." In 1970 (when Bambara edits this anthology), the slogan "No more bombs, guns, pills" would not work in a women's movement that had white women at the center. Birth control pills, in the lens of white women, did not signify genocide. Bambara's essay "The Pill: Genocide or Liberation?" also supports the sign "The Pill: It's a Woman's Choice." Bambara carves out a space in which black women can carry these multiple signs.

In the midst of the Black Power castration and matriarchy blues, *The Black Women* writers boldly made the birth control debate a means of analyzing the deeper layers of the black family crisis. Joanna Clark ends her essay "Motherhood" with the wry suggestion that the birth control pill may be the best alternative to the dowry that "no self-respecting African woman would ever get married without" (71). In the essay Clark writes a memoir about her struggles as a mother that opens up into a poignant commentary on the reasons black women should not allow the more abstract rhetoric of genocide to make them forget about the very concrete violence that black mothers suffer. As Clark refuses to subordinate the suffering tied to the historical trauma of black women being treated as breeders, she refuses to respect the sanctity of the discourse against genocide. Intending to shock and almost blaspheme, she tells her fellow black women a story that is worth quoting in full:

> It's over now, and I have my children back. They have a father who works. And while we haven't come along so far as to get out there in the park every Sunday with a baseball and bat, we do have a go with the frisbee every now and then. It's still very clean living and all-American. But I learned a lot. . . . A friend of mine not too long ago had a vaginal infection and took herself off to a gynecologist. He was good, but he was German. And the lady trembled lest Herr Doktor take one look at her little brown face and decide to practice a bit of "genocide." Black ladies, the last thing we have to worry about is genocide. In fact, we could use a little. Look at what's happened to us in the last hundred years; we've been bravely propagating and all we've gotten are a lot of lumps and a bad name. On the one hand, there are people like Glazer and Moynihan carrying on about matriarchy and inferring that we've botched up the job long enough and that if we insist on doing something, confine ourselves to standing behind the man of the family and bringing him up to par. On the other hand, there are the brothers (from mother to son to brother and sister—what's so hard about being man and woman?). Anyway, there's the brother nattering away about how we've been lopping off balls long enough, it's time to stand aside. (70–71)

This anecdote begins with the normative image of the family that Clark gains after she survives being a struggling mother without the support of her first husband. She emphasizes the seduction of the normative family. When she questions, "From mother to son to brother and sister—what's so hard about being man and woman?," she implies that the identities "man" and "woman" need to be separated from the kinship paradigm. This anecdote shows that the rhetoric of the black family crisis and fear of genocide often negated the health and well-being of black women. If genocide is indeed the systematic killing of a group, then Clark worries that there is a genocide of black women that remains unspoken as the potential genocide of the black race becomes the alleged reason that black women cannot afford to look in the mirror and see that their suffering also matters.

The Ultimate Revision: Not the Pathological Family
Structure but the Pathological Gender Roles

In the preface to *The Black Woman*, Bambara explains that one goal of the anthology is to "set the record straight on the matriarch and the evil Black bitch" (11). When the role of mother and sisters in a family is predicated on the notion of needing a male head of the family, these derogatory positions may be inevitable. In order to imagine a black family structure that does not need a male or female "head," the economic challenges, the generational poverty that too many African American families continue to battle, would have to be separated from the castration and matriarchy blues. In one of the most pointed essays in *The Black Woman*, "Double Jeopardy: To Be Black and Female," Frances Beale advocates this revolutionary work of rewriting the identities "black woman" and "black man" when she writes, "We must begin to rewrite our understanding of traditional personal relationships between man and woman" (100).

The critique of normative gender roles is, finally, inseparable, in *The Black Woman*, from the critique of the 1960s tropes of castration and matriarchy. By deciding to include "Woman Poem," by Nikki Giovanni, as the first poem, Bambara immediately makes *The Black Woman* a response to the rhetoric of castrated black men. Whereas Moynihan argues that black men have been castrated by black matriarchs, in the opening poem, Giovanni writes, "It's having a job / they won't let you work / or no work at all / castrating me / (yes it happens to women too)" (13). The radical edge of this poem is Giovanni's insistence on this unacknowledged castration that happens to black women. It is significant that Giovanni uses the word "castrating" because this poem connects directly with one of the pivotal essays in the anthology, "Is the Black Male Castrated?"

In this essay Jean Carey Bond and Pat Peery question the usefulness of the continued use of the terms "castrated" and "emasculated" as a means of talking about the disempowerment of black men. They wonder if these terms make it difficult to think about the resistance that happens in spite of the oppression. Bond and Peery argue that, contrary to Daniel Patrick Moynihan's insistence on "Black male emasculation" and "Black female matriarchy," black women have never had the power to castrate, and black men have never truly become victims of the "white man's" attempts to castrate them (117–118). Bond and Peery assert, "Indeed, the Black man always surfaces with his manhood not only intact, but much more intact than that of his oppressor, which brings us to the question: just who is the emasculated person in this society? Surely, it is the white man, whose dazzling symbols of power—his goods, his technology—have all but consumed his human essence" (118). Bond and Peery revise the dominant sense of what it means to be a man.

In *The Black Woman*, Bambara, in the essay "On the Issue of Roles," critiques the use of the term "castrated" in the following manner:

> And I wonder if the dudes who keep hollering about their lost balls realize that they probably surrendered them either to Mr. Charlie in the marketplace, trying to get that El Dorado, or to Miss Anne in bed, trying to bang out some sick notion of love and freedom. It seems to me you find your Self in destroying illusions, smashing myths, laundering the head of whitewash, being responsible to some truth, to the struggle. That entails at the very least cracking through the veneer of this sick society's definition of "masculine" and "feminine." (108)

Bambara worries that the Black Power reliance on castration images and the conscious attempt to assert manhood necessarily reinforce a "sick society's" gender script. Black Power feminism, when we remember Bambara's focus on the "dudes who keep hollering about their lost balls," was the insistence on a black revolutionary politics that would not continue to repeat these stale images of what it means to be a man and continue to make the black woman the person responsible for the alleged emasculation.

When Bambara includes this critique in *The Black Woman*, she, like others, guarantees that the critique of this black male performance of masculinity will be recorded as a part of the Black Power movement. As we expose the inseparability of Black Power and the black feminist critiques of masculinism, the following anonymous poem (published in 1969 in *Rat*), like many of the voices in *The Black Woman*, is evidence that black women were responding to the masculinism, with force and frustration, *as* it unfolded.[18] The poem reads:

Some black women feel it is not fair
to the Black men of today to want to
proclaim our Liberation

We still feel sorry for him—as a mother
feels about a crippled child

It is still present in our minds the white
man's emasculation of his manhood

And like a child learning to walk—he is
just now gaining his self-respect.

But listen Black Sisters we held
Black men up for over 300 years

No matter how heavy the Burden
WE HELD HIM UP

　　. . .

But we the Black women of this
country have been the tools of
men long enough—and it's time
they laid these time worn tools
down.

The genuine understanding of why "some black women" feel the need to not "proclaim" their liberation does not prevent the writer from asserting her own sense that 1969 is the precise time for black women's liberation.

Black men also wrestled, during the Black Power movement, with the black family affair. One sign of black male critiques of the sexism stemming from the family affair appears in Bob Bennett's poem "(Title)," in *Black Fire*, a poem seemingly waiting for readers to name. The poem depicts an attempt to move to nonromantic, nonsexual relations between the sisters and brothers (black women and black men). As Bennett counters the script of doomed marriages between matriarchs and emasculated men, he imagines a different kind of marriage with love but no crude romance, a marriage in which men view black women as too much of a family member to be an object of romantic desire. In the last stanza of the poem, he writes:

The girl with the Afro
Without words says she loves our mother
And our mother's children
(She is my sister: I am her brother)
Without romance there is love (423)

Because the stereotype of the matriarch is inseparable from the stereo-type of the asexual mammy, there is clearly a potential canceling out of black women's sexuality and femininity in this depiction of black women as women who should be loved deeply as kin but not as romantic part-ners. Nonetheless, the poet Bennett does represent the transcendent love in kinship as an alternative to the predictably painful romance between those forced to be matriarchs and emasculated men. As he attempts to separate the black family affair from romance, he gestures toward a denat-uralizing of the heterosexual relations between the "sister" and "brother": "(She is my sister: I am her brother) / Without romance there is love."

Audre Lorde's poetry, in *The Black Woman*, also denaturalizes the het-eronormativity of the black family affair.[19] In "Naturally," Lorde "queers" the sheer power of the circulation of "black" as a unifying term that con-nects all blackened subjects regardless of skin color. This queering occurs as Lorde uses "yellow" as a means of thinking about what cannot be said in the "natural black beauty" discourse of the 1960s. Lorde writes:

Since Naturally Black is Naturally Beautiful
I must be proud
And, naturally,
Black and
Beautiful
Who always was a trifle
Yellow
And plain though proud
Before. (18)

The yellowness of the speaker is very different from the imaging of the "high yellow" in the long-standing colorism that sets "high yellow" women on a beauty pedestal and demeans dark-skinned black women. Lorde uses the "low yellow" as a means of questioning the naturalness of any beauty pedestal and the usefulness of a cultural nationalism that assumes that aesthetics and style easily and necessarily translate into viable political revolutionary action (described, at the end of the poem, as "black bread"). The queering mission of this poem is the speaker's multiple identities that collapse categories. She is "Naturally Black [and] Naturally Beautiful," but she remains tied to a past identity coded as "a trifle / Yellow." The speaker in "Naturally" insists, in the last stanza, on her need to not be placed in one category and, more important, on the productive work that can be done in this realm of multiplicity. "A trifle / Yellow" point of view can produce "black bread."

The Black Woman is black bread. When Verta Mae Smart-Grosvenor, in The Black Woman, frames liberation through the metaphor of "kitchen consciousness," she envisions that a certain way of preparing and sharing food might be a model for a kind of politics that would be transformative and entirely nurturing. Smart-Grosvenor's creative nonfiction should not be separated from the critical essays in The Black Woman. As the black family affair is addressed by Gwen Patton, in "Black People and the Victorian Ethos," the need for "black bread" makes Patton insist on breaking the silence as she claims black women's right to critique the gender politics of many "brothers." Patton explains that the late 1960s was the period when some black women felt it was particularly difficult to criticize the "brothers." As she breaks the silence, she insists:

> For almost two years Black women have been cagey about their comments and their contributions to the Movement for fear of de-balling the needed and well-loved new leaders. Black women have crouched in fear trying to do their thing in a passive form, which needs overt action. Meanwhile, white women have resorted to overt actions like guerrilla theater for massive measures like trying to open the road to more communications with their mates. (147)

This language epitomizes the confrontation of the family affair that explodes in The Black Woman. In this family affair, Patton feels that the "crouched" or "cagey" black woman has been the norm "for almost two years." After the Black Power movement gained its thunder by the mid-1960s, Patton feels that the thunder of black women was replaced with "passive" sounds. But the sounds coming from Patton's essay and the collective sounds coming from The Black Woman are not passive. The anthology reveals that many Black Power feminists were "doing their thing" in a radical form even as the "caginess" and the strategic passiveness ("trying to do their thing in a passive form") were being performed by many black women caught in the black family affair.

NOTES

1. Stokely Carmichael, "Notes and Comments," in *Black Nationalism in America*, ed. John H. Bracey Jr., August Meier, and Elliott Rudwick (Indianapolis: Bobbs Merrill, 1970), 472.

2. Kimberlé Crenshaw, "Mapping the Margins: Intersectionality, Identity Politics, and Violence against Women of Color," in *Critical Race Theory: The Key Writings That Formed the Movement*, ed. Kimberlé Crenshaw et al. (New York: New Press, 1995), 358.

3. Benita Roth, *Separate Roads to Feminism: Black, Chicana, and White Feminist Movements in America's Second Wave* (Cambridge: Cambridge University Press, 2004), 77.

4. Toni Cade Bambara, *The Black Woman: An Anthology* (New York: Mentor, 1970), 194. The first edition, published in the same year, has her earlier name, Toni Cade.

5. Farah Jasmine Griffin, "Conflict and Chorus: Reconsidering Toni Cade's *The Black Woman: An Anthology*," in *Is It Nation Time? Contemporary Essays on Black Power and Black Nationalism*, ed. Eddie Glaude Jr. (Chicago: University of Chicago Press, 2002).

6. Griffin cites the passage from a posthumously published interview of Toni Cade Bambara, edited by Toni Morrison (*Is It Nation Time?* 118–119).

7. Cheryl Wall, *Worrying the Line: Black Women Writers, Lineage, and Literary Tradition* (Chapel Hill: University of North Carolina Press, 2005); Griffin, "Conflict and Chorus."

8. Calvin Hernton's poetry and a critical essay, "Dynamite Growing Out of Their Skulls," appear in the seminal Black Arts anthology *The Black Fire: An Anthology of Afro-American Writing*, ed. LeRoi Jones and Larry Neal (New York: William Morrow, 1968). Hernton's *Sex and Racism in America* (New York: Grove Weidenfeld, 1965) is framed as a "study of the psychology of racism." William Grier and Price Cobbs's *Black Rage* (New York: Bantam, 1968) was one of the key texts representing the 1960s emergence of black psychology. The cover of the Bantam first edition included the words "Two black psychiatrists tell it like it is."

9. http://www.dol.gov/oasam/programs/history/webid-meynihan.htm.

10. Donna Franklin, *Ensuring Inequality: The Structural Transformation of the African American Family* (New York: Oxford University Press, 1997), 164.

11. In *Understanding the Black Family* (Oakland, CA: Black Family Institute Publications, 1984), Wade Nobles and Lawford Goddard argue that there was a "paradigmatic shift," beginning in the 1960s and extending to the 1980s, as "black family research [began to be] done by blacks." They understand this shift as a move from white studies of black families and also a move from "an a priori pathological paradigm to a more accurate and representational one" (8). The Moynihan Report is one of the problematic fires that sparks the shift, according to Nobles and Goddard, to this "black on black" family research.

12. In *Ensuring Inequality*, Donna Franklin provides an extensive overview of the range of people who critique Moynihan's pathologizing of nonnuclear black families.

13. Nathan Hare, "Will the Real Black Man Please Stand Up?" *Black Scholar* 2, no. 10 (June 1971): 32.

14. This raw reminder of the materiality of black women's oppression appears in the "working papers" of "Poor Black Women's Study Papers by Poor Black Women of Mount Vernon, NY," written by "Pat Robinson and Group." Bambara captures the grassroots black women consciousness-raising when she includes these working papers in *The Black Woman*.

15. Hernton, *Sex and Racism in America*, 142–143.

16. Grier and Cobbs, *Black Rage*, 70.

17. Jones and Neal, *Black Fire*, 356.

18. *Rat* was founded in March 1968 in New York. It began as a college student militancy magazine and, in late 1969, gained a feminist focus.

19. When Judith Butler, in *Undoing Gender* (New York: Routledge, 2004), wonders, "Is kinship always heterosexual?," she uses the alternative African American kinship structures created

by slavery and its aftermath as an example of an exception to the normative familial bases of heteronormativity. When homophobia shapes the Black Power and Black Arts movement, the notion of African Americans historically being forced into a queer relation to normative (white) kinship competes with an incestuous heterosexuality (the idea that "brothers and sisters" are "always already heterosexual").

9

Retraining the Heartworks
Women in Atlanta's Black Arts Movement

James Smethurst

At some point in her life she was sure Douglass, Tubman, the slave narratives, the songs, the fables, Delaney, Ida Wells, Du Bois, Garvey, the singers, her parents, Malcolm, Coltrane, the poets, her comrades, her godmother, her neighbors, had taught her that. Thought she knew how to build immunity to the sting of the serpent that turned would-be cells, could-be cadres into cargo cults. Thought she knew how to build resistance, make the journey to the center of the circle, stay poised and centered in work and not fly off, stay centered in the best of her people's traditions and not be available to madness, not become intoxicated by the heady brew of degrees and career and congratulations for nothing done, not become anesthetized by dazzling performances with somebody else's aesthetic, not go under. Though the work of the Sixties had pulled the Family safely out of range of the serpent's fangs so the works of the Seventies could drain the poisons, repair damaged tissues, retrain the heartworks, realign the spine.

Toni Cade Bambara, *The Salt Eaters*[1]

Toni Cade Bambara wrote her novel *The Salt Eaters* (1980) during her time in Atlanta when she was a member of the Spelman College faculty and a community political and cultural activist. In fact, the novel began as entries in Bambara's journal, literally rooting it in her day-to-day life in Georgia.[2] The novel meditates on the twinned Black Arts and

Alice Lovelace and Charles "Jikki" Riley perform poetry at the Neighborhood Arts Center. Photo by Jim Alexander.

Black Power movements of the 1960s and 1970s from the perspective of an insider and an activist, reflecting on the shortcomings of those movements, especially for black women, as well as their great contributions to social liberation. The novel, then, does not reject Black Arts and Black Power. Rather, its radical black feminist critiques come from the inside of the movements, seeking to strengthen them. These critiques can be divided into three basic categories: identifying and struggling with male supremacist ideology and practice within the movement; advancing women's leadership within the movement; and recognizing existing networks of women's leadership (e.g., in grassroots neighborhood organizing and in physical and spiritual healing) that function in ways that are not often recognized by those at the putative top of the organizational structure.

That the novel should be set in Claybourne, Georgia, drawing heavily on Bambara's experience in Atlanta rather than, say, New York (which Bambara as a native New Yorker knew well) says something about the

South in general—and Atlanta in particular—as a crucial site of Black Arts and Black Power. It also makes a claim for Atlanta as a locale in which black women had an enormous impact on the Black Arts movement, helping to generate an explicitly black nationalist feminism that offered critical support for the Black Power and Black Arts movements rather than marking them as irredeemably masculinist and misogynist.

The term "Black Arts movement," coined by critic, poet, playwright, and activist Larry Neal, is shorthand for the grassroots explosion of politically and formally radical African American art so closely allied to the Black Power movement during the 1960s and 1970s as to be indistinguishable from it. While there were many regional, aesthetic, and ideological strains of Black Arts, all shared an overriding concern with African American political and cultural empowerment and self-determination that they linked to liberation movements around the world, particularly in Africa and its diaspora. When the subject of the Black Arts movement is discussed by scholars, Atlanta almost never receives the same degree of attention as Chicago, New York, Philadelphia, San Francisco, Oakland, Los Angeles, Detroit, or Cleveland. This is due perhaps to a regionalist bias that undervalued the movement in the South and the fact that all the prominent Black Arts and Black Power journals with a national circulation were located in New York, Chicago, Detroit, and the West Coast. However, some of the most important or most highly visible black artists and intellectuals of the post–Black Arts/Black Power movement, including the writers Toni Cade Bambara and Pearl Cleage, the theater and film workers Andrea Frye, Samuel L. Jackson, Spike Lee, and Bill Nunn, and the literary critic Stephen Henderson began or significantly furthered their careers in the Black Arts institutions of Atlanta. Furthermore, nowhere else was the Black Arts movement so enmeshed with local government as was the case in Atlanta during Maynard Jackson's terms as mayor in the 1970s, providing the occasion for the some of the most intense conversations (and debates) about public support of art in the United States.

As a result, Atlanta went from a city in which the African American arts infrastructure outside of the historically black colleges and universities of Atlanta University Center (AUC) was practically nonexistent except for some venues for black popular music and vaudeville to one recognized as containing one of the most dynamic black cultural scenes in the United States, with galleries, theaters, poetry series, concerts, art classes, and, of course, the National Black Arts Festival. Beyond what might be considered specifically black institutions and events, another legacy of the

Black Arts movement in Atlanta and its institutionalization is that black artists and audiences have access to the institutions of the old-line arts establishment, such as the High Museum of Art, to a degree seldom seen elsewhere. When one looks into the genesis and development of this formidable African American arts infrastructure, one is struck by the key roles that black women played on every level. That in and of itself is not so remarkable. Women were central to the emergence and growth of Black Arts (and Black Power and Black Studies) in practically all major (and many smaller) cities and campuses across the United States.[3] What is striking about the women in the Atlanta Black Arts movement is that so many, like Bambara, proclaimed themselves to be black nationalists and feminists and participated simultaneously in Black Arts, Black Power, *and* feminist institutions and organizations without seeing it as a contradiction—indeed, without it being seen for the most part as a contradiction by the black activist community as a whole.

Undoubtedly, the key institution that made the contribution of black women to the civil rights, Black Power, and Black Arts movements in Atlanta so dynamic, especially early in those movements, was Spelman College, the premier historically black women's college. Its hiring of black women artists to be part of the faculty, especially as artists-in-residence, brought a series of vital woman artists and arts activists to the city and did much to develop both male and female artists who would go on to play key roles in the development of the African American arts infrastructure of the city. Spelman provided financial and institutional support that allowed many of these artists to work in building and supporting community-based institutions and programs. Black women artists and arts educators like Toni Cade Bambara and Barbara Molette also helped train Spelman students, such as Pearl Cleage and Andrea Frye, who in turn went on to immerse themselves in the local Atlanta arts community.

Spelman students active in the civil rights movement also did much to prepare the ground for Atlanta's emergence as a crucial site of Black Power/Black Arts feminism. Like many other women's colleges, Spelman in the 1950s and early 1960s still featured paternalistic administrations and a "finishing school" environment that attempted to severely restrict the behavior of its students. While Spelman women had long rebelled against this coercion individually, the rise of the sit-in movement, the black student movement, and the Student Nonviolent Coordinating Committee (SNCC) in 1960 provided the occasion of a mass rebellion by Spelman students against notions of bourgeois femininity and normative gender roles, often under the threat of expulsion from school and arrest by civil authorities. Women from the college, such as Hershelle Sullivan and Ruby Doris Smith, not only joined the burgeoning student movement but were among its earliest leaders in the city.[4]

Of course, one thing that allowed Spelman faculty and students to have such a large impact on local, regional, and ultimately national black political and cultural life was the relationship of the college to the other historically black schools of AUC: Atlanta University, Morehouse, Clark, and Morris Brown. From the 1930s on, the arts programs of AUC, especially in drama and the visual arts, became the hub of the training of black arts educators who would teach in secondary and postsecondary schools throughout the South. AUC also became the site of some of the most important national showcases of black art.[5]

Such campus-based institutions, programs, and artists provided the bedrock of the African American arts infrastructure before the rise of Black Arts and Black Power, as well as support and training for the grassroots institutions that would emerge in the 1960s and 1970s. In conjunction with Atlanta-based political institutions and organizations with a national profile, such as the Southern Christian Leadership Conference (SCLC), SNCC, and the Institute for the Black World (IBW), these academic programs and institutions helped attract a small but growing community of politically minded artists with close ties to AUC, the civil rights movement, and the nascent Black Power movement. While these artists were ideologically and aesthetically diverse, they shared a desire to do educational, artistic, and political work in the broader black community beyond the college campuses. They began this work first in working-class black areas near AUC in the West End, particularly Vine City, where many of the political organizations and institutions were headquartered, and later in the larger complex of African American neighborhoods in South Atlanta. As the community of local and transplanted black artists grew in Atlanta, many of these artists undertook grassroots-oriented cultural initiatives that attempted to reach beyond University Center—and beyond the city. These efforts were generally formally independent of the schools of AUC but often relied heavily on the academic community for staff, financial support, and an audience. While few of these arts initiatives were explicitly feminist, at least initially, black women who were (or became) feminists (and nationalists) found in them the beginnings of a powerful base in the city's cultural and, ultimately, political infrastructure.

A. B. Spellman founded the journal *Rhythm* in 1970 with the idea of serving this growing local and regional arts community that had no real outlet for the work of its members, especially the writers. A. B. Spellman had distinguished himself as a poet and cultural critic in New York, where he worked closely in the early Black Arts movement with his former Howard University classmate Amiri Baraka. Spellman settled in Atlanta in 1967 after meeting Karen Edmonds (Spellman), a SNCC staff member, whom he later married. He found a job as writer-in-residence at Morehouse College. Edmonds provided a crucial link between black cultural, educational, and civil rights institutions in Atlanta, especially in her work with SNCC and, later, the Southern Education Program. Again, this points out how in Atlanta, as elsewhere, women often facilitated networking and community building between different organizations in different public spheres, in ways that often escape historical notice.

In many respects, *Rhythm* was a more radical forerunner of the journal *Catalyst*, edited by Pearl Cleage and funded by the Fulton County Arts Council in the late 1980s and early 1990s. Like *Catalyst*, *Rhythm* sought to provide an institutional voice for a growing community of black artists in the city. Like the Atlanta Center for Black Art, with which it was affiliated, *Rhythm* was not formally connected to any campus, though many of its staff, contributors, and audience members, such as Cleage and Bernice Reagon, had ties to the AUC schools and the network of civil rights, intellectual, and cultural organizations in the West End/AUC/Vine City area.[6]

The Atlanta Center for Black Art supplied an institutional base for the young, politicized black artists in their attempts to reach out to the larger African American community. It provided arts instruction and performances of poetry, theater, music, and other genres and media aimed at a nonacademic constituency. While its funding and impact were limited, the Atlanta Center helped prepare the ground for the Neighborhood Arts Center that flourished under the Maynard Jackson administration, providing a model of what a grassroots African American arts center might be.[7] It gave such important figures of the new cultural initiatives supported by the Jackson administration as Michael Lomax and Cleage some of their early experience with grassroots artistic efforts in Atlanta's black community. Both Lomax and Cleage served terms as secretary of the center. As Cleage recalls, the center's classes, lectures, performances, and workshops gave artists a chance to get together, become acquainted, and build community, and helped develop a constituency for radical black art in Atlanta, breaking down barriers between campus and grassroots neighborhoods.[8]

Another of these institutions was the radical black bookstore Timbuktu Books, run by Ebon Dooley. Much like Vaughn's Bookstore in Detroit and the Aquarian Bookstore in Los Angeles, Timbuktu was also a meeting place for radical black artists and activists, allowing them to interact and network. It was a place where the various strains of Third World Marxism intersected with Pan-Africanism in Atlanta. Though it was not a large space, it was also the site of readings and discussions. Because the stock of the store was very heavily oriented toward black poetry, it also promoted the notion of art as the center of the new black politics and black community building. Timbuktu, then, was crucial in providing local artists a sense of what was happening in the wider Black Arts movement.[9]

The arts institutions and programs directly affiliated with the AUC schools also increasingly interfaced with local community institutions, as well as with the larger Black Arts and Black Power movements. By the mid-1960s, a dynamic, if somewhat shifting, black theater community began to develop at AUC, particularly through the work of Carlton Molette, Barbara Molette, and Baldwin Burroughs with the Spelman drama program, the Morehouse-Spelman Players, and the AU Summer Theater. The dramatic programs and institutions of AUC provided a training ground for theater workers who went on to national careers as actors and directors much as they always had, but increasingly engaged with new Black Arts theaters and dramatic works.

These AUC graduates went on to start local companies and often retained ties to the Atlanta black theater community even after they attained national recognition. The Black Image Theatre was started in the late 1960s by what was essentially a group of graduates of the AUC schools. One of the founders, the director and actress Andrea Frye, became a mainstay of African American theater in Atlanta. Pearl Cleage was a Spelman graduate in 1971 and later a Spelman faculty member whose career as a playwright was significantly nurtured at AUC and took off in the 1980s. Like Frye, she has remained a pillar of the Atlanta theater community. Again, while obviously the faculty at Spelman (and the Morehouse-Spelman players and the Summer Theater) included men and women, the prominence of Spelman College as an institutional foundation for black theater in the city helped guarantee a place for women theater workers at different levels and in different positions (and not simply as actors) that was not true in many other places.

It was in this climate of black self-reliance, intellectual ferment, and institution building that Maynard Jackson, who was president of the city council, successfully challenged the white mayor Sam Masell in 1973, breaking with the tradition of consensus (and some would say co-optation) politics that dominated Atlanta politics for decades. Early on in his administration Jackson was approached by members of Atlanta's "mainstream" arts community, seeking municipal funding for local cultural institutions. Jackson, whose aunt was a professional opera singer, was sympathetic to their arguments, seeing the arts as both a calling card for Atlanta and a way to bridge the gap between his base in the African American community and white Atlanta, which had largely voted against him. In order to investigate this issue and to come up with a working policy, Jackson established an Ad Hoc Advisory Committee for the Arts, which was charged with planning a Mayor's Day for the Arts, making recommendations for future financial support of the arts, and addressing the particular immediate concerns of Atlanta's arts communities. Jackson put Michael Lomax in charge of the Ad Hoc Advisory Committee—and Shirley Franklin became the chief community volunteer.[10]

Lomax and Pearl Cleage, then his wife, joined the Jackson campaign staff as speechwriters and researchers. Both came from prominent, politically active black families.[11] Both Lomax and Cleage had close ties to the African American arts community on and off the campus, having worked at the Atlanta Center for Black Art and *Rhythm*. Cleage became the city's director of publicity. Jackson appointed Lomax as the director of cultural affairs in 1975. In that capacity, Lomax (with the help of Shirley Franklin and others) consciously sought to create an African American grassroots cultural infrastructure, as well as supporting arts efforts in the city generally, both with money from the city's restaurant and hotel tax and as a conduit of federal, state, and private money. Franklin succeeded Lomax as the head of the city's Bureau of Cultural Affairs after Lomax's 1978 election to the Fulton County Commission, the powerful legislative body of the county that includes Atlanta. After his election to the Fulton County Commission, Lomax, who was eventually elected chair of the commission, successfully pushed for the establishment of the Fulton County Arts Council, which had far more money available for direct grants to artists and arts institutions than the city. The black commissioners on the arts council successfully argued that African American institutions should be funded on the same level as such historically white-dominated institutions.[12]

In short, black women like Cleage and Franklin worked closely with men like Jackson and Lomax in high-level positions promoting African

American political and cultural empowerment in Atlanta. Of course, one might argue that women were, as in other places, relegated to positions dealing with culture and education while men held posts with more executive political authority. However, it is worth noting that because Jackson made culture such a prominent feature of his administration, the arts became a major avenue of political advancement to such positions of executive authority, both for Michael Lomax and for Shirley Franklin. The Bureau of Cultural Affairs provided them valuable lessons in negotiating the political bureaucracy and allowed them to establish close ties with activists, organizations, and institutions directly benefiting from Cultural Affairs programs in a wide range of grassroots communities. These experiences and ties led Lomax to the head of the Fulton County Commission and Franklin to the mayor's office.

Lomax, Franklin, Cleage, the poet Ebon Dooley, and other Black Arts activists pushed for the establishment of the Neighborhood Arts Center (NAC), which was conceived in large part in discussions at the Center for Black Art and Timbuktu Books. Michael Lomax, in fact, describes NAC as "the Atlanta Center for Black Art with funding."[13] These activists were able to take advantage of Maynard Jackson's focus on the arts, the city's desire to put empty school buildings to use, federal employment programs, and government support of the arts, particularly the National Endowment for the Arts (NEA) Expansion Arts Program that A. B. Spellman helped to administer.[14] NAC was a vital black cultural hub and the locus of progressive and radical arts efforts from its beginnings in 1974 until the mid-1980s (although the center officially lasted until 1990, it was only a shadow of its former self in its last few years of existence). For most of its history, NAC was housed in black communities, first in an old school building in Mechanicsville, a working-class black neighborhood in southwest Atlanta, and later on a site on Auburn Avenue, the traditional commercial and civic heart of black Atlanta.[15] While the initial support of NAC came from Jackson's Ad Hoc Advisory Committee on the Arts and a 1974 NEA Expansion Arts grant facilitated by Spellman, much of the funding of NAC staff salaries and internships was made possible through the Comprehensive Employment and Training Act (CETA), which had been enacted by the federal government in 1973.

The excitement and enthusiasm generated by NAC in its heyday are hard to re-create in print. The poet Alice Lovelace, for example, drawn with her husband from St. Louis in the late 1970s by the inspiring figure of Maynard Jackson, recalls getting off a bus and being pulled toward

NAC by the sounds of African drumming, which she followed through the neighborhood until she found the center.[16] NAC ran classes in a wide range of arts and crafts. At different times it housed the most important off-campus black theaters of the 1970s and 1980s, including Jomandi Productions (a theater that survived from 1977 into the 1990s) and the Just Us Theater, as well as the Southern Collective of African American Writers founded by Lovelace, Bambara, and Dooley. Its artists-in-residence included at various times Dooley, Bambara, photographer Jim Alexander, jazz musician Ojeda Penn, and actors Samuel L. Jackson, LaTonya Richardson, and Bill Nunn. Spike Lee, too, participated in its programs. It also brought artists, such as writers Gwendolyn Brooks and Maya Angelou, painter Romare Bearden, and dancer Arthur Miller, to Atlanta, often under the auspices of its Paul Robeson Lecture Series, in which the lectures were generally paired with some sort of performance and/or workshop.[17]

At the same time that these black political and cultural initiatives mushroomed with Jackson's election, the feminist movement also grew exponentially in the city. The year 1974 saw not only the beginnings of NAC but also the establishment of Charis Books and More. The bookstore, now the oldest feminist bookstore in the South, took root in the Little Five Points neighborhood of Atlanta, which was fast becoming a center of radical feminist-lesbian activity in the city and in the region. Charis (as the "and More" suggests) became not only a place where one could buy feminist literature, serving much the same function that the Timbuktu bookstore did for African American literature, but also, again like Timbuktu, a meeting place and the site for readings, lectures, consciousness-raising groups, and so on. While its initial constituency has been described as predominantly white, Charis early on consciously featured antiracist books and was, along with Timbuktu, one of the relatively few bookstores that carried a wide range of titles by black authors, particularly women. In particular, it was a place where one could buy nonracist and nonsexist children's books. Black nationalist feminists like Pearl Cleage early on gravitated toward Charis and the radical feminist community it came to anchor. She gave readings at the bookstore and lent her name to its fund-raising efforts over the ensuing decades—as did anthropologist Johnetta Cole, who served as the first black woman president of Spelman from 1987 to 1997, and Shirley Franklin.[18] Other black women who read their work at Charis over the years included Alice Walker, bell hooks, Tayari Jones, Shay Youngblood, Beverly Guy Sheftall, Gloria Wade

Gayles, Maya Angelou, Nikky Finney, and Octavia Butler—many of them Spelman graduates and/or faculty members.

The development of Atlanta as a center of Black Arts/Black Power feminism took a quantum leap with the arrival of Toni Cade Bambara in 1974. Again, like many other black women artists and intellectuals who settled in Atlanta, her primary institutional base, at least financially, was Spelman College. She was appointed as writer-in-residence at Spelman through the intercession of Michael Lomax after a promised position at Clark College fell through. By the time she reached Atlanta, Bambara had already achieved some considerable reputation as a short-story writer and essayist and as the editor of the groundbreaking black feminist anthology *The Black Woman* (1970).[19]

Almost as soon as Bambara arrived, she looked for a base off campus to do community political and cultural work. She found that base in NAC. Bambara inspired other writers, such as Alice Lovelace and Pearl Cleage, through her energy, her generosity to developing artists, and her commitment to the highest degree of craft even as she remained resolutely a political artist dedicated to grassroots neighborhood work. Bambara constantly promoted networking and community among the younger and older black artists of Atlanta and the South. She conducted writing classes in a wide range of venues, including Spelman, NAC, and her own apartment. Bambara's potluck dinners for local writers at her home were legendary. She organized frequent gatherings of artists and intellectuals and brought writers together in less formal ways, often arranging one-on-one meetings of local artists with more nationally known figures visiting Atlanta to give talks or readings at Spelman or one of the other AUC schools. Pearl Cleage still remembers with a certain amount of amazement the time Bambara brought Toni Morrison over to her apartment for dinner when Morrison was in Atlanta. Cleage found herself simultaneously face-to-face with two of her most idolized authors, the "two Toni's."[20] Such introductions provided local artists contacts outside Atlanta, as well as considerable inspiration and validation of their work as writers.

As mentioned earlier, Bambara and Alice Lovelace were among the chief initiators, in 1978, of the Southern Collective of African American Writers (SCAAW), a regional organization somewhat on the model of the Southern Black Cultural Alliance (SBCA) led by Tom Dent in New Orleans and Wendell Narcisse in Miami. SCAAW institutionalized on a higher level the sort of networking Bambara had promoted. It provided southern black writers in a wide range of genres access to widely acclaimed authors, such as Toni Morrison, Octavia Butler, and Sonia Sanchez. SCAAW published a newsletter and organized a series of annual conferences, the largest of which was the "Conference on Black South Literature and Art," in 1980, at Emory University and the NAC. This conference featured such southern writers as Dent, Narcisse, Kristen Hunter, Alvin Aubert, and John O'Neal (of the Free Southern Theater), as well as nationally known figures (usually with some direct connection to the South) such as Alice Walter and Sonia Sanchez. Though Lovelace did much of the organizing work for SCAAW, she credits Bambara with much of the conceptual work. The organization's egalitarianism (little-known writers received the same billing at SCAAW events as their more famous counterparts), focus on the training of black writers of genres in their respective crafts, dedication to building grassroots networks within and beyond the city and the region, and emphasis on leadership by black women all displayed the imprint of Bambara. Although the organization declined with Bambara's departure in the early 1980s, a sense of community that was the legacy of Bambara's tenure in the city lingered (and is still felt today, particularly among writers who knew her).[21]

Bambara saw her work as explicitly feminist and nationalist. As she explained:

> As black and woman in a society systematically organized to oppress each and both, we have a very particular vantage point and, therefore, have a special contribution to make to the collective intelligence, to the literatures of this historical moment. I'm clumsy and incoherent when it comes to defining that perspective in specific and concrete terms, worse at assessing the value of my own particular pitch and voice in the overall chorus. I leave that to our critics, to our teachers and students of literature. I'm a nationalist; I'm feminist, at least that. That's clear, I'm sure, in the work.[22]

While she allowed the possible value of working with progressive white people, she chose to devote her energies to political and cultural work in the African American community and to building cooperation among people of color, particularly women.[23]

Her fusing of radical black nationalist and feminist politics did much to make a friendly space for black women with similar stances. She was one of the key figures of an underground feminist black liberation group, Sojourner South, which also included Shirley Franklin, Patricia Daly, Janet

Douglas, Jualynne Dodson (research director at the AU School of Social Work and closely associated with the IBW). The group's activities primarily focused around employment discrimination and solidarity with the antiapartheid movement in South Africa. It also provided a space where members could articulate critiques of sexism within the Black Power movement and, even more pointedly, racism in "mainstream" feminism, particularly the failure of many white feminists in Atlanta to see welfare rights as a major feminist concern.[24] In other words, it dovetailed with the project that Bambara undertook in putting together *The Black Woman*.

Pearl Cleage recalls Bambara as someone to whom she could talk about her own combination of nationalism and feminism without having to explain herself.[25] While a commonplace about the antagonism between feminism and black nationalism still has wide circulation, the central role that Bambara, Cleage, Andrea Frye, Alice Lovelace, and other women played in the community cultural and political institutions of the city (and beyond) gave them a credibility and a base of support for their feminist nationalism (or nationalist feminism) that allowed them and these institutions to significantly avoid this antagonism. The sense that these women had made huge contributions to black political and cultural empowerment made it extremely difficult, even if one had been so inclined, to portray them as somehow outside the circle of the African American community in Atlanta. It did not seem to be a contradiction for Bambara and Cleage, say, to work at NAC and other community-based black institutions and be active in the circles around Charis and More.[26] Neither was it a problem for Cleage to articulate her feminist nationalism in columns written for the *Atlanta Tribune*, one of the city's leading African American journals (largely published, edited, and written by black women):[27]

> A sister recently asked me how I am able to balance my Black National-
> ist politics with my Black Feminist politics. I was a little surprised by the
> question, but I tried to explain that I don't see any conflict between the
> two positions. In fact, I don't think you can be a true Black Nationalist,
> dedicated to the freedom of Black people *without* being a feminist, black
> *people* being made up of both men and *women*, after all, and feminism
> being nothing more or less than a belief in the political, social and legal
> equality of women. (*Deals with the Devil*, 180)[28]

As a result of the nationalist feminist participation in the leading African American intellectual, cultural, and political institutions of the city,

Atlanta increasingly became a national locus of black feminism. An example of the city's regional and national importance as a center of Black Power feminism can be seen in the fact that the National Black Feminist Organization, perhaps the first national black organization to explicitly identify itself as feminist in the post–civil rights movement era, chose Atlanta (along with Detroit and Washington, D.C.) as one of the three cities in which it held press conferences in 1974. The group sought to protest what it saw as the stereotypes of black women (and black families), particularly the figure of the domineering black mother drawn from the Moynihan Report and a long line of popular culture representations, as in the television show *That's My Mama*.[29]

Spelman College in particular became an important site for the development of black women's (or Africana women's) studies. When the Women's Research and Resources Center opened there in 1981, it was the first of its kind on a historically black campus. The following years saw the college host a number of national conferences regarding black women in politics, health issues affecting black women, and so on, as well as the tenth conference of the National Women's Studies Association in 1987—the same year that the radical black feminist Johnetta Cole became Spelman's president.[30]

This development of Atlanta as a center of black feminism in the 1970s and 1980s took place at exactly the same time that the city beyond AUC became an increasingly prominent national venue for African American art. Of course, the black campuses continued to be a vital part of this cultural growth. But, increasingly, it was Atlanta as a city and African American arts center, not simply as the home of the schools of AUC, that showed this new profile. Undoubtedly, the prime calling card signaling Atlanta as a major hub of African American art (or any sort of art) was—and is—the National Black Arts Festival. The festival was conceived largely by Michael Lomax in 1987, significantly funded through the Fulton County Arts Council (and other private and public money largely facilitated through the efforts of Lomax, Franklin, and others in city and county government), and inaugurated in 1988. While executive director of the festival Michelle Smith optimistically hoped for an attendance of 250,000, the festival drew a half million viewers.[31] As the name suggests, the founders of the festival wanted to link it to the heyday of the Black Arts movement in the 1960s and 1970s and make a claim to Atlanta's national significance (both to the United States generally and to black people particularly) as well as to the centrality of the African American community to Atlanta's future.[32]

Some of the organizations of the 1970s and 1980s declined and failed under the pressure of economic fluctuations and of a local and national move to the right politically, especially during the Republican administrations of the 1980s and early 1990s and the Republican "tax revolt" of the 1990s. Still, some institutions, like the New Jomandi Theater and the Black Arts Festival, were able to survive financial problems.[33] Similarly, the Bureau of Cultural Affairs, the Fulton County Arts Council, Hammonds House, and other institutions that grew out of the Black Arts initiatives enabled by the election of Maynard Jackson and the rise of black political power in Atlanta and Fulton County also endured and even flourished. Furthermore, the success of black cultural activists and institutions in Atlanta allowed African Americans access to institutions that had once excluded or ignored them, such as the Alliance Theater and the High Museum of Art.

Again, the fact that black women were integral to the development of the Black Arts movement and the grassroots African American cultural infrastructure of Atlanta, or that many of the city's leading black artists were (and are) women was not remarkable. The same could be said about many other cities. What is interesting is that so many of the women who helped build the black arts institutions of the city, which went from virtually nonexistent (at least off campus) to nationally prominent, publicly identified early on as feminists and were active in feminist circles and organizations. Women like Toni Cade Bambara, Pearl Cleage, Alice Lovelace, and Shirley Franklin were not marginal to the movement for black cultural and political empowerment in Atlanta but were right at its center and seen as such, for the most part, by both black women and men. Of course, in other places black culture and political empowerment were closely intertwined, and black artists were also political leaders (and political leaders were deeply committed to the promotion of black art)—one thinks particularly of Newark, New Jersey, and the dual role Amiri Baraka played in its political and cultural life in the Black Power era. However, the way that black feminists tied together feminism and nationalism, art and politics while building grassroots black political, cultural, and educational institutions was remarkable and a crucial part of Atlanta's growth as a center of black art as well as politics. Unquestionably, the most prominent display of this intertwined centrality was the election of Shirley Franklin, the former director of the Bureau of Cultural Affairs and member of Sojourner South, as mayor of Atlanta in 2001. The first black woman to be elected mayor of a major city in the South (unless one counts Washington,

D.C.), Franklin continues to be a strong supporter of black and feminist (and black feminist) cultural institutions and events.

Returning again to *The Salt Eaters*, as Bambara's novel argues, this confluence of feminism and nationalism was not without its contradictions. However, the fact that it was basically triumphant in the movement in Atlanta complicates received narratives about the inherent misogyny and masculinism of Black Arts and Black Power and the conflict between nationalism and feminism. That feminist or protofeminist women were all along at the center of the building of new black political and cultural institutions that grew out of the civil rights movement and the schools of AUC gave these women a particular base of support that insulated them from claims that they were somehow alien to African American interests or owed allegiance to groups primarily located outside the black community. Of course, further research may demonstrate that the case of Atlanta is not so singular as some might imagine.

NOTES

1. Toni Cade Bambara, *The Salt Eaters* (New York: Random House, 1980), 258.

2. Toni Cade Bambara, *Deep Sightings and Rescue Missions* (New York: Pantheon, 1996), 234–235.

3. Sarah Webster Fabio in Oakland, California; Elma Lewis in Boston; Sonia Sanchez in New York and San Francisco; Barbara Ann Teer in New York; Margaret Danner in Detroit; Margaret Burroughs, Gwendolyn Brooks, Val Gray Ward, Johari Amini, Carolyn Rodgers, and Jayne Cortez in Los Angeles, among many other African American women, played central roles in the creation of an African American arts infrastructure during the 1960s and 1970s.

4. For a study of the role of Spelman students and faculty in the civil rights movement, see Harry Lefever, *Undaunted by the Fight: Spelman College and the Civil Rights Movement, 1957–1967* (Macon, GA: Mercer University Press, 2005).

5. In 1934, for example, a member of the Spelman faculty, Anna Cook, founded AU's annual Summer Theater. The Summer Theater staged four plays in six weeks. The majority of these plays were "classic" and modern works by white European and North American playwrights. However, each summer Cook tried to present at least one work with a black author. Some of the most promising younger black writers and directors, Sterling Brown, Owen Dodson, and Baldwin Burroughs, took part in the Summer Theater. Even after Cook moved to Hampton Institute and then Howard University, she continued to direct the Summer Theater. Errol Hill and James Hatch, *A History of African American Theatre* (New York: Cambridge University Press, 2003), 258–261.

6. Author's interview with Ebon Dooley, August 16, 2001, Atlanta, GA; author's interview with A. B. Spellman, December 28, 2000, Washington, DC; author's interview with A. B. Spellman, November 11, 2006, phone interview.

7. Author's interview with Pearl Cleage, August 8, 2007, phone interview; author's interview with Michael Lomax, August 28, 2007, Cambridge, MA.

8. Author's interview with Pearl Cleage.

9. Author's interview with Ebon Dooley; author's interview with Pearl Cleage; and author's interview with Michael Lomax.

10. "Executive Summary," Neighborhood Arts Center Archives, Auburn Avenue Library, Atlanta, GA, box 1, folder 1.

11. Lomax's father was the writer and activist Louis Lomax. His mother, Almena Lomax, was the publisher of the *Los Angeles Tribune* and a protégé of the legendary left-wing publisher of the *California Eagle*, Charlotta Bass. He spent his early years in Los Angeles but graduated from high school in Alabama after his mother moved there to be closer to the center of the civil rights movement. Cleage, a self-described third-generation nationalist, was the daughter of the nationally known founder of the Shrine of the Black Madonna in Detroit, the Reverend Albert Cleage.

12. Author's interview with Michael Lomax; author's interview with Pearl Cleage.

13. Author's interview with Michael Lomax.

14. Author's interview with Pearl Cleage; author's interview with Alice Lovelace, March 4, 2007, phone interview; author's interview with Michael Lomax; author's interview with A. B. Spellman, 2006.

15. Author's interviews with Ebon Dooley; author's interview with Alice Lovelace; "Executive Summary," Neighborhood Arts Center Archives, box 1, folder 1, 5.

16. Author's interview with Alice Lovelace.

17. "Tentative Programming for 1981–82," Neighborhood Arts Center Archives, box 3, folder 1.

18. Author's interview with Pearl Cleage. For an account of the founding and early days of Charis Books and More and the growth of the radical feminist community in Little Five Points, albeit one that perhaps overemphasizes the whiteness of the feminist community in Atlanta, see Saralyn Chesnut and Amanda C. Gable, "'Women Ran It': Charis Books and More and Atlanta's Lesbian-Feminist Community, 1971–1981," in *Carryin' On in the Lesbian and Gay South*, ed. John Howard (New York: NYU Press, 1997), 241–284.

19. *The Black Woman* (New York: New American Library, 1970) was the most important early statement of a Black Power/Black Arts feminism, bringing together the work of a wide range of younger and older black women writers who were united by their use of "the Black Liberation struggle rather than the American Dream as their yardstick, their gauge, their vantage point" (10).

20. Author's interview with Pearl Cleage; author's interview with Alice Lovelace; Winston Grady-Willis, *Challenging U.S. Apartheid: Atlanta and Black Struggles for Human Rights, 1960–1977* (Durham, NC: Duke University Press, 2006), 199–204.

21. Neighborhood Arts Center Archives, box 2, folder 6; author's interview with Alice Lovelace.

22. Toni Cade Bambara, *Black Women Writers at Work*, ed. Claudia Tate (New York: Continuum, 1984), 14.

23. Claudia Tate, ed., *Black Women Authors at Work* (New York: Continuum, 1984), 14–15.

24. Grady-Willis, *Challenging U.S. Apartheid*, 199–201.

25. Author's interview with Pearl Cleage.

26. Ibid.

27. For a collection that contains many of Cleage's columns in the *Atlanta Tribune*, see Pearl Cleage, *Deals with the Devil: And Other Reasons to Riot* (New York: Ballantine, 1993).

28. Author's interview with Pearl Cleage.

29. Kimberly Springer, *Living for the Revolution: Black Feminist Organizations, 1968–1980* (Durham, NC: Duke University Press, 2005), 41.

30. For an account of Spelman's emergence as a locus of Africana women's studies, see Beverly Guy-Sheftall, "A Black Feminist Perspective on Transforming the Academy: The Case of

Spelman College," in *Theorizing Black Feminisms: The Visionary Pragmatism of Black Women*, ed. Stanlie M. James and Abena P. A. Busia (New York: Routledge, 1993), 79–92.

31. Wendell Brock, "NBAF Looks to 2000 and 'New Cadre of Artists,'" *Atlanta Constitution*, June 28, 1988, Arts, 11L; James Flannery, "A Black Arts Festival—and More," *New York Times*, July 31, 1998, Arts and Leisure, 8, 30.

32. Author's interview with Michael Lomax; Brock, "NBAF Looks to 2000 and 'New Cadre of Artists,'" Arts, 11L; Flannery, "A Black Arts Festival," Arts and Leisure, 8, 30.

33. Author's interview with A. B. Spellman, 2006; author's interview with Carlton Molette; Landon Thomas, "Saving the Black Arts Festival," *Atlanta Constitution*, August 15, 1992, A14; Tom Sabulis, "Exit of Theater Pioneer Jolts Jomandi, Community," *Atlanta Constitution*, January 5, 2001, Features, 1E; Dan Hulbert, "Jomandi's JAM Black Theater's in Fight for Its Life," *Atlanta Constitution*, November 13, 1994, Arts, 1.

10

"Women's Liberation or . . . Black Liberation, You're Fighting the Same Enemies"

Florynce Kennedy, Black Power, and Feminism

Sherie M. Randolph

Several decades after the political upheavals of the sixties, very few people recognize the name of the Black feminist lawyer and activist Florynce "Flo" Kennedy (1916–2000). However, during the late 1960s and 1970s, Kennedy was the most well-known Black feminist in the country.[1] When reporting on the emergence of the women's movement, the media covered her early membership in the National Organization for Women (NOW), her leadership of countless guerrilla theater protests, and her work as a lawyer helping to repeal New York's restrictive abortion laws.[2] Indeed, Black feminist Jane Galvin-Lewis and white feminists Gloria Steinem and Ti-Grace Atkinson credit Kennedy with helping to educate a generation of young women about feminism in particular and radical political organizing more generally.[3]

However, presently Kennedy's activism is marginalized or completely erased from most histories of "second-wave" feminism. On the rare occasion that Kennedy is mentioned, it is usually only to reference her exceptional status as one of the few black women involved in the mainstream white feminist movement.[4] Kennedy is a significant exemplar of the exclusion of key Black feminist organizers from most feminist scholarship on the movement: the erasure of her critical role speaks to the ways in which feminist literature has failed to see black women as progenitors of contemporary feminism. In response to such historical effacement, this

Flo Kennedy AP photo.

essay resurrects Kennedy's political contribution to sixties radicalism and uncovers a Black feminist politics and practice that not only were connected to the mainstream feminist movement but also were closely allied to the Black Power struggle. In doing so, it challenges previously held rigid dichotomies between the Black Power and second-wave women's movements and illuminates the centrality of Black feminism and Flo Kennedy to both movements.

Kennedy's assertion that she could "understand feminism [and sexism] better because of the discrimination against Black people"[5] and because of her work in black movements helps us to isolate the Black Power movement as a significant force in shaping contemporary feminist struggles. Earlier feminist movement scholarship ignores or undervalues the connections between Black Power and feminist struggles. Studies of independent black feminists and the predominantly white feminist movements accurately cite the increased masculinity that kept feminism and black nationalism divided.[6] They are not wrong to do so, but positioning Black Power as primarily an antagonistic influence misses what the movement might tell us about how both black and white feminists understood liberation and revolution. Connecting both black and white feminists to organizations such as the Black Panther Party and the Black Power Conferences tells us a great deal about how feminists worked toward reconstructing the society in which they lived. While some recent scholarship has helped to expand our understanding of the Black Power movement's relationship to feminism,[7] there is still much to be understood about the ways in which the Black Power movement was connected to feminist radicalism. I argue that Kennedy's example forces us to see how the strategies and theories understood to have originated in Black Power struggles were absorbed, if at times unevenly, by both black and white feminists.

Kennedy was simultaneously a Black feminist and a black nationalist who built alliances between the mostly white feminist and Black Power movements during the postwar period that Black feminist historian Paula Giddings calls the "masculine decade." The 1960s witnessed a increase in political appeals to black masculinity as many Black Power radicals demanded that black women assume an auxiliary role to black men and address their energy toward the family.[8] Kennedy, like other Black feminists, criticized these antiquated gender norms.[9] Despite her critiques of Black Power and her close relationship to the feminist struggle, Kennedy continued to work inside the Black Power movement as a lawyer for Black Power leaders H. Rap Brown and Assata Shakur, as a fund-raiser for numerous Black Panther Party political campaigns, and as an organizer and delegate of the Black Power Conferences (1967–1972).[10]

Many Black Power advocates were equally critical of the predominantly white women's movement, arguing that feminism was divisive, racist, and a diversion. Black nationalists often accused Black feminists of merely aping white feminist directives.[11] Kennedy, however, maintained that a movement devoted to ending sexist oppression was vital for both women and men. She worked in predominantly white feminist organizations (such as NOW and the October 17th Movement—later known as The Feminists) throughout the 1960s and 1970s and independent Black feminist organizations (such as the National Black Feminist Organization and Black Women United for Political Action) in the 1970s and 1980s.

Years later, Kennedy commented on what many viewed as the incompatibility between her various political locations, noting that despite her close relationship to the feminist movement and white feminists, she was never forced by black nationalists to denounce her feminist affiliations or to "separate . . . as a feminist from the black movement."[12] This was in part because the feminism she espoused was deeply entrenched in the theories and strategies of the Black Power struggle, most notably its commitment to ending white supremacy and imperialism. Indeed, she grounded her critiques of sexism within the Black Power movement's radical criticism of racism and empire. Moreover, like many other radicals, she viewed the Black Power movement as the vanguard movement of the era.[13] As such, her work inside white feminist organizations emphasized challenges to racism and was intricately connected to the Black Power struggle. Much of her activism and writing exemplify how she maneuvered between what most contemporary observers and scholars see as inherently oppositional movements, in an attempt to extend black nationalism outside of Black Power circles and into primarily white feminist spaces.[14]

The midsixties were a watershed period for both the Black Power and women's movements. Civil rights organizations like the Student Nonviolent Coordinating Committee (SNCC) and the Congress of Racial Equality (CORE) rejected their previous integrationist ideology and began to promote black nationalist frameworks and strategies. Even a few black elected officials, including Adam Clayton Powell Jr., began advocating Black Power and held a Black Power Conference at the nation's capitol in hopes of bringing together leaders interested in organizing a nationwide Black Power platform. In the mid-sixties, through the efforts of CORE, SNCC, the Black Power Conference, and other organizations, the Black

Power movement began to occupy the national stage and eclipsed the civil rights movement as the leader of the larger black freedom struggle.

This period was equally pivotal for the predominantly white women's movement. NOW was founded in 1966; several local chapters and women's study groups and organizations emerged throughout the country soon after.[15] The rapid growth of both movements forced shifts in the relationship between postwar radical and liberal organizations: by 1967, both Black Power advocates and feminists were attempting to define new agendas and rethink their ties to the larger postwar struggle. In 1967, important opportunities arose for allegiances between the two movements.

An examination of Kennedy's work as an activist in the Black Power Conference, the National Conference for New Politics (NCNP), and NOW during the summer and fall of 1967 helps us to center Black Power as a pivotal ideological influence on the predominantly white radical feminist and Black feminist politics that emerged in the 1960s.

Florynce Kennedy's Early Radicalism

Born in 1916 in Kansas City, Missouri, Kennedy was raised by working-class parents who taught their five daughters to challenge white authority at every turn. Often the Kennedy girls witnessed their mother and father successfully defending themselves and their family against attacks by the Ku Klux Klan and white employers. In 1942, during the first year of the United States' involvement in World War II, Kennedy moved from Kansas City to New York City, where she found political direction for the lessons she had learned at the feet of her iconoclastic parents.[16]

At the age of twenty-six, Kennedy arrived in New York hoping to benefit from the few wartime opportunities now open to African Americans and women. The city's intellectual and political environment was an escape from the drudgery of Kansas City's unskilled labor market, where she had worked as an elevator operator and a domestic. It was in the political and social milieu of New York City while a student at Columbia University and its law school, and then as an up-and-coming lawyer, that Kennedy politically came of age.

Although Kennedy's work and classes left her little time for political organizing, she took full advantage of Columbia's radical currents. She enrolled in courses on socialism and communism and sought out those professors who were active in New York's Popular Front efforts. She also moved through the city's radical social movements—attending Adam

Clayton Powell's speeches in Harlem and rallies for Progressive Party presidential hopeful Henry Wallace, and voraciously reading anti-imperialist and antiracist literature. Kennedy's experience among the flood of women, most of them white, who entered Columbia University during World War II—and who were barred from admission after the war—led her to connect the oppression of white women and black people. She began to see an alliance of the two as a force that could be tapped against white male hegemony. Her papers in college suggest that she was beginning to make links between all forms of oppression, especially between imperialism, racism, and sexism.[17]

When Kennedy graduated from Columbia Law School in 1951, she became one of the few black women practicing law in the city. Like her peers, including Pauli Murray and Constance Baker Motley, she faced limited opportunities for employment in New York's major law firms and legal aid societies. In 1954 she opened her own firm, defending the rights of black cultural workers (such as Billie Holiday) who had been targeted on the basis of the political import of their work.[18]

In the early and middle 1960s, Kennedy went to work with civil rights organizations (Wednesdays in Mississippi—an interracial group of middle-class women who traveled south during Freedom Summer to help support SNCC workers); white leftist organizations (Youth against War and Fascism and the Workers World Party); and black nationalist organizations (Organization of Afro-American Unity). She published a weekly column in the *Queens Voice*, a local black newspaper, and hosted *Opinions*, a thirty-minute show on WLIB radio. Her frequent guests included activists such as Key Martin (Youth against War and Fascism), Cynthia Epstein (NOW), and Betty Shabazz, widow of Malcolm X. The show was built around heated discussions of various techniques for challenging white backlash against Black Power, strategies for ending the war in Vietnam, and the growth of the women's movement.[19] During the 1960s, Kennedy's column and radio show were among the few Black feminist media channels devoted to examining imperialism, sexism, and racism.

Racism Is "Deadly": The Black Power Movement Should Lead

While Kennedy worked within an array of organizations and advocated ending all forms of oppression, she ultimately believed that racism shaped relationships of power and domination in the United States and was therefore the litmus test for American democracy. Like Black Power leaders and other black radicals Stokely Carmichael, Ella Baker, and W. E. B. Du Bois, Kennedy reasoned that racism contributed to every major social problem in the United States: the exploitation of labor, the policing of sex workers, the abuse of sexual minorities, and the oppression of women as a group.[20]

Frequently, Kennedy used the term "niggerizing" as a synonym for oppression, as a rhetorical strategy meant to force oppressed people to understand how the racist techniques sharpened on the backs of blacks could be deployed against all oppressed people. Although Kennedy understood oppressions as interconnected, she ultimately believed that racism was the primary language scripting American society and was therefore the most "deadly" form of oppression. Further, she argued that "racism will always be worse than sexism until we find feminists shot in bed like [Black Panthers] Mark Clark and Fred Hampton."[21] And, like other Black Power leaders and some white leftists, she argued that black people "started this revolution" and spent more time on the front lines; therefore, the Black Power movement had earned the right to claim vanguard status within the larger struggle.[22]

Though Kennedy privileged black liberation movements and racial oppression, she still argued that it did not matter which oppression was more lethal: they all "hurt like crazy." In her opinion the best strategy was to conquer all forms of exploitation.[23] Kennedy believed that a steady and consistent attack against all forms of oppression from a variety of organizational fronts helped to quicken revolutionary change. Kennedy's theory on challenging oppression helps to explain why she worked in a wide range of organizations and movements throughout her political career.

Her theory on challenging oppression also helps explain her relationship to white leftist—specifically white feminist—organizations. While working in predominantly white left spaces, she demanded that white activists focus on ending racism and support the Black Power struggle. She frequently instructed white radicals on the importance of understanding how power and force circulate in the United States:

If you test the fences of this society and dare to influence the direction of this society, they know you mean business by the extent to which you identify with the black revolution. . . . If you want to absolutely communicate the depth of your determination to bring down this society that is committed to racism, then indicate determination to *frustrate racism with a coalition with the black revolutionary struggle.*[24]

Building the Black Revolutionary Struggle:
The Black Power Conference

When SNCC and CORE began to popularize the term "Black Power" in 1966, Kennedy welcomed the open tenacity, bravado, and revolutionary ambitions of the young radicals. As a representative to the 1967 Black Power Conference in Newark, Kennedy attempted to dispel the media-driven myth that Black Power was a new phenomenon. In an interview with the *New York Times* during the conference, she asserted that Black Power had always existed "but was like the wind that turns no windmill or the waterfall that was not harnessed to run a generator."[25] Like other black radicals, she was frustrated with the Democratic Party's failure to meet the black community's needs and disdained civil rights organizations like the National Association for the Advancement of Colored People (NAACP) that relied primarily on legal strategies in the fight against racism.[26] She welcomed the possibility that young black radicals might "harness" the revolutionary potential of Black Power's assertion that black people constituted a single community within the United States and therefore had a right to determine their own destiny and profoundly shift relationships of power.

During the spring and summer of 1967, Kennedy attended the Black Power Conference planning sessions held in Newark. Alongside Black Power leaders such as Omar Ahmed, Nathan Wright, and Amiri Baraka, she developed workshops, invited black delegates from the United States and abroad, and helped create a publicity plan.[27] Kennedy hoped to find ways to support the Black Power movement's increased momentum.

The Newark rebellion that occurred only days before the meeting helped to virtually triple the registration rolls from the initial projection of 400 participants.[28] From July 20 to July 24, 1967, more than 1,000 black women and men flocked to Newark from other parts of the United States and from the Caribbean and Africa.[29] The delegates represented hundreds of different organizations. The Newark rebellion and the masses of blacks who descended upon the convention forced organizers to engage the concept of Black Power as a tool for revolutionary change and to capitalize on the momentum created by the rebellion. At the workshops, speakers such as Amiri Baraka, H. Rap Brown, and Maulana Karenga (US Organization) stressed black self-defense against white terrorism and warned whites of the radical change in black people. Others stressed a more moderate and reformist view of Black Power, stating that "blacks needed to be like other ethnic groups in America who developed their own solidarity as a basic approach toward entry into the American mainstream."[30]

For Kennedy, the Newark conference and the following Black Power Conferences were important because they emphasized black people's use of collective *power* to challenge American racism and imperialism. It may have been through the conferences that Kennedy more fully defined her thinking on power and oppressed people's ability to make use of their group strength. She advocated a form of Black Power pluralism as represented by leaders as diverse as Malcolm X (after his split from the Nation of Islam), Adam Clayton Powell, and Nathan Wright. Black Power pluralists argued that the United States was monopolized by white power, which had historically served to keep African Americans from true liberation; in order for black people to challenge this oppressive monopoly, they needed to move toward a position of community strength. Most pluralists believed that they could transfer their new racial solidarity and power into national and local decision-making power. They maintained that as a result, black people, the nation, and the world would be fundamentally transformed for the better.[31]

Furthermore, Kennedy credited no other movement with as much potential for illustrating the blatant contradictions of American democracy and thereby rearticulating American democratic principles and ideas not only for black people but for all people. Like many other radicals, she saw the development of Chicano power, Native American power, and women's power as an expected consequence of Black Power's emphasis on liberation and self-determination.[32]

As a facilitator (along with Ossie Davis and Carol Green) of the conference's media workshop, Kennedy used the session to discuss strategies for challenging the media and to stress the importance of sharing tactical information across movement lines.[33] Not long after the media workshop began, Kennedy was interrupted by a commotion in the back of the room. Queen Mother Moore was standing up, demanding that two white intruders seated in the back row be asked to leave. Moore was a powerful voice in black nationalist circles and had been active in black radical politics since the 1920s. Once a member of Marcus Garvey's Universal Negro Improvement Association and the Communist Party (USA), she now was leading the reparations movement through the Reparations Committee she had founded in 1962.[34] Her voice bellowed throughout the room: "These white women have to get out! This meeting is for blacks only!" The activists seated in the front rows turned around to see white feminists and

NOW members Ti-Grace Atkinson and Peg Brennan shrinking into their seats as Moore hovered over them. From the stage Kennedy quickly came to their defense: "These are my guests! I don't invite people some place then tell them to leave!" But Moore and the other attendees did not care whose guests the white women were; they just wanted them out.[35]

For Moore and the other organizers, the Black Power movement was to be unlike the civil rights struggle, where white participation was directly encouraged. In contrast, Black Power promoted independent black politics, and white participation in the conference threatened to disrupt this goal. As the argument between Kennedy and Moore escalated, the room became tense, and bodies began to rise from their seats. Atkinson remembers someone in the crowd threatening to kill Kennedy for bringing the white women to the Black Power Conference. "Do what you have to do," Kennedy responded. "I've lived my life."[36]

There was another unwanted guest in the room, as well, although this other attendee escaped the outrage focused on Atkinson and Brennan. The FBI agent monitoring Kennedy at the conference noted how she became louder and more belligerent as she "directed profanity at Negroes present, and refused to ask whites who were present to leave."[37] Afraid of what might happen next, Brennan "got out of there fast." When Kennedy saw Brennan leave, she ordered Atkinson to "stay where you are!" Shaking, Atkinson froze, not daring to leave her chair. To her surprise, Moore and her backers eventually gave way. Kennedy and the other facilitators returned to their presentations with Atkinson listening quietly, staring at her feet.[38]

Years later Atkinson described her and Brennan's decision to attend the conference as "nuts." Yet she was profoundly appreciative of the opportunity Kennedy provided her to witness the Black Power movement during its formative years. Hearing black activists plot strategies and formulate workshop resolutions "transformed" her burgeoning feminist politics.[39] Atkinson commented: "She was always trying to pull it together and [I] have to say in many ways maybe it was a bad idea or clumsy or difficult. But, it's why people like myself became really transformed not only in terms of politics generally, but because of my feminism. It deepened everything."[40]

Kennedy began helping white feminists learn from the Black Power movement when she first joined NOW's New York chapter only eight months before the Black Power Conference. She frequently invited young feminists like Atkinson, Brennan, and Anselma Dell'Olio to Black Power and anti–Vietnam War meetings and marches. Atkinson remembers how Kennedy wanted the young feminists to witness "a group of people in transition and evolving."[41] The confrontation at the conference workshop reveals a great deal about the value Kennedy placed on white feminists learning from the Black Power struggle and becoming an additional arm in the battle to defeat the repressive state.[42]

Moreover, Kennedy's ability to quiet the room and to have Atkinson remain at the conference over the objections of black participants also suggests that Kennedy held a certain degree of authority in Black Power spaces, authority that was not easily weakened by the confrontation. Hence, Kennedy went on to attend the Black Power Conferences in Philadelphia (1968), Bermuda (1969), and Atlanta (1970) and the related black political caucuses in Gary, Indiana (1968 and 1972).[43] At the Black Power Conference in Bermuda, Kennedy was not only an attendee but also a major voice along with Queen Mother Moore, leading the conference.[44]

Kennedy's involvement in all the Black Power Conferences helped connect her to the larger Black Power movement. Historian Komozi Woodard argues that the conferences served as a key site for the development of movement leadership. The Black Power Conferences mobilized between 1966 and 1969 mark the beginning of what Woodard describes as the modern black convention movement. He argues that this movement served as a center for the creation of national and local leadership, nurtured in many local leaders an identity in a national movement, and created an atmosphere for the development of black united fronts.[45] In many ways Kennedy's organizing work at the conferences substantiates Woodard's conclusions. Through her efforts to develop a black united front, she built relationships with local and national black radicals, became a leader in the larger black convention movement, and went on to share with the white new left, and particularly white feminists, ways they could continue working with the black freedom movement given the rise of Black Power. For Kennedy, Black Power had the potential to end oppression broadly and to create not only a black united front but also a larger radical interracial united front.

Sixties Movements in Flux: The National Conference for New Politics

Only a few weeks after the Newark Black Power Conference, Kennedy and other conference delegates attended the first convention of the National Conference for New Politics in Chicago from August 31 to September 1,

1967. There they engaged in conversations with the white left about ways in which to have meaningful collaborations with the Black Power movement.

An outgrowth of several meetings held during the summer and fall of 1965 between anti–Vietnam War radicals, reform democrats, and civil rights organizers, the NCNP's broad objectives were to end the Cold War and military intervention abroad, to establish racial equality, to encourage both world disarmament and constructive relations between people undertaking revolutionary change, and finally to address the needs of the United States' decaying cities and depressed rural areas.[46] The convention's white organizers were especially hopeful that the meeting would unite the differing sectors of the Black Power and civil rights movements with white liberals and radicals of the peace movement.[47]

As soon as the Black Power radicals arrived at the conference, however, they began to criticize the organizers for failing to include black people in the early planning. Frustrated by the conference's lack of attention to full black participation and black leadership, some black delegates walked out and announced their own convention.[48] The majority, who remained, formed the Black Caucus. Some, like Kennedy and James Forman of SNCC, traveled back and forth between the two black groups.[49]

Black Caucus members met privately to hammer out an agreement. Their strategy recognized the fundamental connections between black liberation and the antiwar movement. The caucus demanded support for the Newark Black Power Conference resolutions, the organization of "white civilizing" committees in white communities to eliminate racism, support for all wars of national liberation worldwide and, finally, 50 percent voting power on all convention committees.[50]

While many white organizers supported these demands, much debate arose over the 50 percent provision, given that black participants made up only 15 to 20 percent of the delegates. Most mainstream news reporters and some white leftists saw the acceptance of the Black Caucus's demands as giving black activists an unfair and undemocratic advantage; some even argued that white leftists were now being forced to "lick [the] boots" of black activists.[51]

For the Black Caucus conferees, however, it was important that black people who fought on the front lines and faced the brunt of the state's attacks be granted significant power in movement leadership. In an essay published in the *Islamic Press International News Gram*, Kennedy challenged those "dissident delegates" and reporters who argued that giving blacks 50 percent of the vote meant white activists had "lick[ed black] boots," asserting that "white people don't lick boots when they make a good alliance, Mr. Racist." The *"constructive rise of black power may be the only hope that America has,"* she answered. "We guess any recognition of the value of the voting power of blacks is 'craven surrender.'"[52]

Organizers like Kennedy, Forman, and H. Rap Brown wanted the white leftists to understand one central message: in order to be effective antiracist allies, white activists had to grasp the importance of black self-determination. The influence of the Black Power movement's ideology and organizing strategies was evident throughout the rest of the convention. In particular, the Black Revolution resolution, created by a majority-white workshop, emphasized black leadership and connected the revolts in Detroit and Newark to the struggles of the South Vietnamese.[53]

"We Were Observing and We Copied": Black Power's Influence on the "Genesis" of the Radical Predominantly White Feminist Movement

The influence of Black Power theories and tactics on white participants at the NCNP was further exemplified when the (mostly white) Women's Workshop demanded 51 percent of the convention votes. The Black Caucus protest provided a framework for feminists to understand how to organize separately, inspiring women to create their own agenda that challenged the hegemony of male leadership, both at the convention and in the new left movement more generally.

Participants such as Kennedy, Jane Adams (Students for a Democratic Society [SDS]), Shulamith Firestone, Ti-Grace Atkinson, and Jo Freeman (Southern Christian Leadership Conference [SCLC]) had been active in organizations or study groups discussing women's liberation while also often working in civil rights and/or new left movements. During the conference most of these women attended the planned Women's Workshop. However, some grew displeased with the workshop, arguing that its leaders were more concerned with challenging the war than with confronting sexist oppression. According to Freeman, she and Firestone stayed up all night after the session, creating new resolutions that took a more direct stance against the oppression of women. Following the example of the Black Caucus, they demanded 51 percent of the convention votes, arguing that women represented 51 percent of the population.[54] They also insisted that the convention support the total equality of women in education and employment, condemn the mass media for perpetuating stereotypes of women, unite with various liberation struggles, and recognize that the majority of black women are doubly oppressed.[55]

The women threatened to tie up the conference with procedural motions if their resolutions were not debated on the convention floor. The conference organizers finally conceded and added the women's resolutions to the agenda. Freeman, Firestone, and several other women handed out 2,000 copies of their resolutions to the delegates.[56]

However, William Pepper, executive director of NCNP, quickly dismissed the women when it was time to read their resolutions. Frustrated, several women ran to the microphone and attempted to make their resolutions heard. Pepper further disregarded the women's concerns when he patted "Shulie [Firestone] on the head and said 'move on little girl we have more important issues to talk about here than Women's Liberation.'" For Freeman, this was the last straw and the incident that represented the "genesis" of the radical, predominantly white women's movement. Through this confrontation, the New Politics Conference became an important moment for the course of the radical, predominantly white women's liberation movement.[57] Hence, a week later some of the women from NCNP met in Chicago and wrote a manifesto, "To the Women of the Left,"[58] which repeated most of their Women's Workshop demands. It was reprinted two months later in *New Left Notes* as "Chicago Women Form Liberation Group."[59] Interestingly, the section that recognized black women as "doubly oppressed" was removed from this version. The excision of any reference to black women in the published manifesto signals the complications many radical white feminists would have in attempting to articulate an understanding of the specific differences among women and the various ways that race and gender oppression intersect.

Kennedy had welcomed the creation of a Women's Workshop and insisted that women's oppression be addressed on the convention floor. Indeed, at the same time Freeman and Firestone were writing their resolutions, Kennedy was in her hotel room, coaching Ti-Grace Atkinson to write and disseminate a statement on the connections between sexism, racism, and imperialism.[60] Each evening Kennedy returned to the room and shared her Black Caucus experiences with Atkinson and two other white feminists from NOW. Atkinson noted that Kennedy had a "profound . . . influence . . . on some of us . . . we were observing and we copied" the Black Caucus strategy. In addition, Atkinson had previously connected with Black Caucus delegates like Omar Ahmed when Kennedy arranged for her to travel to the NCNP on a bus sponsored by Black Muslims from Harlem. On the thirteen-hour bus ride to Chicago Atkinson remembered talking to black nationalists about why a movement for black self-determination was vitally important and their future strategies for achieving the goal of black liberation.[61]

Years later, Atkinson and Brennan remembered that Kennedy helped them to understand the importance of supporting other social justice movements as part of their feminist politics.[62] Atkinson described how Kennedy pushed white feminists to support black movements because for "Flo, [it] was really fundamental . . . to expand understanding and support."[63] Perhaps Kennedy viewed the feminist organizing at the conference as the type of practical borrowing of movement tactics that needed to take place between organizers. Both Kennedy and Atkinson hoped that the (mostly white) Women's Workshop participants would continue fighting to end racism, sexism, and imperialism after they left the conference.

The statement that Kennedy coached Atkinson to write emphasized the struggles black people were waging at the conference and throughout the country, describing racial oppression as the most "justifiably immediately pressing" problem. But the statement went a step further by arguing that "the discrimination against black people should remind us of the discrimination affecting women." Utilizing statistics from NOW's statement of purpose, Atkinson and Kennedy dismissed the then-popular notion that women were not an oppressed group. They urged the Women's Workshop participants to follow the lead of the Black Caucus and press for their own liberation.[64]

Through a detailed list of suggestions for "immediate action," Atkinson and Kennedy emphasized the connections between women's specific oppression and the responsibility of women to support social movements broadly. They called particular attention to the fact that women were not just white. The statement also repeated Kennedy's now commonplace refrain that women should understand their "buying power" as consumers and "enforce their demands on the irresponsible media, business and government"; insisted that women participate in all activities affecting the entire community; and argued that women should "assume leadership in self determination for women and children."[65] However, it was one of the last suggestions that more fully underscored Kennedy's understanding of the ways in which white women should engage in feminist organizing. As feminists, Kennedy maintained, their politics demanded that they be both antiracist *and* anti-imperialist, and be firmly united with these struggles:

New Politics women should assume their political responsibility by actively supporting protest such as those against the draft and those in black communities. This support should be actively demonstrated through protest against criminal policing activities and through appearing in courtroom proceedings involving draft resistors [sic], black protestors, or accused demonstrators. *Women must increase their support of those who bear the real burden of their stated moral commitments.*[66]

Although the statement insisted that white feminists support black social justice movements, Kennedy believed that Atkinson should have been more forceful in supporting the Black Power movement, and even described the statement as racist. Atkinson was confused as to how the very words that Kennedy had dictated to her could now be considered racist. "I'm doing exactly what she told me to do," she remembered. Perhaps Kennedy believed that the statement did not convincingly advocate her insistence that the growing women's movement commit itself fully to ending racism and supporting Black Power. She might have also worried that white feminists were attempting to eclipse the Black Caucus's demands. Setting aside her reservations, whatever they might have been, Kennedy signed and supported the statement because she believed that racism, imperialism, and sexism had to be addressed at the conference.[67]

In spite of Kennedy's disappointment with the final statement, she was encouraged by the burgeoning women's liberation movement. She wanted to do anything she could to create a feminist movement that would eliminate sexism together with racism and imperialism. With the NCNP coming to a close, Kennedy returned to New York, where she would continue to link these agendas as a member of NOW.

National Organization for Women and Black Power

Kennedy had joined the New York chapter of NOW during its first meeting in January 1967. Although the organization had been founded a year earlier in Washington, D.C., the New York chapter quickly became the largest and most active wing.[68] Its early members included black feminists Shirley Chisholm and Pauli Murray and white feminists Kate Millet and NOW's national president, Betty Friedan. Kennedy joined the group with the goal of working with both women and men on issues affecting all women. For her, that meant not only challenging sexist job discrimination and repressive reproductive laws but also protesting the Vietnam

War and the "irresponsible media" and fighting for black liberation. She was especially interested in white feminists supporting the Black Power movement.[69]

Atkinson was inspired by the Black Caucus's success in passing its resolutions at the NCNP and wanted to continue the conference's discussion of Black Power back home. With this experience in mind, Atkinson suggested a panel be held at NOW's November general meeting to discuss Black Power's relationship to the women's movement. Kennedy and Atkinson invited the organizers of the Newark Black Power Conference, Nathan Wright and Omar Ahmed, as well as Betty Shabazz and a delegate from the NCNP Black Caucus, Verta Mae Smart-Grosvenor.[70]

The New York chapter's handwritten and printed minutes from the meeting provide rare insights into what some white feminists took away from the discussion. Next to the name of each speaker, NOW's secretary briefly described that person's affiliation to the Black Power movement and recorded general impressions of her or his presentation. When reporting on Smart-Grosvenor's attendance, the secretary revealed her own disinterest in the discussion when she could not even remember if Smart-Grosvenor attended the event. The secretary wrote, "Did she come?" in the margins next to Smart-Grosvenor's name. For other leaders of the Black Power movement, like Wright, she derisively wrote out what she believed to be the sum total of his talk—"You are O-pressin' me!" The bastardized mimicry of black dialect helps us to see the dismissive ways in which some white feminists viewed Black Power and its specific concerns and in the process failed to challenge their own racism. Furthermore, it helps to give us some insight into NOW's repressive organizational culture and the interpersonal and racist power struggles that would plague the organization.[71]

Though the NOW leadership was not interested in the "Black Power and Women" panel, Friedan still hoped that Atkinson could be an asset to the group's governing board. She viewed Atkinson as a potential protégé who would eventually outgrow the curiosity in Black Power and sixties radicalism that Kennedy had sparked. Friedan was equally confident that Atkinson's "Main Line accent and ladylike blond good looks would be perfect . . . for raising money" from other white women.[72] With these hopes in mind, Friedan voted for Atkinson to assume the presidency of NOW's New York chapter.

It was not long before she regretted her decision. Within months, Friedan tired of Kennedy's and Atkinson's continued attempts to radicalize

NOW. She saw Atkinson's fascination with militant radicalism as potentially impeding the growth of the feminist movement and was also highly critical of the new women's liberation movement. By the summer of 1968, groups like New York Radical Women and Cell 16 were holding protests and study groups challenging traditional ideas of womanhood. Friedan believed that these "hippie" women borrowed too heavily from the Black Power and new left movements and "because they had cut their political eyeteeth on the doctrines of class warfare applied to the problem of race, they tried to adapt too literally the ideology of class and race warfare to the situations of women."[73] Thus, Friedan argued, radical feminists like Atkinson undermined the women's movement with their abstract ideas of women's separatism, "manhatred," and "sex warfare."[74] This insistence on dividing "legitimate" feminist concerns from the radical feminists' interest in Black Power and new left radicalism plagued the New York chapter of NOW. The conflict finally came to a head during the group's membership meeting on October 17, 1968.

Forming the October 17th Movement

Tension between NOW's national leadership and the radical feminists in the New York chapter had been growing steadily ever since the "Black Power and Women" panel. It was sharpened after Atkinson and Kennedy took up the cause of Valerie Solanas. Solanas was the author of *The SCUM* [Society for Cutting Up Men] *Manifesto* and had shot Andy Warhol because she claimed he defrauded her. In the summer of 1968, Kennedy agreed to represent Solanas. She and Atkinson attempted to paint Solanas as a radical feminist taking up arms against sexist oppression. Friedan was infuriated that Atkinson, Kennedy, and a few other NOW feminists were aligning themselves with this cause or with radicalism more generally.[75]

Meanwhile, NOW's more radical feminists were discussing ways to transform the organization so that it would fight not simply to "get women into positions of power" but to "destroy the positions of power."[76] Friedan tried to stop the "crazies" from taking over the organization by voting against Atkinson's reelection to the presidency. Friedan believed that Atkinson knew she would not be reelected and, in an effort to thwart the inevitable, "came up with a proposal to abolish the office of president and the democratic election of officers . . . that would enable the 'crazies' to take over and manipulate decisions, with no accountability to membership."[77] Atkinson, on the other hand, remembered her proposal to restructure the presidency as an effort to help make NOW more efficient and to keep apace of the participatory model of leadership that was a common philosophy circulating in black and new left movements.[78]

A few days before NOW's October meeting, a small group of radical feminists met at Atkinson's apartment to discuss how they could push the chapter in a new direction and resolve the growing factionalism.[79] Some of the women even threatened to leave the organization if their motion for rotating presidents did not pass.[80] On the day of the meeting, Atkinson remained silent while Kennedy and others "urged an experiment in participatory democracy."[81] Kennedy remembers the meeting being very contentious as some of the NOW leaders began a litany of "booing and hissing" as the radical feminists presented their ideas.[82]

Not surprisingly, the motion to create a rotating presidency was defeated. Atkinson left the meeting assuming that her fellow feminists would fulfill their original threat to resign. She went home and wrote a letter resigning from NOW and a press release criticizing NOW for "advocating hierarchy of offices" and not understanding that "the fight against unequal power relationships between men and women necessitates fighting unequal power everyplace."[83] She soon realized that she "was the only one who resigned." Atkinson recalled Friedan being "shocked because . . . [she] thought all of the young women were going to leave with [me]." Emboldened by this discovery, Friedan proceeded to give public statements that described how Atkinson left NOW alone.[84]

Kennedy had never promised to leave NOW if the vote was defeated. She intended to stay even though she was not pleased with the outcome of the meeting.[85] But once Friedan released public statements deriding Atkinson as marginal and insignificant to the women's movement, Kennedy reversed her course and resigned immediately. "I saw the importance of a feminist movement," she says, "and stayed in there because I wanted to do anything I could to keep it alive, but when I saw how retarded NOW was, I thought, 'my God, who needs this?'"[86]

In her resignation letter Kennedy listed many reasons for leaving NOW. High among these was the harassment of radical feminists who attempted to push the organization in a more progressive direction. Kennedy was also outraged at Friedan's racism and her failure to support black liberation and antiwar movements. During a heated executive committee meeting, where Kennedy offered suggestions on how to handle NOW's public relations, Friedan warned her not to interfere with the inner workings of the group and advised Kennedy to instead "focus her attention on matters of Black Power."[87] Kennedy maintained that she was not the type of activist who wrestled for control over an organization and in moments like these, she recalled thinking, "I can't waste my time on this bullshit" and often went "off and set up a [new] committee."[88]

Atkinson and Kennedy were the only two members to officially resign from NOW, forming a new radical feminist group, the October 17th Movement (named for the day Atkinson left NOW). The October 17th Movement's story occupies a prominent place in the birth of the predominantly white radical feminist struggle and is commonly cited as an example of the split between liberal and radical feminism, or between older and younger generations of white feminists.[89]

Missing from this oft-told story is the centrality of Black feminist Flo Kennedy and her leadership in helping to move young feminists in NOW toward a more expansive view of feminism. Indeed, the October 17th Movement reflected Kennedy's concern that the feminist movement concentrate on the connections between sexism, imperialism, and racism. Atkinson often described the October 17th Movement as "an action coalition of the student movement, the women's movement and the Negro movement" and determined to end all forms of oppression.[90]

While NOW's failure to view feminism in more expansive terms helped to fuel the creation of the October 17th Movement and radical feminism, Kennedy stood squarely on the other end, helping to push young white feminists toward an intersectional Black feminist praxis that centered attention on Black Power. It is then not surprising that the new organization attracted Black feminists such as Kay Lindsey, a black writer and producer for Pacifica Radio, whose feminist poem and essay appeared in Toni Cade Bambara's groundbreaking anthology, *The Black Woman*.[91]

The story of how the mostly white radical feminist movement was directly influenced by Black Power and black feminist Flo Kennedy helps us to move Black feminism and Black Power out of the margins of second-wave feminist movement history and closer to its center. While the October 17th Movement would later change its name to The Feminists and lose much of its antiracist ideological agenda—and thus all its black membership—its origins offer a window onto a moment when radical white feminists attempted to create a Black feminist intersectional praxis. As a founder of the radical feminist movement, Kennedy insisted that the movement live up to its "radical" title by looking beyond a limited focus on the oppression of white women.

Kennedy's story also demonstrates that while sixties movements and organizations often erected walls, those boundaries (especially during the nascent period) were far more porous than scholars have previously conceived. Kennedy was a major vehicle circulating the cross-pollination of movement ideas and forging important political alliances. She understood that "whether you're fighting for Women's Liberation or . . . Black Liberation, you're fighting the same enemies." The ultimate goal, for Kennedy, was that organizations and activists focus not on each other but on defeating what she argued was the real oppressor: "the racist sexist genocidal establishment."[92]

NOTES

I would like to thank the following people for their thoughtful comments on this work: Robin Kelley, Beverly Guy-Sheftall, Mary Kelley, Stephen Ward, Timothy Tyson, Sara Clarke Kaplan, James Reische, Ferentz Lafargue, Dayo Gore, Jeanne Theoharis, and Komozi Woodard. I am also especially grateful to Ti-Grace Atkinson and the Kennedy family for allowing me generous access to their personal papers and numerous stories.

1. "Black v. Feminists," *Time*, March 26, 1973.

2. "Marylin Bender, "Valeria Solanis [*sic*] a Heroine to Feminists," *New York Times*, June 14, 1968, 52; Lisa Hammel, "A Class of Fledgling Pickets Gets the Word: 'Make It Exciting, Make It Swing!'" *New York Times*, August 24, 1968, 33; Arleen Abrahams, "The Woman Picketer," *Washington Post, Times Herald*, October 30, 1968, C1; Florynce Kennedy videotape interview titled "Old Black Flo," *60 Minutes*, CBS, July 7, 1976.

3. Ti-Grace Atkinson, interview by author, Cambridge, MA, October 28, 2006; Jane Galvin-Lewis, interview by author, New York, NY, March 15, 2007; Gloria Steinem, "Florynce of America," *Ms.*, April/May 2001, 93.

4. Alice Echols, *Daring to Be Bad: Radical Feminism in America, 1967–1975* (Minneapolis: University of Minnesota Press, 1989), 383. For studies that briefly mention Kennedy's political contribution to the autonomous black feminist and/or the mostly white feminist movements, see Benita Roth, *Separate Roads to Feminism: Black, Chicana, and White Feminist Movements in America's Second Wave* (Cambridge: Cambridge University Press, 2004), 106–107; Jennifer Nelson, *Women of Color in the Reproductive Rights Movement* (New York: NYU Press, 2003), 38–41, 81; Robin Kelley, *Freedom Dreams: The Black Radical Imagination* (Boston: Beacon Press, 2002), 138–139; Marcia Cohen, *The Sisterhood: The True Story of the Women Who Changed the World* (New York: Simon and Schuster, 1988), 160–164.

5. Flo Kennedy interview by Jacqueline Cellabos, 1991, 11, Tully Crenshaw Oral History Project, Schlesinger Library, Harvard University, Cambridge, MA.

6. Roth, *Separate Roads to Feminism*, 83–85; Echols, *Daring to Be Bad*, 49–50.

7. Stephen Ward, "The Third World Women's Alliance: Black Feminist Radicalism and Black Power Politics," in *The Black Power Movement: Rethinking the Civil Rights-Black Power*, ed. Peniel E. Joseph (New York: Routledge, 2006), 119–144; E. Frances White, *Dark Continent of Our Bodies: Black Feminism and the Politics of Respectability* (Philadelphia: Temple University Press, 2001); Matthew Countryman, *Up South: Civil Rights and Black Power in Philadelphia* (Philadelphia: University of Pennsylvania Press, 2006), 258–294; Becky Thompson, *A Promise and a Way of Life: White Antiracist Activism* (Minneapolis: University of Minnesota Press, 2001); Anne M. Valk, *Radical Sisters: Second-Wave Feminism and Black Liberation in Washington, D.C.* (Champaign: University of Illinois Press, 2008).

8. Paula Giddings, *When and Where I Enter: The Impact of Black Women on Race and Sex in America* (New York: Perennial, 1984), 314–324.

9. Toni Cade Bambara, "The Pill: Genocide or Liberation?" and Frances Beale, "Double Jeopardy: To Be Black and Female," in *The Black Woman: An Anthology*, ed. Toni Cade Bambara (New York: Mentor, 1970); The Damned, *Lessons from the Damned: Class Struggle in the Black Community* (New York: Times Change Press, 1973).

10. Kennedy led and participated in fund-raisers and protests in support of Angela Davis, the Panther 21, Fred Hampton, Mark Clark, and various Black Panther Party chapters. She worked in broad-based political alliances such as the Emergency Conference to Defend the Right of Black Panthers to Exist, the Westside Committee to Defend to Panthers, and the Emergency Fall Campaign for Angela Davis. For more information, see Florynce Rae Kennedy FBI File 0977697 (referenced as FRK/FBI), passim. For information in regard to Kennedy's support of H. Rap Brown, see Investigative Report 3/20/1967, 8/20/1967–8/22/1967, 8/29/1969, FRK/FBI; "Don't Let H. Rap Brown Down" flyer, box 13, folder H. Rap Brown, Flo Kennedy Papers, unprocessed manuscript collection, in the possession of Joyce Kennedy-Banks, East Orange, New Jersey (referenced as FKP). For information in regard to Assata Shakur, see The United States of America vs. Joanne Chesimard and Freddie Hilton, December 24, 1973, December 27, 1973, FKP. For information in regard to Kennedy's involvement in the Black Power Conferences, see Flo Kennedy, *Color Me Flo: My Hard Life and Good Times* (Englewood Cliffs, NJ: Prentice-Hall, 1976), 61.

11. Roth, *Separate Roads to Feminism*, 90, 183.

12. Flo Kennedy interview by Sohnya Sayres titled "It's Damn Slick out There," in *The 60s without Apology*, ed. Sohnya Sayres (Minneapolis: University of Minnesota Press, 1984), 352.

13. Ibid.; Dan Berger, *Outlaws of America: The Weather Underground and the Politics of Solidarity* (Oakland, CA: AK Press, 2006), 95.

14. For an example of black feminist Amy Jacque Garvey maneuvering between black nationalism and feminism in the early twentieth century, see Ula Taylor, "Negro Women Are Great Thinkers as Well as Doers": Amy Jacques-Garvey and Community Feminism in the United States, 1924–1927," *Journal of Women's History* vol. 12, no. 2 (Summer 2000): 104–126.

15. Rosalyn Baxandall and Linda Gordon, eds., *Dear Sisters: Dispatches from the Women's Liberation Movement* (New York: Basic Books, 2000), 11.

16. Kennedy, *Color Me Flo*, 24, 29, 31, 37.

17. Florynce Kennedy, "Missouri Message, A Comparative Study—Accentuating the Similarities—of the Societal Position of Women and Negroes," undergraduate papers, box 8, folder Florynce Kennedy Undergraduate Papers, FKP.

18. Kennedy, *Color Me Flo* original tape transcript 6/5, box 5, FKP.

19. " Radio," *New York Times*, June 6, 1965, X18; "Radio—Today's Leading Events," *New York Times*, September 5, 1965, X15; "Radio—Today's Leading Events," *New York Times*, May 2, 1965, X20; Investigative Report, Florynce Kennedy, November 11, 1967, FRK/FBI; "Suggested Highlights from WLIB Public Service Programming," August 6, 1966, box 7, folder WLIB-Radio Listings, FKP.

20. Barbara Ransby, *Ella Baker and the Black Freedom Movement: A Radical Democratic Vision* (Chapel Hill: University of North Carolina Press, 2003), 3; Stokely Carmichael and Charles Hamilton, *Black Power: The Politics of Liberation in America* (New York: Vintage, 1967), 54; Flo Kennedy, audiotape interview, "Speaking for America: Twelve Original Interviews with American Activists" (Berkeley, CA: Visual Corporation, 1976).

21. Fran Moira, "Richmond Women's Festival: An Overflow of Men, Wine, and Blood," *Off Our Backs* 4, no. 9 (September 30, 1974): 11.

22. Kennedy interview by Sayres, 352; Komozi Woodard, *A Nation within a Nation: Amiri Baraka (LeRoi Jones) and Black Power Politics* (Chapel Hill: University of North Carolina Press, 1999), 196.

23. Kennedy interview, "Speaking for America."

24. "A Message for White Radicals," in *Reconstruction* (date unknown), reprinted in Kennedy, *Color Me Flo*, 58; emphasis added.

25. Earl Caldwell, "Two Police Inspectors from Here among the Newark Delegates," *New York Times*, July 22, 1967, 11.

26. Florynce Kennedy, "Once upon a Week," *Queens Voice*, July 10, 1964, 14.

27. Nathan Wright, letter to the Planning Committee for the National Conference on Black Power, box 11, folder National Conference on Black Power, FKP; Kennedy, *Color Me Flo*, 61.

28. Woodard, *A Nation within a Nation*, 86.

29. Chuck Stone, "The National Conference on Black Power," in *The Black Revolt: A Collection of Essays*, ed. Floyd B. Barbour (Boston: Porter Sargent, 1968), 189.

30. This statement is quoted from the National Black Power Conference pamphlet in Robert Allen, *Black Awakening in Capitalist America* (New York: Anchor Books, 1970), 158.

31. William L. Van DeBurg, *New Day in Babylon: The Black Power Movement and American Culture, 1965–1975* (Chicago: University of Chicago Press, 1992), 26.

32. Flo Kennedy, "Chicago's Black Power Conference," *Islamic Press International News Gram*, October 17, 1967, box 8, folder Islamic Press, FKP. For other movements that were influenced by Black Power, see Jeffrey O. G. Ogbar, "Rainbow Radicalism: The Rise of the Radical Ethnic Nationalism," in *The Black Power Movement: Rethinking the Civil Rights–Black Power Era*, ed. Peniel Joseph (New York: Routledge, 2006), 193–228; Thomas Blood McCreary, conversation with author, New York, NY, September 28, 2008.

33. Nathan Wright, *Let's Work Together* (New York: Hawthorn Books, 1968), 146.

34. Kelley, *Freedom Dreams*, 199.

35. Atkinson interview by author.

36. Ibid.; Investigative Report, Newark, NJ, July 27, 1967, FRK/FBI.

37. Investigative Report, Newark, NJ, July 27, 1967, FRK/FBI.

38. Atkinson interview by author.

39. Ibid.

40. Ibid.

41. Ibid.; Peg Brennan, interview by author, San Francisco, CA, January 7, 2008. For quote, see Ti-Grace Atkinson correspondence to author, July 23, 2007.

42. Bender, "Valeria Solanis [*sic*] a Heroine to Feminist."

43. Kennedy, *Color Me Flo*, 62.

44. Elsie Campbell, "Black Bermudians 'Turned On,'" *Contrast*, September 8, 1969; Investigative Report, Bermuda, February 10–13, 1969, FRK/FBI.

45. Woodard, *A Nation within a Nation*, 84.

46. "Don't Mourn for Us . . . Organize: The Call of the National Conference for New Politics Organize," pamphlet, National Conference for New Politics vertical file, Tamiment Library, New York University, New York.

47. Thomas Maier, *Dr. Spock: An American Life* (New York: Basic Books, 2003), 285.

48. Simon Hall, "'On the Tail of a Panther': Black Power and the 1967 Convention of the National Conference for New Politics," *Journal of American Studies* 37 (2003): 65.

49. James Forman, *Making of Black Revolutionaries* (Seattle: University of Washington Press, 1985), 498; Investigative Report, Chicago, IL, September 31, 1967, FRK/FBI.

50. David S. Broder, "Negroes Push Left to 'Genocide' Black," *Washington Post*, September 3, 1967, A1.

51. Walter Goodman, "Yessir, Boss, Said the White Radicals: When Blacks Run the New Left," *New York Times*, September 24, 1967, 257; James A. Wechsler, "No Winners," *New York Post*, September 9, 1967.

52. Kennedy, "Chicago's Black Power Conference"; emphasis added.

53. "National Conference for New Politics Resolutions," 11.

54. Echols, *Daring to Be Bad*, 47–48.

55. "National Conference for New Politics Resolutions," 22–23.

56. Echols, *Daring to Be Bad*, 49.

57. Ibid.; Sara Evans, *Personal Politics: The Roots of Women's Liberation in the Civil Rights Movement and the New Left* (New York: Vintage, 1980), 198–199.

58. Echols, *Daring to Be Bad*, 49; Evans, *Personal Politics*, 198–199.

59. "Chicago Women Form Liberation Group," *New Left Notes*, November 13, 1967, 2.

60. Ti-Grace Atkinson, *Amazon Odyssey: The First Collection of Writings by the Political Pioneer of the Women's Movement* (New York: Links Books, 1974), 97–98. Atkinson credits their statement with forcing the creation of the Women's Workshop. Her description conflicts with the NCNP's printed resolutions that detailed how the Women's Workshop was planned before the convention started. See "National Conference for New Politics Resolutions."

61. Atkinson interview by author.

62. Ibid.; Brennan interview by author.

63. Atkinson interview by author.

64. Florynce Kennedy and Ti-Grace Atkinson, letter to New Politics Women, September 1967, National Organization for Women/New York Chapter Papers, Tamiment Library, New York University, New York, box 5, folder 3 (referenced as NOW/NY).

65. Ibid.

66. Ibid.; emphasis added.

67. Atkinson interview by author.

68. Atkinson interview by author.

69. Atkinson and Kennedy, letter to New Politics Women.

70. Atkinson interview by author; "Women and Black Power" flyer, NOW/NY, box 5, folder 13.

71. "Women and Black Power" flyer; NOW/New York meeting minutes (handwritten), November 11, 1967, and NOW/New York meeting minutes (typed) November 21, 1967, NOW/NY, box 5, folder 13.

72. Echols, *Daring to Be Bad*, 167.

73. Betty Friedan, *It Changed My Life: Writings on the Women's Movement* (New York: Random House, 1979), 108.

74. Ibid.

75. Betty Friedan, telegram to Florynce Kennedy, June 1968, Ti-Grace Atkinson Papers, unprocessed manuscript collection, in the possession of Ti-Grace Atkinson, Cambridge, MA.

76. Atkinson, *Amazon Odyssey*, 10; "'Young, Black and Beautiful' Organize," *Los Angeles Times*, October 31, 1968, C4.

77. Friedan, *It Changed My Life*, 109.

78. Atkinson interview by author.

79. Atkinson, *Amazon Odyssey*, 9.

80. Atkinson interview by author.

81. Ibid.; Florynce R. Kennedy, Memorandum to the Officialdom of NOW: National and New York, November 18, 1968, Dolores Alexander Papers, Schlesinger Library, Harvard University, Cambridge, MA, box 7, folder 12.

82. Ibid.

83. Atkinson, *Amazon Odyssey*, 10.

84. Atkinson interview by author.

85. Ibid.

86. Kennedy, *Color Me Flo*, 62.

87. Kennedy, Memorandum to the Officialdom of NOW.

88. Kennedy, *Color Me Flo*, 62.

89. Flora Davis, *Moving the Mountain: The Women's Movement in America since 1960* (Champaign: University of Illinois Press, 1999), 97; Ruth Rosen, *The World Split Open: How the Modern Women's Movement Changed America* (New York: Viking, 2000), 84–85.

90. "'Young, Black and Beautiful' Organize."

91. "October 17 Movement Bi-weekly Meeting Schedule," box 7, FKP; Kay Lindsey, "Poem," "The Black Woman as Woman," in *The Black Woman: An Anthology*, ed. Toni Cade Bambara (New York: Mentor, 1970).

92. "Black v. Feminists," *Time*, March 26, 1973; Florynce Kennedy, unorganized notes, box 7, folder Unorganized Notes, FKP.

11

To Make That Someday Come
Shirley Chisholm's Radical Politics of Possibility

Joshua Guild

I used to be a moderate. I spent twenty years going to all kinds of meetings, trying to find ways all of us, black and white, could work together. Thousands like me kept saying, "Let us in a little. Give us a piece of that pie." What happened? Watts, Newark, Hartford. . . . Today I am a militant. Basically I agree with what many of the extremist groups are saying—*except* that their tactics are wrong and too often they have no program. But people had better start to understand that if this country's basic racism is not quickly and completely abolished—or at least controlled—there will be a real, full-scale revolution in the streets.

Shirley Chisholm, 1970[1]

In the summer of 1971, with a pivotal national election looming on the horizon, an embattled Republican in the White House, and the nation mired in a costly and deeply unpopular war, the black newsweekly *Jet* wondered whether America was finally ready for a black president. If the answer was in the affirmative, the magazine asked its readers, who should it be? An overwhelming 98 percent of readers responding to the magazine's national poll replied that they supported the idea of a black candidate running for president in the upcoming election. Of the prominent figures offered up as potential contenders, the clear favorite chosen by readers from Philadelphia to Los Angeles was a young, handsome, charismatic legislator who had delivered a stirring speech at the most recent Democratic National Convention.[2]

The person described as African Americans' preferred presidential candidate was veteran civil rights activist Julian Bond, a cofounder of the Student Nonviolent Coordinating Committee (SNCC) and a member of the Georgia House of Representatives. Although Bond was in favor of a black candidate competing for the nation's highest office and personally flattered by the broad popular support reflected in the magazine poll results, there was just one problem. At just thirty-one years of age, Bond was constitutionally disqualified from running for president.

Beyond the ineligibility of the top vote getter, the *Jet* survey was beset by another weakness. Of the nine proposed presidential candidates—a list that included Cleveland's Carl Stokes, the first black mayor of a major American city, Supreme Court justice Thurgood Marshall, and activist-comedian Dick Gregory—eight were men. The lone exception was Shirley Chisholm, the first black woman to ever serve in the U.S. Congress. The representative from Bedford-Stuyvesant, Brooklyn, finished fifth in the *Jet* poll, tallying a mere 5 percent of the vote. And yet, six months later, it was Chisholm—not one of the more heralded male political figures—who would make history.

On January 25, 1972, Shirley Anita St. Hill Chisholm took the podium in front of a bank of microphones inside Brooklyn's Concord Baptist Church to formally announce her intention to seek the Democratic nomination for president. The intrepid former educator and daughter of working-class Caribbean immigrant parents declared that, though she was equally proud of her blackness and her womanhood, she was not running for president in order to represent any one constituency. "I am the candidate of the people," Chisholm proclaimed, "and my presence before you now symbolizes a new era in American political history."[3] With these words, Shirley Chisholm officially embarked on a pathbreaking journey. In pursuing a major party's nomination, Chisholm became the first black American and the first woman to make a serious, sustained bid for the presidency of the United States, entering primaries in several major states and campaigning across the country.[4] She did so with a tiny, almost exclusively volunteer campaign staff, and a budget inconceivably small by today's standards.

But the significance of Shirley Chisholm's run for president, and of her broader political career, goes far beyond mere "firsts." Chisholm was passionate, outspoken, courageous, and ambitious. In many respects, she was a visionary who dared to imagine a different kind of politics and pursued such a path in her 1968 campaign for Congress and her improbable bid for the White House four years later. Despite frequent pressures to act otherwise, Chisholm insisted upon the equal salience of her racial and gender identities. Chisholm became a pioneer in developing an intersectional black feminist praxis as she labored to forge unlikely coalitions and struck difficult political compromises for the sake of a larger good.

By standing for the fundamental right of everyday people to determine their own futures by participating in the political process, Shirley Chisholm represented a radical democratic politics of possibility. Chisholm emphatically believed that politics—and, by extension, the power to shape the world—should not be the exclusive preserve of the wealthy, or men, or a dominant racial group. As a consequence, she used her campaigns to open a door through which people could imagine themselves as legitimate stakeholders in an imperfect American democracy.

While Chisholm clearly appreciated the importance of grassroots movements and their ability to effect change from outside the gates, she believed that blacks, women, and other marginalized groups in the United States would achieve meaningful political power only via the ballot box. Chisholm thus helped revise the meanings of militancy in the Black Power era, both by highlighting the connections between racism and sexism and through her commitment to concrete action in the realm of formal politics. Chisholm cherished her independence and maverick reputation yet always viewed her own political legitimacy through her ability to represent a larger constituency in spaces where such voices had rarely, if ever, been represented.

Chisholm's faith in the elasticity of the American political system did not prevent her from passionately critiquing its shortcomings. On the campaign trail, on college campuses, and on the floor of Congress, Chisholm advocated for the rights of the poor, women, youth, and people of color, promoting more humane domestic policies in the face of spiraling militarism abroad and worsening urban abandonment at home. Emerging on the national political scene at the height of Black Power, while charting what many perceived to be a traditional path to influence, Shirley Chisholm strikingly identified herself as a "militant." Chisholm refused to be circumscribed by either race or gender, helping to redefine black radicalism through an expansive politics of possibility.

The future congresswoman was born Shirley Anita St. Hill in Bedford-Stuyvesant, Brooklyn, on November 30, 1924. Shirley's father was a native of British Guiana (now Guyana) who came of age in Cuba and Barbados and worked as an unskilled laborer in New York. Her Barbadian mother was trained as a seamstress and supplemented the sewing she took in with domestic work for white families in Brooklyn. To mitigate the financial strains on the family, the St. Hills sent Shirley and her three younger sisters to live temporarily with their maternal grandmother in Barbados. Shirley spent ages three to eleven on the small island, before returning to her parents' Brooklyn home in the mid-1930s.[5]

For Shirley, coming back to Brooklyn meant joining the small but well-rooted West Indian immigrant community later chronicled by writer Paule Marshall in her novel *Brown Girl, Brownstones.*[6] More important, it meant reestablishing her relationship with her parents. Although lacking in formal education, Charles St. Hill was a "remarkable man" and a major influence in his eldest daughter's life.[7] Chisholm affectionately remembered her father's voracious consumption of newspapers and his deep interest in politics. Many a night Chisholm fell asleep to the spirited conversations of her father and his friends as they cataloged the evils of British colonialism. Charles St. Hill was a fierce Garveyite who believed in black unity, exuded racial pride, and inspired his children with these notions despite the fact that such professions were "not as fashionable at that time" as they would become in later years. Racial uplift and anticolonialist aspirations were not the only wellsprings of political conversation, however. "Much of the kitchen-table talk had to do with unions," Chisholm reflected. "Papa belonged to the Confectionery and Bakers International Union, and there was nothing he was more proud of than being a union man."[8] These tenets of working-class solidarity and racial unity would greatly inform Chisholm's own politics as a public figure.

After graduating from Girls' High School, one of Brooklyn's premier public schools, Chisholm went on to Brooklyn College. She had won scholarships to both Oberlin and Vassar but, unable to afford the necessary living expenses, elected to attend the nearby public college. Chisholm later wondered how her life might have otherwise turned out: "If I had gone to Vassar . . . [w]ould I have become one of the pseudo-white upper-middle-class black women professionals, or a doctor's wife, with furs, limousines, clubs, and airs?"[9]

Chisholm first became interested in politics at Brooklyn College, where she majored in sociology and joined the debating club and the Harriet Tubman Society, a black student organization. Before long, the petite young West Indian woman who lived with her parents and attended church thrice weekly was making a name for herself on campus as a forceful debater unafraid to speak her mind on the issues of the day.

She joined the Brooklyn chapter of the National Association for the Advancement of Colored People (NAACP) yet remained somewhat ambivalent about its program and not particularly active in the organization. Chisholm later attributed this ambivalence to a broader impatience with many community organizations she worked with over the course of more than two decades. In her estimation, most groups expended far too much energy on meetings and the pronouncements of leaders and not enough time distributing resources or effecting real change.[10]

Upon her graduation in 1946, Chisholm pursued a teaching career, one of the few professional avenues then open to educated black women. She took a job at a Harlem nursery school while also enrolling in evening classes at Columbia University's Teachers College, from which she would receive a degree in early childhood education.[11] (It was during this time that she met an unassuming Jamaican-born private investigator named Conrad Chisholm whom she married in 1949.) She left full-time teaching in 1953 to pursue administrative duties, eventually directing one of the city's largest day care centers.[12] At the same time that Chisholm was blossoming into leadership roles professionally, she was beginning to emerge politically in Brooklyn.

Concerned about the inequities that plagued her Brooklyn neighborhood, Chisholm gained valuable experience by participating in community organizing efforts related to issues such as schools and sanitation. She furthered her political education by joining the local Democratic Party club, undaunted by the smoke-filled clubhouse scene presided over by mostly Irish men who exchanged favors and patronage for voter loyalty in the majority-black district.[13] Chisholm initially entered this strange realm out of a desire to see resources leveraged for the benefit of her central Brooklyn community. When party leaders realized that this unusually assertive black woman could not be discouraged from opposing business as usual, they attempted to co-opt her with a leadership position. These efforts ultimately failed, and in 1953 Chisholm joined a burgeoning movement to challenge the white-dominated political machine and elect Brooklyn's first black civil court judge.

This successful campaign spawned a new group, the Bedford-Stuyvesant Political League (BSPL), dedicated to increasing local black political representation. Led by a veteran political strategist named Wesley McDonald "Mac" Holder, the BSPL fell short of ousting the machine from power.[14] In 1960, however, after a dispute with Holder, Chisholm helped establish the Unity Democratic Club "to do what the [BSPL] had never managed to do": seize control of the district from the corrupt machine while ensuring black Brooklynites political representation commensurate with the community's rapidly growing population.[15] Chisholm and her colleagues in the Unity Club built their organization up from the grassroots and, after some initial defeats, broke through in 1962 with a successful slate of candidates for both state and county offices.[16] Two years later, Shirley Chisholm was elected to the New York State Assembly, carried into office by the Unity Democratic organization.

These experiences in the rough-and-tumble of local politics helped shape Chisholm's views about political change. She came to appreciate the importance of personal, door-to-door organizing and campaigning. The work was thankless and hardly radical in any conventional sense. Yet the lesson of these campaigns was that local people did not have to accept the leadership presented to them and could, instead, cultivate their own leaders. Chisholm also experienced the resistance of entrenched political power to someone of her sensibilities. As she learned how to navigate these male-dominated spaces as an independent woman of color, Chisholm advocated for women's issues in Albany, even while her self-identification as a "feminist" remained on the horizon. Though she would continue to learn these lessons in the state legislature, Chisholm would be most dramatically tested in her 1968 bid to become Brooklyn's first black representative in Washington.

For more than two decades, the combination of political party maneuvering and district gerrymandering had effectively minimized black electoral representation in Brooklyn, despite the remarkable growth of the borough's black population. By the late 1960s, however, court rulings mandating proportional congressional districts had finally made the situation untenable. In early 1968, state legislators agreed to create a new Twelfth Congressional District in central Brooklyn.[17] The new district included a large swath of mostly black Bedford-Stuyvesant, as well as portions of more racially mixed Crown Heights, Flatbush, Bushwick, Greenpoint, and Williamsburg. Estimates placed the overall proportion of black and Puerto Rican residents in the district at close to 80 percent. Most observers believed that the realignment would virtually guarantee the election of Brooklyn's first black member of Congress.

The Citizens' Committee for a Negro Congressman in Brooklyn was formed in December 1967 and took as its self-appointed charge the vetting of possible aspirants for the congressional seat.[18] The committee interviewed upwards of a dozen hopefuls for the Democratic nomination.

Shirley Chisholm, then a three-year veteran of the state legislature, was the only woman considered.[19] Chisholm's long-standing ties to central Brooklyn, her position in state government, and her experience as a political organizer made her uniquely suited to represent the area.[20]

When the citizens' committee "unanimously" pegged Chisholm to represent the community, it was an important, albeit largely symbolic, expression of support.[21] The committee was an ad hoc group with no organizational muscle behind its endorsement. Chisholm still faced a host of obstacles in her eventual path to Washington. As it would turn out, the 1968 congressional campaign in Brooklyn foreshadowed in a number of important ways the opportunities and challenges Chisholm would meet on the national stage in 1972.

Chisholm's two opponents in the primary were state senator William Thompson, the favored candidate of the local Democrats, and Dollie Robinson, a former state labor official supported by another of the borough's influential black politicians. The challenge for Chisholm was to distinguish herself from her well-supported rivals while simultaneously confronting the power of the county machine.[22] Defying Democratic Party hierarchies would be a common theme throughout Chisholm's career.

Chisholm emphasized two main strategies during the primary. The first—a hallmark of all her political campaigns—was to get out into the community to present herself directly to voters. Chisholm visited street corners, businesses, parks, and housing projects, attended tiny fundraisers in supporters' living rooms, and spoke to an array of community groups large and small. In the evenings and on weekends, she traveled the district in a caravan of cars with her volunteers, using a sound truck to introduce herself to residents. A relentless campaigner, Chisholm set herself apart with the intensity and extent of her outreach efforts.

Everywhere she went, Chisholm stressed her independence and her lack of affiliation with any larger political organization. She coined the motto "unbought and unbossed" to describe her political orientation.[23] More than a casual campaign slogan, Chisholm would employ the phrase throughout her career to underscore her autonomy. While offering a strong rejection of the closed and corrupt system of urban machine politics, Chisholm's trademark saying also signified upon ideas of racial and gender liberation. To be "unbought" meant to be unencumbered by political debts, to "owe nothing to the traditional concentrations of capital and power," as she put it, and thus free to speak and act independently.[24] Yet it also signaled freedom from a collective legacy of slavery and colonialism.[25]

Not only was Chisholm her own "boss," unburdened by the dictates of an organizational hierarchy, she was an outspoken woman (whose husband remained contentedly in the background) in a time of rapidly evolving gender expectations. A phrase born in her watershed Brooklyn congressional campaign, "unbought and unbossed" would be key to the organizing logic of Chisholm's presidential bid four years later.[26]

The Chisholm campaign's second important strategic choice in the 1968 primary was its special effort to reach out to white voters in the Bushwick neighborhood. Chisholm and her sage political adviser, "Mac" Holder, reasoned that with three black candidates in the race, including two women, the black vote would likely be fairly evenly split.[27] By targeting whites in the fringes of the district, while outworking her opponents, Chisholm hoped to cut into the support for the favorite, William Thompson. In making these entreaties to voters beyond the black community, Chisholm gained valuable experience in crafting a broadly appealing message that resonated across lines of race, gender, and class, experience that would prove useful when she staged her run for president.

Following months of aggressive campaigning, Chisholm achieved a significant upset by winning the June primary.[28] In virtually any other postwar election, earning the Democratic nomination in Kings County would have all but guaranteed victory in the general election. But the shifting tides of racial politics in 1968 intersected with intensifying public opposition to the war in Vietnam to create an unpredictable electoral terrain.

The year had already seen the assassinations of Martin Luther King Jr. and, just weeks before the local primary, presidential hopeful and New York senator Robert F. Kennedy.[29] Burdened by Vietnam, Democratic president Lyndon Johnson had declined to seek reelection. Meanwhile, with Black Power in its ascendancy, activists from across the black freedom struggle debated the most effective routes to social, political, and economic transformation. In Brooklyn, the entry of James Farmer into the local congressional contest as a Republican made the 1968 election even more anomalous. It was within this context that Shirley Chisholm began to hone her radical democratic vision, offering an important alternative to the masculinist black militancy of the period.

In the late 1960s, James Farmer was a highly respected national figure, well known for his participation in the southern Freedom Rides and his leadership of the Congress of Racial Equality (CORE). He boasted instant name recognition and a sterling civil rights pedigree. He also had no connection whatsoever to Brooklyn. Therefore, local residents had to ask themselves who was best suited to represent this rapidly expanding community so often overshadowed by Harlem. Was it the experienced, committed, and outspoken local politician, a native of the area who also happened to be a black woman? Or was it the towering figure of the national civil rights establishment, one who embodied the ideal of the assertive black male? Complicating this equation was Farmer's outsider status and his endorsement by the Republican Party.

Farmer had resigned his position as chairman of CORE in 1966, hoping to head up a new national War on Poverty literacy project. When the proposed initiative was scuttled, Farmer, a Harlem resident, turned to lecturing and university teaching. In early 1968, New York's Liberal Party approached Farmer to run as its congressional candidate in central Brooklyn. Farmer accepted the offer, anxious to get back into the daily fray of politics. Because state laws permitted candidates to run on multiple parties' tickets, Farmer invited both the Democrats and the Republicans to endorse him.[30] With more established local candidates already lining up, Brooklyn Democrats declined to endorse the civil rights leader. Republicans, on the other hand, seeing a golden opportunity in a district dominated by Democrats, jumped at the chance to add Farmer's name to their ticket. Farmer used the endorsement to call for a new era in black politics, emphasizing black independence from the dictates of either major party.[31] The face-off between James Farmer and Shirley Chisholm was thus set.

In their own ways, both candidacies were products of the black freedom struggle and the rising expectations that accompanied it. Having never held elected office, James Farmer was a veteran of the southern civil rights movement and national policy debates who—much like CORE—was now redirecting his energies toward the problems of urban black communities. Chisholm, for her part, had entered public life through her involvement in neighborhood activism and local politics. That she, a black woman, could now mount a challenge for a congressional seat was in no small measure a function of the pressure the era's vital social movements had placed on American democracy from below. Both candidates cast themselves as independent political rebels ready to seize upon the historic opportunity to join Adam Clayton Powell Jr. as New York State's second black congressional representative.

On the major issues there was little substantive disagreement between Farmer and Chisholm. Both candidates opposed the war in Vietnam, criticized the inadequacies of the War on Poverty and the welfare system, and supported the idea of local community control of public schools.

Although Farmer was running on the Republican ticket, he took pains to distance himself from Richard Nixon, under whose name he would appear on the November ballot, and ultimately endorsed Democrat Hubert Humphrey.[32] The campaign, therefore, turned on questions of personality, experience, and leadership, questions that were debated through the language of gender. The masculinist overtones of the Farmer campaign undercut the candidate's otherwise progressive platform. At the same time, it symbolized a growing fissure in black politics nationwide—one that cast a compromised black manhood as the metaphor for black oppression.

One *New York Times* headline crudely summed up the campaign for many: "Farmer and Woman in Lively Bedford-Stuyvesant Race."[33] While Farmer insisted that he respected the hardworking assemblywoman and personally made few overt appeals to gender, such a framing was in fact central to his campaign. According to Chisholm, Farmer "toured the district with sound trucks manned by young dudes with Afros, beating tom-toms: the big, black, male image."[34] Meanwhile, his campaign literature argued for "a 'strong male image' and 'a man's voice' in Washington."[35] These assertions of black masculinity appeared both in the aftermath of the Moynihan Report, which had attributed the ills of urban black communities to the predominance of female-headed households, and within the context of Black Power's rise.[36]

Chisholm, who had prepared to mount her campaign on the issues and had hoped to beat Farmer with her superior organization and strong Brooklyn roots, resented the gendered refrain. "It's too bad, my friends, that this question of sex has to enter into a campaign," she remarked to a local women's organization, insisting on her preference to be evaluated solely as an individual and on her record.[37] Elsewhere, Chisholm challenged the zero-sum gender framework, declaring, "Of course we have to help black men, but not at the expense of our own personalities as women. The black man must step forward, but that does not mean we have to step back."[38]

As she repudiated the sexism of the Farmer campaign, Chisholm was attempting to craft an expansive black woman's politics at a time when the goals of "feminism" and "black liberation" were still routinely deemed to be incompatible. Although black women in the United States had been articulating feminist consciousness since the time of enslavement, it was not until the late 1960s that a discernible black feminist movement began to take shape.[39] The emergence of black feminist politics was partly a response to the male-centered rhetoric and marginalization of women, and women's issues, embedded within the most popular manifestations of black power.[40] By rejecting the notion that feminist concerns were the exclusive domain of middle-class white women, black women activists and theorists refused to subsume the pursuit of gender equality in the service of the supposed collective racial good. Chisholm's response to the gendered framing of her campaign against James Farmer must be understood within this context.

Chisholm's emergent radicalism derived from her resistance to a kind of black militant rhetoric—and to a formulation of black politics more generally—that privileged male leadership, while ignoring the specific concerns of women. In terms of the campaign, Chisholm recognized the need to respond effectively to her opponent's strategy. She did so by using her gender as a positive feature of her appeal to voters. "It was not my original strategy to organize womanpower to elect me," she later wrote, "it was forced on me by time, place, and circumstances."[41] Chisholm honed her feminism through this experience, learning how to speak effectively to women's issues within the context of a wider political campaign, something she had not done in her previous runs for public office.[42] By the time she decided to run for president, Chisholm had come to understand herself as uniquely positioned to advocate for both women and people of color, often emphasizing the plight of poor women and families to highlight the relevant intersections of these concerns.[43]

On November 5, 1968, Shirley Chisholm made history. Following an exhausting campaign through the summer and early fall, Chisholm defeated James Farmer by a margin of 2.5 to 1 to become the first black woman elected to Congress.[44] Given Farmer's national prominence, Chisholm's victory was unexpected, attributable to her superior organization, strong local ties, and the failure of Farmer's masculinist appeals to resonate with district voters. Less evident was the path that Chisholm would chart for herself as a first-term legislator in Washington. She had touted herself as both an "unbossed" independent and the people's candidate, committed to confronting the status quo. Yet the reality was that Chisholm would arrive in the House as a lone black woman in a patriarchal, racist, tradition-bound institution, a single voice amid a chorus of 435.

In many ways, the inherent constraints of her position obscured Chisholm's militancy. She had made a conscious choice, reflective of her particular radical democratic philosophy, to pursue social change from within the corridors of power. Nevertheless, Chisholm tried to leverage her newfound national profile to implicitly challenge fundamental presuppositions about what it meant to be "militant" or to exercise "Black Power." With her penchant for outspokenness, Chisholm staked a number of strong positions that underscored her independence and her willingness to risk popularity for principle. Although virtually no one at the time of her election would have predicted a serious bid for the White House fours years later, Chisholm's early years in Congress provided her with a platform that she would eventually use to seize the political moment that materialized in 1972.

Savoring her victory over James Farmer, Chisholm promised not to be a "quiet freshman Congressman."[45] She made good on that guarantee promptly after being sworn in when she volubly resisted her initial assignment on the House Agriculture Committee. Chisholm argued that such a placement would prevent her from representing the needs of either her Brooklyn constituents or African Americans more broadly. In publicly objecting to her assignment, Chisholm demonstrated a willingness to challenge both her own party's leadership and one of Congress's defining characteristics, what she called the "petrified, sanctified system of seniority."[46] Despite receiving criticism for her oppositional stance, Chisholm was reassigned to the veterans' affairs committee, a position she believed more favorable to her district's needs.[47]

Far more than the committee assignment flap, it was Chisholm's maiden address on the House floor later that spring that illustrated her convictions and connected her to the radical tenor of the times. Chisholm used the occasion to deliver a powerful antiwar message. In the speech, she castigated the Nixon administration for promoting costly new weapons systems at the same as it was announcing cuts to Head Start. In unsparing language, she criticized a culture of militarism that funneled resources away from education, antipoverty programs, and urban redevelopment initiatives to pay for needless foreign wars. It was a critique that had been leveled by a wide range of antiwar, civil rights, and Black Power activists.[48] What made Chisholm's words stand out was the site of their delivery and the passion with which they were conveyed.

The first-year congresswoman concluded her remarks by promising to vote against any defense appropriation bill that should come to the floor until the country's values had been sufficiently realigned to "use its strength, its tremendous resources, for people and peace, not for profits and war."[49] Chisholm recalled that she received little encouragement from her House colleagues after her speech but did garner considerable attention from students.[50] The antiwar speech propelled Chisholm to speaking engagements on college campuses, establishing a circuit that would remain a critical source of support for her in the years to come.[51] In public appearances Chisholm continued to drive home the message that the "immoral war" in Vietnam was distracting attention from the "even greater war which must be battled at home," warning that "we could actually have bloodshed in our country" unless her fellow politicians took steps to "cure our domestic crisis."[52]

Chisholm liked to refer to herself as America's "first black woman congressman," an ironic label intended to highlight the unique crossroads of race, gender, and power she occupied. The designation also implicitly underscored Chisholm's distance from her peers. When she entered Congress in January 1969, Chisholm was one of ten women in the House and one of nine African Americans (then the largest contingent of black representatives in history), but the only black woman. Later that year, Chisholm joined such colleagues as Representative John Conyers of Michigan and Representative William Clay of Missouri to create an informal black caucus.[53] The group, initially known as the Democratic Select Committee, was formalized the following year. Its ranks grew further after the 1970 election, and in 1971 it became the Congressional Black Caucus (CBC).[54] Despite the fact that she was one of its founding members, Shirley Chisholm had a strained relationship with the CBC. She felt marginalized as a woman and sometimes quarreled with her colleagues based on what she believed to be their old-line, clientist approach to black politics. CBC members like William Clay, on the other hand, considered Chisholm arrogant, selfish, and difficult to work with.[55] The tensions between Chisholm and her black colleagues in Congress, steeped in gendered conceptions of leadership, became most acute in the context of the impending presidential election as black leaders sought a strategy to ensure the advancement of African American interests.

Shirley Chisholm's decision to run for president arose out of the swirling waters of black political possibility that defined the early 1970s, a moment when national power brokers and grassroots activists alike were strategizing ways to translate the insurgent promise of civil rights victories and the kinetic force of urban uprisings into concrete political power. As the sixties gave way to the seventies, widespread calls for black unity brought integrationists into dialogue with nationalists, while radicals who had previously eschewed electoral politics began to dramatically reconsider their positions.[56] In this way, a wide array of individuals and organizations were redefining the contours of black militancy.

The election of African American mayors in cities like Cleveland, Newark, Atlanta, and Detroit and the increase in black representation in Congress were among the first fruits of these efforts. The Black Panther Party's striking turn to electoral politics in Oakland, running Bobby Seale for mayor and Elaine Brown for city council in 1973, further underscored the fluidity of black politics during this era.[57] Perhaps no single event better exemplified both the excitement and the uncertainty of this transitional period than did the National Black Political Convention held in Gary, Indiana, in March 1972, described by one scholar as "the shotgun wedding of the radical aspirations of Black power and conventional modes of politics."[58] Spearheaded by Newark's Amiri Baraka, Gary mayor Richard Hatcher, and Michigan congressman Charles Diggs, the Gary Convention brought together some 8,000 delegates from around the country, including nearly 2,000 black elected officials, with the goal of forging a unified political agenda on the eve of a crucial national election.[59]

Yet even before the momentous gathering in Gary, political leaders and prospective voters were intensely debating the prospect of running a black candidate for president in 1972. Inspired by many of the aforementioned political gains, such discussions were part of a larger strategic and philosophical debate about how African Americans could influence the coming campaign. Given the enduring bitterness stemming from the unfulfilled promises and cynical compromises that marred the 1964 and 1968 Democratic conventions, black leaders were determined to capitalize on the increasing concentrations in black voting strength to shape the national political agenda. In closed-door meetings, prominent black gatekeepers argued the merits of various electoral strategies.

These secret, largely male gatherings took place throughout the early fall of 1971 in cities like Detroit, Cleveland, and Washington, D.C. Attendees included such figures as Rev. Jesse Jackson, Julian Bond, Amiri Baraka, Manhattan borough president Percy Sutton, House delegate Walter Fauntroy of the District of Columbia, and select members of the nascent Congressional Black Caucus, along with local black leaders in each host city.[60] The most noteworthy of these strategy meetings was convened in Northlake, Illinois, in September 1971, a two-day affair attended by the broadest cross section of black elected officials and national leaders prior to the Gary Convention.[61]

The substance of these conversations ranged from identifying an acceptable Democratic candidate for black leaders to endorse to the creation of an independent black third party.[62] Eventually, two principal competing strategies emerged from these discussions. The first position, advanced by Julian Bond, called for African Americans to run "favorite son or daughter" candidates in the presidential primaries. The idea was for popular black politicians to enter individual primaries in states with significant black voting strength with the goal of capturing enough delegates to use as leverage at the national convention. Alternatively, others advocated rallying behind a single black presidential candidate and using that person's campaign to influence the Democratic Party platform and the selection of the eventual nominee.

Despite—or perhaps because of—her political acuity and ambitions, Chisholm opted out of active participation in this ongoing debate. She did not attend the Northlake summit or any of the other meetings to discuss strategies for the 1972 election.[63] Somewhat self-servingly, Chisholm later justified her absence by the gatherings' failure to reach a productive consensus and "because I divined that if I attended I would be the focus of much of the dissension."[64]

Chisholm also decided to forgo the Gary Convention, after having formally declared her presidential candidacy two months earlier. Rather than viewing the historic assembly as an opportunity to win black support for her fledgling campaign, Chisholm saw opposition to her candidacy as rooted in sexism and an overly narrow conception of black politics. She repeatedly insisted that she was "more than the black candidate" and was determined to fashion a more diverse coalition. "While I would have welcomed the support of these [black male leaders], I did not seek it because, even if they had offered me their backing (as I knew they would never do), I would have been locked into a false and limiting role," Chisholm contended, concluding that the idea of black leadership coalescing behind a woman was "unthinkable!"[65] Some black leaders thought that Chisholm made a major strategic error by not attending the Gary conference to rally support for her candidacy. Looking back, convention organizer Amiri Baraka remarked, "I think that by not coming to Gary, she played into their hands. Because, you know, Coretta King was there, Betty Shabazz was there—Shirley Chisholm should have been there.[66]

Chisholm's run for president had much in common with the campaign of Charlotta Bass twenty years earlier. As the 1952 vice presidential nominee of the Progressive Party, Bass became the first black woman to campaign for one of the top two spots on a national ticket. Active in publishing and civil rights in California for more than four decades, Bass used the Progressive Party platform to critique the Cold War militarism and civil rights gradualism of the two major parties.[67] But whereas Bass represented a marginalized third party, Shirley Chisholm hoped to inject a similarly critical voice in the center of the national political conversation. Reflecting the tenor of her time, Chisholm also spoke more directly to women's issues in her campaign than had her predecessor. Like Bass before her, however, Chisholm's realism about her electoral prospects in no way constrained the reach of her vision.

Chisholm thus forged ahead with limited support from influential black leaders and against a Democratic Party that had little patience for an insurgent black female candidate. As she campaigned throughout the winter and spring of 1972, she relied on an outpouring of volunteers to staff local offices, organize rallies and fund-raisers, and petition to get her name on the ballot in various primaries. In between her legislative duties in Washington, Chisholm made campaign stops in Massachusetts, New Jersey, Pennsylvania, Michigan, Minnesota, North Carolina, Florida, and California.[68]

A cofounder of the National Women's Political Caucus (NWPC) and a member of the National Organization for Women (NOW), Chisholm attracted a diverse array of women to her campaign and earned backing from members of the women's movement. But whereas white female support was sometimes tentative, women of color were among her most ardent champions. The difference, Chisholm argued, was that white women "felt that they were fighting for a lost cause," knowing that Chisholm had no chance of securing the nomination and recognizing that they would ultimately have to throw their support behind one of the male candidates. On the other hand, women of color—like "some of the black and brown women on the NWPC Policy Council"—used their experiences in the civil rights movement and other struggles to make sense of Chisholm's campaign. These women were accustomed to confronting "seemingly impossible challenges" and knew that "success" could not be measured solely in the final outcome but in the progress achieved in the fight along the way. Chisholm affectionately cited women like Chicana feminist Lupe Anguiano and Mississippi civil rights activist Fannie Lou Hamer as allies in this mold.[69]

While not wanting to be pigeonholed as the black candidate, Chisholm still actively recruited African American voters to her unlikely coalition. Speaking to a majority-black crowd of 1,700 in Pittsburgh, Chisholm lashed out at the failures of the Nixon administration and shared her "non-negotiable demands" for the ultimate Democratic nominee.

Chisholm announced that she intended to leverage her electoral support to ensure that a black man be named vice presidential nominee, a woman secretary of the Department of Health, Education, and Welfare, and a Native American head of the Interior Department.[70] Chisholm's statement signaled her willingness to pursue a somewhat uncomplicated politics of group representation, a politics not so dissimilar to that practiced by urban machines across the land—including the one in Brooklyn that gave Chisholm her political education.

Later that spring, Chisholm won an important endorsement that signified not only the broad appeal of her progressive vision but also the uniqueness of the political moment. The Black Panther Party, which had recently begun to demonstrate an interest in electoral politics, officially voiced its support for Chisholm. In the May 13, 1972, issue of the Party newspaper, *The Black Panther*, resident artist Emory Douglas produced a poignant image that dramatized what was at stake for African Americans in the election. In the full-page pen-and-ink drawing, Douglas depicted a disheveled black girl, with threadbare clothes, holding a broken, empty plate and spoon. A cockroach crawls on the wall above one shoulder. Over the other shoulder hangs a photo of Shirley Chisholm. A simple message appears at the top of the page: "A Vote for Chisholm Is a Vote for Survival."[71] In Chisholm, the Panthers saw a leader committed to principles of social justice, one who could be counted on to advocate for the poor and the marginalized.

By most conventional measures, Shirley Chisholm's 1972 run for the presidency was a failure. Most obviously, she fell well short of winning the Democratic nomination, which went instead to South Dakota senator George McGovern. Furthermore, Chisholm picked up only a small parcel of delegates for her efforts, nowhere near the number needed to influence the nominating process at the Party convention in Miami.[72] By her own frank admission, Chisholm's barebones, amateurish, largely volunteer-run campaign lacked both organization and resources, making numerous errors along the way that alienated would-be supporters and translated into lost votes.[73] Chisholm's candidacy also reflected the obstacles to realizing a unified black political strategy, particularly one that did not subsume the voices of women under the "universal" banner of racial progress. Most of all, Chisholm failed to ignite the kind of multiracial, multigenerational, national coalition necessary to shake up the two-party status quo.

Yet looked at from a different angle of vision, Chisholm's campaign— and, indeed, her political career as a whole—was anything but a failure. As historian Robin D. G. Kelley poignantly reminds us, "Too often our standards for evaluating social movements pivot around whether or not they 'succeeded' in realizing their visions, rather than on the merits or the power of the visions themselves."[74] Such a focus on end results, Kelley continues, both leads us to underestimate the enormity of the opposition faced by social movements and restricts our appreciation for the future struggles these movements frequently inspire. If Shirley Chisholm and her grassroots campaign failed to transform wholesale the electoral system in 1972, she nonetheless presented a trenchant critique of what existed and an inspiring vision for what was possible. In the process, Chisholm politicized her supporters in important ways and paved the way for future insurgent candidacies.

In her decision to run for president and in the development of her campaign, Shirley Chisholm fused a radical democratic philosophy with a pragmatism honed by more than two decades of political experience in Brooklyn, Albany, and Washington. Above all, Chisholm's bid for the White House capitalized on the dynamism of the political moment by forging a series of unlikely coalitions—most notably between black radicals and white feminists. The Chisholm campaign was ultimately undone by the candidate's inability to sustain such precarious alliances in the face of a broad constellation of outside pressures and internal fissures. Nevertheless, Chisholm's campaign for the presidency, like her initial run for Congress in 1968, was significant for the ways in which she resisted the prevailing gender norms in black America and in American politics.

By boldly reimagining the possible, Chisholm represented the highest ideals of the black freedom struggle. In the radical democratic tradition of Ella Baker, Bayard Rustin, and Fannie Lou Hamer, she believed ordinary people had a right to shape their own futures by participating in the political process. Chisholm thus emphasized principled engagement from within the system. It was a position she derived from experience and studied observation of both history and the surrounding political landscape.

If Shirley Chisholm has been insufficiently remembered and recognized, it is due to a combination of her sometimes-defiant independence, the uneasy coalitions she attempted to forge, and the difficult compromises required of a sitting legislator.[75] She was a champion of women's involvement in politics who appealed to both middle-class feminists and public assistance recipients. Although few would have described the former schoolteacher as a militant—indeed, those who identified themselves as such frequently criticized her—she nevertheless saw herself in that tradition. Chisholm courageously defended the rights of black radicals like Angela Davis and Joan

Bird and won the endorsement of the Black Panther Party during her run for president.[76] Although unusually outspoken as a junior member of Congress, Chisholm recognized the inherent limits of her position and leveraged votes in exchange for a platform from which she could fight for change.

Through her example, Chisholm inspired and helped politicize many who, despite the advances wrought by the civil rights and women's liberation movements, remained disconnected from formal politics. One such individual was Barbara Lee, a young single mother on public assistance attending Mills College in Oakland when Chisholm ran for president. Taken by the audacity of the candidate and her message, Lee volunteered on Chisholm's California campaign and learned invaluable lessons of electoral possibility and political independence that would shape her life's path.[77] Three decades later, Representative Barbara Lee cast the lone vote in Congress against granting President George W. Bush unfettered authority to carry out military reprisals in the aftermath of the September 11 terrorist attacks. The Chisholm campaign provided unique, transformative experiences to countless other volunteers—women and men, young and older, black, white, and Latino—in Brooklyn and across the country.

Beyond her impact on individuals, Shirley Chisholm paved the way for subsequent major party presidential contenders who did not fit the traditional politician's profile. Most notably, Chisholm laid a blueprint for Rev. Jesse Jackson's 1984 and 1988 campaigns. In ways that analysts have greatly undervalued, Chisholm's bold attempt at progressive, multicultural coalition politics in the early 1970s anticipated Jackson's Rainbow Coalition. Likewise, Chisholm helped make possible the groundbreaking 2008 Democratic nomination contest between Senator Hillary Clinton, a white woman, and Senator Barack Obama, a black man.

Ironically, the election of Barack Obama to the presidency threatens to further obscure Shirley Chisholm's radical legacy by relegating her to a historical footnote. Each in their own way has been understood as a product of the civil rights era. Like Chisholm, Obama built a multiracial coalition that relied upon grassroots volunteerism and youth mobilization to propel his campaign. At the same time, the differences between the campaigns—and the eras—are unmistakable. A mastery of new communication technologies, an unprecedented fund-raising apparatus, and the news media's boundless attention all helped Obama ascend to the White House. Equally striking, however, is the contrast between Chisholm's candor and Obama's relative cautiousness on various issues affecting society's most marginalized. Whereas Chisholm was unyielding in her attention to questions of poverty and urban regeneration, for example, Obama framed his campaign around an ill-defined "middle class" and rarely, if ever, addressed the needs of the poor or of cities in his public statements. Though certainly no stranger to political expediency or personal ambition, Shirley Chisholm nonetheless remained steadfast in her radical vision, speaking powerful truths and fighting for a more just and equitable America.

Chisholm's ascension to the national stage came at a crucial transitional moment in black politics, a time when African Americans were attempting to translate the symbolic and legislative gains of the black freedom struggle into tangible political power capable of improving the lives of America's dispossessed. Chisholm sought the nation's highest office not because she thought she could win but because she hoped to be an agent of change. Hers was a radicalism of possibility. "I ran because somebody had to do it first," she explained. "In this country everybody is supposed to be able to run for President, but that's never really been true. I ran *because* most people think the country is not ready for a black candidate, not ready for a woman candidate. Someday. . . . It was time in 1972 to make that someday come."[78]

NOTES

I would like to thank the editors and the anonymous reviewer for the press for their useful comments. Thanks also to Derek Musgrove, Tera Hunter, Valerie Smith, Daphne Brooks, Ferentz Lafargue, Tavia Nyong'o, and Alondra Nelson for exceedingly helpful suggestions on earlier drafts.

1. Shirley Chisholm, *Unbought and Unbossed* (Boston: Houghton Mifflin, 1970), 146; emphasis in original.

2. *Jet*, August 26, 1971, 13–16.

3. Shirley Chisholm, "Statement of Candidacy for the Office of President of the United States," January 25, 1972, Shirley Chisholm Papers, Rutgers University Library Special Collections, box 3, folder 24.

4. Senator Margaret Chase Smith of Maine was the first woman to appear on the ballot of a major party when she sought the Republican nomination for president in 1964. Chase campaigned in New Hampshire and remained on the ballot up through the national convention, when the nomination went to Barry Goldwater. See Jo Freeman, "Mrs. Smith Runs for President," January 30, 2000, http://www.jofreeman.com/polhistory/smith.htm (accessed March 23, 2008). Besides being the first black candidate to do so, Chisholm was the first woman to run a truly national campaign, entering primaries, establishing campaign offices, and making appearances in multiple states. See also Paula D. McClain, Niambi M. Carter, and Michael C. Brady, "Gender and Black Presidential Politics: From Chisholm to Moseley Braun," *Journal of Women, Politics and Policy* 27, nos. 1–2 (2005): 51–68.

5. Chisholm, *Unbought and Unbossed*, 3–10; *Current Biography*, October 1969, Brooklyn Public Library, Shirley Chisholm clippings file.

6. Paule Marshall, *Brown Girl, Brownstones* (1959; New York: Feminist Press, 1981).

7. Shirley Chisholm interview, n.d. [ca. 1968], C-169, Schomburg Center for Research in Black Culture Oral History Tape Collection, New York Public Library (hereafter SC-OH).

8. Chisholm, *Unbought and Unbossed*, 13–14.

9. Ibid., 22.

10. Ibid., 27.

11. Chisholm often recounted her difficulties in securing a job after graduation, dismissed by potential employers on account of her race, youthful looks, and small stature. In later years Chisholm used these experiences as examples of her determination. See Chisholm interview, 1968, C-161, SC-OH.

12. Chisholm interview, 1968, C-161, SC-OH; Chisholm, *Unbought and Unbossed*, 43.

13. Chisholm, *Unbought and Unbossed*, 29–31, 36–38.

14. Holder mentored Chisholm and, after a falling-out and reconciliation, would later serve as her campaign manager and chief political strategist.

15. Chisholm, *Unbought and Unbossed*, 47.

16. Harold X. Connolly, *Ghetto Grows in Brooklyn* (New York: NYU Press, 1977), 172–173.

17. *New York Times*, February 23, 1968. The legislature's action on redistricting was the capstone of more than twenty years of community activism to expand black electoral representation. See Connolly, *Ghetto Grows in Brooklyn*, 102–110, 162–167; Jeffrey Gerson, "Bertram L. Baker, the United Action Democratic Association, and the First Black Democratic Succession in Brooklyn, 1933–1954," *Afro-Americans in New York Life and History* 16, no. 2 (1992): 17–46; and Julie A. Gallagher, "Women of Action, in Action: The New Politics of Black Women in New York City, 1944–1972" (Ph.D. diss., University of Massachusetts–Amherst, 2003), 176–177.

18. *New York Amsterdam News*, December 30, 1967.

19. Redistricting had forced Chisholm to run for the same seat in consecutive years in special elections.

20. Other possible candidates included a popular state senator; Chisholm's predecessor in the State Assembly, Judge Thomas Jones; and former Brooklyn NAACP president Rev. Milton A. Galamison, a well-known local civil rights advocate.

21. Chisholm interview, 1968, C-161, SC-OH.

22. *New York Times*, February 26, 1968, April 13, 1969; Chisholm, *Unbought and Unbossed*, 66–67; Chisholm interview, 1968, C-161, SC-OH.

23. Chisholm, *Unbought and Unbossed*, 68–69; Chisholm interview, C-161, SC-OH.

24. Chisholm, *Unbought and Unbossed*, 176.

25. Thanks to my colleague Daphne Brooks for suggesting this critical reading of Chisholm's rhetoric.

26. While undoubtedly an evocative tagline, the symbolism of "unbought and unbossed" eventually came to outweigh its substance. By the end of her congressional career in 1982, the notion of "independence" had become something of a fetish for Chisholm, a convenient way to explain unpopular positions or her distance from would-be allies.

27. This strategy was also motivated by the reality that white voter registration outpaced that of blacks in the district, despite their significantly lower proportion of the population. *New York Times*, June 12, 1968.

28. In spite of all the attention given to the race, voter turnout was exceedingly low, with only 12,000 total votes cast, less than a third of the number of votes tallied in a neighboring district. *New York Times*, June 22, 1968.

29. Kennedy was well known in central Brooklyn for his efforts to direct private capital into a major community development initiative, the Bedford-Stuyvesant Restoration Corporation, established in 1967 with major funding from the Ford Foundation.

30. James Farmer, *Lay Bare the Heart: An Autobiography of the Civil Rights Movement* (New York: Arbor House, 1985), 300–311; *New York Times*, March 9, 1968.

31. *New York Times*, May 20, 1968, and July 26, 1968.

32. Farmer, *Lay Bare the Heart*, 312. While Farmer endorsed Humphrey for president, he also made public appearances with Republican senator Jacob Javits and was endorsed by

Governor Nelson Rockefeller. See *New York Times*, September 26, 1968, and October 3, 1968. The Chisholm campaign tried to capitalize on these ambiguities by hammering home Farmer's connection to the Nixon-Agnew slate.

33. *New York Times*, October 26, 1968.

34. Chisholm, *Unbought and Unbossed*, 71.

35. *New York Times*, October 26, 1968.

36. See Steve Estes, *I Am a Man! Race, Manhood, and the Civil Rights Movement* (Chapel Hill: University of North Carolina Press, 2005), esp. chaps. 5 and 7.

37. "Emma Lazarus meeting, Brooklyn, October, 1968," C-168, SC-OH.

38. *New York Times Magazine*, April 13, 1969.

39. See, for example, Paula Giddings, *When and Where I Enter: The Impact of Black Women on Race and Sex in America* (New York: Bantam Books, 1985); Deborah Gray White, *Too Heavy a Load: Black Women in Defense of Themselves, 1894–1994* (New York: Norton, 1999); and Kimberly Springer, *Living for the Revolution: Black Feminist Organizations, 1968–1980* (Durham, NC: Duke University Press, 2005), 1–44.

40. Kimberly Springer, "Black Feminists Respond to Black Power Masculinism," in *The Black Power Movement: Rethinking the Civil Rights–Black Power Era*, ed. Peniel Joseph (New York: Routledge, 2006), 105–118.

41. Chisholm, *Unbought and Unbossed*, 75.

42. Historian Julie Gallagher documents Chisholm's legislative work in Albany on behalf of working women in "Waging 'The Good Fight': The Political Career of Shirley Chisholm, 1953–1982," *Journal of African American History* 92 (Summer 2007): 399. Notwithstanding these important efforts, I contend that the 1968 campaign represented a crucial turning point in the development of Chisholm's feminist politics.

43. In discussing her strong pro-choice views, for example, Chisholm stressed the disparate impact abortion and family planning restrictions had on low-income women and women of color. See *Congressional Record*, 91st Cong., 1st sess., 1969, 115, no. 206.

44. *New York Times*, November 6, 1968. Amazingly, Chisholm had been bedridden and prevented from making public appearances for more than a month during the campaign as she recovered from surgery to remove a large benign tumor in her abdomen. Chisholm, *Unbought and Unbossed*, 71–73.

45. *New York Times*, November 6, 1968.

46. *New York Times*, January 30, 1969.

47. One commentator suggested that Chisholm was "naïve" about the ways of Congress, arguing that the Agricultural Committee would have been an ideal place from which the first-term lawmaker could have begun to accumulate political debts. *New York Daily News*, January 31, 1969. What the writer failed to appreciate was the strategic importance of both *symbolic* and *real* power for Chisholm as a pioneering black politician.

48. See Simon Hall, *Peace and Freedom: The Civil Rights and Antiwar Movements in the 1960s* (Philadelphia: University of Pennsylvania Press, 2005).

49. Chisholm, *Unbought and Unbossed*, 97. Chisholm's speech reprinted in full as "The Business of America Is War, and It Is Time for a Change," in *Freedom on My Mind: The Columbia Documentary History of the African American Experience*, ed. Manning Marable (New York: Columbia University Press, 2003), 368–371.

50. Chisholm, *Unbought and Unbossed*, 98–99.

51. In her first term Chisholm spoke strongly in favor of lowering the national voting age to eighteen, a step that was eventually taken with the passage of the Twenty-sixth Amendment in 1971. *Congressional Record*, 91st Cong., 1st sess., 115, no. 127. Chisholm specifically targeted students and younger voters during her presidential campaign.

52. *New Pittsburgh Courier*, April 26, 1969.

53. *New York Sunday News*, November 9, 1969.

54. William L. Clay, *Just Permanent Interests: Black Americans in Congress, 1870–1991* (New York: Amistad Press, 1992), 116–117, 121–122.

55. Ibid., 194–199, 225.

56. See Cedric Johnson, *Revolutionaries to Race Leaders: Black Power and the Making of African American Politics* (Minneapolis: University of Minnesota Press, 2007).

57. Robert O. Self, *American Babylon: Race and the Struggle for Postwar Oakland* (Princeton, NJ: Princeton University Press, 2003), 303–308.

58. Johnson, *From Revolutionaries to Race Leaders*, 129.

59. Komozi Woodard, *A Nation within a Nation: Amiri Baraka (LeRoi Jones) and Black Power Politics* (Chapel Hill: University of North Carolina Press, 1999), 184–185, 203–221; Peniel E. Joseph, *Waiting 'Til the Midnight Hour: A Narrative History of Black Power in America* (New York: Henry Holt, 2006), 276–283; Marguerite Ross Barnett, "The Congressional Black Caucus," *Proceedings of the Academy of Political Science* 32, no. 1 (1975): 34–50.

60. Clay, *Just Permanent Interests*, 220. Clay, who entered Congress with Chisholm, was a member of the CBC and participant in these meetings.

61. Woodard, *A Nation within a Nation*, 190–192; Shirley Chisholm, *The Good Fight* (New York: Harper and Row, 1973), 28–31.

62. Moderates at Gary strongly opposed the call for a separate black third party, which had been debated by nationalists in other venues. As Komozi Woodard notes, although Amiri Baraka was a key proponent of a version of this idea, he would ultimately play an essential role in bridging the divide between nationalists and more moderate political elites in Gary. See Woodard, *A Nation within a Nation*, 185–187; Johnson, *From Revolutionaries to Race Leaders*, Ch. 3.

63. After some initial controversy about her place on the program, Chisholm did speak at a CBC-sponsored national conference of black elected officials in November 1971.

64. Chisholm, *The Good Fight*, 30.

65. Ibid., 37–38.

66. Quoted in *Chisholm '72: Unbought and Unbossed*, DVD, directed by Shola Lynch, Twentieth Century Fox Home Entertainment, 2004.

67. Gerald R. Gill, "'Win or Lose—We Win': The 1952 Vice Presidential Campaign of Charlotta A. Bass," in *The Afro-American Woman: Struggles and Images*, ed. Sharon Harley and Rosalyn Terborg-Penn (1978; Baltimore: Black Classic Press, 1997), 109–118.

68. Chisholm, *The Good Fight*, 77–78.

69. Ibid., 77.

70. *New Pittsburgh Courier*, March 11, 1972.

71. Sam Durant, ed., *Black Panther: The Revolutionary Art of Emory Douglas* (New York: Rizzoli, 2006), 159.

72. Ronald W. Walters, *Black Presidential Politics in America: A Strategic Approach* (Albany: State University of New York Press, 1988), 116.

73. Chisholm, *The Good Fight*, 159.

74. Robin D. G. Kelley, *Freedom Dreams: The Black Radical Imagination* (Boston: Beacon Press, 2002), iv.

75. Scholarly attention to Chisholm has been sparse to date. A small handful of doctoral theses have explored her career and ideas, usually within a larger constellation of political figures. Meanwhile, Chisholm's presidential run was the focus of Shola Lynch's important 2004 documentary film, *Chisholm '72: Unbought and Unbossed*.

76. *New York Amsterdam News*, June 13, 1970, and July 31, 1971.

77. See *Chisholm '72: Unbought and Unbossed*.

78. Chisholm, *The Good Fight*, 3.

12

Denise Oliver and
the Young Lords Party
Stretching the Political Boundaries of Struggle

Johanna Fernández

Revered in movement circles for her political acuity and leadership in the Young Lords Party (YLP)—the Puerto Rican organization
that consciously fashioned itself after the Black Panther Party—Denise
Oliver is at once one of the most locally influential and least acknowledged *African American* radicals of the sixties. As an African American,
Oliver's prominent membership in a Puerto Rican organization captured
the imagination of her contemporaries because it bespoke of the political
dynamism and open racial and ethnic consciousness in the Young Lords.
(Approximately 30 percent of the YLP was composed of African American and non–Puerto Rican Latinos.) Both as an African American and as
the first woman elected to the YLP's official leadership body, the central
committee, she possessed enormous symbolic power. She seemed to em-
body the possibilities for building an equitable multiracial society.

However, because conventional histories of the Black Power movement
often overlook nationalism's pliability and fail to look for black activism in
unlikely places, Oliver's political evolution and important presence within
the movement have eluded historians. Ironically, it is precisely her crossover—during a period that profoundly challenged racial norms—that has
rendered her invisible in history. Yet, despite Oliver's relative anonymity,
her contributions to the movement were exceptional. From her activism
in a local branch of the National Association for the Advancement of
Colored People (NAACP) as a teenager and participation in the Student
Nonviolent Coordinating Committee (SNCC) while a student at Howard

University, to her activism in the Young Lords and Black Panther parties, Oliver helped build some of the most important freedom organizations of the period. Oliver's leadership in the YLP contributed to a radical reformulation of gender politics and practice within the organization. In 1970, Oliver helped pen a comprehensive position paper on gender inequality that theorized the intersection of race and class in the lives of women of color. The arc of Oliver's life—from her early political formation in a black household with communist leanings in Queens, to her work in the black freedom movements of the 1960s and her later membership in the Young Lords Party—offers a view of the forces that created a generation of men and women who embraced the varied calls of Black Power and with it contributed to the transformation of American society.

During Oliver's tenure in the YLP's central committee, she served first as minister of finance and later as minister of economic development. Her ascendance was a product of a pitched battle over the role of women in the organization, but also of Oliver's confidence, breadth of knowledge, and undeniable experience in the black freedom movement. Her membership in some of the most important organizations of the period—meant that she came to the organization grounded in the major issues and debates of the civil rights and Black Power movements. And because she was a red-diaper baby, Oliver was familiar with the classic theoretical texts that were becoming required reading among young radicals.

Oliver's membership in the Young Lords points to a kind of racial and ethnic crossover that may have been more common in the movements of the 1960s than we currently acknowledge, a mingling that is not yet reflected in the historiography of the Black Power movement. The history of the Young Lords is a telling example of this underdocumented phenomenon, as approximately 25 percent of the group's members was African American, and more than 10 percent of this Puerto Rican organization was composed of Latino men and women who were not Puerto Rican. While we do not have corresponding statistics for the Black Panther Party, we have abundant anecdotal evidence that many Latinos claimed membership in that organization. By examining such instances of racial and ethnic crossing, we can gain a more complete understanding of the potential of the civil rights movement and the dreams these organizations inspired in their participants.

Political Evolution

Oliver was born in Brooklyn in 1947. Her parents were newcomers to postwar New York who became part of the city's growing and vibrant black left. They came of age politically amid the explosion of black urbanization produced by the war and the expansion of civil rights protest and black unionization led by New York's black Popular Front.[1] In many ways, her parents imparted to her the belief in the possibilities for social change and cross-racial coalition generated by the second great migration, the expectations for freedom raised by World War II, and the political inroads achieved by the Communist Party in Harlem. Her father, George Bodine Oliver, was either a member of the Communist Party or a fellow traveler. Like many black servicemen of his generation, Mr. Oliver's commitment to conscious political organizing grew following a near-fatal assault while stationed at a military base in the South. The light-complected Mr. Oliver, a Tuskegee Airman, was mistaken for a "nigger lover" by the unschooled eye of a white supremacist and was beaten within an inch of his life as he deboarded a bus alongside his recognizably black fellow soldier.

After the war, Mr. Oliver turned his attention to acting. In the 1950s he integrated Broadway alongside a cohort of black actors and later became a professor of drama. After moving to New York following his service in the army, Mr. Oliver became a part of the CP-influenced cultural milieu of the 1940s and 1950s. His firstborn child, Denise, thus grew up in a rich cultural and political environment, "a world," as she put it, "of folk songs, jazz, and political expression." Actors and folk singers, including Paul Robeson, Leon Bibb, Theodore Bikel, Odetta, Peter, Paul, and Mary, and Pete Seeger, were friends of the family. Not only was Oliver's world expanded by her father's circle, but he also insisted that Denise learn Spanish as a child. Because to be "truly literate" one had to know multiple languages, he even insisted that his daughter learn to read Cervantes in Spanish. Her father could not have foreseen, however, how prescient his insistence would be in Denise's development as an activist.

The quintessential red-diaper baby, Oliver "grew up . . . around people who had very different ideas." Despite having experienced the pall of silence and secrecy forced on progressives by McCarthyism, her household continued to be a gathering point for left-wing activists and artists. It was this 1950s culture that tendered her formative political training. As she recalled:

> The dinner table at our house was a place where you engaged in political debates. . . . a number of white leftists who are red babies . . . had that kind of upbringing, predominantly Jewish in New York; I'm one of the black red babies. And there were a few of us.[2]

Oliver fondly remembers that her godparents were Jewish social workers in the settlement house movement and that the first word she uttered was in Yiddish. The vigorous political culture of the Old Left ignited Oliver's lifelong dedication to radical politics. Her life's path—and her parents' influence—was evident early on; as a child, her first act of protest was to challenge the rationale behind "duck and cover" drills at her elementary school:

> I remember moving back to New York and being told that you had to get under your desk because the reds were going to bomb us . . . .a group of my little friends, we all refused . . . to take cover . . . because we had been told at home that that was hogwash.[3]

Oliver's parents' connections to the rich political and cultural world of the 1940s and 1950s imparted to her an expansive vision of a just and multiracial society. But by the 1950s, as the Cold War narrowed political discourse in American society, the hopes for a radical multiracial politics, which had sustained the interests of progressive black Americans in the Communist Party, dimmed. The massive relocation of working- and middle-class white Americans to racially exclusive suburbs and the insular orientation of their lives around home ownership, consumerism, and domestic cold war politics made the progressive call for interracial struggle with white Americans more and more difficult to imagine.

In the late 1950s, an optimistic, teenage Oliver witnessed the fallout produced by residential and school integration in New York. Against the backdrop of the televised saga of school integration in Little Rock and with the help of a white proxy, Oliver's parents purchased a home in Hollis, a predominantly white neighborhood in Queens. Hollis was one of a cluster of residential enclaves in New York experiencing an influx of first-time black and Puerto Rican home buyers. Ironically, despite having lived in the South as a child, Oliver came face-to-face with white racial aggression against blacks on the well-kept sidewalks and in the public schools of southeastern Queens. Her recollections of cross burnings on lawns and fire-bombings that destroyed the homes of black families in adjacent neighborhoods are corroborated by countless local news reports. Oliver's new borough also became an experiment in school integration, as the New York City Board of Education declared in 1959 that black and Puerto Rican children from severely overcrowded Brooklyn schools were to be bused to Queens.[4]

The records left behind by journalists and observers of the time describe a white community fiercely opposed to and organized against these measures. With racially antiseptic language that echoed southern demands for states' rights, Queens residents maintained that measures to bus Brooklyn children into Queens schools undermined the concept of "neighborhood schools" and local autonomy.[5] In protest, thousands of white parents in Oliver's new community held mass rallies and informational meetings at local churches, hundreds kept their children at home on the first day of school, and in one instance 2,000 white parents picketed city hall. For their part, the hundreds of black and Puerto Rican parents whose children were bused to Queens from Brooklyn demanded assurances from New York City mayor Wagner that their children would be protected from acts of white aggression. Amid the hostilities, a local newspaper reported that "racist scribbling greeted the Brooklyn students," and according to Oliver, students rioted in the school courtyards during her first day at Junior High School 59:[6]

> I remember getting off the bus . . . commotion going on . . . and . . . a white kid with blood streaming down his face . . . .there were fights going on in the yard. There were white students who had jumped on some black students, there were black students fighting back, there were [white] parents . . . protesting the bussing of kids into their neighborhood. . . . the bus monitor rushed us into the building. . . . you could feel the hostility immediately.[7]

A decade before the Olivers settled there, the cluster of neighborhoods in southeastern Queens had become a major battleground in the national struggle against housing discrimination. In 1946, the NAACP successfully argued a suit on behalf of a prospective black home buyer in St. Albans, Queens, that challenged restrictive covenants, barring the "sale, lease, or gift of property to 'Negroes or persons of the Negro race or blood or descent.'" In 1948 the Supreme Court ruled in *Shelly v. Kramer* that the lower court decisions upholding discriminatory covenants were a form of "state action" that violated the Fourteenth Amendment and therefore were unenforceable.[8] Soon thereafter, St. Albans became a kind of new suburban frontier where famous black artists, athletes, and entertainers, including Count Basie, Jackie Robinson, and Lena Horne, purchased their fabulous homes. Nestled next to St. Albans in Hollis, the Olivers' move to Queens from Brooklyn demonstrates the opening the 1948 decision created for ordinary black Americans. The Olivers were representative of the larger movement of black middle-class professionals, including post office employees, civil servants, transit workers, teachers, and professors, away from worsening housing conditions in Manhattan, Brooklyn, and the Bronx.

Oliver's political worldview thus was forged by the growing contradictions of life for many black northerners in the 1950s: just as the strength of political and artistic communities grew, the rising hopes of blacks for a better future were frustrated as a result of their exclusion from the good life afforded to their white counterparts through suburban home ownership. In postwar northern cities, the politics of Oliver's generation were shaped by white resistance to African American advances in education, employment, and housing. As a witness to the fierce Queens battle against school and housing integration in Queens, Oliver understood viscerally that her life had to unfold in a different setting and soon pursued admission into the specialized New York City public high schools:

> The racialization at that time was palpable, white students were privileged. . . . at a certain point in time it became very difficult to function in the context of school. . . . the group of us who were in this little [black] cadre of people meeting with our black teacher, who was a member of the NAACP . . . were not given permission to be away from school [to take the exam for the specialized high schools in New York]. . . . I was given what was called a blue referral card for being absent without permission [on that day] and sent . . . for detention.[9]

According to Oliver, her entire cohort of gifted, middle-class black students all gained admission to the specialized public high schools; she enrolled at Music and Art High School in September 1960. Alongside this cohort who weathered the storm of Queens integration, Oliver joined the youth section of the Queens branch of the NAACP, which was led by former New York City judge and civil rights advocate William Booth. In 1963, she took part in a civil disobedience action demanding the employment of black workers at a major construction project in Queens's Rochdale

Village. Led by William Booth and other members of the NAACP, the protesters, among them the seventeen-year-old Oliver, sat in front of construction site bulldozers.[10]

In many ways, Denise Oliver's early life experiences speak to the continuities and ruptures between the Old Left and the New. While shaped by the world of CP-influenced New York radicals of the fifties, when Oliver entered politics she never considered joining the youth chapter of the CP. Instead, she joined her local chapter of the NAACP. In college, Oliver joined Students for a Democratic Society and SNCC, and eventually the Young Lords Party and the Black Panther Party. Membership in the CP had little appeal for Oliver because she perceived her parents to be proverbial armchair Marxists, and because the CP had very little to offer her growing disquietude around issues of race. "The CP had a very straight sort-of Stalinist line. Questions of race were not necessarily addressed in the way that we, as young people, felt they were supposed to be addressed."[11] In discussing its shortcomings, Oliver tellingly conflates the perspective and orientation of the CP with that of the wing of the civil rights movement led by Martin Luther King:

> Remember that the agenda of civil rights was pacifist militancy in a sense. Kneel down, get beat over the head . . . and pray to Jesus [that] "We shall overcome." Well I was into "we shall overrun." By the time I got to D.C. and came into contact with Rap, who was from Bogalusa, Louisiana [and] had an example in Louisiana, the Deacons of Black Defense, I had been exposed to new ideas: Robert Williams and the Deacons [of Black Defense] . . . that it's not about lay down and get kicked in the head, that you have a right to self defense . . . to stop the fight before it starts by being aggressive as opposed to passive.[12]

Oliver's recollections support the historiographical consensus, which links the increasing popularity of Black Power with the mounting unrest and growing political confidence of a younger generation of African Americans. The CP's inability to relate to a new movement in the 1960s—with a different character and social base than that of the 1930s—meant that it would play a marginal ideological role during a new wave of radicalization in the second half of the sixties.[13] As Oliver indicates:

> The Communist Party worldview wasn't about Black Power. And their . . . presence . . . in the civil rights movement was a shadow presence . . .

coming out of the McCarthy period. . . . you had communists in the anti-war movement . . . in the unions . . . but [not] openly so.[14]

But the practical, commonsense politics of self-defense, which Oliver associates with Robert Williams and the Deacons of Defense in the 1950s, appears to have another antecedent. Despite her parents' strong affiliation with the Communist Party, the Olivers had their own story of struggle and survival, which had been passed down orally from mother to daughter.

My mother taught me from the time I was born that her father and her uncles armed themselves in Salisbury, Maryland, to fight against the Klan . . . later when we were on the Southern campus [my father] and some young professors banded together to keep the Ku Klux Klan off the campus . . . in 1957.[15]

For Oliver, as for many African Americans, such oral recollections functioned as incubators of a militant tradition of struggle and defiance that were instrumental in shaping her radical outlook on issues of justice and race.

Also crucial to Oliver's political formation was the gathering pace of nationalist sentiments, exemplified by Malcolm X's meteoric rise in the late 1950s. During her time at Music and Art, Oliver encountered a female student "who was following some new man who had showed up on the Harlem scene named Malcolm X. And she had changed her last name to 'X.'" Oliver developed a political relationship with her classmate and subsequently took a summer job at the Truth Coffee Shop, which Oliver describes as the "beatnik café for the new black, cultural nationalist intelligentsia of Harlem."[16] "What was much more exciting, as I got a little bit older, was being exposed to this concept of revolutionary nationalism and the idea of Black Power, because remember the Communist Party worldview wasn't about Black Power."[17]

Having discovered the politics that captured her generation's imagination, Oliver convinced her parents to allow her to transfer to a historically black university, Howard, after only a year at Hunter College. Starting at Howard in the fall of 1965, she arrived "with all these dreams" of finding a like-minded world of activists committed to transforming society. She found, instead, an asphyxiating environment where Victorian-era etiquette was common among what she deemed "the beige aristocracy." Shocked by the conservative black elite within the student body, and in the university administration, she and a small group of black activists (among them Hubert Brown—later H. Rap Brown), began a campaign to change Howard's political and cultural "regime." Their aim was to get Howard "to be a black school and not a Negro Institution," a place where both students and administration might employ a greater awareness about the "role those schools play in nurturing and sustaining black struggle."[18]

Perhaps not surprisingly, Oliver was suspended early in the spring semester of 1968 by the dean of women, ostensibly for refusing to "behave like a nice Howard lady." Nevertheless, she rented an apartment in the D.C. area and slipped back onto campus a few months later, as more than a thousand students occupied an administrative building. The student activism that culminated in the building "takeover" was a protest over single-sex dorms and the restrictive parietals that accompanied the policing of the dorms, the absence of black studies, and the presence of the ROTC on campus. In addition, the protesters successfully called for the college president's dismissal on account of his accommodations to the racially retrograde politics of Washington, D.C.'s white elite.

Oliver attributes the power and success of the student movement at Howard and the diversity of its demands, in part, to the campus's confluence of perspectives from different worlds. During her brief time at Howard, she was witness to the convergence of a black Diaspora.

> I remember those progressive students on campus, Babington-Johnson and Hubert Brown, they were from the Bahamas. . . . and then of course, there was Harry Quintana, and he was a black Puerto Rican from New York, and he had an afro. . . . there was this core group of students on scholarship from the West Indies, some of [whom] were key in [later] implementing the rebellion in Granada. So the interplay . . . between African American students, in the sense of U.S. students, who had an axe to grind against Uncle Tom-ism [with] input from these "international students" who had a whole history of their own sense of black pride . . . [because] they're coming from a majority culture—which influences how you look at things—was incredible.[19]

The rich analysis and experience that this diverse group of black students brought to Howard echoed, in many ways, the vibrancy of the multiracial and multicultural world represented by the best of her parents' internationally oriented left-wing politics. Though she may not have been conscious of the similarities at the time, the heady mix of ideas and ethnically diverse personalities on campus likely resembled the raucous parade of artists and intellectuals that trooped through her parents' home. The dynamism of ideas swirling around her childhood, combined with the varieties of consciousness-raising at Howard, predisposed her to joining a predominantly Puerto Rican organization. The racial temper of her life experiences was consistently fluid, and thus significantly different from the hardened racial nationalism that came to dominate certain activist politics in the late 1960s.

Soon after the occupation, Oliver left Howard. She had impressed an older architectural student, Harry Quintana, who recommended her for a job as a VISTA volunteer. In her new occupation, she joined efforts to reform youth gangs in New York with University of the Streets and with Real Great Society, a Puerto Rican East Harlem social service organization affiliated with federal antipoverty programs. In collaboration with University of the Streets, she began to teach black and Puerto Rican history to African American and Puerto Rican youth in East Harlem who had been permanently expelled from New York's public school system. Both the site and the topic of her work would foreshadow much of what was to come.

Shortly after her employment at University of the Streets, and as a result of her associations with the Real Great Society, Oliver was swept into a college education program at the State University of New York at Old Westbury. At Old Westbury, Oliver entered a markedly different stage in her political evolution, one that led to a full-fledged embrace of revolutionary nationalism and membership in the Young Lords. Oliver became part of a network of activists at Old Westbury who formed a precursor to the Young Lords, the Sociedad de Albizu Campos (SAC),[20] a reading circle named after the father of the Puerto Rican national independence movement, Don Pedro Albizu Campos, composed of students who were interested in Puerto Rican history and the politics of Puerto Rico's national liberation movements.[21] At the same time, a number of the members of SAC, including future Young Lords Pablo Guzman and Bob Bunkley, were increasingly interested in the Black Panther Party.

At Old Westbury, Oliver quickly became part of a tightly knit network of budding revolutionaries of color. Many were Puerto Rican, but a significant core was African American. What they shared, however, trumped race: they knew each other intimately, they had grown together politically, and they were looking to make their mark right where they were.

An Organization's Rise, a Woman's Emergence

In the spring of 1969, an interview in the Panther newspaper, *Black Panther*, piqued the attention of a number of members of the SAC. The interview featured Jose "Cha Cha" Jimenez, the leader of a Puerto Rican group in Chicago modeled after the Black Panther Party that called itself the Young Lords Organization (YLO).[22] Of particular interest to SAC members were Jimenez's statements concerning the colonial relationship between Puerto Rico and the United States.[23] In response, a small group of the male members of SAC decided to drive to Chicago to learn more about the Young Lords. After convening with Cha Cha Jimenez and securing permission to launch a chapter of the YLO back home, the New York radicals, who were eager to connect theoretical understandings of power and politics with urban community organizing as the next phase in the movement, reported back with excitement on the mission and work of the Chicago group.

The New York Lords announced their formation on Saturday, July 26, 1969, at the East Village's Tompkins Square Park.[24] Eventually, they duplicated the organizing efforts of the Chicago group in East Harlem and the South Bronx and renamed themselves the Young Lords Party. Their most famous campaign featured their audacious garbage-dumping protests, which forced the city to conduct regular neighborhood garbage pickups. A quieter but more significant victory was their anti–lead poisoning campaign, which the *Journal of Public Health* deemed instrumental in the passage of anti–lead poisoning legislation in New York during the early 1970s. At Lincoln Hospital in the Bronx, the Young Lords were among the first activists to challenge the advent of draconian spending cuts and privatization policies in the public sector. In addition to carrying on a long tradition of struggle at Lincoln, the Young Lords were continuing the work of the BPP and other activists who in the winter of 1969 spearheaded a battle over control of the Community Mental Health Clinic affiliated with Lincoln. In short, the YLP identified with the Black Power movement and exposed the structures of racism and economic inequality that disproportionately harmed African Americans and Latinos in American cities.

Oliver was one of a number of members of the SAC who welcomed its transformation from reading group to revolutionary organization, and eventually decided to leave Old Westbury to become a full-time member of the organization. Like the group of SAC members who traveled to

Chicago to meet Jimenez, she was anxious to connect ideological discussions with grassroots activism in New York's neighborhoods. And because she was in SAC and had developed close personal and political ties with its members, transitioning to the Young Lords seemed an automatic extension of her activism and commitments.

Once we recognize the YLP's conscious modeling on the Black Panther Party, Oliver's crossover to the Young Lords should not surprise us. Despite its largely Puerto Rican membership and determined Puerto Rican nationalism, the organization possessed a rare multiracial and multiethnic composition that presaged the contemporary demographic character of American cities. Operating in the interstices of the late 1960s and early 1970s, the YLP attracted Chicanos, African Americans, and other Latinos. According to Iris Morales, former member of the YLP and producer of the documentary film on the Young Lords, ¡Palante, Siempre, Palante!, "activists who had participated in the civil rights, Black liberation, and cultural nationalist movements joined." Puerto Ricans made up the majority of the members, but African Americans, Morales estimates, "made up about 25 percent of the membership. Other Latinos—Cubans, Dominicans, Mexicans, Panamanians, and Columbians—also joined. One member was Japanese-Hawaiian."[25]

Most important, non–Puerto Rican members were not merely passive participants in the organization but were integral to its lifeblood. As mentioned previously, Oliver was the first woman elected to the Young Lords' central committee. Pablo Yoruba Guzman, one of the founders of the New York branch and a member of the central committee was of Afro-Cuban parentage, and Omar Lopez, the primary strategist of the Chicago YLO, was Mexican American. The ethnic crossover embodied by Oliver's later membership in the Young Lords was incubated in the shared experiences between blacks and Puerto Ricans in New York. These groups came to develop a unique relationship, shaped by both groups' condition before the dominant society as racialized and colonial subjects.[26] But, before finding widespread political expression in the 1960s, the common currents between African Americans and Puerto Ricans were expressed in music, as they for decades worked, lived, and created alongside each other despite their differences. As noted by sociologist and cultural theorist Juan Flores, "African Americans and Puerto Ricans in New York had been partying together for many years . . . since the musical revolution of the late 1940s, when musical giants like Mario Bauza, Machito, and Dizzie Gillespie joined forces in the creation of 'Cubop' or Latin Jazz."[27]

From the time she enrolled at Music and Art High School, Oliver immersed herself in the rich cultural world of black and Spanish Harlem. It was there that the experiences of a generation of blacks and Puerto Ricans reared in a moment of racial struggle and solidarity gave shape to the boogaloo, which combined R & B and soul traditions with Afro-Cuban musical idioms. Boogaloo became hugely popular among both groups with Joe Cuba's "Bang Bang" and Pete Rodriguez's "I Like It Like That."[28] In his recollections of those years, Felipe Luciano, an Afro–Puerto Rican and former chairman of the Young Lords, remembers that "Denise loved Latin music. Danced her pants off. . . . had an affinity for a culture that was African, but had another patina to it. That is, she understood the African nature of Puerto Rican society when they didn't." Because Luciano and Oliver both had an abiding affinity for each other's cultural and racial worlds, each was attentive to the organic manifestations of this intercultural solidarity. As Luciano says:

> Panamanians were the first Latinos who came who developed an affinity, an intrinsic, jugular, umbilical connection to African Americans. They were the first. But they almost wholly went into Afro America, to the extent that you almost forgot that they were Latinos. Puerto Ricans were different. They kept a nugget of their culture and their aesthetic deep within them, but the relationships that they developed with black people were so deep and so loving and so contradictory and so enmeshed that it developed a new culture, and you could hear it in the music. . . . Blacks and Puerto Ricans in New York, when you say the word, it already connotes a whole experience.[29]

The hybridity of experience between blacks and Puerto Ricans to which Luciano refers was anchored materially in the shared condition of social and economic disadvantage that these groups endured, together with the onset of deindustrialization that began during World War II, just as many of them were starting new lives in New York.[30]

While historical accounts offer a painful but necessary examination of the depth of conflict and racism that existed between different peoples of color; Feliciano and Oliver and many others are elegant witnesses to the solidarity that accompanied the crowded conditions and dimmed economic prospects in New York's ethnic neighborhoods. Although interracial conflict is important to acknowledge, it is also important to draw our scholarly attention to the equally profound moments of mingling, and the relationships forged across racial boundaries. As Oliver explains, growing up in New York, these combined experiences established a compelling precedent for Oliver's eventual membership in the Young Lords Party.

> I had connections in East Harlem, I had partied in East Harlem, spent my summers at my cousin Jean's house . . . my friends who were Puerto Rican—to me, we were all black folks. So people have asked me, "How did you feel being a black person in the Young Lords?" I said, "It wasn't a problem." I mean, you have people like Carl Pastor, he was black. Pablo, his father, was Cuban; his mother was Puerto Rican—he was black. Felipe was black. Felipe was Last Poets. He was black; . . . Bob Bunkley (Muntu) was African American.[31]

As an African American woman, Oliver's prominent membership in the YLP bespoke of the increasingly complex racial panorama of American cities. Over the course of the 1940s, the Puerto Rican population in New York City quadrupled, and throughout the 1950s Puerto Ricans migrated to the city in larger numbers than African Americans.[32] The transfer of more than one-third of Puerto Rico's population to New York between 1943 and 1960 produced a unique generation of Puerto Ricans who identified primarily with the mainland. Out of this vast demographic dislocation of Puerto Ricans emerged an urban experience distinct to the mainland United States, and an identity whose expression was unleashed with the rise of the Young Lords Party in the late 1960s. As sons and daughters of the migration after World War II, their consciousness was shaped by an unlikely combination of politicizing experiences, both from global events—namely, the rise of the civil rights movement and the Vietnam War—and from their own particular experiences in an urban setting beset by industrial decline and greater economic and racial segregation. Though not always acknowledged, the shared dilemmas of African Americans and Puerto Ricans were articulated by the Young Lords in their politics and publications. For Oliver, the parallel themes of oppression inherent in the experiences of African Americans and Puerto Ricans called for common cause rather than separate struggle.

Always attentive to the big picture, Oliver recognized early on the importance of media as an organizing tool. In the production of the organization's newspaper, *Pa'lante*, Oliver was indispensable and functioned as jack-of-all-trades because she possessed both political competence and technical know-how. Oliver's early training in one of the highly politicized and learned households of the Old Left, not to mention her ability to speak and write Spanish, proved an asset to an organization that produced a bilingual newspaper. According to Felipe Luciano, "Denise was just erudite. I mean, she was so smart and people loved her."[33] As one of the organization's best writers, she regularly wrote and edited articles, and as an artist she produced much of the paper's politically conscious artwork. Since she had previously been trained in graphics and design at Music and Art, she was part of the original team of Young Lords who created the first layouts of the newspaper.

The confidence she gained in a home that subverted the traditional gender roles of the 1950s also determined the role she would later play in the Young Lords Party. Unlike many women in the organization—who, in Oliver's generous phrasing, "had to work through issues of female passivity"—she was reared in a household where there was always an egalitarian distribution of chores, in which her father provoked political debates with her, and where "nobody told [her] to wash the dishes . . . while [her] brother read a book." Oliver recalls, "I never learned how to type; I didn't want to learn how to type because I didn't want to be typecast." And so, because of her refusal to type and perform secretarial duties during her early membership in the YLP, because of her assertive disposition, and because she was known to be "very organized" and fiercely serious about the work of the organization, she was assigned the prominent and strategic position of Officer of the Day (OD) when incompetency led to the dismissal from that position of a male member of the group late in 1969.

Oliver's work as Officer of the Day gave her a bird's-eye view of the organization; the position also enabled her to expand her responsibilities exponentially. Because of the broad oversight of the organization that the position required, the OD worked closely with members of the central committee. The OD was charged with overseeing the day-to-day work of the organization; delegating assignments to each of its members; handling crises as they emerged; and keeping track of the sales of newspapers. Like a staff sergeant in the military, the OD was also charged with enforcing discipline both on the membership *and* on members of the central committee for failure to tend to assigned duties. Therefore, as a woman in a male-dominated paramilitary organization like the YLP, Oliver exercised rare power. The job of OD afforded Oliver, a woman, a measure of visibility and authority that few in the organization possessed. In 1970 the YLP was engulfed in an internal and overdue struggle against male chauvinism waged by women in the organization; the women demanded, among other things, the election of a woman to the YLP's central committee. Oliver's appointment to the central committee was a logical choice.

Because she had lived a life of struggle in the movement and had straddled many worlds, Oliver's election was also a strategic choice for the Young Lords central committee. According to Felipe Luciano:

> Denise knew how to live the double life: one of the revolutionary, one of the streets . . . the dope fiends loved her, and then she knew just about everyone there was to know in the black movement . . . .Remember, when you're thinking of a Central Committee—let's make it equivalent to a board of directors—you need someone who has access, you need someone who has skills, and you need someone who is a worker. She fulfilled all of those things, plus she was close to us . . . so there really was no other choice.[34]

And in the atmosphere of fatal danger and suspicion produced by police infiltration of radical organizations in the sixties, trust was the paramount requisite for the appointed leadership of organizations like the Young Lords and Black Panthers. In the words of Felipe Luciano,

> Denise hung with us when we were nothing. And the one thing about Puerto Ricans that you can put your money on is their understanding of loyalty. . . . there were other women of comparable political experience, but no one as close to us as Denise. Denise was family.[35]

During her tenure as OD, Oliver became especially aware of the gendered assumptions made by the central committee about who could and could not perform particular tasks. She came to understand that "part of the problem wasn't just that men automatically took the sort of macho role, but [that] women were used to submissive behavior . . . and weren't opening their mouths."[36] In response, Oliver resolved, alongside a number of other women of the organization, to address the problem: "We used to talk about some of the young women in the organization; what we would need to do to get them to speak up, to take a more forward-moving role, not to drop to the back, not to defer to male privilege." The male-centric culture of the group encouraged the learned passivity of the least confident and self-aware female members, even as the organization's activist orientation provided openings for its more politically confident female members.

From the time of its earliest political formulations in October 1969, when Pablo Guzman drafted the YLO's Thirteen Point Program and Platform, the issue of women's oppression figured prominently in the organization's literature. By 1969, the subject of women's oppression and the subordinate role accorded to women within the civil rights movement writ large was a major consideration in the era's political discourse. Though not always willingly, the Young Lords were forced to address the issue in order to keep up with the era's quickly developing political consciousness.[37] Point 10 of the group's platform read: "We Want Equality for Women. Machismo Must Be Revolutionary . . . Not Oppressive."[38] Despite the YLO's continued embrace of "machismo," albeit an ostensibly reformed version of it, the organization determined that "our men must support their women in their fight for economic and social equality, and must recognize that our women are equals in every way within the revolutionary ranks."[39]

As the history of the Young Lords suggest, even though the ideas of the women's movement gained rhetorical acceptance, the old patterns of interaction and inequality continued to arrest the goal of social parity between the sexes both in society and within the movement. Despite the vast experience of Denise Oliver and Iris Morales, among several outspoken female members, in civil rights work and student activism, women in the Young Lords were not represented in the formal leadership until Oliver's election in the summer of 1970. The political prominence of women simply did not grow in proportion to their growth in the ranks of the organization. And when women were assigned to posts in various ministries, including the Defense Ministry,[40] they were disproportionately assigned traditional women's work like child care and secretarial tasks. Even worse was the group's flagrant male chauvinism. Women in the group were routinely humiliated by the behavior of their male counterparts, as potential female recruits seeking information about the group were routinely objectified and sexually propositioned upon arrival at the organization's headquarters. This behavior was later identified by women in the organization as "sexual fascism."[41] Yet despite these conditions, the women of the YLO were reticent to lay bare the discrepancy between the organization's professed ideals and its day-to-day practices, to force the organization to adopt a policy against sexual misconduct.

In part as a result of Oliver's role as OD, the issue of gender oppression, which had been considered in the New York group from its emergence, began to be addressed more forthrightly by women. When the women of the Young Lords began to insist in 1970 that the conduct of men had to change, they formed a women's caucus, which they believed would allow them the space necessary to discuss these hard issues openly and carve out a strategy for reforming the YLP. At the same time, they began to publish *La Luchadora*, a circular that addressed the experience of gender in the organization as well as more theoretical issues of women's oppression. They also identified the absence of women on the central committee as a grievance requiring immediate redress. Simultaneously, women became aware of their own blind spot in allowing the language of the organization's platform to stand unchallenged. According to Oliver, amid debates and discussion in the women's caucus, "We looked in our own faces and we could kick ourselves; we had allowed this thing that said, 'Machismo should be revolutionary, not oppressive' . . . it became patently clear to us that that was the stupidest . . . thing we had read in our lives, and we had let it slide by. They didn't mean anything by it; they were trying to be feminist in that statement. But we realized it was not." The group's platform was eventually changed to read, "Down with Machismo and Male Chauvinism."[42]

Under the leadership of Oliver, the Young Lords Party distinguished itself from other revolutionary nationalist organizations by listening to the demands that the organization adopt an aggressive campaign to reeducate its members and challenge men and women to defy socially prescribed gender roles. While they initially formed a women's caucus, the women of the organization successfully argued, thereafter, for a men's caucus because without the participation of men in similar discussions, very little progress would be made. As Oliver explains:

> Men's caucus came after we recognized that it was all well and good that women were changing, coming to grips with their own passivity, coming to grips with learning how to say "no" to machismo, asserting themselves, but that doesn't do you any good if men aren't changing right along with it, and how do you change men? Men are going to have to take responsibility for changing themselves.[43]

The caucuses refashioned the culture of the group and the behavior of its members with regard to gender parity. Sexist behavior in the organization was denounced formally, and those guilty of it were tried, charged, and disciplined accordingly.

A turning point for the Young Lords came when an issue of the *Rat*, a feminist underground publication of the early 1970s, asked whether the women of the Young Lords were "Young Ladies." Responding to the feminist critique of nationalist women, the Young Lords emphasized that crucial factors of race and class cast a complexity on their oppression, which could not be understood or analyzed by Anglo feminism. Oliver and others argued that these "right-wing" women's groups did not, for example, take into account the exploited condition of Third World women who, by virtue of race, were used as a cheap source of labor and paid significantly lower wages than white women. The Young Lords also highlighted the manipulation of Puerto Rican women in the state-sanctioned campaign to control the Puerto Rican population through the sterilization of women. With the implementation of Operation Bootstrap in 1947 the island became a laboratory for testing pharmaceuticals in Latin America, including unethical research on birth control methods and sterilization technology.[44]

On the basis of what they perceived as a genocidal threat, the Young Lords also disagreed with the position of the women's movement on abortion. Denise Oliver explained, "We feel we can't have a dogmatic approach on abortion. It would be incorrect for us to either be completely in favor of abortion or completely against it."[45] Suspicious of the potential uses of abortion as a form of population control, the group maintained a critical support of it. The organization's preoccupation with the threat of genocide fostered indirect arguments against abortion, maintaining that with society's social and economic constraints on women, the decision to abort was not one made freely by the individual.[46] They also argued that legal abortions were a threat to the lives of poor women whose color and class limited them to substandard medical care. As explained in their position paper on women's liberation:

> Abortions in hospitals that are butcher shops are little better than the illegal abortions our women used to get. The first abortion death in NYC under the new abortion law was Carmen Rodriguez, a Puerto Rican sister who died in Lincoln Hospital. Her abortion was legal, but the conditions in the hospital were deadly.[47]

"Community control" of health care institutions, they argued, was the solution to botched abortions and poor health care: "We believe that abortions should be legal if they are community controlled, if they are safe, if our people are educated about the risks, and if doctors do not sterilize our sisters while performing abortions." In some ways, the Young Lords failed to appreciate the broader political significance implicit in a legal decision around abortions—that legislation would either extend or curtail the power of the state in general and in particular over women's bodies. Despite its shortsightedness, the Young Lords' position was comprehensive and offered potent connections not only between broader issues of race, gender, and class but between those issues and the democratic control of local institutions. Oliver was instrumental in conceptualizing the Young Lords' position paper on women of color and reproductive rights. In this paper, which remains one of the clearest political expositions on the subject by any group of the period, the Young Lords articulated a comprehensive reproductive rights program calling for access to adequate health care, child care, community control of abortion clinics and contraception options alongside education geared at raising consciousness about state-sponsored sterilization campaigns that disproportionately targeted women of color and Puerto Rican women, in particular.

Conclusion

Denise Oliver's role within the YLP is all the more potent when we acknowledge its brevity. Two years after she became a member, and a mere six months after she joined the central committee, the YLP moved its operations to Puerto Rico, in order to focus its attention on the island's struggle for independence. The decision came after a bitter internal struggle over the organization's direction, which drove a wedge between many of its members. Oliver was crushed, since she had no intention of continuing to work with the Young Lords if it was to abandon a political orientation focused primarily on the U.S. mainland. Her urge to foment change, however, was not dimmed. Oliver walked across town and joined the Black Panther Party. The Black Panther Party promised a continuation of the work that had drawn her to the Young Lords. A few months later she was recruited to fly to Paris and then to Algiers, where she eventually joined Eldridge and Kathleen Cleaver. They traveled together in Africa, where they met with the growing number of new postcolonial governments. Because so many nations in Africa were in the throes of revolution, Oliver identifies the mid-1970s as one of the most important political periods of her life.

Despite being associated primarily with the YLP, Oliver's political trajectory is expansive, and rich with activist connections and involvement spanning approximately two decades before the Young Lords and years beyond. From her first act of protest in elementary school against "duck

and cover" nuclear bomb drills, to the experience of witnessing white ri-
oters protesting desegregation on her first day at St. Albans Junior High in
Queens; and from her agitations with Hubert Brown (later H. Rap Brown)
while a student at Howard University in the mid-1960s to her deep commitment in the Young Lords Party and then the Black Panther Party, Oliver's life in struggle is a revealing microcosm. The variety of her engagements mirror many of the problems that engaged black northern radicals
and reflects the ebb and flow and character of the myriad movements of
the postwar period and beyond.

Oliver's participation as an African American woman in a self-defined
Puerto Rican revolutionary nationalist organization continues to puzzle
students of the era. But confusion stems from narrow and static understandings of nationalist politics in the 1960s. The reality of cross-racial and
ethnic membership in nationalist organizations suggests that revolutionary nationalist groups were not always homogeneous entities, as is commonly understood. One of the widespread misconceptions of 1960s nationalist groups is that they employed a reductionism in their analysis of
racial oppression that led to a categorical rejection of multiracial alliances.
While many nationalist groups embraced such views, the most recognized
nationalist group of the period, the Black Panther Party, spearheaded the
Rainbow Coalition, which included the Young Patriots (a group of politicized white migrants from Appalachia) and the Young Lords. Historically, nationalism has emerged during moments of widespread pessimism
about the possibility for multiracial struggle, but in the sixties revolutionary nationalist organizations defined their call for separate race-based organizations as a political strategy rather than an essentialist creed. The era
has left us with numerous examples of nationalist rhetoric, but if we look
more closely, we will see how Oliver's example is not an isolated one. Activists of this era routinely declared their faith in nationalist politics even
as they were forging connections along shared class interests and across
racial and ethnic lines. Such simultaneity and apparent contradiction only
deepen our understanding of nationalism's complexities. Ironically, while
many revolutionary nationalist groups called for separate race-based organizations as a political strategy, these same organizations often failed
to appreciate the changing racial character of American cities, and the
many ways that separatist politics were no longer sustainable in a changing world. The story of Denise Oliver and her intimate involvement in
the Young Lords Party suggests that amid the dominant nationalist currents of the time, and indeed even within them, there existed fissures and

contradictions that created spaces for interethnic solidarity along class lines that advanced a broader and more inclusive vision of struggle toward racial, gender, and economic equality in the United States.

NOTES

1. Martha Biondi, *To Stand and Fight: The Struggle for Civil Rights in Postwar New York City* (Cambridge, MA: Harvard University Press, 2003), 3–16.

2. Denise Oliver, interview by author, August 11, 2006, and August 18, 2007.

3. Denise Oliver, interview by author, August 18, 2007.

4. Ibid.

5. "2,000 Rally in School Fight," *Long Island Daily Press*, June 24, 1959; "Transfer of Students Opposed," *Long Island Daily Press*, July 26, 1959; "State to Review School Transfers," *Long Island Press*, August 27, 1959; "White Pupils End Queens Boycott," *Long Island Daily Press*, September 16, 1959.

6. "Let the Children Go Back to School," *Long Island Daily Press*, September 15, 1959; Denise Oliver, interview by author, August 18, 2007.

7. Denise Oliver, interview by author, August 18, 2007.

8. Biondi, *To Stand and Fight*, 120–121.

9. Denise Oliver, interview by author, August 18, 2007.

10. Ibid.; Robert D. McFadden, "William Booth, Judge and Civil Rights Leader, Dies at 84," *New York Times*, December 27, 2006.

11. Denise Oliver, interview by author, August 11, 2006.

12. Ibid.

13. This also meant that the Party's political experiences and lessons of previous attempts at a multiracial, working-class movement could not be imparted to the new radicals.

14. Denise Oliver, interview by author, August 18, 2007.

15. Ibid..

16. Denise Oliver, interview with author, August 11, 2006.

17. Denise Oliver, interview by author, August 18, 2007.

18. Ibid.

19. Ibid.

20. Michael Abramson, *Palante: Young Lords Party* (New York: McGraw-Hill, 1971), 8; Alfredo Lopez, *The Puerto Rican Papers: Notes on the Re-emergence of a Nation* (New York: Bobbs Merrill, 1973), 324.

21. This history of the Young Lords builds on a number of works on the subject, including Agustin Lao, "Resources of Hope: Imagining the Young Lords and the Politics of Memory," *Centro* 7, no. 1 (1995): 34–49; Carmen Teresa Whalen, "Bridging Homeland and Barrio Politics: The Young Lords in Philadelphia," in *The Puerto Rican Movement: Voices from the Diaspora*, ed. Andres Torres and Jose E. Velazquez (Philadelphia: Temple University Press, 1998), chap. 7; Johanna Fernández, "Between Social Service Reform and Revolutionary Politics: The Young Lords, Late Sixties Radicalism and Community Organizing in New York City," in *Freedom North: Black Freedom Struggles Outside of the South, 1940–1980*, ed. Jeanne Theoharis and Komozi Woodard (New York: Palgrave Macmillan Global Publishing of St. Martin's Press, 2003); and Fernández, "Radicals in the Late 1960s: A History of the Young Lords Party in New York City, 1969–1974" (Ph.D. diss., Columbia University, 2004).

22. For a discussion of the Chicago Lords and their activities, see Frank Browning, "From Rumble to Revolution: The Young Lords," in *The Puerto Rican Experience*, ed. Eugene Cordasco and Eugene Bucchioni (Totowa, NJ: Littlefield, Adams, 1973), 231–245.

23. "Interview with Cha Cha Jimenez Chairman of the Young Lords Organization," *Black Panther*, June 7, 1969, 17.

24. Felipe Luciano and Hiram Maristany, "The Young Lords Party, 1969–1975," *Caribe* 7, no. 4 (1983): 7; Agustin Lao, "Resources of Hope: Imagining the Young Lords and the Politics of Memory," *Centro* 7, no. 1 (1995): 36.

25. Iris Morales, "¡Palante, Siempre, Palante! The Young Lords," in *The Puerto Rican Movement: Voices from the Diaspora*, ed. Andres Torres and Jose E. Velazquez (Philadelphia: Temple University Press, 1998), 214–215.

26. For a fuller discussion, see Ramon Grosfoguel, *Colonial Subjects: Puerto Ricans in a Global Perspective* (Berkeley: University of California Press, 2003), chap. 5.

27. Juan Flores, *From Bomba to Hip Hop: Puerto Rican Culture and Latino Identity* (New York: Columbia University Press, 2000), 80.

28. Ibid., 82.

29. Felipe Luciano, interview by author, September 21, 2008.

30. For a fuller discussion, see Andres Torres, *Between Melting Pot and Mosaic: African Americans and Puerto Ricans in the New York Political Economy* (Philadelphia: Temple University Press, 1995).

31. Denise Oliver, interview by author, August 18, 2007.

32. Nathan Glazer and Daniel P. Moynihan, *Beyond the Melting Pot: The Negroes, Puerto Ricans, Jews, Italians, and Irish of New York City* (Cambridge, MA: MIT Press, 1970), 93; Torres, *Between Melting Pot and Mosaic*, 66.

33. Felipe Luciano, interview by author, September 21, 2008.

34. Ibid..

35. Ibid..

36. Denise Oliver, interview by author, August 18, 2007.

37. See Jennifer Nelson, *Women of Color and the Reproductive Rights Movement* (New York: NYU Press, 2003), chap. 4; Casey Hayden and Mary King, "Sex and Caste: A Kind of Memo," in *Takin' It to the Street: A Sixties Reader*, ed. Alexander Bloom and Wini Breines (New York: Oxford University Press, 2003), 38–43.

38. See 13-Point Program in *Palante* 2, no. 2 (May 8, 1970).

39. See, revised 13-Point Program in Abramson, *Palante*, 150; see also discussion in Judy Clemserud, "Young Women Find a Place in High Command of Young Lords," *New York Times*, November 11, 1970, 52.

40. "Women in the Colonies," May 1970. Palante Radio Program Recording on New York's WBAI, Pacifica Radio Archives.

41. Clemserud, "Young Women Find a Place in High Command of Young Lords," 52.

42. Abramson, *Palante*, 51.

43. Denise Oliver, interview by author, August 18, 2007.

44. Discussed in Iris Lopez, "Agency and Constraint: Sterilization and Reproductive Freedom among Puerto Rican Women in New York City," *Urban Anthropology* 22 (1993): 320. For a comprehensive history of birth control in Puerto Rico, see Annette Ramirez de Arellano and Conrad Scheipp, *Colonialism, Catholicism, and Contraception: A History of Birth Control in Puerto Rico* (Chapel Hill: University of North Carolina Press, 1983). See also "Puerto Rican Genocide," *Palante* 2, no. 2 (May 8, 1970): 8.

45. Abramson, *Palante*, 50.

46. "Young Lords Party Position Paper on Women," *NACLA Newsletter* 4, no. 6 (October 1970): 14–17; "Young Lords Party Position Paper on Women," *Rat*, October 6, 1970, 3–5.

47. "Young Lords Party Position Paper on Women," *Rat*, 5.

13

Grassroots Leadership
and Afro-Asian Solidarities
Yuri Kochiyama's Humanizing Radicalism

Diane C. Fujino

Life magazine's coverage of the assassination of Malcolm X
bore a striking photograph of the slain Black leader lying prone, his head
resting gently on the lap of a middle-aged Asian woman.[1] The visibility of
Malcolm's gigantic impact juxtaposed with the invisibility of this woman
is symbolic of the erasure of Asian American activism. That the woman in
the photo is Yuri Kochiyama, one of the most prominent Asian American
activists, though obscure to all but certain activist and Asian American
circles, speaks to the continuing invisibility of Asian American struggles.
Asian American participation disrupts two conventional narratives about
Black nationalist movements. First, the caring pose of Kochiyama in *Life*
is suggestive of a deeply humanizing practice, one that enabled her to dis-
regard her own safety to rush to help others. Her practice promotes an
alternative form of leadership, one that embodies nurturance and what
Karen Sacks calls "centerperson" skills.[2] Second, Kochiyama's presence as
an Asian American in the Black Power movement contests the common
equation of nationalism with racial exclusion. To the contrary, significant portions of the Black Power movement exhibited commitments to
unifying allies across racial divides, particularly deploying Third World
solidarities.

In this study of Kochiyama's political ideas and practice, I seek to present a gendered analysis of leadership and to discuss the role of race, in this
case of Asian Americans, in the Black Power movement, questioning the
meaning of exclusion, self-determination, and autonomous organizing. In

Yuri Kochiyama (right) with Muhammad Ahmad (Max Stanford, leader of the Revolutionary Action Movement) and Diane Fujino at the founding rally of the Jericho movement for political prisoners, Washington, D.C., 1998. At the rally, Kochiyama was swarmed by veteran black radicals and younger activists alike.

doing so, this study offers an expanded view of the Black Power movement by contesting conventional narratives about gender, race, and leadership in the nationalist movements of the 1960s.

Transforming the Political: Kochiyama's Political Development

Based on Kochiyama's early life, one would predict a strong opposition to Black Power politics. In fact, at the moment of her introduction to Malcolm X, Kochiyama, a newly baptized civil rights activist, criticized Malcolm for his "harsh stance on integration." Born Mary Yuri Nakahara in 1921 to middle-class Japanese immigrants, Kochiyama was well integrated into her largely working-class White community in San Pedro in South Los Angeles. While her Nisei (second-generation Japanese American) peers experienced an uneven racial reception—with some integration into schools, some interracial friendships, and some harsh discrimination— Kochiyama was unusually assimilated into American life. She became the first female student body officer at her high school, was active in a multitude of integrated extracurricular activities, and even broke the romantic barrier of interracial dating. Kochiyama's racial experiences contrasted sharply with those of Malcolm X, whose autobiography is filled with vivid stories of racism and the hardships of poverty. Still, both their fathers died prematurely surrounded by racialized violence. Malcolm's father, a Garveyite organizer hounded by the Ku Klux Klan, had his body almost split in two across streetcar rails. Kochiyama's father, like other Japanese American community leaders, was falsely imprisoned by the FBI on the day of the attack on Pearl Harbor and died six weeks later.[3] Whereas Malcolm reacted with anger and hatred for his father's White supremacist killers, Kochiyama responded rather blandly, all but dismissing any governmental culpability. This coincides with her responses to other racial encounters. When Kochiyama and other Nisei women were asked to leave an organization shortly *before* the bombing of Pearl Harbor, they left without incident. She recounted: "We wrote a nice letter saying we understand that our Japanese background makes us suspect. We wished all the women good luck and thanked them for our short-lived experience."[4] On the eve of Pearl Harbor, Kochiyama's apolitical views, nonconfrontational style, and integration into mainstream activities enabled her blind spot to racism.

She was awakened to racial inequality, though only gradually, through the forced removal and incarceration of 110,000 West Coast Japanese Americans during World War II. From inside the former Santa Anita racetrack, with its horse stables hastily converted into subpar housing, Kochiyama listened to other internees discuss the political and racial context of incarceration and the long history of anti-Japanese racism. Still, as is typical with any process of change, her transformation from a color-blind to a race-conscious worldview was precarious and uneven. From behind barbed wire she wrote, "But not until I myself actually come up against prejudice and discrimination will I really understand the problems of the Nisei."[5]

After the war, she moved to New York City to marry Bill Kochiyama, a strikingly handsome Nisei soldier she had met at the Jerome, Arkansas, concentration camp.[6] Along with raising six children, Kochiyama's experiences living in low-income housing projects and waitressing in working-class neighborhood restaurants schooled her in the realities of U.S. racism. From customers, she learned of Jim Crow segregation; from her mainly Black and Puerto Rican neighbors, she heard stories of everyday racism. This new understanding of racial injustice prompted Kochiyama to rethink her own experiences. Yuri and Bill spoke openly about their concentration camp experiences years before it become fashionable to discuss within Japanese American circles. They wrote in their family newsletter in 1951: "As we look back to Christmas of 10 years ago, we of Japanese ancestry can recall with almost vivid painfulness, the uneasy, frustrating, insecure experiences we were forced to undergo."[7] At the time, her recognition of discrimination did not detract from a patriotic faith in U.S. institutions. To the contrary, she saw these institutions as able to remedy any deviations from its professed goals of "democracy and justice for all." Their article concluded: "A grateful nation's thanks, her recognition and acceptance of an equally grateful minority completes the wartime saga, and opens the way whereby Niseis may continue their campaign for rights still denied."[8]

Kochiyama's social consciousness continued to evolve as the media covered the unfolding civil rights movement. She began inviting civil rights speakers to her family's weekend "open houses," formerly exclusively social gatherings. But it was not until 1963, a couple of years after her family moved to Harlem, that she developed an activist practice. Given her proclivity for interracial unity and nonviolent tactics, it is surprising how quickly her initial entry into civil rights turned to radicalism. The day after she met Malcolm X in October 1963, Kochiyama heard him speak for the first time on a radio debate among civil rights advocates. It was Malcolm—and not the traditional civil rights leaders—who captured her imagination. She felt compelled to write, though her letter reveals the influence of civil rights ideology on her own beliefs: "It may be possible that non-Negroes may wake up and learn to treat all people as human beings. And when that time comes, I am sure that your pronouncement for separation will be changed to integration. If each of us, white, yellow, and what-have-you, can earn our way into your confidence by actual performance, will you . . . could you . . . believe in 'togetherness' of all people?"[9] It is significant that, while striving for integration, she locates the source of the social problem not in people of color failing to adapt to the mainstream, but in "non-Negroes" failing to treat Black people humanely.

The mythology assumes a close relationship between Kochiyama and Malcolm X. But my research reveals that she actually had few direct interactions with Malcolm, who spent half of 1964 in Africa, the Middle East, and Europe. But Malcolm's visit to the Kochiyama's home in June 1964, to visit survivors of the Hiroshima atomic bomb and peace advocates, and Malcolm's eleven postcards sent to the Kochiyamas during his travels abroad provoked a process of radical transformation in her. She began attending Malcolm's Organization of Afro-American Unity (OAAU) Liberation School every Saturday. After hearing a tape recording of the vicious jailhouse beating of Fannie Lou Hamer and after OAAU teacher James Campbell depicted racism as this country's "congenital deformity," Kochiyama began viewing racism no longer as an aberrant mark in a society otherwise committed to democracy and equality but as structurally embedded in its very history.[10] As she learned about the partitioning of Africa by European leaders at the 1884–1885 Berlin Conference without regard to geographic or cultural boundaries or the desires of African people, she came to locate domestic and global oppression in the context of "racism, colonialism, capitalism, and imperialism."[11]

In honor of Malcolm X, Kochiyama began an annual eight-page political newsletter. More than a "family news-sheet," as she modestly called it, the North Star chronicled the revolutionary nationalist movement in Harlem in a period of historical significance (1965–1969) and disseminated the ideas of Black Power to Black, Asian American, and other progressive audiences. This activity built on her interests as a journalism major at Compton Junior College in the prewar years and her family's production of an eight- to twelve-page socially oriented Christmas newsletter (1950–1968). The North Star captures the rapid changes in Kochiyama's politics since her introduction to Malcolm X. More than a personal political transformation, her ideological development reflected the nationwide tectonic shifts in the Black freedom movement. The front page of the 1966 North Star shouted the call for "Black Power," popularized by Stokely Carmichael (later Kwame Ture). In a dramatic reversal of her denouncement of Malcolm's "harsh stance on integration," Kochiyama now agreed with Black Power's condemnation of integrationism as a major "frailty" of the civil rights movement. Quoting Carmichael, she wrote: "Integration is irrelevant to the freedom of Black people. Negroes have always been made to believe that everything better is always white. If integration means moving to something white is moving to something better, then integration is a subterfuge for white supremacy."[12] Kochiyama advocated Black Power as "an idea to inspire a new image; assert a Black self; create basic changes; govern one's own destiny; achieve not for personal attainments, but for all Black people."[13] When the Asian American movement began in the late 1960s, Kochiyama's words would inspire many of its young activists to adopt the politics of self-determination and autonomy over integration into Martin Luther King's beloved community.

After Malcolm's assassination in 1965, Kochiyama continued her political education under the tutelage of social critic Harold Cruse at Amiri Baraka's (LeRoi Jones's) short-lived but significant Black Arts Repertory Theater/School in Harlem, became embroiled in political prisoner and other antiracist and anti-imperialist solidarity work, and transformed her family's weekend "open houses" into gatherings for Black radicals. When the Republic of New Africa (RNA) formed in 1968, advocating a separate Black nation in the U.S. South as the pathway to Black liberation, Kochiyama saw in the RNA's emphasis on nationhood and land the clearest strategy for implementing Malcolm's politics. That Malcolm himself no longer supported Black nationalism by 1964 did not deter those in the RNA from claiming Malcolm's vision as the basis of their ideology.[14] Out of respect for Black self-determination, Kochiyama initially joined the Friends of RNA. But when the RNA began accepting non-Blacks in 1969, she was quickly invited to join. It was then, at the age of forty-eight, that she began using her Japanese middle name, Yuri, in solidarity with political and cultural self-definition and the RNA's practice of adopting African and Muslim names.

In the late 1960s and early 1970s, Kochiyama's life was an invigorating and exhausting whirlwind of political activities—attending weekly RNA classes on nation building, revolutionary first aid, and gun control; working with the newly formed Asian Americans for Action; speaking at antiwar rallies, supporting Puerto Rican freedom fighters; staying up until the wee hours of the night corresponding with political prisoners; writing articles for numerous movement publications; and making leaflets and picket signs. On top of this, she also maintained a family life and worked part-time as a waitress. By integrating family life with political activism (though not always smoothly) and by bringing a culture of caring to Black militancy, she came to exemplify the women's movement's famous axiom, "the personal is political," even as she rejected identification with the feminist movement.[15]

"Centerperson" Leadership and a Culture of Caring

Anthropologist Karen Sacks, in her study of Duke Medical Center clerical workers, argues that social networks are critical to building social movements, in this case a unionization campaign. Aware of the gendered nature of leadership, she labeled these leaders "centerwomen"—as opposed to "spokesmen."[16] Sacks used the latter term to refer to public and masculine forms of leadership associated with power and visibility and emphasized in the social movement literature, namely, charismatic speakers, confrontational negotiators, decision makers, and those with official titles. By contrast, the centerwomen in her study emphasized talking to coworkers, usually one-on-one, signing them up for the union, and asking them to organize others. They brought people together, raised critical consciousness through personal conversations, and disseminated information through social networks. As one woman expressed to Sacks, "Women are organizers and men are leaders."[17]

Sacks's concept of the "centerwomen" allows us to discuss Kochiyama's activist contributions as a form of leadership, though she was not an official leader, theoretician, strategist, or spokesperson for the radical Black movement. Instead, Kochiyama exemplified the dedicated activist, willing to do the behind-the-scenes work, with little public recognition or reward. Mutulu Shakur, RNA activist, stated: "I done spent many a cold night when it was just me and Yuri walking the streets of Harlem and Brooklyn trying to get things done. [She was there doing] the mundane small things, consistent in being there, that's the practice."[18] Indeed, her practice involved being an on-the-ground grassroots organizer who talked to people one-on-one, recruited through personal networks, and welcomed people into her home. Some may interpret Kochiyama's activism as emanating from a position of weakness, one that reproduces stereotypes of submissive women and passive Asian Americans. I admit being disappointed to discover that she had not played a more formidable and dazzling role in the Black Power movement. In doing so, I was inadvertently privileging spokesmen over centerwomen leadership and erroneously equating political leadership with power and visibility. Ella Baker is renowned for her sharp criticism of the charismatic leader model, asserting that such hero worship reinforced dominant society's emphasis on individualism and narcissism (usually personified by the male body) and, most significantly, diminished ordinary people's belief in their own power to effect change. Baker insisted, "Strong people don't need strong leaders."[19] Kochiyama demonstrated in practice, though less often in words, her understanding of Baker's ideas.

Kochiyama is famed for her unparalleled hospitality and the relentless flow of visitors into her home, dubbed "Grand Central Station." In 1962, the year before she plunged into political activism, a complete stranger, a teacher from a school near Kochiyama's hometown, had heard of her family's generosity and wrote to ask if they would host a terminally ill teenager with a dream of visiting New York City museums. In her typical fashion, Kochiyama enthusiastically offered to house him, enlisted the help of friends, and organized an engaging schedule of activities.[20] Kochiyama relied on her centerperson leadership to fulfill this teenager's dream. Those around her were unusually receptive to her requests for help in large part because they recognized her generosity to others. Over the years, hundreds of overnight guests—medically ill children, single mothers and their children, soldiers passing through town, vacationing friends, students, and even strangers—stayed at the Kochiyamas' modest apartment, sleeping on the floor or anywhere they could find a space, even on a mattress in the bathtub. She recalled regularly leaving her home so others could stay: "Our friends would say, 'Gee your place is so crowded, why don't you [sleep] over [at] our place and bring the youngest one.'"[21] In addition, scores of people, half of whom were newcomers, would drop by their weekly Friday and Saturday night "open houses."[22] A neighbor recalled: "Yuri was the key person who made things happen. Bill made sure everyone was comfortable and had a drink . . . . But Yuri was the one who brought people in from all over."[23]

Kochiyama has a long history of exhibiting centerperson leadership, whether working as a Sunday school teacher in the late 1930s, arranging housing for Nisei soldiers during World War II, or opening her house to overnight guests and social events in the 1950s. When she gained a critical consciousness, she did not subsume her nurturing ways to what might be seen as hard-core political causes. Instead, she understood the need to nurture the individual in the process of creating societal change. In this, she moved the feminist slogan "the personal is political" beyond rhetoric into the realm of practice. The frequent meetings at the Kochiyamas' turned from organizing services for Asian American soldiers to hosting numerous Black militant groups. They continued their massive open houses, now overflowing with activists—the famous like Stokely Carmichael (Kwame Ture), poet LeRoi Jones (Amiri Baraka), and Malcolm's sister and OAAU leader Ella Collins, as well as the unknown.[24] Kochiyama was also a magnet for messages, an important function in a period before e-mail and answering machines and in a community where not everyone had reliable access to a telephone. One RNA activist recounted: "Yuri used to waitress at Thomford's. That became like our meeting place. Everybody would come in and talk to Yuri. So when you'd come in, Yuri would have the most recent information for you. If we wanted to set up a meeting, she would set it up. If you had a message for someone, you'd just leave it with Yuri. She must have received fifteen, twenty messages a day."[25] Since she was known for traveling throughout town, dropping off flyers or running errands, people would leave messages for her at various Harlem establishments—a highly unorthodox practice indeed.[26] This extraordinary ability to cultivate social relations made her a central figure with up-to-date movement news and a valuable source for recruiting new members. Just as the centerwomen in Sacks's study organized baby showers and biweekly dinners that built the social networks that fueled union organizing, Kochiyama's efforts to nurture individuals and create a community were vital to the arduous work of sustaining activists and movements over time.

Nowhere did Kochiyama's work as a centerperson shine as brightly as in the political prisoner movement, where she became the "central figure" to many political prisoners.[27] "Yuri was our internet in those days" proclaimed an RNA activist, referring to her ability to disseminate information and connect people.[28] Kochiyama was the first person many turned to when arrested or when released from prison, either calling her home or dropping by her work. "When we were captured by the enemy, our first call went to WA6-7412," recounted political prisoner Mutulu Shakur, rattling off her telephone number from memory thirty years after his first postprison phone call to Kochiyama. "Everybody just remembered that number. Anybody getting arrested, no matter Black, Puerto Rican, or whatever, our first call was to her number. Her network was like no other. She would get a lawyer or get information out to our family and the movement. You knew she wasn't going to stop until somebody heard from you."[29] Mtayari Shabaka Sundiata wrote to Kochiyama in 1975: "After visiting with you Sunday, I felt so good knowing that someone beyond this cement grave knows that I am alive and very much a part of the movement for a better life for all oppressed people . . . .You are the only person on the outside that I have any contact with. Everyone else seems to have considered me legally dead."[30] These words of Sundiata, head of the Brooklyn RNA when Kochiyama joined and a Black Liberation Army member, strengthened her resolve to support those facing adversity.

Kochiyama also functioned as an informal archivist. "You should have seen the files she had on political prisoners," remarked one activist. "She had everybody's case, when they went to the parole board, their whole file. So if you wanted information on a political prisoner, say to organize a conference or a tribunal, all we had to do was go to Yuri."[31] Another remembered the clutter of papers that Kochiyama's packrat behavior produced: "She had little cardboard boxes [of files] stacked up everywhere. One of her back rooms was just filled with these boxes. And there used to be boxes in the hallway and in the kitchen. The kitchen table always had bunches of stuff on it, and underneath it. But . . . it was amazing how quickly she could put her hands on information."[32] Not only did she save countless movement documents, but her razor-sharp memory, in decline only after a stroke in 1999, enabled her to remember facts about events and cases that eluded most people.

Her tendency to focus on the individual at times eclipsed larger debates about strategy and theory. During the planning of an international political prisoner conference in 2001, for example, a divisive debate emerged: Are political prisoners those targeted and imprisoned because of their activism, or can they also include those who become politicized as a result of harsh prison conditions? This was a troubling debate to Kochiyama, who feared that such conflict would lead to irreparable divisions, as she has witnessed during her many years of activism. So after one particularly contentious meeting, rather than engaging a political discussion, Kochiyama chitchatted with people from "both sides" of the issue, inquiring about their families and health. While Kochiyama has been criticized for sidestepping political debates, and rightly so, her strength as a centerperson lies in building community and emphasizing the common social bonds and political causes that unify those working for justice.[33] Though it sounds clichéd, she is someone who actually practices the method; as she puts it, "There's more that unites us than divides us." Few are as masterful at humanizing the struggle or at maintaining optimism about the potential for change as Kochiyama.

In gendering centerwomen and spokesmen styles, I, like Sacks, do not intend to essentialize or polarize these sets of skills. I am not advocating that nurturance and networking are essentially feminine or that public speaking and hard-hitting negotiations are essentially masculine. As discussed later, Kochiyama also emerged as a public speaker and writer— skills usually considered more masculine. Historically, the idea of "separate spheres," centering on women's domesticity and men's breadwinning roles, arose as industrialization created factory and other work spaces away from the household.[34] Because this historic context continues to govern the conventional thinking about femininity and masculinity and serves to devalue the feminine, it becomes necessary to discuss it through a gendered lens. Women often did the unheralded, unglamorous, hard everyday work that enabled organizations and movements to succeed and

enabled men to become visible leaders. While recognizing women's contributions, this view reproduces a hierarchical relationship between men
as leaders in the public sphere and women as nurturers in the private
sphere, as in "behind every great man is a great woman." Instead, I am
arguing that networking, communicating, and the nurturing of activists,
communities, and social movements are equal in importance to speaking,
theorizing, negotiating, and holding formal titles when creating societal
and personal transformation. Both centerperson and spokesperson skills
ought to be valued and recognized as leadership.[35]

Afro-Asian Solidarities and the Politics of Self-Determination

Despite her own internment experience, it was from living in working-
class Black communities in postwar New York and listening to her neighbors' stories of daily subjugations that Kochiyama became consciously
aware of widespread U.S. racism. After becoming radicalized in Harlem
though the influence of Malcolm X and learning about the long and
vigorous history of Black resistance, Kochiyama became convinced that
Black Power was the most revolutionary U.S.-based social movement at
the time. Black radicalism exerted such a strong impact in part because
in 1963, when she plunged into activism, the Japanese American activism that existed was less visible and, to Kochiyama, less urgent than the
Black activism encircling her in Harlem and exploding in the South.[36] So
when the Asian American movement emerged in the late 1960s, Kochiyama was already firmly embedded in the Black Power movement. In that
movement, she was mentored by advanced organizers, eloquent spokes-
persons, and sophisticated theoreticians. In the nascent Asian American
movement, young activists looked to elders like Kochiyama, who had experience beyond her relative short life in the movement. It is not surprising, then, that to her Black Power was the most advanced movement and
contained the potential for far-reaching revolutionary transformation.
Thus, even as she worked intensely in the Asian American Movement, she
placed her priority with the radical Black movement.

Kochiyama's behind-the-scenes work in the Black movement reflects
her strong belief in Black self-determination. In the *North Star*, she explained: "We realize the urgency and need for the privacy and intimacy
of Black people. We hope we have not ever trespassed. We have tried to
help only when asked; and especially in the periphery role of support,
fund-raising and notifying."[37] Though my analysis places centerperson

leadership on a par with spokesperson leadership, Kochiyama saw the two sets of skills in hierarchical ways. She would help with "notifying" and "support" rather than primary leadership and with "fund-raising" rather than decision making.

Kochiyama's work on the periphery, beyond exhibiting centerperson leadership and a respect for Black self-determination, also stemmed from an internalization of cultural style. While this self-effacing style is often attributed to Japanese or women's culture, it also reflects the ways subordinated groups exhibit their options and power. Since childhood, Kochiyama displayed a tendency toward modesty, collectivity, and behind-the-scenes work, even as she held positions of institutional power (first female student body officer) and was widely respected for her selfless support of others. She befriended new students, provided candy to the poor at Easter, wrote notes to cheer up athletes, and inspired optimism and a sense of purpose to Japanese American teenagers confined inside concentration camps. In continuously meeting new people through her broad networks, Kochiyama played an important role in recruiting people to radical Black organizations. One RNA comrade recalled that after meeting a potential member and providing background information, Kochiyama would call a Black leader to "do a workshop" for them at her home.[38] She saw herself as being able to contribute, but in a peripheral way.

The common association of Black nationalism with racial exclusion raises the question of how Kochiyama as an Asian American was received in the Black Power movement. The overwhelming response is that she was "absolutely accepted," as exclaimed by Black activist Nyisha Shakur.[39] Kochiyama's respect for Black self-determination and her tireless work for Black liberation endeared her to Black activists. Many were awed by her dedication to, in their view, a community that was not her own. Her willingness to do support work and to readily relinquish decision making and power to Black activists reduced potential conflicts with fellow activists and rendered her less threatening to this movement's leadership. That she was seen as a Third World (read not White) person further facilitated a positive reception by Black nationalists. In Malcolm X's Organization of Afro-American Unity, A. Peter Bailey observed: "Yuri didn't try to out Black everyone, like many Whites do. So many Whites—Right, Left, or center—interacted with the Black movement with such paternalism. They'll do anything for you as long as they run it. That's why most Black people didn't trust alliances with Whites. But people came to trust Yuri, to respect her as a strong supporter of the Black movement."[40]

But did her willingness to do support work and her self-effacing ways simultaneously reinforce stereotypes of model minority passivity ascribed to Asian Americans and internalized by Black activists? The multiple and at times contradictory layers of racial politics in the Black Power movement require a complex response. Laura Pulido, in her racial comparative study of radical organizing in Los Angeles, found that many Black and Chicano activists viewed Asian Americans as model minorities.[41] This perception interfered with the formation of Third World solidarities because in assuming the nonexistence of anti-Asian racism, Blacks and Chicanos saw little common ground around which to unify. Moreover, in internalizing the model minority logic—which promotes hard work, frugality, and self-reliance, instead of protest, as pathways to upward mobility—they could not see the Asian American activism that did exist. By ascribing to the model minority image of Asian Americans, popularized in 1966 in two nationally respected and widely read magazines, some Black activists viewed her humble work as evidence of culturally prescribed practices.[42]

But more so, by living in a Harlem housing project unit and participating in the militant Black struggle, Kochiyama was seen as outside of the model minority construct. To those who saw her as exceptional, her presence did not change their overarching view of Asian Americans as model minorities and non-allies in the struggle for justice. But others developed complex thinking about racial politics, moving beyond the militant minority versus model minority divide. For Black radicals, including the revolutionary nationalists with whom Kochiyama worked, the enduring presence of Afro-Asian alliances forged at the 1955 Bandung conference and the revolutionary fervor occurring in China, North Korea, and Vietnam in the 1960s, compelled a view of Asia that contrasted sharply with the model minority image. This view extended, in uneven ways, to Asian Americans. Kochiyama, with her unrelenting devotion to Black liberation, reinforced the view of Asian Americans as resisters.

From her earliest experiences in the militant Black movement, Kochiyama saw Black radicals express alliances with Asians and Asian Americans. Her first extended contact with Malcolm X took place at the Kochiyamas' home when Malcolm accepted an invitation to speak to Hiroshima atomic bomb survivors and peace advocates. She recalls Malcolm saying to the Hiroshima survivors: "You were bombed and have physical scars. We too have been bombed and you saw some of the scars in our neighborhood. We are constantly hit by the bombs of racism." He went on to express his admiration of Japan, recounted Kochiyama:

He explained that almost all of Asia had been colonized by Europeans except Japan. The only reason Japan wasn't colonized was because Japan didn't have resources that Europeans wanted. All over Southeast Asia, European and American imperialists were taking rubber and oil and other resources. But after World War II, Japan did provide valuable military bases for America, especially on the island of Okinawa. It was because Japan hadn't been colonized that Japan was able to stay intact and become so strong until her defeat in World War II.[43]

Malcolm X's sentiments echo the earlier ideas of Black internationalists, who viewed Japan as the champion of the dark nations against the rise of U.S. and European imperialism and global white supremacy.[44] While Kochiyama noted that Malcolm's one-sided admiration of Japan overlooked its history of anti-Korean oppression and heinous military treatment of Asian nations and people, she also understood that Malcolm was expressing commonalities between African American and Japanese experiences and liberation struggles.

When she attended the OAAU Liberation School, Kochiyama was surprised that at her first class the instructor, James Shabazz, who spoke some Japanese, Korean, and Chinese, wrote the characters for Tao on the board. When he explained that "the spirituality underlying these martial arts . . . were exercises to help one move towards God similar to how Islam did," she, as the only non-Black in the room, appreciated that Shabazz emphasized parallels, rather than separateness, among various cultures.[45] A few months earlier, Max Stanford (later Muhammad Ahmad), leader of the Revolutionary Action Movement (RAM), had approached Kochiyama to enlist her help in building his organization in Harlem. While Stanford mistakenly thought that OAAU meetings were held at Kochiyama's home, he did not overestimate the importance of her centerperson leadership and networks. Stanford credits Kochiyama with facilitating the formation of the RAM Black Panther Party in Harlem: "Yuri opened up her apartment as a meeting place, where we met for lunch two or three times a week. She'd fix sandwiches and we would listen to Malcolm's unedited speeches . . . . She could introduce people to us. She would circulate any information that we had to a whole network of people . . . .Yuri was a constant communicator, constant facilitator, constant networker."[46] In those early months of her budding activism, and with uncertainty about her racial location in the nationalist movement, Stanford's invitation signaled her relevance to the local Black movement.

By 1969, Kochiyama was promoting Afro-Asian solidarities in, for example, an article she wrote on Robert F. Williams for the newsletter of the newly formed Asian-Americans for Action. Williams was renowned within activist circles for his daring actions to arm southern Blacks against Ku Klux Klan attacks, including establishing an all-Black chapter of the National Rifle Association and teaching self-defense to no less than members of the NAACP, known for their polite resistance through legislative means. As Williams gained strength and notoriety, the police ran him out of town in 1961. He fled to Cuba and later China.[47] After the Republic of New Africa selected Williams as its president, despite his location in exile, Kochiyama began corresponding with him and distributing his banned publication, the *Crusader*. Based on his relationship with Mao Tse-tung, Williams solicited two statements from the Chinese leader in 1963 and 1968 in support of Black liberation.[48] Aware of Williams's importance to Afro-Asian solidarity, Kochiyama focused her article on, as she titled it, "Who Is Rob Williams, and What Is His Relationship to Asians?" She wrote, "Williams moved Mao to publicly vociferate support of the Black people's struggle in America, and also reciprocally, he helped Black people to better view the Chinese people's revolution and goals."[49] Williams told the American public: "China impressed me as a variety of worlds with a variety of people bound by profound human qualities, some of which the Western world must cultivate if it is to survive. I think that the greatest human qualities being manifested in China today are those of morality and selflessness."[50] In stating that Williams "symbolizes the internationalism of people's struggles globally," she was expressing her own position on the need for global unity in struggle, particularly Afro-Asian alliances.[51] She quickly learned that, contrary to the widespread view that Black Power singularly promoted Black issues and racial separatism, this movement, particularly its revolutionary wing, drew heavily on Bandung's promotion of anticolonialism, antiracism, self-determination, and Third World unity.

Such an ideology was appealing to the Asian American movement as it developed in the late 1960s and 1970s, so much so that Black Power and Third Worldism—more than civil rights—exerted the strongest influence on this budding movement.[52] Richard Aoki, for example, brought ideas developed as an early Japanese American leader of the Black Panther Party into the Third World Liberation Front strike for ethnic studies at UC Berkeley.[53] Berkeley's Asian American Political Alliance used hard-hitting language to advocate Third World unity and the principles of self-determination: "We Asian Americans refuse to cooperate with the White Racism in this society, which exploits us as well as other Third World people," and "We Asian Americans support all oppressed people and their struggles for Liberation and believe that Third World People must have complete control over the political, economic, and educational institutions within their communities."[54] In New York, I Wor Kuen's twelve-point platform and program, modeled after the Black Panther Party, stated: "We want liberation of all Third World peoples and other oppressed peoples"; "We want community control of our institutions and land"; and "We want a socialist society."[55]

Though Kochiyama was not distinctive in forging Afro-Asian solidarities, it can be said that she, more than any other activist, infused Black Power politics into the Asian American Movement through her writings, speeches, everyday conversations, social-political networks, and frequent gatherings at her home.[56] From its start, Asian Americans for Action, founded in New York City in 1969 by longtime activists Kazu Iijima and Min Matsuda, recognized the Black struggle "as the most critical struggle at this point;" accused U.S. foreign policy of being "imperialistic" because it gained "profits accrued from the people and materials of . . . the Third World," and indicted U.S. domestic policies as "token, minimal gestures used as pacification devices which serve only to perpetuate the oppressed condition of the poor and minorities."[57] In such a radical space, Kochiyama found comrades to help forge Third World alliances, to organize Asian American support for Black liberation, and, for the first time, to develop her own politics around Asian and Asian American issues. Though not a core leader, Kochiyama regularly attended meetings, frequently contributed to its newsletters, and was often a featured speaker and public representative of the organization.

While Kochiyama promoted Black liberation within Asian American circles, she has been criticized, particularly by Asian American activists, for failing to develop Black support for Asian American liberation. This stems from Kochiyama's view of the pervasiveness and brutality of anti-Black racism and the revolutionary potential of the Black freedom struggle—ideas that parallel the position of Asian-Americans for Action. In the post-Bandung movement, Kochiyama's location as a Third World person enabled her to see identity as well as solidarity in the struggles for Black, Asian, and Third World liberation. Her steadfast support for political prisoners, her most intense area of struggle in a life filled with support for a multitude of issues, was motivated by her own experience of incarceration during World War II. She reflected: "I cannot help but feel strongly about this because I can never forget what we, peoples of Japanese ancestry, experienced during World War II because of hysteria, isolation, and absolutely no support . . . .Yes, we were also political prisoners."[58]

To respond to the increased arrests of many of her comrades—those "captured" in the "anticolonial" war of national liberation—Kochiyama helped form the National Committee to Defend Political Prisoners (NCDPP) in the early 1970s. "Yuri, out of all of us, was in touch with prisoners and supporters the most," observed an NCDPP member. "People would call her relentlessly, just all the time . . . .She was seemingly writing and visiting most of the political prisoners and really staying on top of it."[59] In the 1990s, she generated Asian American support for the renowned Black political prisoner Mumia Abu-Jamal and, for the first time, organized support groups for Asian American political prisoners, namely, David Wong and Yu Kikumura.

So rather than seeing support for Black or Asian American liberation in additive or competing ways, Kochiyama's practice connected and expanded these struggles. As the Asian American Movement grew and as she spoke out against U.S. imperialism in Asia, she helped raise awareness of Asian and Asian American oppression and resistance. She wrote, for example, about the work of newly formed Asian American political groups to the predominantly Black readership of the *North Star*.[60] In the 1980s, as the struggle to right the wrongs of the World War II concentration camps gained momentum, she linked Japanese American redress with Black reparations. By broadcasting the work of the Asian American Movement, she helped to repeal the blind spot of Black and Chicano activists to Asian American activism.

In her speeches and writings, she was particularly effective at drawing connections between Asian liberation and Black struggles. Her Hiroshima-Nagasaki Week speech, for example, promoted Black Power, Third World radicalism, and Asian liberation. She condemned American militarism in Vietnam and Okinawa, radioactive fallout in Micronesia, and the slaughter of half a million Indonesians in 1965. Then, with a boldness reminiscent of Malcolm X, she denounced "the recent so-called 'good-will' tour by President Nixon" and proclaimed that "The U.S. must understand that Asia does not need American leadership or *any* Great White Father. They know that American involvement is not for the concern of Asia but to benefit themselves." Borrowing from Marcus Garvey, she stated, "Just as Africa must be for Africans, Asia must be for Asians." She ended with a strategy for building Third World collaborations: "When nations can feel unity for self-determination among themselves, [only then] can there be interdependence in trade and positive rapport in inter-race and international relations."[61] Her vocal opposition to U.S. imperialism in Vietnam, Hiroshima-Nagasaki, Okinawa, and other parts of Asia helped build Black support for Asian liberation. In the *North Star*, she called Vietnam "a North Star to liberation movements" in Africa, South America, and Black America, published the program of the National Liberation Front of South Vietnam, and discussed Ho Chi Minh in glowing terms.[62]

Significantly, it was the Asian American Movement that enabled Kochiyama to develop and display spokesperson leadership in addition to her already extensive centerperson leadership. She became a coveted speaker on the national circuit—a role she neither asked for nor would have accepted in the black freedom movement. By the 1990s, she rose to national stature as a Movement leader. By the early twenty-first century, her own memoir, two biographies, one in English and one in Japanese, and a U.S.-based documentary focused on her life.[63]

Conclusion

Yuri Kochiyama's life is so important because, with extraordinary consistency, she practiced the kinds of skills that empower ordinary people, nurture activists, and ultimately sustain social movements. While we remember the magnificent marches, fiery speeches, and provocative images, we often forget the undramatic, everyday work involved in creating social change. Centerperson leadership is particularly vital to organizing, or the ongoing development of groups to build and sustain a larger vision, by contrast to mobilizing, or the pulling together of relatively large numbers of people for a relatively short-term goal. By encouraging subordinated people to think boldly and imaginatively, by attending to their personal well-being, and by enthusiastically and passionately caring about those facing hardships, especially those besieged by racism and state repression, Kochiyama inspired many toward an activist practice. Significantly, she also reminds us to be understanding—critical yes, but always understanding—about people's shortcomings. Historian Charles Payne observed: "Unless we do a better job of responding to the human contradictions and weaknesses of the people we work with, we are likely to continue to create politics that are progressive in the ideas expressed but disempowering in the way individuals expressing those ideas relate to one another."[64] While

Kochiyama has tended to avoid offering criticism, even when needed, her ability to understand human contradictions and to nurture, in gentle and supportive ways, people's inclination for social justice helped to build the kind of social movement that, in its process, embodied the values and vision of a liberating and egalitarian society.

NOTES

I borrow from Payne's discussion of Ella Baker in noting, that Yuri Kochiyama could have contributed so much, yet remain so obscure even among the politically informed reminds us of "how much our collective past has been distorted—and distorted in disempowering ways."[65] By focusing our vision on centerperson leadership skills, the complicated positioning of Asian Americans within the Black nationalist movement, and the need to work humanely with the very real human frailties contained in individuals and in social movements, Kochiyama's radical humanism helps recenter these distorted and invisible elements of the Black freedom struggle.

1. "The Violent End of the Man Called Malcolm X," *Life*, March 5, 1965, 26.

2. Karen Sacks, "Gender and Grassroots Leadership," in *Women and the Politics of Empowerment*, ed. Ann Bookman and Sandra Morgen (Philadelphia: Temple University Press, 1988), 77–94.

3. Kochiyama believes her father's death resulted from the prison's inadequate medical treatment for his recent ulcer surgery; for other explanations, see Diane C. Fujino, *Heartbeat of Struggle: The Revolutionary Life of Yuri Kochiyama* (Minneapolis: University of Minnesota Press, 2005).

4. Yuri Kochiyama, interview with author, June 29–July 6, 1997, Harlem, NY.

5. Diary by Yuri Kochiyama (Mary Nakahara), "The Bordered World," vol. 2, September 9, 1942, Japanese American National Museum, Los Angeles.

6. Most internees were first placed in temporary "assembly centers," often hastily converted fairgrounds or racetracks, and, about half a year later, moved to the more permanent "relocation centers" or "concentration camps."

7. Kochiyamas, *Christmas Cheer*, 1951, 2. If not otherwise specified, Kochiyama's materials come from her personal archive.

8. Ibid.

9. "Mrs. Mary Kochiyama & family," letter to Malcolm X, October 17, 1963.

10. Yuri Kochiyama, class notes, OAAU Liberation School, December 12, 1964; March 13, 1965. Kochiyama's handwritten notes show she attended every Saturday from December 5, 1964, until April 3, 1965, except for three Saturdays in late December and early January. On Hamer's beating, see Chana Kai Lee, *For Freedom's Sake: The Life of Fannie Lou Hamer* (Urbana: University of Illinois Press, 1999), 45–53.

11. Kochiyamas, editorial, *North Star*, 1968, 7.

12. Kochiyama, "And Then We Heard the Thunder 'Black Power': SNCC's New Battle Cry!" *The North Star*, December 1966, 1; Stokely Carmichael and Charles V. Hamilton, *Black Power: The Politics of Liberation in America* (New York: Vintage, 1967), 54–55.

13. Kochiyama, "And Then We Heard the Thunder 'Black Power,'" 1.

14. Imari Obadele, *Foundations of the Black Nation* (Detroit, MI: House of Songhay, 1975); George Breitman, *The Last Year of Malcolm X* (New York: Schocken, 1967), 64–65; George Breitman, ed., *Malcolm X Speaks* (New York: Grove Press, 1965), 197.

15. Kochiyama incorrectly equated feminism with gender segregation. Liberal feminism's neglect of race and class issues and radical feminism's call for separation from men loomed so large that many women of color in the 1970s felt alienated by the women's movement. But by the 1990s, when Kochiyama expressed this view, many women of color had transformed feminism to encompass the intersectionality of race, class, and gender. See Diane C. Fujino, "Revolution's from the Heart: The Making of an Asian American Women Activist, Yuri Kochiyama," in *Dragon Ladies: Asian American Feminists Breathe Fire*, ed. Sonia Shah (Boston: South End Press, 1997), 169–181.

16. Social networking was especially important in Durham County, where 22 percent of the labor force worked in health care. Workers had multiple relationships as family and friends forged through church, school, and other social institutions. It was widely acknowledged that women did most of the behind-the-scenes work that was critical to the unionization campaign, though they infrequently held traditional leadership positions. See Karen Brodkin Sacks, *Caring by the Hour: Women, Work, and Organizing at Duke Medical Center* (Urbana: University of Illinois Press, 1988); Sacks, "Gender and Grassroots Leadership."

17. Sacks, *Caring by the Hour*, 119.

18. Mutulu Shakur, interview with author, October 19, 1998.

19. Quoted in Barbara Ransby, *Ella Baker and the Black Freedom Movement: A Radical Democratic Vision* (Chapel Hill: University of North Carolina Press, 2003), 188. On grassroots leadership, see Ransby's discussion of the contrasting leadership models of Ella Baker and Martin Luther King Jr. (pp. 189–192); Charles Payne, "Men Led, but Women Organized: Movement Participation of Women in the Mississippi Delta," in *Women in the Civil Rights Movement: Trailblazers and Torchbearers, 1941–1965*, ed. Vicki L. Crawford, Jacqueline Anne Rouse, and Barbara Woods (Brooklyn, NY: Carlson, 1990); Dolores Delgado Bernal, "Grassroots Leadership Reconceptualized: Chicana Oral Histories and the 1968 East Los Angeles Blowouts," *Frontiers* 19 (1998): 113–142.

20. Kochiyamas, "New Faces of '62," *Christmas Cheer*, 1962, 1; Kochiyamas, "Sequel to the Mike Hernandez Story," *Christmas Cheer*, 1963, 1, 10; Yuri Kochiyama, interview with author, November 3–10, 1997.

21. Kochiyama, interview with author, November 3–10, 1997.

22. Kochiyama, *Christmas Cheer*, 1959, 6. The pages of *Christmas Cheer* document the massive flow of people into their home, including some eighty overnight guests in a single year (Kochiyamas, *Christmas Cheer*, 1954, 6).

23. Genevieve Hall-Duncan, interview with author, January 17, 2000.

24. Kochiyamas, "Black Leadership Blazes Pathways Lighting Minds," *The North Star*, 1965, 4, 5, 8.

25. Ahmed Obafemi, interview with author, February 7, 2000.

26. Bibi Angola, interview with author, December 6, 1999.

27. Ahmed Obafemi, interview with author, February 7, 2000.

28. Bolanile Akinwole, interview with author, February 21, 2000.

29. Mutulu Shakur, interview with author, October 19, 1998.

30. Mtayari Shabaka Sundiata, letter to Yuri Kochiyama, April 27, 1975.

31. Ahmed Obafemi, interview with author, February 7, 2000.

32. Bolanile Akinwole, interview with author, February 21, 2000.

33. Author's participant-observation, Tear Down the Walls meeting, Oakland, CA, and conversations with Kochiyama, 2001.

34. Michael Kimmel, *Manhood in America: A Cultural History* (New York: Oxford University Press, 2006).

35. Sacks, *Caring by the Hour*; Sacks, "Gender and Grassroots Leadership," 77–94; Payne, "Men Led, but Women Organized"; Bernal, "Grassroots Leadership Reconceptualized," 113–142.

36. Japanese Americans were participating in civil rights activism at the time, but there was no guarantee of support from the wider community. When the March on Washington organizers invited the Japanese American Citizens League (JACL) to send representatives to the rally, the JACL leadership did accept, but only over the objections of numerous local chapter presidents and after much internal struggle. Also in 1963, the San Francisco *Hokubei Mainichi* editor Howard Imazeki created a stir when he published an editorial, widely reprinted, rejecting Black claims of racism and blaming Blacks for their own situation (Greg Robinson, "Nisei and the Black Freedom Movement"). Bill and Yuri Kochiyama wrote a letter to the editor of the *New York Nichi Bei* (September 26, 1963) strongly denouncing Imazeki's views. That they believed the article "may be representative of the thinking of many Nisei in California and across the country" reveals the distance Kochiyama felt between her budding political activism and the majority of Japanese Americans. On the demise of the Japanese American Left, see Diane C. Fujino, "The Black Liberation Movement and Japanese American Activism: The Radical Activism of Richard Aoki and Yuri Kochiyama," in *Afro Asia: Revolutionary Political and Cultural Connections between African Americans and Asian Americans*, ed. Fred Ho and Bill V. Mullen (Durham, NC: Duke University Press, 2008), 165–197. On early Japanese American radicalism, see Yuji Ichioka, "A Buried Past: Early Issei Socialists and the Japanese Community," *Amerasia Journal* 1 (1971): 1–25; Josephine Fowler, *Japanese and Chinese Immigrant Activists: Organizing in American and International Communist Movements, 1919–1933* (Brunswick, NJ: Rutgers University Press, 2007).

37. Kochiyamas, "Warm Greetings," *North Star*, 1968, 2.

38. Ahmed Obafemi, interview with author, February 7, 2000.

39. Nyisha Shakur, interview with author, October 15, 1998.

40. A. Peter Bailey, interview with author, March 3, 2000; Malcolm X, "Message to the Grass Roots," in *Malcolm X Speaks*, ed. George Breitman (New York: Grove Press, 1965), 16; Clayborne Carson, "The Time Has Come," in *The Eyes on the Prize Civil Rights Reader*, ed. C. Carson, David J. Garrow, Gerald Gill, Vincent Harding, and Darlene Clark Hine (New York: Penguin Books, 1991), 245–246.

41. Laura Pulido, *Black, Brown, Yellow, and Left: Radical Activism in Los Angeles* (Berkeley: University of California Press, 2006).

42. The model minority image of Asian America, popularized in two widely read newsmagazines in 1966, extols the educational and occupational achievements of Asian Americans. By promoting hard work, delayed gratification, and assimilationism as pathways to success, its logic functioned to denounce political protest at the moment of the rise of Black Power. See William Petersen, "Success Story, Japanese-American Style," *New York Times Magazine*, January 9, 1966; "Success Story of One Minority Group in U.S.," *U.S. News & World Report*, December 26, 1966.

43. Yuri Kochiyama, interview with author.

44. Black internationalists mistakenly elevated Japan as a symbol of triumph over global White racism; see Marc Gallicchio, *The African American Encounter with Japan and China: Black Internationalism in Asia, 1895–1945* (Chapel Hill: University of North Carolina Press, 2000).

45. Yuri Kochiyama, class notes from the OAAU Liberation School, December 5, 1964; Yuri Kochiyama, interview with author.

46. Muhammad Ahmad (Max Stanford), interview with author, January 30, 2000; Yuri Kochiyama, interview with author. On RAM, see Muhammad Ahmad (Maxwell Stanford), *We Will Return in the Whirlwind: Black Radical Organizations, 1960–75* (Chicago: Charles H. Kerr, 2007); Robin D. G. Kelley, *Freedom Dreams: The Black Radical Imagination* (Boston: Beacon, 2002).

47. Timothy B. Tyson, *Radio Free Dixie: Robert F. Williams and the Roots of Black Power* (Chapel Hill: University of North Carolina Press, 1999); Robert F. Williams, *Negroes with Guns* (Chicago: Third World Press, 1962/1973).

48. Mao Tse-tung, "Calling upon the People of the World to Unite to Oppose Racial Discrimination by U.S. Imperialism and Support the American Negroes in Their Struggle against Racial Discrimination," August 1963, in Robert Williams, *The Crusader*, October 1964, 1; Mao, "In Support of the Afro-American Struggle against Violent Repression," *April 1968* (Peking: Foreign Language Press, 1968); both reprinted in Ho and Mullen, *Afro Asia*, 91–96. For more on Afro-Asian political connections, see Ho and Mullen, *Afro Asia*; Bill V. Mullen, *Afro-Orientalism* (Minneapolis: University of Minnesota Press, 2004); Max Elbaum, *Revolution in the Air: Radicals Turn to Lenin, Mao, and Che* (London: Verso, 2002); and Vijay Prashad, *Everybody Was Kung Fu Fighting: Afro-Asian Connections and the Myth of Cultural Purity* (Boston: Beacon Press), 2001.

49. Mary (Yuri) Kochiyama, "Who Is Rob Williams, and What Is His Relationship to Asians?" *Asian Americans for Action Newsletter*, October 1969, 4, 8, in author's possession.

50. Robert F. Williams, "On the Platform with Mao Tse-tung," *New York Times*, February 20, 1971.

51. Kochiyama, "Who Is Rob Williams?"

52. Those arguing for Black Power's strong influence include Glenn Omatsu, "The 'Four Prisons' and the Movements for Liberation," *Amerasia Journal* 15, no. 1 (1989): xvi, xv–xxx; Fred Ho, "The Inspiration of Mao and the Chinese Revolution on the Black Liberation Movement and the Asian Movement on the East Coast," in Ho and Mullen, *Afro Asia*; Fred Ho, ed., *Legacy to Liberation: Politics and Culture of Revolutionary Asian Pacific America* (San Francisco: AK Press, 2000); and Diane C. Fujino, "Who Studies the Asian American Movement? A Historiographical Analysis," *Journal of Asian American Studies* 11 (June 2008): 127–169. By contrast, William Wei presents a civil rights framing for the Asian American movement (*The Asian American Movement* [Philadelphia: Temple University Press, 1993]), which I critique in "Who Studies the Asian American Movement?" For a spatial analysis of the formation of Afro-Asian political relations, see Diane C. Fujino, "Race, Place, Space, and Political Development: Japanese American Radicalism in the 'Pre-Movement' 1960s," *Social Justice*, forthcoming.

53. Diane C. Fujino, "The Black Liberation Movement and Japanese American Activism." My current research is a book project on Richard Aoki.

54. "AAPA Perspectives," *AAPA* newspaper, November 1969, 3. The AAPA newspaper reprinted Kochiyama's article on Robert Williams (November 1969, 2) and included other articles reflecting their support of "Third World Power" (February 1969, 1); a front-page picture of Black Panther leader Bobby Seale with the article, "Free All Political Prisoners" (November 1969, 1); an article on "Would You Believe Concentration Camps for Americans," denouncing concentration camps to detain "militants, black or white" (November–December 1968, 3); and several articles supporting the struggle for Third World studies at UC Berkeley. Diane C. Fujino, "The Black Liberation Movement and Japanese American Activism: The Radical Activism of Richard Aoki and Yuri Kochiyama," in Ho and Mullen, *Afro Asia*, 165–197; Asian-Americans for Action newsletters; Asian American Political Alliances newspapers.

55. I Wor Kuen, "12 Point Platform and Program," in Ho, *Legacy to Liberation*, 405–407.

56. Renowned Chinese American activist Grace Lee Boggs exerted a powerful influence on radical thought and the Black labor and radical movements in Detroit. While she minimally participated in the Asian American movement, in recent years, her ideas and stature in the movement have influenced Asian American activism. See Grace Lee Boggs, *Living for Change: An Autobiography* (Minneapolis: University of Minnesota Press, 1998); Mullen, *Afro-Orientalism*; Jennifer Jung Hee Choi, "At the Margins of the Asian American Political Experience: The Life of Grace Lee Boggs," *Amerasia Journal* 25, no. 2 (1999): 18–40.

57. *Asian-Americans for Action Newsletter* 1, no. 1 (June 1969): 1.

58. Yuri Kochiyama, "Statement for the Subpoenees for the Forum on Political Repression," speech, Saint Mark's Church, New York, February 6, 1975.

59. Nyisha Shakur, interview with author, October 15, 1998.

60. Kochiyamas, "Asians Organize in NY," *North Star*, 1969, 3, 7, 8.

61. Mary Kochiyama, "Hiroshima-Nagasaki Week speech," August 9, 1969, New York City, in *Asian-Americans for Action Newsletter* 1, no. 3 (October 1969): 3-4.

62. Kochiyamas, "Brave New World," *North Star*, 1966, 2, 3; "Ho Chi Minh," *North Star*, 1969, 3.

63. Rea Tajiri and Pat Saunders, *Yuri Kochiyama: Passion for Justice* (video, 1993); Mayumi Nakazawa, *Yuri: The Life and Times of Yuri Kochiyama* (Tokyo: Bungenshugu, 1998); *Passing It On—A Memoir*, ed. Marjorie Lee, Akemi Kochiyama-Sardinha, and Audee Kochiyama-Holman (Los Angeles: UCLA Asian American Studies Center, 2004); Fujino, *Heartbeat of Struggle*.

64. Charles Payne, "Ella Baker and Models of Social Change," *Signs: Journal of Women in Culture and Society* 14 (1989): 898.

65. Ibid.

14

"We Do Whatever Becomes Necessary"

Johnnie Tillmon, Welfare Rights, and Black Power

Premilla Nadasen

I was forty-six years old and in the nation's capital before I was ever called a nigger. I politely took off my coat, handed my bag to my attorney, and went and had me a fist city on the man's head. He didn't hit me back or nothin', but he ran. Never had been called that by a white person out of all the thirty-five years I lived in Little Rock and Arkansas. But many years ago I had decided that's what I was going to do.

Brian Lanker[1]

Welfare rights leader Johnnie Tillmon relayed this story to Brian Lanker, photographer and author of *I Dream a World: Portraits of Black Women Who Changed America*, about an incident that occurred at the height of her political activity in 1973. Tillmon's decision to stand up for herself and her refusal to passively accept racial slurs are characteristic of the racial consciousness and assertiveness that Black Power instilled in many African Americans during the postwar era.

Yet, even more important than Tillmon's obvious racial pride and practice of self-defense was her commitment to autonomy and self-determination for poor women. She and other welfare rights activists organized mass-based, confrontational campaigns to demand economic resources to give poor women control over their lives. Her philosophy of Black Power encompassed defending her children from the perils of poverty and protecting her civil rights as a single mother. Activists nurtured a pride in who they were as black welfare recipients and sought to reclaim their womanhood. Tillmon's political vision offers a fresh angle from which to view the practice of Black Power. It provides an opportunity to look beyond the banners and headlines and to explore how Black Power was understood, adopted, and theorized by poor black women. Tillmon adopted the rhetoric of self-determination but developed its meaning through her own lens as a poor black woman struggling for economic justice and personal dignity. For Tillmon, gender—in particular female independence and autonomy—were central to her philosophy of black radicalism. She was unable to parcel out her struggle for women's rights, Black Power, and economic justice. For women in the welfare rights movement, these goals were interlocking and mutually reinforcing and formed the basis for a radical black feminism. The history of the welfare rights movement forces us to expand our understanding and definition of second-wave feminism and Black Power politics to include grassroots welfare rights campaigns. It also encourages us to recognize how the boundaries between women's liberation and Black Power activism were fluid, overlapping, and permeable.

Over the past decade Black Power scholars have been rethinking the nature and the trajectory of Black Power politics. They have analyzed the ways in which women in Black Power organizations carved out a space for self-empowerment, how black women activists in "non–Black Power" organizations articulated their own version of Black Power, and how grassroots activists across the country engaged with the ideas of Black Power. This scholarship illustrates that the roots of Black Power can be located not only in the shifting priorities of the national civil rights organizations but also in the ongoing community activism in cities around the country.[2] A long tradition of black protest often preceded and laid the foundation for the "official" turn to Black Power. So Black Power was not simply a reaction to the perceived victories or failures of the southern-based civil rights movement, and the Black Panther Party for Self-Defense was not its only organizational manifestation. Instead, as numerous scholars are demonstrating, activism around housing, tenants' rights, education, and welfare rights activism can be counted as part of the broader, more nuanced, definition of Black Power politics.[3]

Tillmon's distinctive Black Power politics placed poor black women at the center—a political view that was cultivated over the course of her life. Tillmon's childhood and early adulthood in a rural black community in Arkansas instilled in her a deep sense of independence, autonomy, and self-pride. She labored from a very early age, picking cotton, ironing shirts in a laundry, and, briefly, working as a domestic. She observed black people, sometimes related, sometimes not, pulling together to help one another in times of need. She also witnessed white poverty alongside black poverty. As a single mother, she juggled her many responsibilities of working, mothering, and caring for a home. These experiences propelled her to help launch and lead a political movement for welfare rights. They also laid the basis for a political analysis that combined race, class, gender, sexuality, and political and economic autonomy. Tillmon advocated a Black Power politics that encompassed not only racial pride and self determination but also a commitment to class politics attuned to the specific interests of poor women. She saw independence for poor black women as crucial for their self-determination. This included government financial support that provided them freedom from economic vulnerability in order to raise their children. She also advocated independence in the form of personal autonomy, whether in the arena of intimate relations, welfare administration, or organizational politics. Women in the welfare rights movement pushed for reproductive rights, an easing of caseworker control over the lives of AFDC recipients, and welfare recipient control of the decision making within the National Welfare Rights Organization (NWRO). They posited a radically different conception of freedom and liberation from what other feminist or Black Power activists of the 1960s articulated. Thus, Tillmon crafted an expansive vision of Black Power—one that defies easy categorization and calls into question the binary opposition of integration/nationalism and self-defense/nonviolence. Her vision challenges the masculine posture that has become so closely identified with Black Power and expands our understanding of self-determination.[4] Through her articulation of a radical black feminist politics, she sought to empower poor women—especially poor black women—and provide them with economic security and personal autonomy.[5]

The Making of an Organizer—and a Movement

Born in 1926 in Scott, Arkansas, Johnnie Lee Percy was a sharecropper's daughter, whose itinerant farming family was forever in search of a better economic situation. The rural black traditions of self-reliance and self-determination that decades later would inspire organizers in the Student Nonviolent Coordinating Committee to embrace Black Power were the bedrock of Tillmon's early life.[6] Although poor, she had fond childhood memories of her family's self-sufficiency, since they made or grew nearly everything they needed—clothing, soap, lard, fruit, and vegetables. When she was five years old, her mother died in labor. Her father and stepmother raised her and her two younger brothers. Tillmon's upbringing instilled in her a strong sense of racial pride. She learned her family's history of slavery from her father. Johnnie Tillmon recalled, "Most of my black history came from . . . my father. My father's mother . . . [was one] of the last slaves on the ship that docked in South Carolina. . . . They handed the information down to him and he passed it on to me, which I find quite unusual 'cause most dark people never talked about their African inheritance to their children."[7] Segregation was prevalent in Arkansas, especially in urban areas, and early on Tillmon encountered separate facilities for blacks and whites. But she learned to live with these publicly drawn racial boundaries. Moreover, formal segregation might not have been as profound in shaping her worldview as the larger structural forces that impoverished families like hers. She observed white poverty firsthand, and recognized some of the similarities between her own economic situation and that of poor white people: "Some of the white people in Little Rock were just as poor as I was . . . where I lived there was always white people who worked on the farms. They weren't treated any better . . . than I was."[8]

As Tillmon tells it, far from being "shiftless and lazy"—as welfare recipients were often described in the 1960s—she began her working career in the cotton fields at the age of seven. She attended one- or two-room schoolhouses in rural Arkansas until she moved in with her aunt in Little Rock to attend high school. Although a good student, she took a job and never graduated. For a short time she did domestic work, but when the family asked her to eat lunch with the dog, she promised to never again work in anybody's house. During World War II she was employed in a war plant, then got a job in a laundry, where she remained until she left Little Rock. At the laundry, an integrated workplace, Tillmon noticed little racial animosity: "For those of us who worked there, it wasn't about white and black. It was about green. Were you going to get paid at 12:00 on Saturday?"[9] In 1946, she married James Tillmon and had two children, but she and her husband separated after two years. She subsequently had four more children. Tillmon worked during her marriage and after it ended and also supported her father, who lived with her. When her father died in 1960, she headed to California to join her two brothers.

While pregnant with her sixth child, Tillmon moved in with her brother in Los Angeles. To support herself and her five children, she worked as a shirt line operator—a job her sister-in-law helped her land—where she ironed 120 shirts an hour. She eventually moved into a place of her own but found it impossible to care for an infant and five other children while working full-time. She sent her six-month-old baby girl to live with her youngest brother in Richmond, California. At her job in the laundry, where African Americans, Mexican Americans, and poor whites worked side by side, Tillmon advocated for better working conditions and wages and quickly rose to a position as union shop steward. She also helped register voters and joined a community association, the Nickerson Gardens Planning Organization, which planted flowers, arranged after-school activities for children, and improved living conditions in her housing project.

In 1963, Tillmon contracted a severe case of tonsillitis and was hospitalized. The president of the neighborhood association, Mr. Garringer, suggested that Tillmon apply for welfare so she could devote more time to raising her children. Her teenage daughter—who had been skipping school—needed her attention. In addition, with welfare assistance she could be reunited with her two-year-old daughter, who was still living in northern California with her brother. Imbued with negative ideas about welfare, she hesitated but eventually agreed because of concern for her children.

Tillmon was struck by the differences between her life as a recipient and as a working woman. Caseworkers inventoried Tillmon's refrigerator, questioned such decisions as purchasing a television, and provided her with a welfare budget that outlined how she should spend her money. She contrasted this constant supervision to her relative independence as a worker: "When I left my job in the evening, I was through until the next morning. And on the weekend I didn't have no one peeping and peering, telling me what to do or what I couldn't do."[10] The policing of her intimate life angered Tillmon. She later recounted: "When I was working every day, if I wanted to have male company, then I had male company. But when you're on welfare, you can't have too much male company."[11]

Tillmon's experiences with the welfare system were not unique. Welfare officials treated recipients alternately as children or criminals. Intake workers produced piles of application documents and often nastily asked probing questions about the candidate's personal and sexual history. Welfare department investigators searched recipients' homes, violating their privacy and in the process stripping them of their dignity. Recipients whom caseworkers believed had an intimate partner or an alternate source of income, or those whom they believed were able to work, were routinely denied assistance. These policies disproportionately affected African American women, who had historically been denied access to welfare.[12] Caseworkers routinely applied stricter eligibility criteria to African American women and consistently allotted them smaller monthly payments.

In the early and mid-1960s, poor single mothers such as Tillmon participated in and witnessed the civil rights movement, a renewed labor movement, burgeoning feminist activism, and many other grassroots campaigns. Inspired by the countless examples of ordinary people refusing to submit to unjust, unfair, or racist policies, they began to agitate for themselves. Disgruntled recipients came together in small neighborhood and community groups across the country to share grievances, show one another support, and influence the policies and practices of the welfare department.

Just eight months after getting on welfare, Tillmon began to organize her fellow recipients. She and five of her friends surreptitiously obtained a list of all Aid to Dependent Children (ADC)—as AFDC was known prior to 1962—recipients in the housing project. They sent out letters asking the women to come to a meeting to discuss their lease and grant. Three hundred people showed up at the first meeting.[13] In August 1963, Aid to Needy Children (ANC) Mothers Anonymous opened an office staffed by welfare recipients to help people who had been cut off assistance, had not gotten a grocery order, or had similar welfare problems. As Tillmon explained, her goal was "to be independent and if you weren't independent, to be treated with dignity."[14] Johnnie Tillmon's advocacy of respect and economic security for poor women without government intrusion embodied a vision of self-determination and black pride—one premised on a revamped social policy that treated people as human beings.

Shortly after Tillmon established ANC Mothers Anonymous in Los Angeles, groups across California formed a statewide organization. But California was not the only site of welfare organizing in the mid-1960s. Recipients in Ohio, New York, Mississippi, Nevada, Michigan, and New Jersey were also mobilizing.[15] Civil rights activist George Wiley, who had recently left the Congress of Racial Equality (CORE) and formed the Poverty/Rights Action Center, brought together these disparate groups into a national coalition. Tillmon joined other welfare rights leaders from around the country at a meeting in Chicago in 1966. This initial contact laid the basis for a national network of welfare rights groups. These local groups eventually coalesced in 1967 to form the National Welfare Rights Organization (NWRO). The membership, paid organizers, and staff of NWRO included men and women, African Americans, other people of color, and whites. The best estimates suggest that African Americans constituted 85 percent of the membership, whites 10 percent, and Latinas 5 percent, and there were a few Native Americans. While a handful of men joined, women constituted the overwhelming majority—around 98 percent.

The NWRO's elected leaders emerged from the ranks of the membership, initially limited to welfare recipients and later broadened to include any poor person. The National Coordinating Committee met four times a year and included delegates from each state. The annual conventions elected a nine-member executive committee, which met eight times a year and carried out policies decided by the membership. Johnnie Tillmon became the organization's first chairman.[16] Although the founders designed this structure to ensure recipient participation, in reality much of the power in NWRO rested with the paid field organizers and staff in the national office, most of whom were middle-class men, often white.[17] The NWRO's first executive director, George Wiley, an African American from a predominantly white, relatively privileged community in Rhode Island, was a chemistry professor at Syracuse University who gave up his faculty position to organize the poor.

Together Wiley, Tillmon, and a cadre of other organizers and recipients built a nationwide movement that challenged the paternalism and racism that were central to the welfare program. NWRO chapters and other unaffiliated welfare rights groups around the country fought for higher welfare benefits, better treatment from caseworkers, and protection of recipients' civil rights. They organized campaigns to ensure that recipients had all the items the welfare department deemed part of a basic minimum standard of living. Thousands of recipients were given additional "special grant" allowances for household items they did not have. Welfare rights activists pushed for participation in shaping welfare policy by issuing position papers, organizing conferences, participating in client advisory groups, and meeting with high-level welfare officials. They initiated credit campaigns to force department stores to extend credit to welfare recipients, who had little disposable cash, so they could purchase big-ticket consumer products. They also mapped a legal strategy and, with assistance from lawyers, overturned some particularly egregious welfare regulations, such as the "substitute father" rules, which denied assistance to a woman for having a relationship with a man under the presumption that he could support her, and residency laws, which denied aid to recent migrants. On the national level, they won a Supreme Court victory that guaranteed them the right to due process, entitling recipients to a hearing before termination of their benefits. They also fought, unsuccessfully, for a guaranteed annual income. Most important, they empowered recipients to think differently about AFDC and poverty and encouraged them to seek and claim their rights. Overall, these campaigns sought to instill pride in welfare recipients by debunking the racial and sexual stereotypes of AFDC, and affording recipients a degree of control and autonomy over their lives. The welfare rights movement is a powerful example of mass-based feminist and Black Power organizing by poor black women. Its ideology encompassed black pride, women's liberation, and poor people's economic justice. By 1968 the movement counted 30,000 members and had chapters across the country in both rural and urban areas. Its membership rolls greatly exceeded that of many other women's liberation and Black Power groups and rivaled mass-based organizations, such as Students for a Democratic Society.

Violence and Nonviolence

The welfare rights movement employed multiple strategies: lobbying Congress, holding sit-ins, and planning marches and public demonstrations. It used mass-based direct-action tactics patterned after civil rights protests to wage special-grants campaigns. In New York City, for example, recipients came together, determined what winter clothing items they did not have that welfare regulations specified they should have—such as a coat for every child, five long-sleeve shirts, or a pair of snow boots—and submitted their requests. If the department refused to give them the money to purchase these items, recipients held a sit-in until they were given checks. In most cases, welfare administrators—their offices disrupted, mobbed by the press, and facing irate welfare mothers—conceded to avoid the unenviable situation of having to explain why they did not enforce their own rules. At the height of the special-grant protests in New York City in 1968, recipients won $12 to 13 million a month in special grants from the welfare department—five times more than disbursed the previous year.[18]

While most welfare rights organizations relied on nonviolent direct action, activists did not limit their strategies in this way. The welfare rights movement's use of multiple strategies complicates the simplistic violent/nonviolent trajectory that has framed popular understandings of the black freedom movement. Welfare rights activists, as Rhonda Y. Williams argues, had a "tactical flexibility" and "enacted divergent strategies and verbal postures," including self-defense and threats of violence, to win concessions and counter state violence.[19] In many public demonstrations, welfare rights activists adopted a militant posture. With their children in tow, they marched in downtown centers and in front of city halls, "shopped-in" at department stores, blocked entrances to public welfare buildings, and took over the offices of high-ranking politicians. Their angry calls for justice were broadcast on the evening news. One famous photo printed on the front page of the *Washington Post* showed a group of black women on welfare sitting with their feet on the desk of Health, Education, and Welfare (HEW) secretary Elliot Richardson. Their opponents used this as evidence that they had no respect for lawmakers and seemed indifferent to laws as well. In one incident welfare recipients took over a welfare office in the Bronx, overturned furniture, and ripped telephones off the walls.[20]

At first glance, it might seem that the turn to violence or threat of violence on the part of some welfare recipients was born of frustration and anger. But more often than not, activists consciously deliberated over the most fruitful strategy and turned to violence only when more tame protests seemed ineffective. The Bronx protest occurred after welfare officials replaced the special-grant system, which had yielded countless victories for activists, with annual flat grants. When welfare officials dug in their heels and refused to negotiate with protesters, organizers began to contemplate more radical alternatives. Welfare rights activists had also learned through observation that violence or the threat of violence can actually be quite effective. Tillmon expressed this sentiment: "It is true that when we're not heard we have to make people hear us. We do whatever becomes necessary. We're not a violent group . . . even sometimes we might have to throw a rock to get attention. We don't want to throw rocks to hit anybody. But just to make a noise. . . . People don't seem to hear us if we don't demonstrate."[21] So while some welfare rights activists preferred nonviolence, they were not beyond employing violence if they felt it was necessary, appropriate, or more likely to win concessions. Welfare rights activists' thoughtful and intentional use of violence, in fact, parallels that of other Black Power activists who did not seek out confrontational violence but held it in a strategic reserve arsenal.[22]

Self-Determination

The welfare rights movement also harnessed as a central goal self-determination—a core principle of Black Power. As Tillmon succinctly put it, "I always preach and teach independence."[23] For welfare recipients, independence meant having the resources and political space to make decisions about their day-to-day lives. The struggles for a minimum standard of living, a guarantee of reproductive rights, and protection of recipients' right to privacy and due process also were designed to give poor women autonomy and control over their lives. Quite simply, welfare recipients wanted to live their lives with economic security but without interference from welfare caseworkers and administrators.

These early campaigns and the language they adopted to claim welfare and government assistance reflected a sense of entitlement by recipients. They saw welfare as a right and argued that the prosperity of the country and its commitment to equality required that it bring all of its citizens up to a basic minimum standard of living; they also claimed entitlement to governmental assistance as the right of mothers engaged in meaningful and important work that deserved support; and they questioned the value of formal political equality and equal access to schools if people were impoverished or if children went to school hungry.

The demand for a right to welfare targeted most directly AFDC's history of monitoring poor women. Since the program's inception, caseworkers had conducted investigations to determine recipients' worthiness, sometimes showing up unexpectedly in infamous "midnight raids" to determine if clients were engaged in so-called unethical behavior. This might have included poor housekeeping, reluctance to look for employment, lavish spending, or intimate relations with a man. These moral and cultural criteria became a basis on which to exclude women considered unworthy of support. The popular cultural discourse suggested that black women on welfare were lazy, promiscuous, and looking for a free ride. Tillmon's own experience diverges from this view: "I will never accept that I got a free ride. It wasn't free at all. My ancestors were brought here against their will. They were made to work and help build this country. I worked in the cotton fields from the age of seven. I worked in the laundry for twenty-three years. I worked for the national organization for nine years. I just retired from city government after twelve-and-a-half years."[24]

To counter the historically stingy disbursement of AFDC funds, welfare rights activists fought for higher monthly benefits and a decent standard of living. They wanted poor single mothers to have an adequate level of assistance to properly feed, clothe, and house their families. They argued that "real" equality meant providing recipients' children with the same opportunities available to other children, such as attending summer camp and participating in graduation exercises. When caseworkers denied their applications or cut off their assistance without notice, recipient organizers demanded fair hearings. Such hearings—a formal nonjudicial hearing before a state board of welfare to overturn a caseworker's decision—challenged the discretionary power of caseworkers and shifted the balance of power between caseworker and client.

Tillmon and other welfare rights activists attempted to debunk the notion that welfare receipt or single motherhood was a sign of cultural deficiency. Since the early 1960s, popular images painted the stereotypical welfare recipient as an African American mother with multiple sexual partners, unwilling to work, and quite content to live off the government's largesse. These cultural representations had a damaging impact both on the administration of welfare programs, which became more punitive, and on the self-esteem of welfare recipients. By their public presence *as welfare recipients*, women in the welfare rights movement began to break the silence and stamp out the personal shame that shrouded the welfare program. Just as other Black Power activists reclaimed their racial identity by asserting "black is beautiful," black welfare recipients reclaimed a positive understanding of black womanhood and elevated their position as welfare recipients by bringing recognition to their work as mothers. In part to dispel the misconception that most welfare recipients were black women, Tillmon frequently pointed to the larger number of white women on welfare. Highlighting the presence of white women on the rolls transformed welfare from a "black woman's problem" into a "poor women's problem." So, the welfare rights movement employed a dual strategy. It asserted a positive view of black motherhood while still trying to debunk the myth that most recipients were black.

Tillmon defended single motherhood in part because of her own experiences as a single mother. But, in addition, as a child in a rural black Arkansas community, she witnessed more expansive definitions of family. As she explained in an interview: "People in those days you didn't have adoptions . . . and if there was a child who needed care, then people raised the child. Sometime it lose [*sic*] the mother or the father, it didn't have to be an aunt or an uncle to pick the child up. It was people saw a child needed some assistance and helped them."[25] Tillmon drew on these experiences of elastic family forms to question the stigma attached to single motherhood, as well as the assumption that poor women needed a male breadwinner. Women on welfare who failed to conform to conventional norms were acutely aware of the social expectations to marry and establish traditional family relationships, but they believed that such relationships often served to subordinate women. Tillmon argued that an unmarried woman was led to believe that she had "failed as a woman because [she has] failed to attract and keep a man. There's something wrong with [her]." The meager benefits and stigma attached to welfare served as an "example" to let any woman know what would happen "if she tries to go it alone without a man."[26] While she recognized that some women wanted a partner to "help pay the bills," she rejected this option for herself: "I have never depended on nobody like that. I was raised to be an independent person."[27] By crafting self-determination to include respect for alternative notions of family and female independence, Tillmon's philosophy broadened the definition of both Black Power and black feminism

In addition to expanding the boundaries of acceptable personal relationships, welfare rights activists wanted the right to determine under what circumstances they would have a child. In the 1960s, poor women's childbearing was often blamed for the "welfare crisis." Welfare officials used strategies such as forced sterilizations and caps on welfare payments to prevent or discourage poor women from having children. Welfare rights activists resisted such pressure and consequently articulated a version of Black Power that called for reproductive autonomy for poor women. Tillmon argued in 1971: "Nobody realizes more than poor women that all women should have the right to control their own reproduction."[28] Tillmon supported poor women's access to an array of birth control methods but also sought to protect their right to bear children. She explained the NWRO's position on the issue. "We know how easily the lobby for birth control can be perverted into a weapon against poor women. The word is choice. Birth control is a right, not an obligation. A personal decision, not a condition of a welfare check."[29] In 1973 Tillmon issued a statement jointly with Charles Fanueff, executive director of the Association for Voluntary Sterilization, opposing forced sterilization of welfare recipients.[30] Years before the mainstream women's movement came to this position, the welfare rights movement articulated a broad-based politics of reproductive rights.

The demand for a guaranteed annual income, an income floor below which the government would not allow families to fall, most clearly embodied Tillmon's goal of self-determination. Many groups in the 1960s, including the Black Panther Party, discussed and endorsed the guaranteed annual income. This demand reflected activists' beliefs that a minimum standard of living was a fundamental right regardless of family status or work history, and the federal government had the responsibility to provide it. The guaranteed income represented a truly radical call for self-determination. It promised to alleviate the most extreme cases of poverty and provide a measure of economic security for poor families, give people a viable alternative to degrading and exploitative labor conditions, and liberate poor women from economic dependence on men. Moving beyond calls for self-determination premised on political autonomy, it suggested that substantive self-determination required economic resources—particularly for single mothers with children. Tillmon explained: "I believe in rhetoric to a certain extent. But you can only rhetoricize so long and then you have to deal with fact." Tillmon, like other Black Power leftists, maintained that material conditions must be central to any program for self-determination.[31]

The "facts" for welfare recipients included juggling child care and work, managing a meager monthly budget, and contending with a demoralizing public stigma that denigrated poor women's work as mothers. The guaranteed income would ameliorate some of this difficulty by enabling welfare recipients to decide whether they should work outside the home or stay home and raise their children. To assist mothers wanting paid employment, the NWRO supported the creation of child care centers; this was "one of the first priorities" of Tillmon's welfare rights organization in California.[32] But they also wanted welfare officials and critics of welfare to recognize poor women's work as mothers.[33] Tillmon proposed in 1971 that we could resolve the "welfare crisis" and "go a long way toward liberating every woman" in the country if the president issued "a proclamation that women's work is *real* work" and if government paid women "a living wage for doing the work we are already doing—child raising and housekeeping."[34]

These demands collectively would have put greater power and control in the hands of poor women on welfare. Women in the welfare rights movement called for transformation of the welfare program and demanded a prominent role in its re-creation. Participation became a rallying cry for women in the welfare rights movement. They secured seats on local governing boards. They spoke at welfare and social work conferences. They met with state and national policy makers to give their input on the implementation of reforms. Welfare rights activists' demands to shape social welfare policy were in essence a call for community control of welfare, dovetailing with a broader pattern of Black Power politics that advocated community control of schools, housing projects, and policing.

Struggle for Power within the NWRO

The struggle for self-determination not only informed welfare rights activists' political positions vis-à-vis the welfare state but also came to influence the internal politics of the movement. Although welfare recipients held elected leadership positions within the NWRO, the middle-class staff wielded disproportionate power through running the day-to-day operations in the national office. Middle-class staff, most of whom were white men, dominated the NWRO administrative and organizing positions, controlled the purse strings, and held paid staff positions. In some instances, the staff handpicked recipient leaders, or failed to carry out decisions made by them. Women in the welfare rights movement began to suspect that they were denied self-determination in their very own organization and became increasingly critical of the role of middle-class organizers—both black and white—within the NWRO. Since NWRO's inception, the predominantly white, middle-class male staff and the overwhelmingly poor black female constituency had wrestled for control and disagreed about the movement's strategies and goals. In 1966, when white male organizers in California called a meeting of welfare activists to form a county-wide organization, Johnnie Tillmon and several ANC mothers showed up unexpectedly. Tillmon remembers that after organizer Tim Sampson read to the group the bylaws he had written, "I stood up and took them by-laws and ripped them apart and told the ladies, write it yourself."[35] She then turned to the organizers and said: "You don't just come into somebody's neighborhood and run it."[36]

The tensions over control and decision making came to a head most overtly between black and white staff members in the national office in 1969. According to white organizer Rhoda Linton, who began working in the national office in 1968, "There were a lot of white people involved in making decisions about what the organization was going to do. And there were a lot of people of color doing the 'do'—doing the work."[37] This reality fostered a racial divide that mirrored that of black freedom organizations such as the Student Nonviolent Coordinating Committee (SNCC) and the Congress of Racial Equality (CORE). John Lewis, an African American who worked for NWRO, wrote in an article in the *Washington Afro American* that, feeling "manipulated by white people," black staff members believed that "at national headquarters, professionals have a paternalistic frequently racist attitude about recipients, consistently making policy decisions the recipients themselves should have made."[38] He pointed out that only one recipient out of a total of forty staff members worked for NWRO. "Recipients should have been brought in from the beginning to learn the administrative jobs, but they weren't. The issue is not just race, but whether a recipient should be executive director . . . and have a person like Dr. Wiley to give him assistance if he needs it."[39]

Tillmon and the NWRO Executive Committee took issue with the actions of the black staff members who, by 1969, organized to express dissatisfaction with white control within the organization. Tillmon disagreed with the critique of Wiley and the white staff and dismissed the importance of paid staff positions, arguing that staff salaries were so low, "they weren't living high off the hog."[40] She professed support for Wiley, who not only had important contacts and brought invaluable fund-raising skills to the movement but had proven his ongoing commitment to the welfare rights struggle. Throughout the entire brouhaha, she recounted, "I believed in George." The welfare recipient leadership generally and Tillmon specifically refused to align themselves with the black staff members who they saw as calling for racial exclusion. The roots of the tensions within the organization were many. Race alone cannot adequately explain the increasingly fraught dynamics. Many women welfare rights activists, concerned about recipient control and autonomy, did not see hiring more African Americans to work in the national office as an adequate solution. But gender was also an issue. According to Tim Sampson, Wiley's policy of almost always hiring male organizers created a backlash.[41] But hiring only female organizers would not have satisfied recipients either. They were not committed to a crass racial exclusion or female separatism. Instead, they wanted to invest recipients, who had the most experience and knowledge of the welfare system, with greater decision-making power. Tillmon articulated her concern with the staff in terms of class: "Most of those kids were college kids who was rich. None of them was poor."[42] But recipients did not want to be directed by middle-class black staff any more than they wanted to be controlled by white staff. Tillmon saw her struggle as inclusive of race, class, and gender. She explained in an interview: "It wasn't women organizers versus men organizers. Or it wasn't white organizers versus black organizers. . . . Our thing was recipient versus the establishment."[43] Acutely aware of welfare's impact on both black and white women, Tillmon explained in a 1971 interview: "NWRO is not a black organization, not a white organization. . . . We are all here together and we are fighting the people who are responsible for our predicament. . . . We can't afford racial separateness. I'm told by the poor white girls on welfare how they feel when they're hungry, and I feel the same way when I'm hungry."[44]

By the early 1970s, Tillmon and other welfare rights activists pressed for autonomy, self-sufficiency, and, consequently, control of NWRO by recipients. Consistent with the rhetoric of self-determination, both nationally and internationally, Johnnie Tillmon argued that the nonpoor should serve only in supportive, not leadership, roles. She proposed that women on welfare "try and do something for ourselves and by ourselves to the extent that we could."[45] Because of the ongoing discontent of welfare rights activists, in 1972 George Wiley resigned as executive director. Johnnie Tillmon replaced him and moved to Washington to take charge of the national office. After this, black women recipients had firm control over the organization. Tillmon's leadership solidified NWRO as an organization controlled by welfare recipients. As executive director, Tillmon continued striving for self-determination for welfare rights activists. Outlining to the Executive Board her most important goal of recommitting NWRO to its grassroots base, she pledged to make the organization self-supporting through membership dues rather than relying primarily on private and institutional philanthropy. In 1974 Tillmon organized the "Half-A-Chance" campaign and appealed to all poor people in the country to give fifty cents to NWRO. Little came of the campaign, however.[46] For the next several years, welfare rights activists continued to push for autonomy and self-determination for AFDC recipients, articulating a black feminist politics that combined race, gender, class, and sexuality.

Race, Nationalism, and Black Women's Power

Tillmon's political philosophy embodies a black radical feminist tradition. Although committed to interracial organizing, Tillmon acknowledged the central role race played in structuring welfare policies and poor women's life chances. Since its inception, the welfare rights movement had addressed the disproportionate number of impoverished black people, racially discriminatory welfare policies, and racialized and sexualized stereotypes of welfare recipients. For Tillmon, addressing race and racism and the way in which black women bore the brunt of AFDC's punitive policies did not mean disregarding the reality of white poverty. Empowering poor black women did not necessarily require erecting racially exclusive boundaries. Tillmon often referred to one of her visits to Appalachia, where she met poor white women on welfare who implored her "not to leave them out." She never wavered from her belief in an inclusive movement: "One thing I want to say about our organization is there is no color line. We don't look at the color of skin when a person needs help. We don't look at religious background."[47]

Similarly, Tillmon saw gender as indispensable for understanding the politics of the welfare rights movement. In 1971 she wrote in an article in *Ms. Magazine* that women in the welfare rights movement were "the front line troops of women's freedom" and that ensuring the right to a living wage for women's work concerned all women.[48] In the article Tillmon articulated her political position on welfare and how it undermines self-determination:

> The truth is that AFDC is like a super-sexist marriage. You trade in *a* man for *the* man. But you can't divorce him if he treats you bad. He can divorce you, of course, cut you off anytime he wants. *The* man runs everything. In ordinary marriage sex is supposed to be for your husband. On AFDC you're not supposed to have any sex at all. You give up control of your own body. It's a condition of aid. You may even have to agree to get your tubes tied so you can never have more children just to avoid being cut off welfare. *The* man, the welfare system, controls your money. He tells you what to buy, what not to buy, where to buy it, and how much things cost. . . . *The* man can break into your house anytime he wants to and poke into your things. You've got no right to protest. You've got no right to privacy when you go on welfare."[49]

This quote by Tillmon is widely cited as incontrovertible evidence of her gendered analysis of welfare. The analogy between welfare and marriage makes clear her perspective that the welfare system entails the same kind of patriarchal control over women as marriage. But it is no coincidence that Tillmon makes continual reference to "the man." In 1960s black radical rhetoric, "the man" came to symbolize the white male power structure. When the Black Panther Party and other revolutionary black nationalist groups situated material conditions at the center of their Black Power politics, "the man" became a shorthand reference not only for white power but for the political, social, and economic control of black communities. It connoted a system in which black people were marginalized and disempowered. Tillmon's use of the phrase "the man" reveals her understanding of the racial and economic nature of the welfare system and its particular impact on poor women.

Johnnie Tillmon articulated a variant of Black Power politics that placed female independence and power at the center. Although Tillmon did not endorse black nationalism, she modeled a positive black identity that integrated class, gender, and sexuality. She rejected calls to restore the two-parent heterosexual black family and for black men to reassert their masculinity. Her radical black feminism proposed autonomy for poor women to make decisions about childbearing, child rearing, and their intimate lives. She waged campaigns to enable poor women to live their lives with dignity, respect, and economic security. And she worked tirelessly to debunk the stereotypes that had become associated with receipt of welfare. If Black Power, at its core, is about empowering black people, striving for self-determination, and giving them a sense of self-worth, then Johnnie Tillmon was one of its most important advocates.

Despite Tillmon's valiant efforts at reviving NWRO, the internal struggles, financial strains, and more hostile political climate made ongoing national welfare rights work difficult. Welfare recipients on the local level continued to organize, to build community institutions, and, in the words of historian Annelise Orleck, "fight their own War on Poverty."[50] After NWRO closed its doors in 1975, Tillmon returned to California. She bought a house with her new husband, Harvey Blackston, the famous jazz musician better known as "Fats Harmonica," just a few blocks from the Nickerson Gardens public housing complex where she first organized welfare recipients. She continued to work with the local welfare rights chapter and became a paid legislative aide on welfare issues for city councilman Robert Farrell. She later served on a welfare advisory committee under Governor Jerry Brown and subsequently under the administration of Republican governor George Deukmejian. She died of diabetes in 1995 at the age of sixty-nine.[51]

Conclusion

Black Power is not a discrete ideology that operates only in opposition to other political perspectives around which we can draw clear boundaries. Instead, it is a more diffuse force that permeated many local, global, and intimate spaces. It worked in concert with and at times in opposition to feminism, class, sexuality, and coalition work. Although Black Power is most commonly associated with the Black Panther Party, a study of Johnnie Tillmon's ideology illustrates alternative understandings of Black Power that circulated during this period. Welfare rights activists like Tillmon charted a course independent of other Black Power advocates to mold a Black Power politics to empower poor black women.

Tillmon's upbringing in rural Arkansas instilled in her an abiding belief in female independence and a racial consciousness that underpinned her black radical feminist politics. Welfare rights activists began to organize in the late 1950s and early 1960s in response to economic inequities and racially discriminatory administrative practices. They advocated a community-controlled welfare program that treated people with dignity and respected their personal autonomy. They worked to transform the psychological and social stigma attached to welfare and nurture pride and a positive self-image among recipients. They defended poor women's reproductive control over their bodies. They relied on both violence and nonviolence and were willing to do "whatever becomes necessary." Although overwhelmingly black, the welfare rights movement did not draw racially exclusive boundaries but maintained a commitment to interracial organizing—inclusive of African American, white, Latina, Asian, and Native American women. Tillmon's radical black feminist politics was the basis for a vision of Black Power that fostered independence and self-determination for all poor women.

As economically vulnerable poor mothers who were closely monitored by welfare officials, welfare rights activists had fewer choices about the kind of militancy in which they could engage. Welfare rights activists did not posture with assault rifles or wear black berets, but they relied on the ammunition of ideology to articulate a transformative vision of social policy and family relations. Their grassroots campaign offers us a different way to conceptualize black radicalism and women's liberation. It shows black women not only as actors and practitioners of Black Power but as theoreticians as well. They articulated a philosophy that combined racial power, economic justice, and women's liberation. Johnnie Tillmon's political ideology integrating race, class, gender, and sexuality redefines our notion of self-defense and self-determination and redraws the boundaries of second-wave feminism and Black Power, complicating and expanding the traditional understanding.

NOTES

Many thanks to Rhonda Y. Williams and Robyn C. Spencer for their thoughtful and insightful comments on this essay. They have both influenced my thinking greatly. Thanks also to Sherna Berger Gluck, who had the foresight to interview Johnnie Tillmon before Tillmon passed away.

1. Brian Lanker, *I Dream a World: Portraits of Black Women Who Changed America* (New York: Stewart, Tabori and Chang, 1989), 92

2. Rhonda Williams, "Black Women, Urban Politics, and Engendering Black Power," in *The Black Power Movement: Rethinking the Civil Rights–Black Power Era*, ed. Peniel Joseph (New York: Routledge, 2006).

3. See, for example, Jeanne Theoharis and Komozi Woodard, eds., *Freedom North: Black Freedom Struggles Outside the South, 1940–1980* (New York: Palgrave Macmillan, 2003); Robyn Spencer, "Repression Breeds Resistance: The Rise and Fall of the Black Panther Party in Oakland, CA, 1966–1982" (Ph.D. diss., Columbia University, 2001); Peniel Joseph, ed., *The Black Power Movement: Rethinking the Civil Rights–Black Power Era* (New York: Routledge, 2006); Rhonda Y. Williams, *The Politics of Public Housing: Black Women's Struggles against Urban Inequality* (New York: Oxford University Press, 2004); Barbara Ransby, *Ella Baker and the Black Freedom Movement: A Radical Democratic Vision* (Chapel Hill: University of North Carolina Press, 2003); Chana Kai Lee, *For Freedom's Sake: The Life of Fannie Lou Hamer* (Urbana: University of Illinois Press, 1999); Matthew Countryman, *Up South: Civil Rights and Black Power in Philadelphia* (Philadelphia: University of Pennsylvania Press, 2005); Tracye Matthews, "'No One Ever Asks What a Man's Role in the Revolution Is': Gender Politics and Leadership in the Black Panther Party, 1966–1971," in *Sisters in the Struggle: African American Women in the Civil Rights–Black Power Movement*, ed. Bettye Collier-Thomas and V. P. Franklin (New York: NYU Press, 2001); Robyn Spencer, "Engendering the Black Freedom Struggle: The Black Panther Party and Revolutionary Black Womanhood," *Journal of Women's History* (forthcoming); Jeffrey Ogbar, *Black Power: Radical Politics and African American Identity* (Baltimore: Johns Hopkins University Press, 2004); Christina Greene, *Our Separate Ways: Women and the Black Freedom Movement in Durham, North Carolina* (Chapel Hill: University of North Carolina Press, 2005); Robert Self, *American Babylon: Class, Race, and Power in Oakland and the East Bay, 1945–1978* (Princeton, NJ: Princeton University Press, 2003); Timothy Tyson, *Radio Free Dixie: Robert F. Williams and the Roots of Black Power* (Chapel Hill: University of North Carolina Press, 1999); Paniel Joseph, *Waiting 'Til the Midnight Hour: A Narrative History of Black Power in America* (New York: Henry Holt, 2006); Martha Biondi, *To Stand and Fight: The Struggle for Civil Rights in Postwar New York* (Cambridge, MA: Harvard University Press, 2003).

4. Emilye J. Crosby, "'This Nonviolent Stuff Ain't No Good. It'll Get Ya Killed': Teaching about Self-Defense in the African American Freedom Struggle," in *Teaching the American Civil Rights Movement: Freedom's Bittersweet Song*, ed. Julie B. Armstrong, Susan H. Edwards, Houstan B. Roberson, and Rhonda Y. Williams (New York: Routledge, 2002), 159–169.

5. For more on black feminism outside "traditional" Black Power organizations, see Rhonda Williams, "'We're Tired of Being Treated Like Dogs': Poor Women and Power Politics in Black Baltimore," *Black Scholar* 31, nos. 3–4 (Fall/Winter 2001): 31–41; and Williams, "Black Women, Urban Politics and Engendering Black Power"; Kimberley Springer, "Black Feminists Respond to Black Power Masculinism," in Joseph, *The Black Power Movement*; Stephan Ward, "The Third World Women's Alliance," in Joseph, *The Black Power Movement*; and Sharon Harley, "'Chronicle of a Death Foretold': Gloria Richardson, the Cambridge Movement, and the Radical Black Activist Tradition," in Collier-Thomas and Franklin, *Sisters in the Struggle*.

6. Hasan Kwame Jeffries, "SNCC, Black Power, and Independent Political Party Organizing in Alabama, 1964–1966," *Journal of African American History* 91 (2006): 171–193.

7. Sherna Berger Gluck, Interview no. 2 with Johnnie Tillmon, 1991, the Virtual Oral/Aural History Archive, University of Southern California.

8. Ibid.

9. Gluck Interview no. 3 with Tillmon, 1991.

10. Ibid.

11. Hobart Burch, "Insights of a Welfare Mother: A Conversation with Johnnie Tillmon," *Journal* 14 (January–February 1971): 13–23, quotation on p. 14.

12. For more on the history of AFDC, see Frances Fox Piven and Richard Cloward, *Regulating the Poor: The Functions of Public Welfare* (New York: Pantheon, 1971); Mimi Abramovitz, *Regulating the Lives of Women: Social Welfare Policy from the Colonial Times to the Present* (Boston: South End Press, 1989); Ellen Reese, *Backlash against Welfare Mothers Past and Present* (Berkeley: University of California Press, 2005); Jennifer Mittelstadt, *From Welfare to Workfare: The Unintended Consequences of Liberal Reform, 1945–1965* (Chapel Hill: University of North Carolina Press, 2005); Gwendolyn Mink, *The Wages of Motherhood: Inequality in the Welfare State, 1917–1942* (Ithaca, NY: Cornell University Press, 1995); Lisa Levenstein, "From Innocent Children to Unwanted Migrants and Unwed Moms: Two Chapters in the Public Discourse on Welfare in the United States, 1960–1961," *Journal of Women's History* 11 (Winter 2000): 10–33; Linda Gordon, *Pitied but Not Entitled: Single Mothers and the History of Welfare* (New York: Free Press, 1994); Kenneth Neubeck and Noel A. Cazenave, *Welfare Racism: Playing the Race Card against American's Poor* (New York: Routledge, 2001), chap. 3; Robert Lieberman, *Shifting the Color Line: Race and the American Welfare State* (Cambridge, MA: Harvard University Press, 1998).

13. *New York Times*, November 21, 1995.

14. Gluck Interview no. 3 with Tillmon, 1991.

15. See Premilla Nadasen, *Welfare Warriors: The Welfare Rights Movement in the United States* (New York: Routledge, 2004); Williams, *Politics of Public Housing*; Annelise Orleck, *Storming Caesar's Palace: How Black Mothers Fought Their Own War on Poverty* (Boston: Beacon Press, 2005); Felicia Kornbluh, *The Battle for Welfare Rights: Politics and Poverty in Modern America* (Philadelphia: University of Pennsylvania Press, 2007); Nick Kotz and Mary Lynn Kotz, *A Passion for Equality: George A. Wiley and the Movement* (New York: Norton, 1977); Frances Fox Piven and Richard Cloward, "The Welfare Rights Movement," in *Poor People's Movements: Why They Fail and How They Succeed* (New York: Vintage, 1977); Guida West, *The National Welfare Rights Movement: The Social Protest of Poor Women* (New York: Praeger, 1981); Lawrence Neil Bailis, *Bread or Justice: Grassroots Organizing in the Welfare Rights Movement* (Lexington, MA: Heath., 1972).

16. At the founding of the NWRO, the women adopted the title "chairman." In the early 1970s, when they articulated feminist goals, they changed the title to "chairwoman."

17. See Nadasen, *Welfare Warriors*, chap. 5; West, *The National Welfare Rights Movement*, 57–64.

18. *New York Times*, August 30, 1968.

19. Rhonda Williams, "Nonviolence and Long Hot Summers: Black Women and Welfare Rights Struggles in the 1960s," *Borderlands E Journal* 4, no. 3 (2005): 2–4.

20. *New York Times*, August 31, 1968.

21. Johnnie Tillmon, speech, United Presbyterian Woman National Meeting, 1970, NWRO Papers, Moorland-Spingarn Research Center (MSRC), Howard University.

22. See Tyson, *Radio Free Dixie*; Ransby, *Ella Baker and the Black Freedom Movement*; Lee, *For Freedom's Sake*; Simon Hall, "The NAACP, Black Power, and the African American Freedom Struggle, 1966–1969," *Historian* 69 (2007): 49–82.

23. Gluck Interview no. 1 with Tillmon, 1984.

24. Lanker, *I Dream a World*, 92.

25. Gluck Interview no. 2 with Tillmon, 1991.

26. Johnnie Tillmon, "Welfare Is a Woman's Issue," *Ms. Magazine*, Spring 1972, 111–116.

27. Gluck Interview no. 3 with Tillmon, 1991.

28. Tillmon, "Welfare Is a Woman's Issue."

29. Ibid.

30. "Strategies for Survival," NWRO pamphlet, 1973, Wiley Papers, box 7. For more on black women and reproductive rights, see Jennifer Nelson and Dorothy Roberts, *Killing the Black Body: Race, Reproduction and the Meaning of Liberty* (New York: Vintage, 1997); Jael Silliman, Marlene Gerber Fried, Loretta Ross, and Elena Gutierrez, *Undivided Rights: Women of Color Organize for Reproductive Justice* (Cambridge, MA: South End Press, 2004); Johanna Schoen, *Choice and Coercion: Birth Control, Sterilization, and Abortion in Public Health and Welfare* (Chapel Hill: University of North Carolina Press, 2005); Anna Marie Smith, *Welfare Reform and Sexual Regulation* (New York: Cambridge University Press, 2007).

31. Lanker, *I Dream a World*, 92.

32. West, *National Welfare Rights Movement*, 253.

33. Eileen Boris, "When Work Is Slavery," in *Whose Welfare?* ed. Gwendolyn Mink (Ithaca, NY: Cornell University Press, 1999), 36–55.

34. Tillmon, "Welfare Is a Woman's Issue," 115; also available at www.albany.edu/faculty/cb598342/tillmon.doc, p. 3.

35. Interview no. 4 with Tillmon, 1991.

36. West, *National Welfare Rights Movement*, 84.

37. Author interview with Rhoda Linton, New York City, 2003.

38. John Lewis, "Black Voices," *Washington Afro American*, August 19, 1969.

39. Ibid.

40. Gluck Interview no. 5 with Tillmon, 1991.

41. Author interview with Tim Sampson, San Francisco, 1997.

42. Gluck Interview no. 4 with Tillmon, 1991.

43. Ibid.

44. Burch, "Insights of a Welfare Mother," 13–23.

45. Johnnie Tillmon, interview with Guida West, quoted in West, *National Welfare Rights Movement*, 101.

46. NWRO, Welfare Fighter, 4 (February 1974), NWRO Papers, MSRC, Howard University; NWRO Press Release, July 18, 1974, MSRC.

47. Tillmon, speech, United Presbyterian Woman National Meeting.

48. Tillmon, "Welfare Is a Woman's Issue," 111–116.

49. Ibid.

50. Orleck, *Storming Caesar's Palace*.

51. *New York Times*, July 9, 1995; *New York Times*, November 21, 1995.

About the Contributors

MARGO NATALIE CRAWFORD is Associate Professor in the Department of English at Cornell University. She is the author of *Dilution Anxiety and the Black Phallus* and coeditor, with Lisa Gail Collins, of *New Thoughts on the Black Arts Movement.*

PRUDENCE CUMBERBATCH is Assistant Professor in the Department of Africana Studies at Brooklyn College, City University of New York. She is currently completing a book on black women's activism in Baltimore, Maryland.

JOHANNA FERNÁNDEZ is Assistant Professor in the Department of Black and Hispanic Studies at Baruch College, City University of New York. Her forthcoming book on the Young Lords will be published by Princeton University Press.

DIANE C. FUJINO is Chair and Associate Professor of the Department of Asian American studies at the University of California, Santa Barbara. She wrote *Heartbeat of Struggle: The Revolutionary Life of Yuri Kochiyama* and edited *Wicked Theory, Naked Practice: A Fred Ho Reader.*

DAYO F. GORE is Assistant Professor of Women, Gender, Sexuality Studies at the University of Massachusetts-Amherst. Her forthcoming book on the political thought and activism of black women affiliated with the U.S. left during the 1940s and 1950s will be published by NYU Press.

JOSHUA GUILD is Assistant Professor of history and African American studies at Princeton University. He is currently completing a book on the politics of black community formation in postwar Brooklyn and London.

GERALD HORNE is Moores Professor of history and African American studies at the University of Houston. He is the author of several books, including *Race Woman: The Lives of Shirley Graham Du Bois* and *Race War! White Supremacy and the Japanese Attack on the British Empire*.

ERICKA HUGGINS is a former Black Panther Party member and political prisoner, human rights activist, poet, lecturer, and teacher. She currently teaches women's studies at California State University–East Bay and sociology at Laney College in Oakland, California. She is working on an autobiography entitled *Fearless*.

JOY JAMES is the John B. and John T. McCoy Presidential Professor of the Humanities and College Professor in Political Science, and Senior Research Fellow in the Center for African and African American Studies at the University of Texas–Austin. Her publications include *Resisting State Violence: Gender, Race, and Radicalism in U.S. Culture*; *Transcending the Talented Tenth: Black Leaders and American Intellectuals*; and *Shadowboxing: Representations of Black Feminist Politics*.

ANGELA D. LEBLANC-ERNEST is former Director of the Black Panther Party Research Project at Stanford University, an independent scholar, and a home-schooling mother of three. She is working on a book about the Black Panther Party's community programs.

ERIK S. MCDUFFIE is Assistant Professor in African American studies and in the Gender and Women's Studies Program at the University of Illinois at Urbana-Champaign. His forthcoming book is tentatively entitled *Toward a Brighter Dawn: Black Women and American Communism, 1919–1956*.

PREMILLA NADASEN is Associate Professor of history at Queens College, City University of New York, and is the author of *Welfare Warriors: The Welfare Rights Movement in the United States*. She is writing a book on the history of domestic worker organizing in the United States.

SHERIE M. RANDOLPH is Assistant Professor of history and African American and African studies at the University of Michigan, Ann Arbor. She is writing a book on Florynce "Flo" Kennedy and black feminist politics in the postwar United States.

JAMES SMETHURST is Associate Professor in the W. E. B. Du Bois Department of Afro-American Studies at the University of Massachusetts–Amherst. He is the author of *The Black Arts Movement: Literary Nationalism in the 1960s and 1970s and The New Red Negro: The Literary Left and African American Poetry, 1930–1946.*

MARGARET STEVENS is currently completing her dissertation with the American Civilization Department at Brown University. Her research focuses on transnational Communist and black radical organizations in New York City and the Caribbean between the two world wars.

JEANNE THEOHARIS is Associate Professor of Political Science at Brooklyn College, City University of New York. She is coeditor with Komozi Woodard of *Groundwork: Local Black Freedom Movements* and *Freedom North: Black Freedom Struggles Outside the South, 1940–1980.* She is also the coauthor of *Our Schools Suck: Students Talk Back to a Segregated Nation on the Failures of Urban Education.*

KOMOZI WOODARD is Professor of American History, Public Policy, and Africana Studies at Sarah Lawrence College. He is the author of *A Nation within a Nation: Amiri Baraka (LeRoi Jones) and Black Power Politics.* He is also coeditor with Jeanne Theoharis of *Freedom North* and *Groundwork.*

Index

CPSIA information can be obtained
at www.ICGtesting.com
Printed in the USA
BVOW03s0818200217

476563BV00003B/4/P